SOURCES FOR CULTURES OF THE WEST

VOLUME 1: TO 1750

EDITED BY

Clifford R. Backman
BOSTON UNIVERSITY

Christine Axen
BOSTON UNIVERSITY

NEW YORK   OXFORD
OXFORD UNIVERSITY PRESS

Oxford University Press is a department of the University of Oxford.
It furthers the University's objective of excellence in research,
scholarship, and education by publishing worldwide.

Oxford   New York
Auckland   Cape Town   Dar es Salaam   Hong Kong   Karachi
Kuala Lumpur   Madrid   Melbourne   Mexico City   Nairobi
New Delhi   Shanghai   Taipei   Toronto

With offices in
Argentina   Austria   Brazil   Chile   Czech Republic   France   Greece
Guatemala   Hungary   Italy   Japan   Poland   Portugal   Singapore
South Korea   Switzerland   Thailand   Turkey   Ukraine   Vietnam

For titles covered by Section 112 of the US Higher Education
Opportunity Act, please visit www.oup.com/us/he for the
latest information about pricing and alternate formats.

Published by Oxford University Press
198 Madison Avenue, New York, New York 10016
http://www.oup.com

Oxford is a registered trademark of Oxford University Press.

Library of Congress Cataloging-in-Publication Data
Sources for cultures of the west / edited by Clifford R. Backman, Boston University,
Christine Axen, Boston University.--Second edition.
     volumes cm
   Contents: Volume 1: To 1750 --
     ISBN 978-0-19-024049-3 (vol. 1 : pbk.) 1. Civilization, Western—Sources. 2. Religion and
civilization—Sources. 3. Science and civilization—Sources. 4. Philosophy and civilization—
Sources. I. Backman, Clifford R., editor of compilation. II. Axen, Christine, editor of
compilation. III. Backman, Clifford R. The cultures of the West.
   CB245.S5696 2015
   909'.09821--dc23
                                                                            2015020916

Printing number: 9 8 7 6 5 4 3 2 1

Printed in the United States of America
on acid-free paper

CONTENTS

HOW TO READ A PRIMARY SOURCE

This sourcebook is composed of sixty-seven primary sources. A primary source is any text, image, or other source of information that gives us a firsthand account of the past by someone who witnessed or participated in the historical events in question. Although such sources can provide significant and fascinating insight into the past, they must also be read carefully to limit modern assumptions about historical modes of thought. Here are a few elements to keep in mind when approaching a primary source.

AUTHORSHIP

Who produced this source of information? A male or a female? A member of the elite or of the lower class? An outsider looking *in* at an event or an insider looking *out*? What profession or lifestyle does the author pursue, which might influence how he is recording his information?

GENRE

What type of source are you examining? Different genres—categories of material—have different goals and stylistic elements. For example, a personal letter meant exclusively for the eyes of a distant cousin might include unveiled opinions and relatively trivial pieces of information, like the writer's vacation plans. On the other hand, a political speech intended to convince a nation of a leader's point of view might subdue personal opinions beneath artful rhetoric and focus on large issues like national welfare or war. Identifying genre can be useful for deducing how the source may have been received by an audience.

AUDIENCE

Who is reading, listening to, or observing the source? Is it a public or private audience? National or international? Religious or nonreligious? The source may be geared toward the expectations of a particular group; it may be recorded in a language that is specific to a particular group. Identifying audience can help us understand why the author chose a certain tone or why he included certain types of information.

HISTORICAL CONTEXT

When and why was this source produced? On what date? For what purposes? What historical moment does the source address? It is paramount that we approach primary sources in context to avoid anachronism (attributing an idea or habit to a past era where it does not belong) and faulty judgment. For example, when considering a medieval history, we must account for the fact that in the Middle Ages, the widespread understanding was that God created the world and could still interfere in the activity of mankind—such as sending a terrible storm when a community had sinned. Knowing the context (Christian, medieval, views of the world) helps us to avoid importing modern assumptions—like the fact that storms are caused by atmospheric pressure—into historical texts. In this way, we can read the source more faithfully, carefully, and generously.

BIAS AND FRAMING

Is there an overt argument being made by the source? Did the author have a particular agenda? Did any political or social motives underlie the reasons for writing the document? Does the document exhibit any qualities that offer clues about the author's intentions?

STYLISTIC ELEMENTS

Stylistic features such as tone, vocabulary, word choice, and the manner in which the material is organized and presented should also be considered when examining a source. They can provide insight into the writer's perspective and offer additional context for considering a source in its entirety.

Clifford Backman
Christine Axen
Boston University

CHAPTER 1

WATER AND SOIL, STONE AND METAL: THE FIRST CIVILIZATIONS

1.1. SHAMASH HYMN, CA. 2000–1600 BCE

Shamash, the Babylonian sun-god of justice, is the subject of this two-hundred-line ode. Depicted as the god of gods, Shamash rules everything, all the way from the lesser divinities to the daily practices of mortal merchants. In fact, the density of economic references in this religious hymn corresponds to an economic boom during this era. Consider how the hymn depicts the powerful god's concern for the moral welfare of his devotees.

Shamash, at your arising mankind bows down,
[. . .] every land.
Illuminator, dispeller of darkness of the vault of
    heavens,
Who sets aglow the beard of light, the corn field,
    the life of the land.
Your splendor covers the vast mountains,
Your fierce light fills the lands to their limits.
You climb to the mountains surveying the earth,
You suspend from the heavens the circle of the
    lands.
You care for all the peoples of the lands,
And everything that Ea [god of wisdom], king of
    the counselors, had created is entrusted to you,

Whatever has breath you shepherd without
    exception,
You are their keeper in upper and lower regions.
Regularly and without cease you traverse the
    heavens,
Every day you pass over the broad earth. . . .
In the underworld you care for the counselors of
    Kusu, the Anunnaki,
Above, you direct all the affairs of men,
Shepherd of that beneath, keeper of that above,
You, Shamash, direct, you are the light of
    everything. . . .
Among all the Igigi there is none who toils but
    you,

From Nels M. Bailkey and Richard Lim, eds. *Readings in Ancient History: Thought and Experience from Gilgamesh to St. Augustine*, 7th ed. Andover: Cengage Learning, 2011, pp. 25–8.

None who is supreme like you in the whole
     pantheon of gods.
At your rising the gods of the land assemble;
Your fierce glare covers the land.
Of all the lands of varied speech,
You know their plans, you can scan their way.
The whole of mankind bows to you,
Shamash, the universe longs for your light. . . .
You stand by the traveller, whose road is
     difficult,
To the seafarer is dread of the waves you give [. . .]
It is you who patrol the unseen routes,
You constantly tread paths which confront
     Shamash alone.
You save from the storm the merchant carrying
     his capital,
The [. . .] who goes down to the ocean you equip
     with wings.
You point out settling-places to refugees and
     fugitives,
To the captive you point out routes that only
     Shamash knows. . . .
A man who covets his neighbor's wife
Will [. . .] before his appointed day.
A nasty snare is prepared for him [. . .]
Your weapon will strike at him, and there will be
     none to save him.
     . . .
The merchant who practices trickery as he holds
     the corn measure,
Who weighs out loans of corn by the minimum
     standard, but requires a large quantity in
     repayment,
The curse of the people will overtake him before
     his time,

If he demanded repayment before the agreed
     date, there will be guilt upon him. . . .
The honest merchant who weighs out loans
     of corn by the maximum standard, thus
     multiplying kindness,
It is pleasing to Shamash, and he will prolong
     his life.
He will enlarge his family, gain wealth,
And like the water of a never failing spring his
     descendants will never fail. . . .
The progeny of evil-doers will fail.
Those whose mouth says "No"—their case is
     before you.
In a moment you discern what they say;
You hear and examine them; you determine the
     lawsuit of the wronged.
Every single person is entrusted to your hands;
You manage their omens; that which is perplexing
     you make plain.
You observe, Shamash, prayer, supplication, and
     benediction,
Obeisance, kneeling, ritual murmurs, and
     prostration.
The feeble man calls you from the hollow of his
     mouth,
The humble, the weak, the afflicted, the poor,
She whose son is captive constantly and
     unceasingly confronts you. . . .
Which are the mountains not clothed with your
     beams?
Which are the regions not warmed by the
     brightness of your light?
Brightener of gloom, illuminator of darkness,
Dispeller of darkness, illuminator of the broad
     earth.

STUDY QUESTIONS

1. Which specific groups is Shamash enjoined to thwart? Why?
2. How might the hymn be read as a warning to the living *lugals* in Sumerian culture?

1.2. "POEM OF THE RIGHTEOUS SUFFERER,"
CA. 2000–1600 BCE

This religious lament was recorded in cuneiform (a pictograph, or picture-based, language written with a stylus in clay that was developed ca. 3000 BCE) by the Babylonians, who dominated the Near East in the 3rd and 2nd millennia BCE. The concept of a broken bond between man and the gods, which is mourned here, was absorbed from the great Sumerian culture that preceded the Babylonian Empire. The poignant, bitter lament reveals an individual trying to comprehend the absence and silence of the god Marduk, who promises prosperity and joy to those who pray to him, despite the individual's adherence to traditional religious rite.

My god has forsaken me and disappeared,
My goddess has failed me and keeps at a
    distance.
The benevolent angel who walked beside me has
    departed,
My protecting spirit has taken to flight, and is
    seeking someone else.
My strength is gone; my appearance has become
    gloomy;
My dignity has flown away, my protecting made
    off. . . .
The king, the flesh of the gods, the sun of his
    peoples,
His heart is enraged with me, and cannot be
    appeased.
The courtiers plot hostile action against me,
They assemble themselves and give utterance to
    impious words. . . .
They combine against me in slander and lies.
My lordly mouth have they held as with reins,
So that I, whose lips used to prate, have become
    like a mute.
My sonorous shout is reduced to silence,
My lofty head is bowed down to the ground,
Dread has enfeebled my robust heart. . . .
If I walk the street, ears are pricked;

If I enter the palace, eyes blink.
My city frowns on me as an enemy;
Indeed my land is savage and hostile.
My friend has become foe,
My companion has become a wretch and a devil. . . .
As I turn round, it is terrible, it is terrible;
My ill luck has increased, and I do not find the
    right.
I called to my god, but he did not show his face,
I prayed to my goddess, but she did not raise her
    head.
The diviner with his inspection has not got to the
    root of the matter,
Nor has the dream priest with his libation
    elucidated my case.
I sought the favour of the *zaqiqu*-spirit, but he did
    not enlighten me;
And the incantation priest with his ritual did not
    appease the divine wrath against me.
What strange conditions everywhere!
When I look behind, there is persecution, trouble.

Like one who has not made libations to his god,
Nor invoked his goddess at table,
Does not engage in prostration, nor takes
    cognizance of bowing down;

From Nels M. Bailkey and Richard Lim, eds. *Readings in Ancient History: Thought and Experience from Gilgamesh to St. Augustine,* 7th ed. Andover: Cengage Learning, 2011, pp. 20–2.

From whose mouth supplication and prayer is
 lacking,
Who has done nothing on holy days, and
 despised sabbaths,
Who in his negligence has despised the gods' rites,
Has not taught his people reverence and worship,
But has eaten his food without invoking his god,
And abandoned his goddess by not bringing a
 flour offering,
Like one who has grown torpid and forgotten his
 lord,
Has frivolously sworn a solemn oath by his god,
 like such a one do I appear.
For myself, I gave attention to supplication and
 prayer:
To me prayer was discretion, sacrifice my rule.
The day for reverencing the god was a joy to my
 heart;
The day of the goddess's procession was profit
 and gain to me.
The king's prayer—that was my joy,
And the accompanying music became a delight
 for me.
I instructed my land to keep the god's rites,
And provoked my people to value the goddess's
 name.
I made praise for the king like a god's

And taught the populace reverence for the palace.
I wish I knew that these things were pleasing to
 one's god!

What is proper to oneself is an offence to one's
 god,
What in one's heart seems despicable is proper to
 one's god.
Who knows the will of the gods in heaven?
Who understands the plans of the underworld
 gods?
Where have mortals learnt the way of a god?
He who was alive yesterday is dead today.
For a minute he was dejected, suddenly he is
 exuberant.
One moment people are singing in exaltation,
Another they groan like professional mourners.
Their condition changes like an opening and
 shutting the legs.
When starving they become like corpses,
When replete they vie with the gods.
In prosperity they speak of scaling heaven,
Under adversity they complain of going down to
 hell.

I am appalled at these things; I do not understand
 their significance.

STUDY QUESTIONS

1. In what sense has the *lugal* failed to fulfill his role as protector?
2. What is the responsibility of the gods to this worshipper, and what can he do if the gods renege on the contract?

CHAPTER 2

LAW GIVERS, EMPERORS, AND GODS: THE ANCIENT NEAR EAST[1]

2.1. "TALE OF SINUHE," EARLIEST MS
CA. 1800 BCE

This Egyptian story recounts the adventures of Sinuhe, a member of a princely entourage, who flees his homeland yet longs to return. This tale, which may be a historical account, describes Sinuhe's departure; a copy of the kingly decree calling him home is repeated; and his safe return culminates in the promise that he will be buried among his own people. Consider how Sinuhe's identity is intertwined with his proximity to his homeland.

. . .
I travelled southwards.
I did not plan to reach this Residence,
expecting strife would happen;
I did not think to live after him.
. . .
Thirst's attack overtook me,
and I was scorched, my throat parched.
I said, "This is the taste of death."
But I lifted up my heart, and gathered my limbs together,
as I heard the noise of cattle lowing, caught sight of Syrians,
and a leader of theirs, who had once been in Egypt, recognized me.

Then he gave me water,
while he boiled milk for me.
I went with him to his tribe,
and what they did was good.
Country gave me to country.
I set out for Byblos; I got to Qedem.
I had spent half a year there,
when Amunenshi carried me off.
He was the ruler of upper Retjenu,
and he told me, "You'll be happy with me,
for you'll hear the speech of Egypt."
He said this, knowing my character
and having heard of my understanding,
and the Egyptians who were with him there
had vouched for me.

[1]Parkinson, R. B. 1997. *The Tale of Sinuhe and Other Ancient Egyptian Poems 1940–1640* BC (Oxford World Classics). Oxford: Oxford University Press.

Then he said to me, "Why did you come here?
Has anything happened in the Residence?"
Then I said to him, "It's that the Dual King
    Sehotepibre
has gone to the horizon,
and how this all happened is unknown."
But I spoke in half-truths.
"I have come from the expedition to the Libyan
    land:
it was reported to me, and my heart failed
and carried me off on the ways of flight.
I had not been talked of, and my face had not
    been spat upon;
I had heard no reproaches; my name had not
    been heard in the herald's mouth.
I do not know what brought me to this country—
    it is like a plan of God."

. . .

Now, he is a God who is peerless,
before whom no other exists.
He is a lord of understanding, excellent of plans,
    effective of orders;
coming and going are by his command.
He subjugates the countries.
His father stayed within his palace,
and he reported to him that what he had
    ordained was done.

Now he is a hero, active with his strong arm,
a champion without compare,
seen descending on barbarians, approaching the
    combat.
He curbs horns, weakens hands;
his foes cannot marshall troops.
He is vengeful, a smasher of foreheads;
close to him no one can stand.
He is far-striding, destroying the fugitive;
there is no end for the man who shows him his
    back.
He is firm-hearted at the moment of forcing
    retreat.
He turns back again and again; he shows not his
    own back.
He is stout-hearted, seeing the masses;
he allows no rest around his heart.

. . .

He is a lord of kindness, great of sweetness.
Through love he has conquered.
His city loves him more than its own members;
it rejoices at him more than at its God.
Men and women pass by, exulting at him.
He is a king, who conquered in the egg,
his eyes on it from birth.
He makes those born with him plentiful.
He is unique, God-given.
How joyful this land, since he has ruled!
He extends its borders.

. . .

And he said unto me, "Well, Egypt is certainly
    happy,
knowing of his success.
But look, you are here,
and you will stay with me; I shall do you good."
He placed me at the head of his children.
He joined me to his eldest daughter.
He had me make my choice of his country,
from the choicest of what was his,
on his border with another country.
It was a good land,
called Iaa.
Figs were in it, and grapes;
its wine was more copious than its water;
great its honey, plentiful its moringa-oil,
with all kinds of fruit on its trees.
Barley was there, and emmer, and numberless
    were its cattle of all kinds.
Now, what came to me as a favourite was great.
He appointed me the ruler of a tribe
of the choicest of his country.

. . .

I spent many years there,
and my children became heroes,
each man subjugating his tribe.

. . .

in his heart I attained high regard;
he loved me, knowing my valour.
He placed me at the head of his children, having
    seen the strength of my arms.

. . .

For now God has acted so as to be gracious to one
    with whom He was offended,
whom He led astray to another country.

Today, He is satisfied.
A fugitive takes flight because of his surroundings;
     but my reputation is in the Residence.
A creeping man creeps off because of hunger; but
     I give bread to my neighbour.
A man leaves his land because of nakedness; but
     I have bright linen, white linen.
A man runs off because of lack of someone to
     send; but I am plentiful of serfs.
Good is my house, spacious my dwelling place,
     and memory of me is in the palace.
Whatever God fated this flight—be gracious, and
     bring me home!
Surely You will let me see the place where my
     heart still stays!
What matters more than my being buried
in the land where I was born?
This is my prayer for help, that the good event befall,
that God give me grace!
May He act in this way, to make well the end of
     someone whom He made helpless,
His heart sore for someone He compelled to live
     in a foreign country!

. . .

**Copy of the Decree Brought to This Humble
Servant about His Being Brought Back to Egypt:**
"Horus Living-of-Incarnations;
Two Ladies Living-of-Incarnations;
Golden Horus Living-of-Incarnations;
Dual King Kheperkare;
Son of Re Senwosret
—may he live for all time and eternity!
Royal Decree to the Follower Sinuhe:
Look, this decree of the king is brought to you
to inform you that your roving through countries,
going from Qedem to Retjenu,
country giving you to country,
was at the counsel of your own heart.
What had you done, that you should be acted
     against?
You had not cursed, that your speech should be
     punished.
You had not spoken in the officials' council, that
     your utterances should be opposed.
This idea carried off your heart—

it was not in my heart against you.

. . .

Return to Egypt!
And you will see the Residence where you grew up,
kiss the earth at the Great Portal,
and join the Friends.
For today you have already begun to be old, have
     lost your virility,
and have in mind the day of burial,
the passing to blessedness.

A night vigil will be assigned to you, with holy oils
and wrappings from the hands of Tayet.
A funeral procession will be made for you on the
     day of joining the earth,
with a mummy case of gold,
a mask of lapis lazuli,
a heaven over you, and you placed in a hearse,
with oxen dragging you,
and singers going before you.

. . .

Your death will not happen in a foreign country;
Asiatics will not lay you to rest;
you will not be put in a ram's skin when your
     coffin is made.
This is too long to be roaming the earth!
Think of your corpse—and return!

. . .

This flight which your humble servant made—
I had not planned it. It was not in my heart.
I had not thought of it. I know not what parted
     me from my place.
It was like the nature of a dream,
like a Delta man seeing himself in Elephantine,
a man of the marshy lagoons in Southern Egypt.
I had no cause to be afraid; no one had run
     after me.
I had heard no reproaches; my name had not
     been heard in the herald's mouth.
Only—that shuddering of my limbs,
my feet hastening,
my heart overmastering me,
the God who fated this flight dragging me away!
I was not presumptuous before,
for a man respects him who is acknowledged by
     his land,

and the Sungod has put respect for you
    throughout the land,
and terror of you in every country.
Whether I am at home,
whether I am in this place—
it is you who veils this horizon of mine.
The sun shines for love of you;
the water of the river
is drunk when you wish;
the air of heaven
is breathed when you say.

. . .

I was given the house of a Governor,
such as belongs to a Friend.
Many craftsmen were building it,
all its trees were freshly planted.
Meals were brought to me from the
    palace,
three and four times a day,
as well as what the royal children gave,
without making a moment's ceasing.
A pyramid of stone was built for me,
in the midst of the pyramids.
The masons who construct the pyramid measured
    out its foundations;
the draughtsman drew in it;
the overseer of the works which are in the burial
    grounds busied himself with it.
All equipment to be put in a tomb shaft—
its share of these things was made.
I was given funerary priests;
a funerary demesne was made for me,
with fields in it and a garden in its proper place,
as is done for a Chief Friend.
My image was overlaid with gold,
and its kilt with electrum.
It is his Majesty who has caused this to be done.
There is no other lowly man for whom the like
    was done.
I was in the favours of the king's giving,
until the day of landing came."

So it ends, from start to finish,
as found in writing.

STUDY QUESTIONS

1. How does the document draw attention to international relations in Middle Kingdom Egypt and the general view of outsiders in this culture?
2. Why do the gods of Egypt take special responsibility for the Nile, and in what terms do they exercise that power?

2.2. "EPIC OF GILGAMESH,"
18TH CENTURY–7TH CENTURY BCE

A heroic epic about King Gilgamesh of Uruk (modern Iraq), this work is one of the earliest surviving works of literature, from the origins of civilization in Mesopotamia. Accompanied by his friend Enkidu, Gilgamesh embarks on adventures and interacts personally with the gods. After the death of Enkidu as punishment for Gilgamesh's rejection of the goddess Ishtar, the protagonist turns his focus toward immortality. The Epic's flood narrative is often compared with the Biblical tale of Noah.

From *Myths from Mesopotamia: Creation, the Flood, Gilgamesh, and Others.* Ed. Stephanie Dalley. New York: Oxford University Press, 1989, pp. 50–6, 71, 74, 77–84, 86–8, 95, 100–1, 107–19, 123–4.

[Of him who] found out all things, I [shall te]ll
the land,
[Of him who] experienced everything, [I shall
tea]ch the whole.
He searched (?) the lands (?) everywhere.
He who experienced the whole gained complete
wisdom.
He found out what was secret and uncovered
what was hidden,
He brought back a tale of times before the Flood.
He had journeyed far and wide, weary and at last
resigned.
He engraved all toils on a memorial monument
of stone.

. . .

The story of that man, Gilgamesh, who went
through all kinds of sufferings.
He was superior to other kings, a warrior lord of
great stature,
A hero born of Uruk, a goring wild bull.
He marches at the front as leader,
He goes behind, the support of his brothers,
A strong net, the protection of his men,
The raging flood-wave, which can destroy even
a stone wall.
Son of Lugalbanda, Gilgamesh, perfect in
strength,
Son of the lofty cow, the wild cow Ninsun.
He is Gilgamesh, perfect splendor,
Who opened up passes in the mountains,
Who could dig pits even in the mountainside,
Who crossed the ocean, the broad seas, as far as
the sunrise.
Who inspected the edges of the world, kept
searching for eternal life,
Who reached Ut-napishtim the far-distant, by
force.
Who restored to their rightful place cult centres
(?) which the Flood had ruined.
There is nobody among the kings of teeming
humanity
Who can compare with him,
Who can say "I am king" beside Gilgamesh.
Gilgamesh (was) named from birth to fame.
Two-thirds of him was divine, and one-third
mortal.

. . .

He had no rival, and at his *pukku*
His weapons would rise up, his comrades have to
rise up.
The young men of Uruk became dejected in their
private [quarters(?)].
Gilgamesh would not leave any son alone for his
father.
Day and night his [behavior(?)] was overbearing.
He was the shepherd (?)[ ]
He was their shepherd (?) yet [ ]
Powerful, superb, [knowledgeable and expert],
Gilgamesh would not leave [young girls alone],
The daughters of warriors, the brides of young
men.
The gods often heard their complaints.
The gods of heaven [ ] the lord of Uruk.
    "Did [Aruru (?)] create such a rampant wild
    bull?
    Is there no rival? At the *pukku*
    His weapons rise up, his comrades have to
    rise up.
    Gilgamesh will not leave any son alone for
    his father.
    Day and night his [behaviour (?)] is
    overbearing.
    He is the shepherd of Uruk the Sheepfold,
    He is their shepherd, yet [ ]
    Powerful, superb, knowledgeable [and
    expert],
    Gilgamesh will not leave young girls [alone],
    The daughters of warriors, the brides of
    young men.
    Anu often hears their complaints."
They called upon great Aruru:
    "You, Aruru, you created [mankind (?)]!
    Now create someone for him, to match (?) the
    ardour (?) of his energies!
    Let them be regular rivals, and let Uruk be
    allowed peace!"
When Aruru heard this, she created inside herself
the word (?) of Anu.
Aruru washed her hands, pinched off a piece of
clay, cast it out into open country.
She created a [primitive man], Enkidu the warrior:
offspring of silence (?), sky-bolt of Ninurta.

His whole body was shaggy with hair, he was
    furnished with tresses like woman,
His locks of hair grew luxuriant like grain.
He knew neither people nor country; he was
    dressed as cattle are.
With gazelles he eats vegetation,
With cattle he quenches his thirst at the watering
    place.
With wild beasts he presses forward for water.

. . .

Gilgamesh spoke to him, to the hunter,
    "Go, hunter, lead forth the harlot Shamhat,
    And when he approaches the cattle at the
        watering place,
    She must take off her clothes and reveal her
        attractions."

. . .

Then wild beasts arrived at the water; they
    satisfied their need.
And he, Enkidu, whose origin is the mountain,
(Who) eats vegetation with gazelles,
Drinks (at) the watering place with cattle,
Satisfied his need for water with wild beasts.
Shamhat looked at the primitive man,
The murderous youth from the depths of open
    country.
    "Here he is, Shamhat, bare your bosom,
    Open your legs and let him take in your
        attractions!
    Do not pull away, take wind of him!
    He will see you and come close to you.
    Spread open your garments, and let him lie
        upon you,
    Do it for him, the primitive man, as women do.
    Then his cattle, who have grown up in open
        country with him, will become alien to
        him.
    His love-making he will lavish upon you!"
Shamhat loosened her undergarments, opened
    her legs and he took in her attractions.
She did not pull away. She took wind of him,
Spread open her garments, and he lay upon her.
She did for him, the primitive man, as women do.
His love-making he lavished upon her.
For six days and seven nights Enkidu was aroused
    and poured himself into Shamhat.

When he was sated with her charms,
He set his face towards the open country of his
    cattle.
The gazelles saw Enkidu and scattered,
The cattle of open country kept away from his
    body.
For Enkidu had stripped (?); his body was too
    clean.
His legs, which used to keep pace with (?) his
    cattle, were at a standstill.
Enkidu had been diminished, he could not run as
    before.
Yet he had acquired judgment (?), had become
    wiser.
He turned back (?), he sat at the harlot's feet.
The harlot was looking at his expression,
And he listened attentively to what the harlot
    said.
The harlot spoke to him, to Enkidu,
    "You have become [profound] Enkidu, you
        have become like a god.
    Why should you roam open country with
        wild beasts?
    Come, let me take you into Uruk the Sheepfold,
    To the pure house, the dwelling of Anu and
        Ishtar,
    Where Gilgamesh is perfect in strength,
    And is like a wild bull, more powerful than
        (any of) the people."
She spoke to him, and her speech was acceptable.
Knowing his own mind (now), he would seek for
    a friend.

. . .

They stood at the edge of the forest,
Gazed and gazed at the height of the pines,
Gazed and gazed at the entrance to the pines,
Where Humbaba made tracks as he went to
    and fro.
The paths were well trodden and the road was
    excellent.
They beheld the Pine Mountain, dwelling-place of
    gods, shrine of Irnini.
The pines held up their luxuriance even on the
    face of the mountain.
Their shade was good, filling one with happiness.
Undergrowth burgeoned, entangling the forest.

. . .

He struck (?) (his) head (?), and matched him [ ].
They stirred up the ground with the heels of their
    feet,
Sirara and Lebanon were split apart at their
    gyrations,
White clouds grew black,
Death dropped down over them like a fog.
Shamash summoned up great tempests against
    Humbaba,
South Wind, North Wind, East Wind, West Wind,
    Moaning Wind,
Gale, *šaparziqqu*-Wind, *imhullu*-Wind, . . . -Wind
Asakku, Wintry Wind, Tempest, Whirlwind,
Thirteen winds rose up at him and Humbaba's
    face grew dark.
He could not charge forwards, he could not run
    backwards.
Thus the weapons of Gilgamesh succeeded
    against Humbaba.

. . .

He washed his filthy hair, he cleaned his gear,
Shook out his locks over his back,
Threw away his dirty clothes and put on fresh
    ones.
He clothes himself in robes and tied on a sash.
Gilgamesh put his crown on his head
And Ishtar the princess raised her eyes to the
    beauty of Gilgamesh.
    "Come to me, Gilgamesh, and be my lover!
    Bestow on me the gift of your fruit!
    You can be my husband, and I can be your
      wife.
    I shall have a chariot of lapis lazuli and gold
      harnessed for you,
    With wheels of gold, and horns of *elmēšu*-
      stone."

. . .

Gilgamesh made his voice heard and spoke,
He said to Ishtar the princess,
    "What could I give you if I possessed you?
    I would give you body oil and garments,
    I would give you food and sustenance.
    Could I provide you with bread fit for gods?
    Could I provide you with ale fit for kings?"

. . .

Which of your lovers [lasted] forever?
Which of your masterful paramours went to
    heaven?
Come, let me [describe (?)] your lovers to you!
He of the sheep (?) [. . . ..]
    knew him:
For Dumuzi the lover of your youth
You decreed that he should keep weeping year
    after year.
You loved the colourful *allallu*-bird,
But you hit him and broke his wing.
He stays in the woods crying "My wing!"
You loved the lion, whose strength is complete,
But you dug seven and seven pits for him.
You loved the horse, so trustworthy in battle,
But you decreed that he should gallop seven
    leagues (non-stop),
You decreed that he should be overwrought and
    thirsty,
You decreed endless weeping for his mother Sililu.
You loved the shepherd, herdsman, and chief
    shepherd
Who was always heaping up the glowing ashes
    for you,
And cooked ewe-lambs for you every day.
But you hit him and turned him into a wolf,
His own herd-boys hunt him down
And his dogs tear at his haunches.
You loved Ishullanu, your father's gardener,
Who was always bringing you baskets of dates.
They brightened your table every day;
You lifted your eyes to him and went to him.
"My own Ishullanu, let us enjoy your strength,
So put out your hand and touch our vulva!"
But Ishullanu said to you,
"Me? What do you want of me?
Did my mother not bake for me, and did I
    not eat?
What I eat (with you) would be loaves of
    dishonor and disgrace,
Rushes would be my only covering against the cold."
You listened as he said this,
And you hit him, turned him into a frog (?),
Left him to stay amid the fruits of his labours.
But the pole (?) goes up no more, [his] bucket
    goes down no more.

And how about me? You will love me and then
    [treat me] just like them!"
When Ishtar heard this,
Ishtar was furious, and [went up] to heaven.
Ishtar went up and wept before her father Anu,
Her tears flowed before her mother Antu.
    "Father, Gilgamesh has shamed me again and
        again!
    Gilgamesh spelt out to me my dishonour,
    My dishonour and my disgrace."
Any made his voice heard and spoke,
He said to the princess Ishtar,
    "Why (?) didn't you accuse Gilgamesh the
        king for yourself,
    Since Gilgamesh spelt out your dishonour,
    Your dishonour and your disgrace?"
Ishtar made her voice heard and spoke,
She said to her father Anu,
    "Father, please give me the Bull of Heaven,
        and let me strike Gilgamesh down!
    Let me . . . Gilgamesh in his dwelling!
    If you don't give me the Bull of Heaven,
    I shall strike (?) [ ]
    I shall set my face towards the infernal
        regions,
    I shall raise up the dead, and they will eat the
        living,
    I shall make the dead outnumber the living!"
. . .
At the snorting of the Bull of Heaven a chasm
    opened up, and one hundred young men of
    Uruk fell into it,
Two hundred young men, three hundred young
    men.
At its second snorting another chasm opened up,
    and another hundred young men of Uruk fell
    into it,
Two hundred young men, three hundred young
    men fell into it.
At its third snorting a chasm opened up,
And Enkidu fell into it.
But Enkidu leapt out. He seized the Bull of
    Heaven by the horns.
The Bull of Heaven blew spittle into his face,
With its thick tail it whipped up its dung.
. . .

Then Gilgamesh, like a but[cher (?)] heroic and
    [ ]
Plunged his sword in between the base of the
    horns and the neck tendons.
When they had struck down the Bull of Heaven
    they pulled out its innards,
Set them before Shamash,
Backed away and prostrated themselves before
    Shamash.
Then the two brothers sat down.
Ishtar went up on to the wall of Uruk the
    Sheepfold.
She was contorted with rage, she hurled down
    curses,
    "That man, Gilgamesh, who reviled me has
        killed the Bull of Heaven!"
Enkidu listened to Ishtar saying this,
And he pulled out the Bull of Heaven's shoulder
    and slapped it into her face:
    "If I could only get at you as that does,
    I would do the same to you myself,
    I would hand its intestines on your arms!"
. . .
Then daylight came. [And] Enkidu said to
    Gilgamesh,
    "O my brother, what a dream [I saw] last
        night!
    Anu, Elil, Ea, and heavenly Shamash [were in
        the assembly].
    And Anu said to Ellil, 'As they have slain the
        Bull of Heaven,
    So too they have slain Huwawa, who [guarded]
        the mountains pla[nted] with pines.' "
And Anu said, "One of them [must die]."
Ellil replied: "Let Enkidu die, but let Gilgamesh
    not die."
Then heavenly Shamash said to valiant Ellil,
"Was it not according to your word that they slew
    the Bull of Heaven and Huwawa? Should now
    innocent Enkidu die?"
But Ellil turned in anger to heavenly Shamash
    saying,
"(The fact is), you accompanied them daily, like
    one of their comrades."
Enkidu lay down before Gilgamesh, his tears
    flowing like streams.

"O my brother, my brother is so dear to me.
But they are taking me from my brother."
And: "I shall sit among the dead, I shall [ ] the
threshold of the dead;
Never again [shall I see] my dear brother with my
own eyes."

. . .

He decided to curse the harlot too.
"Come, Shamhat, I shall fix a fate for you!
[Curses(?)] shall not cease for ever and ever.
I shall curse you with a great curse!
Straight away my curses shall rise up against
you!
You shall never make your house voluptuous
again,
You shall not release [ ] of your young bulls,
You shall not let them into the girls' rooms.
Filth shall impregnate your lovely lap (?),
The drunkard shall soak your party dress
with vomit,

. . .

You shall never obtain the best cosmetic [oil (?),]
Bright silver, people's affluence, shall not
accumulate in your house,

. . .

The crossroads (?) shall be your only sitting
place,
Waste ground your only lying place, the shade
of a city wall your only sitting place.
Thorns and spikes shall skin your feet,
The drunkard and the thirsty shall slap your
cheek,

. . .

Because you defiled me when I was pure,
Because you seduced me in the open country
when I was pure."
Shamash heard the utterance of his mouth.
Immediately a loud voice called down to him
from the sky:
"Enkidu, why are you cursing my harlot
Shamhat,
Who fed you on food fit for gods,
Gave you ale to drink, fit for kings,
Clothed you with a great robe,
Then provided you with Gilgamesh for a fine
partner?

And now Gilgamesh, the friend who is a
brother to you
Will lay you to rest on a great bed
And lay you to resent on a bed of loving care,
And let you stay in a restful dwelling, the
dwelling on the left.
Prices of the earth will kiss your feet.
He will make the people of Uruk weep for
you, mourn for you,
Will fill the proud people with woe,
And he himself will neglect his appearance
after you(r death).
Clothed only in a lionskin, he will roam the
open country."
Enkidu listened to the speech of Shamash the
warrior.
[His anger abated (?)]; his heart became quiet
(*about 2 lines missing*)
"Come, Shamhat, I shall change your fate!
My utterance, which cursed you, shall bless
you instead.
Governors and princes shall love you,
The single-league man shall smite his thigh
(for you),
The double-league man shall shake out his
locks (for you).
The herdsman shall not hold back for you, he
shall undo his belt for you.
He shall give you ivory, lapis lazuli, and gold,
Rings (and) brooches (?) shall be presents for
you.

. . .

Gilgamesh mourned bitterly for Enkidu his friend,
And roamed open country.
"Shall I die too? Am I not like Enkidu?
Grief has entered my innermost being,
I am afraid of Death, and so I roam open
country.
I shall take the road and go quickly
To see Ut-napishtim, son of Ubara-Tutu.

. . .

[Gilgamesh spoke to her, to Siduri the alewife],
"[How could my cheeks not be wasted, nor my
face dejected],
[Nor my heart wretched, nor my appearance
worn out],

[Nor my grief in my innermost being],
[Nor my face like that of a long-distance
      traveller],
[Nor my face weathered by cold and heat . . .],
[Nor roaming open country, clad only in a
      lionskin?]
[My friend whom I love so much, who
      experienced every hardship with me],
[Enkidu, whom I love so much, who
      experienced every hardship with me—]
[The fate of mortals conquered him!] Six days
      [and seven nights I wept over him],
[I did not allow him to] be buried, [until a
      worm fell out of his nose].
[I was frightened and].
I am afraid of Death, [and so I roam open
      country].
The words of my friend [weigh upon me].
[I roam open country] for long distances; the
      words of my friend Enkidu weigh upon me.
I roam open country on long journeys.
[How, O how] could I stay silent, how, O how
      could I keep quiet [ ]?
My friend whom I love has turned to clay:
Enkidu my friend whom I love [has turned to
      clay.]
Am I not like him? Must I lie down too,
Never to rise, ever again?"
Ut-napishtim spoke to him, to Gilgamesh,
      "Why do you prolong grief, Gilgamesh?
      Since [the gods made you] from the flesh of
      gods and mankind,
      Since [the gods] made you like your father
      and mother,
      [Death is inevitable (?)] at some time, both
      for Gilgamesh and for a fool,
      But a throne is set down [for you (?)] in the
      assembly [ ].

      . . .

      [Why (?)] have you exerted yourself? What
      have you achieved (?)?
      You have made yourself weary for lack of
      sleep,
      You only fill your flesh with grief,
      You only bring the distant days (of reckoning)
      closer.

Mankind's fame is cut down like reeds in a
      reed-bed.

. . .

Nobody sees Death,
Nobody sees the face of Death,
Nobody hears the voice of Death.
Savage Death just cuts mankind down.
Sometimes we build a house, sometimes we
      make a nest,
But then brothers divide it upon inheritance.
Sometimes there is hostility in [the land],
But then the river rises and brings flood-water.
Dragonflies drift on the river,
Their faces look upon the face of the Sun.
(But then) suddenly there is nothing.
The sleeping (?) and the dead are just like
      each other,
Death's picture cannot be drawn.
The primitive man (is as any) young man (?).
      When they blessed me,
The Anunnaki, the great gods, assembled;
Mammitum who creates fate decreed
      destinies with them.
They appointed death and life.
They did not mark out days for death,
But they did so for life."

. . .

Ut-napishtim spoke to him, to Gilgamesh,
"Let me reveal to you a closely guarded
      matter, Gilgamesh,
And let me tell you the secret of the gods.
Shuruppak is a city that you yourself know,
Situated [on the bank of] the Euphrates.
That city was already old when the gods
      within it
Decided that the great gods should make
      a flood.
There was Anu their father,
Warrior Ellil their counsellor,
Ninurta was their chamberlain,
Enuugi their canal-controller.
Far-sighted Ea swore the oath (of secrecy)
      with them,
So he repeated their speech to a reed hut,
"Reed hut, reed hut, brick wall, brick wall,
Listen, reed hut, and pay attention, brick wall:

(This is the message:)
'Man of Shuruppak, son of Ubara-Tutu,
Dismantle your house, build a boat.
Leave possessions, search out living things.
Reject chattels and save lives!
Put aboard the seed of all living things, into
    the boat.
The boat that you are to build
Shall have her dimensions in proportion,
Her width and length shall be in harmony,
Roof her like the Apsu.'
I realized and spoke to my master Ea,
'I have paid attention to the words that you
    spoke in this way,
My master, and I shall act upon them.
But how can I explain myself to the city, the
    men and the elders?'
Ea made his voice heard and spoke,
He said to me, his servant,
'You shall speak to them thus:
"I think that Ellil has rejected me,
And so I cannot stay in your city,
And I cannot set foot in Ellil's land again." '

. . .

When the first light of dawn appeared
The country gathered about me.
The carpenter brought his axe,
The reed-worker brought his stone,

. . .

On the fifth day I laid down her form.
One acre was her circumference, ten poles
    each the height of her walls,
Her top edge was likewise ten poles all round.
I laid down her structure, drew it out,
Gave her six decks,
Divided her into seven.
Her middle I divided into nine,
Drove the water pegs into her middle.
I saw to the paddles and put down what was
    needed:
Three *sar* of bitumen I poured into the kiln,
Three *sar* of pitch I poured into the inside.
Three *sar* of oil they fetched, the workmen
    who carried the baskets.
Not counting the *sar* of oil which the dust (?)
    soaked up,

The boatman stowed away two more *sar* of oil.
At the [ ] I slaughtered oxen.
I sacrificed sheep every day.
I gave the workmen ale and beer to drink,
Oil and wine as if they were river water
They made a feast, like the New Year's Day
    festival.
When the sun [rose (?)] I provided hand oil.
[When] the sun went down the boat was
    complete.
[The launching was (?)] very difficult;
Launching rollers had to be fetched (from)
    above (to) below.
Two-thirds of it [stood clear of the water line
    (?)].
I loaded her with everything there was,
Loaded her with all the silver,
Loaded her with all the gold
Loaded her with all the seed of living things,
    all of them.
I put on board the boat all my kith and kin.
Put on board cattle from open country, wild
    beasts from open country, all kinds of
    craftsmen.

. . .

When the first light of dawn appeared,
A black cloud came up from the base of the sky.
Adad kept rumbling inside it.
Shullat and Hanish were marching ahead,
Marched as chamberlains (over) (?) mountain
    and country.
Erakal pulled out the mooring (?) poles,
Ninurta marched on and made the weir(s)
    overflow.
The Anunnaki had to carry torches,
They lit up the land with their brightness.
The calm before the Storm-god came over the sky,
Everything light turned to darkness.
[ ]
On the first day the tempest [rose up],
Blew swiftly and [brought (?) the flood-weapon],
Like a battle force [the destructive *kašūšu*-weapon]
    passed over [the people]
No man could see his fellow,
Now could people be distinguished from the sky.
Even the gods were afraid of the flood-weapon.

They withdrew; they went up to the heaven of Anu.
The gods cowered, like dogs crouched by an
    outside wall.
Ishtar screamed like a woman giving birth;
The Mistress of the Gods, sweet of voice, was
    wailing,
"Has that time really returned to clay,
Because I spoke evil in the gods' assembly?
How could I have spoken such evil in the gods'
    assembly?
I should have (?) ordered a battle to destroy my
    people;
I myself gave birth (to them), they are my own
    people,
Yet they fill the sea like fish spawn!"
The gods of Anunnaki were weeping with her.
The gods, humbled, sat there weeping.
Their lips were closed and covered with scab.
For six days and [seven (?)] nights
The wind blew, flood and tempest overwhelmed
    the land;
When the seventh day arrived the tempest, flood
    and onslaught
Which had struggled like a woman in labour,
    blew themselves out (?).
The sea became calm, the *imhullu*-wind grew
    quiet, the flood held back.
I looked at the weather; silence reigned,
For all mankind had returned to clay.
The flood-plain was flat as a roof.
I opened a porthole and light fell on my cheeks.
I bent down, then sat. I wept.
My tears ran down my cheeks.
I looked for banks, for limits to the sea.
Areas of land were emerging everywhere (?).
The boat had come to rest on Mount Nimush.
. . .
When the seventh day I arrived,
I put out and released a dove.
The dove went; it came back,
For no perching place was visible to it, and it
    turned around.
I put out and released a swallow.
The swallow went; it came back,
For no perching place was visible to it, and it
    turned round.

I put out and released a raven.
The raven went, and saw the waters receding.
And it ate, preened (?), lifted its tail and did not
    turn round.
Then I put (everything ?) out to the four winds,
    and I made a sacrifice,
Set out a *surqinnu*-offering upon the mountain
    peak,
Arranged the jars seven and seven;
Into the bottom of them I poured (essences of ?)
    reeds, pine, and myrtle.
The gods smelt the fragrance,
The gods like flies gathered over the sacrifice.
. . .
As soon as Ellil arrived
He saw the boat. Ellil was furious,
Filled with anger at the Igigi gods.
"What sort of life survived? No man should have
    lived through the destruction!"
Ninurta made his voice heard and spoke,
He said to the warrior Ellil,
"Who other than Ea would have done such a
    thing?
For Ea can do everything?"
Ea made his voice heard and spoke,
He said to the warrior Ellil,
"You are the sage of the gods, warrior,
So how, O how, could you fail to consult, and
    impose the flood?
Punish the sinner for his sin, punish the criminal
    for his crime,
But ease off, let work not cease; be patient,
    let not [ ]
Instead of your imposing a flood, let a lion come
    up and diminish the people.
Instead of your imposing a flood, let a wolf come
    up and diminish the people.
Instead of your imposing a flood, let famine be
    imposed and [lessen] the land.
Instead of your imposing a flood, let Erra rise up
    and savage the people.
I did not disclose the secret to the great gods,
I just shows Atrahasis a dream, and thus he heard
    the secret of the gods."
Now the advice (that prevailed) was his advice.
Ellil came up into the boat,

And seized my hand and led me up.

He led up my woman and made her kneel down
at my side.

He touched our foreheads, stood between us,
blessed us:

"Until now Ut-napishtim was mortal,

But henceforth Ut-napishtim and his woman
shall be as we gods are.

Ut-napishtim shall dwell far off at the mouth of
the rivers."

. . .

Ut-napishtim spoke to him, to Gilgamesh,
"Gilgamesh, you came, weary, striving,
What can I give you to take back to your
country?
Let me reveal a closely guarded matter,
Gilgamesh,
And let me tell you the secret of the gods.
There is a plant whose root is like camel-thorn,
Whose thorn, like a rose's, will spike [your
hands].
If you yourself can win that plant, you will
find [rejuvenation (?)]."

When Gilgamesh heard this, he opened the pipe,

He tied heavy stone to his feet.

They dragged him down into the Apsu, and [he
saw the plant].

He took the plant himself: it spiked [his hands].

He cut the heavy stones from his feet.

The sea threw him up on its shore.

Gilgamesh spoke to him, to Ur-shanabi the
boatman,
"Ur-shanabi, this plant is a plant to cure a
crisis!
With it a man may win the breath of life.
I shall take it back to Uruk the Sheepfold; I
shall give it to an elder to eat, and so try
out the plant.

Its name (shall be): "An old man grows into
a young man."
I took shall eat (it) and turn into the young
man that I once was."

At twenty leagues they ate their ration.

At thirty leagues they stopped for the night.

Gilgamesh saw a pool whose water was cool,

And went down into the water and washed.

A snake smelt the fragrance of the plant.

It came up silently and carried off the plant.

As it took it away, it shed its scaly skin.

Thereupon Gilgamesh sat down and wept.

His tears flowed over his cheeks.

[He spoke to (?)] Ut-shanabi the boatman,
"For what purpose (?), Ur-shanabi, have my
arms grown weary?
For what purpose (?) was the blood inside me
so red (?)?
I did not gain an advantage for myself,

. . .

And the spirit of Enkidu came out of the Earth
like a gust of wind.

They hugged and kissed (?),

They discussed, they agonized.
"Tell me, my friend, tell me, my friend,
Tell me Earth's conditions that you found!"
"I can't tell you, my friend, I can't tell you!
If I tell you Earth's conditions that I found,
You must sit (and) weep!
I would sit and weep!
[Your wife (?),] whom you touched, and your
heart was glad,
Vermin eat [like (?)] an old [garment].
[Your son (?) whom] you touched, and your
heart was glad,
[Sits in a crevice (?)] full of dust.
'Woe' she said, and grovelled in the dust.
'Woe' he said, and grovelled in the dust."

STUDY QUESTIONS

1. What are the gods' reasons for their humbling of Gilgamesh?
2. Contrast the relationship between Enkidu and Gilgamesh with those between Gilgamesh and
   female figures in the narrative. What does the document suggest about the superiority of
   same-sex friendship to heterosexual encounters?

2.3. FROM LAWS OF HAMMURABI, CA. 1772 BCE

This law code, assembled by King Hammurabi of Babylon, consists of almost three hundred laws and accompanying punishments. It is recorded in the Akkadian language in cuneiform on several tablets (one of which is on display at the Louvre Museum in Paris). Although the most famous of these laws—"An eye for an eye, a tooth for a tooth"—deals with responses to harmful acts, many of the laws deal with economic peace, such as proper payment of wages, or social peace, such as the framework for divorce.

When the lofty Anu, king of the Anunnaki gods, and Enlil, lord of heaven and earth, he who determines the destiny of the land, committed the rule of all mankind to Marduk, the chief son of Ea; when they made him great among the Igigi gods; when they pronounced the lofty name of Babylon; when they made it famous among the quarters of the world and in its midst established an everlasting kingdom whose foundations were firm as heaven and earth—at that time, Anu and Enlil named me, Hammurabi, the exalted prince, the worshipper of the gods, to cause justice to prevail in the land, to destroy the wicked and the evil, to prevent the strong from oppressing the weak, to go forth like the sun over the black-headed people, to enlighten the land and to further the welfare of the people. Hammurabi, the shepherd named by Enlil, am I, who brought about plenty and abundance; . . . obedient to the mighty Shamash; . . . who rebuilt Ebabbar for Shamash, his helper; . . . the powerful king, the sun of Babylon, who cause light to go forth over the lands of Sumer and Akkad; the king who cause the four quarters of the world to render obedience; the favorite of Ishtar, am I.

When Marduk sent me to rule the people and to bring help to the country, I established the law and justice in the language of the land and promoted the welfare of the people. At that time (I decreed):

THE ADMINISTRATION OF JUSTICE

1. If a man accuse a man, and charge him with murder, but cannot convict him, the accuser shall be put to death.

3. If a man in a case before the court, offer testimony concerning deeds of violence, and do not establish the testimony that he has given—if that case be involving like, the man shall be put to death.

4. If he offer testimony concerning grain or money, he shall himself bear the penalty imposed in that case.

5. If a judge pronounce a judgment, render a decision, deliver a sealed verdict, and afterward reverse his judgment, they shall prosecute the judge for reversing the judgment which he has pronounced, and he shall pay twelvefold the damages which were awarded in said judgment; and publicly they shall expel him from his seat of judgment, and he shall not return, and with the judges in a case he shall not take his seat.

PROPERTY

9. If a man who has lost anything that which was lost in the hand of another man; and the man in whose hand the lost property is found say, "A man sold it to me, I purchased it in the presence of

From Nels M. Bailkey and Richard Lim, eds. *Readings in Ancient History: Thought and Experience from Gilgamesh to St. Augustine*, 7th ed. Andover: Cengage Learning, 2011, pp. 28–36.

witnesses"; and the owner of the lost property say, "I will bring witnesses who know the lost property"; if the purchaser produce the seller who has sold it to him and the witnesses in whose presence he purchases it, and the owner of the lost property produce witnesses who know his lost property, the judges shall look into their matters. The witnesses in whose presence the purchase was made and the witnesses who know the lost property shall declare what they know in the presence of god. The seller shall be put to death as a thief; the owner of the lost property shall receive his lost property; the purchases shall take from the estate of the seller the money which he paid out.

10. If the alleged purchases do not produce the seller who sold it to him, and the witnesses in whose presence he purchased it, and if the owner of the lost property produce witnesses who know the lost property, the purchaser is a thief, he shall be put to death; the owner of the lost property shall receive his lost property.

11. If the alleged owner of the lost property do not produce witnesses who know his lost property, he is a mischief-maker, he has stirred up strife, he shall be put to death.

22. If a man practice brigandage and be captured, that man shall be put to death.

23. If the brigand be not captured, the man who has been robbed shall establish the amount of his loss before the god, and . . . the governor, in whose land or border the robbery was committed, shall compensate him for whatsoever was lost.

24. If there were loss of life, the city and governor shall pay one mina of silver to his heirs.

IRRIGATION

53. If a man neglect to strengthen his dike, and do not strengthen his dike, and a break be made in his dike and he let the water carry away farmland, then man in whose dike the break has been made shall restore the grain which he has damaged.

54. If he be not able to restore the grain, they shall set him and his goods, and the farmers whose grain the water has carried away shall divide the results of the sale.

55. If a man open his canal for irrigation and neglect it and he let the water carry away an adjacent field, he shall measure out grain on the basis of the adjacent fields.

56. If a man open up the water and he let the water carry away the preparations of an adjacent field, he shall measure out ten *kor* of grain for each *gan* [of damaged land].

HOUSE RENTAL

78. If a man who is a tenant have paid the full amount of money for his rent for the year to the owner of the house, and he the owner say to him before his days are full, "Vacate," the owner of the house, because he made the tenant move out of his house before his days were full, shall lose the money which the tenant paid him.

CAPITAL AND INTEREST

86. If a merchant put out grain at an interest, for one *kor* he shall receive one hundred *sila* of grain as interest [*i.e.* 20 percent].

87. If he put money out at interest, for one shekel of silver he shall receive one-fifth of a shekel as interest.

89. If a merchant increase the interest on grain beyond one hundred *sila* for one *kor*, for the interest on silver beyond one-sixth shekel plus six *she* [*i.e.*, one-fifth of a shekel] and take his interest, he shall lose whatever he put out at interest.

93. If a merchant put out grain or silver at interest and when he puts it out at interest he give silver by the small stone and grain by the small measure but when he receives it back he receive silver by the large stone and grain by the large measure, that man shall lose whatever he put out.

REGULATION OF TRADE

104. If a merchant give an agent grain, wool, oil, or goods of any kind with which to trade, the agent shall write down the money received and return it to the merchant. The agent shall take a sealed receipt for the money which he gives to the merchant.

105. If the agent be careless and do not take a receipt for the money which he has given to the merchant, the money not receipted for shall not be placed to his account.

108. If a barmaid do not take grain in payment of drink, but if she take money by the great stone, or make the measure of drink smaller than the measure of grain, they shall prosecute that barmaid, and they shall throw her into the water.

109. If outlaws hatch a conspiracy in the house of a wine-seller, and she do not arrest these outlaws and bring them to the palace, that wine-seller shall be put to death.

110. If a priestess or a nun who is not resident in a convent open a wineshop or enter a wineshop for a drink, they shall burn that woman.

DEBT SLAVERY

117. If an obligation of a man mature and he give his wife, his son, or his daughter, or bind them over to service, for three years they shall work in the house of their purchaser or master; in the fourth year their freedom shall be given to them.

118. If he bind over to service a male or female slave, and if the merchant transfer or sell such a slave, there is no ground for a suit.

MARRIAGE AND THE FAMILY

128. If a man take a wife and do not draw up a contract with her, that woman is not a wife.

129. If the wife of a man be taken in lying with another man, they shall bind them and throw them into the water. If the husband of the woman spare the life of his wife, the king [also] shall spare the life of his servant.

131. If a man accuse his wife and she have not been taken in lying with another man, she shall take an oath in the name of god and she shall return to her house.

136. If a man desert his city and run away, and afterward his wife enter into another house, if that man return and seize his wife, because he hated his city and fled, the wife of the fugitive shall not return to her husband.

138. If a man put away his wife who has not borne him children, he shall give her money to the amount of her marriage settlement and he shall make good to her dowry which she brought from her father's house and then he may put her away.

141. If the wife of a man who is living in his house set her face to go out, playing the fool, ruining her house, and belittling her husband, they shall convict her; if her husband announce her divorce, he may put her away. For her journey home no alimony shall be given to her. If her husband do not announce her divorce, her husband may take another woman. That woman [the first wife] shall dwell in the house of her husband as a maidservant.

142. If a woman hate her husband and say, "Thou shalt not have me," her past shall be inquired into for any deficiency of hers; and if she have been careful and be without past sin and her husband have been going out and greatly belittling her, that woman has no blame. She shall take her dowry and go to her father's house.

143. If she have not been careful, have been going out, ruining her house and belittle her husband, they shall throw that woman into the water.

145. If a man take a wife and she do not present him with children, and he set his face to take a concubine, that man may take a concubine and bring her into his house. That concubine shall not take precedence of his wife.

146. If a man take a wife and she give a maidservant to her husband and she bear children and afterward that maidservant would take precedence of her mistress; because she has borne children, her mistress may not sell her for money, but she may reduce her to bondage and count her among the maidservants.

150. If a man make his wife a present of a field, garden, house, and goods and deliver to her a sealed deed, after the death of her husband her children may not make any claim against her. The mother after her death may give them to her child whom she loves, but to a brother she may not give them.

159. If a man who has brought a present to the house of his [prospective] father-in-law and has given the marriage settlement look with longing upon another woman and say to his father-in-law, "I will not take thy daughter," the father of

the daughter shall take to himself whatever was brought to him.

160. If a man bring a present to the house of his [prospective] father-in-law and give a marriage settlement and the father of the daughter say, "I will not give thee my daughter," he the father-in-law shall double everything which was brought to him and return it.

162. If a man take a wife and she bear him children and that woman die, her father may not lay claim to her dowry. Her dowry belongs to the children.

165. If a man make a present of field, garden, and house to his son who is first in his eyes and write for him a sealed deed; after the father dies, when the brothers divide, he shall take the present which the father gave him, and over and above they shall divide the goods of the father's house equally.

168. If a man set his face to disinherit his son and say to the judges, "I will disinherit my son," the judges shall inquire into his past, and if the son have not committed a crime sufficiently grave to cut him off from sonship, the father may not cut off his son from sonship.

170. If a man's wife bear him children and his maidservant bear him children, and the father during his lifetime say to the children which the maidservant bore him, "My children," and reckon them with the children of his wife; after the father dies the children of the wife and the children of the maidservant shall divide the goods of the father's house equally. The child of the wife shall have the right of choice at the division.

ADOPTION

185. If a man with his father's consent take a young child for sonship and rear him, one may not bring claim for that adopted son.

191. If a man who has taken a young child for sonship and reared him establish a house and later have children; if he set his face to cut off the adopted son, that son shall not go away empty. The father who reared him shall give to him of his goods one-third the portion of a con, and then he shall go. He need not give him of field, garden, or house.

PERSONAL INJURY AND MANSLAUGHTER

195. If a man strike his father, they shall cut off his hand.

196. If a man destroy the eye of another man, they shall destroy his eye.

197. If he break a man's bone, they shall break his bone.

198. If he destroy the eye of a common man or break a bone of a common man, he shall pay one mina of silver.

199. If he destroy the eye of a man's slave or break a bone of a man's slave, he shall pay one-half his price.

206. If a man strike another man in a quarrel and wound him, that man shall swear, "I did not strike him intentionally," and he shall be responsible for the physician.

207. If he die as a result of the blow, he shall swear as above, and if it were the son of a gentleman, he shall pay one-third mina of silver.

PHYSICIAN'S FEES

215. If a physician make a deep incision upon a man with his bronze lancet and save the man's life; or if he operate on the eye socket of a man with his bronze lancet and save that man's eye, he shall receive ten shekels of silver.

216. If it were a common man, he shall receive five shekels.

217. If it were a man's slave, the owner of the slave shall give two shekels of silver to the physician.

218. If a physician make a deep incision upon a man with his bronze lancet and cause the man's death, or operate on the eye socket of a man with his bronze lancet and destroy the man's eye, they shall cut off his hand.

221. If a physician set a broken bone for a man or cure a sprained tendon, the patient shall give five shekels of silver to the physician.

222. If it were a common man, he shall give three shekels of silver.

223. If it were a man's slave, the owner of the slave shall give two shekels of silver to the physician.

228. If a builder erect a house for a man and complete it, he shall give him two shekels of silver per *sar* of house as his wage.

229.   If a builder erect a house for a man and do not make its construction firm and the house which he built collapse and cause the death of the owner of the house, that builder shall be put to death.

233.   If a builder erect a house for a man and do not surround it with walls of proper construction, and a wall fall in, that builder shall strengthen that wall at his own expense.

EPILOGUE

The righteous laws, which Hammurabi, the wise kind, established and by which he gave the land stable support and good government. Hammurabi, the perfect king, am I. I was not careless, nor was I neglectful of the black-headed people, whose rule Enlil presented and Marduk delivered to me.

The great gods proclaimed me, and I am the guardian shepherd whose scepter is righteous and whose beneficent shadow is spread over my city. In my bosom I carried the people of the land of Sumer and Akkad; under my protection I brought their brethren into security; in my wisdom I sheltered them.

That the strong might not oppress the weak, and that they should give justice to the orphan and the widow, in Babylon, the city whose turrets Anu and Enlil raised, in Esagila, the temple whose foundations are firm as heaven and earth, for the pronouncing of judgments in the land, for the rendering of decisions for the land, and to give justice to the oppressed, thy weighty words I have written upon my monument, and in the presence of my image as king of righteousness have I established it.

The king who is preeminent among kings am I. My words are precious, my wisdom is unrivaled. By the command of Shamash, the great judge of heaven and earth, may I make righteousness to shine forth on the land. By the order of Marduk, my lord, may no one efface my statuses, may my name be remembered with favor in Esagila forever.

Let any oppressed man, who has a cause, come before my image as king of justice! Let him read the inscription on my monument! Let him give heed to my weighty words! And may my monument enlighten him as to his cause and may he understand his case! May he set his heart at ease! (and he will exclaim): "Hammurabi indeed is a ruler who is like a real father to his people; he has given reverence to the words of Marduk, his lord; he has obtained victory for Marduk in north and south; he has made glad the heart of Marduk, his lord; he has established prosperity for the people for all time and given good government to the land." . . .

In the days that are yet to come, for all future time, may the king who is in the land observe the words of justice which I have written upon my monument! May he not alter the judgments of the land which I have pronounced, or the decisions of the country which I have rendered! May he not efface my statuses! If that man have wisdom, if he wish to give his land good government, let him give attention to the words which I have written upon my monument! And may this monument enlighten him as to procedure and administration, the judgments which I have pronounced, and the decisions which I have rendered for the land! And let him rightly rule his black-headed people; let him pronounce judgments for them and render for them decisions! Let him root out the wicked and the evil from his land! Let him promote the welfare of his people!

Hammurabi, the king of justice, to whom Shamash has committed truth, am I. My words are weighty; my deeds are unrivaled; only to the fool are they vain; to the wise they are worthy of every praise.

STUDY QUESTIONS

1.   How, specifically, is Hammurabi proclaiming himself an agent of divine power, especially at the document's beginning and conclusion?
2.   What does the document suggest about the relative status of women in Babylonian society at this period?
3.   When are financial and capital punishments applied in the code, and is there a consistent principle at work here?

2.4. "LOYALIST TEACHING," CA. 1550–1000 BCE

An Egyptian set of instructions, this text speaks as a father to his children. Two subjects are advised on: first, that loyalty and obedience to the pharaoh are absolutely necessary (because the pharaoh will protect his supporters); and second, that a member of society must also be respectful of his fellow citizens and participate in civic duty. Thus, all the teachings encourage order in the face of chaos. Although fragmented, these teachings exude the zeal and devotion of the "father" for a harmonious society.

Praise the king within your bodies! 2
Be close to his Majesty in your hearts!
Put terror of him throughout the day!
Create acclamation for him at every season!
He is the Perception which is in breasts:
his eyes probe every body.
He is the Sungod under whose governance one
    lives:
the man under his shade will have great
    possessions.
He is the Sungod by whose rays one sees:
he illuminates the Two Lands more than the sun.
. . .
The king is Sustenance; his speech is Plenty. 5
The man he makes is someone who will always
    exist.
He is the heir of every god,
the protector of his creators.
They strike his opponents for him.
. . .
Fight for his name! Respect his oath! 6
Make no opposition against a reward of his
    giving.
Acclaim the Red-king! Worship the White
    Crown!
Pay homage to the uplifter of the Double Crown!
You should do these things, so that your limbs
    may prosper!
You will find this good for all time—
being on earth, without sorrow,
passing lifetime in peace!

Enter into the earth which the king gives! 7
Rest in the place of all time!
Join with the eternal cavern!—
with your children's homes full of love for you,
your heirs remaining in your positions.
Conform [to] my example! Do not neglect my
    words!
Make good the rule of my making!

May you speak to your children! 8
Speech has taught, since the time of the God.
I am a noble to be listened to,
whose understanding is recognized by his lord.
Do not overstep my example! Do not be
    indifferent to my pattern!
You should be free from disloyal action!
The son who hears will be a faultless man.
Can any plan of his not succeed?
    *
You will praise these things after years, 9
for this soundness gives landfall.
Another method for developing your hearts,
—which is even better—concerning your servants:
care for men, organize people,
that you may secure servants who are active!
It is mankind who create all that exists;
one lives on what comes from their hands.
They are lacking, and then poverty prevails.

The professions are what provide provisions. 10
A house is empty, with its foundations uprooted,

and the very sound of them re-establishes its
walls!
The man who sleeps until dawn is a lord of many;
there will be no sleep for the solitary man.
No one sends a lion on a mission.
No herd can isolate himself from the walled
enclosure;
its voice is like the thirsty creature's outside the
well,
with [decay] around it, and the wailing of birds.

One must long for the Nileflood, then one profits
by it;   11
no ploughed field exists of itself.
The cattle who belong to a cowherd are great:
it is the cattleherd who can drive the wild bull.
it is [the herdsman] who brings [the animals]
across to land.
[The shepherd] will be a plentiful flock, without
number!
To God, [these are] excellent professions.
Someone who is capable in them is a clever man.
Do not make a field-worker wretched with taxes—
let him be well off, and he will still be there for
you the next year.
If he lives, you have his hands;
you ruin him, and then he plans to turn
vagabond.
. . .

It is the evil man who destroys his own
mound   13
a town is founded for the man who is loved.
Patience is a man's monument.
Quietness is excellent, [calmness] is good.
The man who foresees what will come [has never
been thwarted];
the man with powerful authority prevails.
The merciful—the cow bears for him;
the bad herdsman—his herd is small.

Fight for men in every respect!   14
They are a flock, good for their lord.
Evidently by them alone one lives;
they are good also when joining the earth.
You should look to [your . . . who . . .]!
You should watch over your funerary priests:
the son is disloyal, but the priest remains!
It is a kind man who is named "heir."
Lay the noble dead to rest; make invocations in
their name;
[honour] the blessed dead; bring food-offer[ings]!
[This is better for] the doer than for the man for
whom it is done—
the beneficiary protects the man who is still on
earth."

So it ends, from start to finish,
as found in writing.

STUDY QUESTIONS

1. Why should a man be loyal to the pharaoh, and what specific benefits can he expect to gain?
2. How does the document elevate seemingly ignoble professions and relate them to the king's job?

2.5. EGYPTIAN *BOOK OF THE DEAD*: "NEGATIVE CONFESSION," IN USE CA. 1550–50 BCE

Used in the Egyptian funeral rite for a millennium, the *Book of the Dead*—perhaps more properly translated as the *Book of Going Forth into Day*—corresponds to the various steps to the Egyptian afterlife. Most commonly written in *hieroglyphics*,[2] the *Book of the Dead* provides spells for the departed soul's journey. This selection, the "Negative Confession," represents the dead person's oath to the god Osiris that he had not committed any of the forty-two sins that would bar his way to the afterlife. The rational path of the *Book of the Dead* reflects the Egyptian concept that the gods are not merely capricious beings unconcerned with the well-being of humanity.

Homage to thee, O Great God [Osiris], Lord of Double Maati, I have come to thee, O my Lord, I have brought myself hither that I may behold thy beauties. I know thee, and I know thy name, and I know the names of the two and forty gods who exist with thee in this Hall of Double Maati, who live as warders of sinners and who feed upon their blood on the day when the lives of men are taken into account in the presence of the god Un-nefer [Osiris]: in truth, ["Lord of Justice"] is thy name. In truth I have come to thee, and I have brought *maat* to thee, and I have expelled wickedness for thee.

1. I have not done evil to mankind.
2. I have not oppressed the members of my family.
3. I have not wrought evil in the place of right and truth.
4. I have no knowledge of worthless men.
5. I have not wrought evil. . .
7. I have not brought forward my name for exaltation to honors.
8. I have not ill-treated servants.
9. I have not belittled a god.
10. I have not defrauded the oppressed one of his property.
11. I have not done that which is an abomination unto the gods.
14. I have made no man to suffer hunger.
15. I have made no one to weep.
16. I have done no murder.
17. I have not given the order for murder to be done for me.
18. I have not inflicted pain upon mankind.
22. I have not committed fornication.
26. I have not encroached upon the fields of others.
27. I have not added to the weight of the scales [to cheat the seller].
28. I have not misread the pointer of the scales [to cheat the buyer].
29. I have not carried away the milk from the mouths of children.
30. I have not driven away the cattle which were upon their pastures.
33. I have not turned back water at the time [when it should flow].
34. I have not cut a cutting in a canal of running water.
37. I have not driven off the cattle from the property of the gods.
38. I have not obstructed a god in his procession.
   I am pure! I am pure! I am pure! I am pure!

Nels M. Bailkey and Richard Lim, eds. *Readings in Ancient History: Thought and Experience from Gilgamesh to St. Augustine*, 7th ed. Andover: Cengage Learning, 2011, pp. 53–5.

[2] A language written using symbols (images) that each stand for meanings, sounds, or a combination.

STUDY QUESTIONS

1. In what ways does this document lack "any positive sense of morality," addressing the nonperformance of evil rather than the active doing of good?
2. Should the pharaoh play an economic role, facilitating progress for his people in certain respects?

2.6. GREAT HYMN TO THE ATON, 14TH CENTURY BCE

This hybrid hymn and poem to the Egyptian sun-god Aton is attributed to the founder of Egyptian monotheism, King Akhenaten, whose name means "living spirit of Aton." Athough this brand of monotheism did not persist, this poem expresses an appreciation of a world attuned to the rising and setting of the sun—the embodiment of Aton—and inhabited by a multitude of cultures united in their devotion to this single deity. Consider the individual elements that the author praises Aton for creating.

Hymn to the Aton

Thou appearest beautifully on the horizon of
   heaven,
Thou living Aton, the beginning of life!
When thou art arisen on the eastern horizon,
Thou has filled every land with thy beauty.
Thou art gracious, great, glistening, and high over
   every land;
Thy rays encompass the lands to the limit of all
   that thou hast made:
As thou art Re, thou reachest to the end of them;
Thou subduest them for thy beloved son.
Though thou art far away, thy rays are on earth;
Though thou art in their faces, no one knows thy
   going.

When thou settest in the western horizon,
The land is in darkness, in the manner of death.
They sleep in a room, with heads wrapped up,
Nor sees one eye the other.

All their goods which are under their heads might
   be stolen,
But they would not perceive it.
Every lion is come forth from his den;
All creeping things, they sting.
Darkness is a shroud, and the earth is in stillness,
For he who made them rests in his horizon.

At daybreak, when thou arisest on the horizon,
When thou shinest as the Aton by day,
Thou drivest away the darkness and givest thy rays.
The Two Lands are in festivity every day,
Awake and standing upon their feet,
For thou hast raised them up.
Washing their bodies, taking their clothing,
Their arms are raised in praise at thy appearance.
All the world, they do their work. . .

Creator of seed in women,
Thou who makest fluid into man,

From Nels M. Bailkey and Richard Lim, eds. *Readings in Ancient History: Thought and Experience from Gilgamesh to St. Augustine*, 7th ed. Andover: Cengage Learning, 2011, pp. 55–8.

Who maintainest the son in the womb of his
    mother,
Who soothest him with that which stills his weeping,
Thou nurse even in the womb,
Who givest breath to sustain all that he has made!
When he descends from the womb to breathe
On the day when he is born,
Thou openest his mouth completely,
Thou suppliest his necessities.
When the chick in the egg speaks within the shell,
Thou givest him breath within it to maintain him.
When thou hast made him his fulfillment within
    the egg, to break it,
He comes forth from the egg to speak at his
    completed time;
He walks upon his legs when he comes forth
    from it. . .

How manifold it is, what thou hast made!
They are hidden from the face of man.
O sole god, like whom there is no other!
Thou didst create the world according to thy desire,
Whilst thou wert alone:
All men, cattle, and wild beasts,
Whatever is on earth, going upon its feet,
And what is on high, flying with its wings.

The countries of Syria and Nubia, the land of
    Egypt,
Thou settest every man in his place,
Thou suppliest their necessities:
Everyone has his food, and his time of life is
    reckoned.
Their tongues are separate in speech,
And their natures as well;
Their skins are distinguished,
As thou distinguished the foreign peoples.
Thou makest a Nile in the underworld,
Thou bringest it forth as though desirest
To maintain the people of Egypt
According as thou madest them for thyself,
The lord of all of them, wearying himself with them,

The lord of every land, rising for them,
The Aton of the day, great of majesty.

All distant foreign countries, thou makest their
    life also,
For thou hast set a Nile in heaven,
That it may descend for them and make waves
    upon the mountains,
Like the great green sea,
To water their fields in their towns.
How effective they are, thy plans, O lord of eternity!
The Nile in heaven, it is for the foreign peoples
And for the beasts of every desert that go upon
    their feet;
While the true Nile comes from the underworld
    for Egypt. . .

Thou art in my heart,
And there is no other that knows thee
Save thy son [Akhenaton],
For thou hast made him well-versed in thy plans
    and in thy strength.

The world came into being by thy hand,
According as thou hast made them.
When thou hast risen they live,
When thou settest they die.
Thou art lifetime thy own self,
For one lives only through thee.

Eyes are fixed on beauty until thou settest.
All work is laid aside when thou settest in the
    west.
But when thou risest again,
Everything is made to flourish for the king, . . .
Since thou didst found the earth
And raise them up for thy son,
Who came forth from thy body:
the King of Upper and Lower Egypt, . . . Akh-en-
    Aton, . . . and the Chief Wife of the King . . .
    Nefert-iti, living and youthful forever and ever.

STUDY QUESTIONS

1. How is Aton described?
2. Are Aton's qualities that of an impersonal god or a god that enjoys intimate relations with
human beings?

CHAPTER 3

THE PEOPLE OF THE COVENANT

3.1. THE BIBLICAL TALE OF NOAH AND THE GREAT FLOOD, GENESIS 6.1–9.28

The origins of the Bible remain subject to debate even after three thousand years of intense study. The first books to be composed, scholars agree, were the five books of Torah, which began to appear in various forms around 950 BCE and perhaps a bit later. Dating the texts is challenging because several authors and editors had a hand in the process. Most Biblical scholars hold to the so-called "Documentary Hypothesis," which postulates that the texts as they survive result from the intertwining of several writers' work, writers known by the initials J, E, D, and P. The readings below, from the Book of Genesis, include selections identified with the J author (known as the "Yahwist"), the E author (the "Elohist"), and the P author (the "Priestly Author").

> **Note to Reader:**
> Normal type = J author. *Italic type = E author.*
> **Bold type = P author.**

CHAPTER 6

¹When men began to increase on earth and daughters were born to them, ²the divine beings saw how beautiful the daughters of men were and took wives from among those that pleased them. ³The LORD said, "My breath shall not abide in man forever, since he too is flesh; let the days allowed him be one hundred and twenty years." ⁴It was then, and later too, that the Nephilim appeared on earth—when the divine beings cohabited the daughters of men, who bore them offspring. They were the heroes of old, the men of renown.

⁵The LORD saw how great was man's wickedness on earth, and how every plan he devised by his mind was nothing but evil all the time. ⁶And the LORD regretted that He had made man on earth, and His heart was saddened. ⁷The LORD said, "I will blot out from the earth the men whom I created—men together with beasts, creeping things, and birds of the sky; for I regret that I made them."

⁸But Noah found favor with the LORD. **⁹This is the line of Noah: Noah was a righteous man; he was blameless in his age; Noah walked with God. ¹⁰Noah begot three sons: Shem, Ham, and Japheth.**

¹¹The earth became corrupt before God; the earth was filled with lawlessness. ¹²When God saw

---

The Jewish Study Bible, *Tanakh*. Published by The Jewish Publication Society.

how corrupt the earth was, for all flesh had corrupted its ways on earth, ¹³God said to Noah, "I have decided to put an end to all flesh, for the earth is filled with lawlessness because of them: I am about to destroy them with the earth. ¹⁴Make yourself an ark of gopher wood; make it an ark with compartments, and cover it inside and out with pitch. ¹⁵This is how you shall make it: the length of the ark shall be three hundred cubits, its width fifty cubits, and its height thirty cubits. ¹⁶Make an opening for daylight in the ark, and terminate it within a cubit of the top. Put the entrance to the ark in its side; make it with bottom, second, and third decks. ¹⁷For my part, I am about to bring the Flood—waters upon the earth—to destroy all flesh under the sky in which there is breath of life; everything on earth shall perish. ¹⁸But I will establish My covenant with you, and you shall enter the ark, with your sons, your wife, and your sons' wives. ¹⁹And of all that lives, of all flesh, you shall take two of each kind into the ark to keep alive with you; they shall be male and female. ²⁰From birds of every kind, cattle of every kind, every kind of creeping thing on earth, two of each shall come to you to stay alive. ²¹For your part, take of everything that is eaten and store it away, to serve as food for you and for them."

²²Noah did so; just as God commanded him, so he did.

CHAPTER 7

¹Then the LORD said to Noah, "Go into the ark, with all your household, for you alone have I found righteous before Me in this generation. ²Of every clean animal you shall take seven pairs, males and their mates, and of every animal that is not clean, two, a male and its mate; ³of the birds of the sky also, seven pairs, male and female, to keep seed alive upon all the earth. ⁴For in seven days' time I will make it rain upon the earth, forty days and forty nights, and I will blot out from the earth all existence that I created." ⁵And Noah did just as the LORD commanded him.

⁶**Noah was six hundred years old when the Flood came, waters upon the earth.** ⁷Noah, with his sons, his wife, and his sons' wives, went into the ark because of the waters of the Flood. ⁸Of the clean animals, of the animals that are not clean, of the birds, and of everything that creeps on the ground, ⁹**two of each, male and female, came to Noah into the ark, as God had commanded Noah.** ¹⁰And on the seventh day the waters of the Flood came upon the earth.

¹¹**In the six hundredth year of Noah's life, in the second month, on the seventeenth day of the month, on that day**

> All the fountains of the great deep burst apart,
> And the floodgates of the sky broke open.

¹²The rain fell on the earth forty days and forty nights. ¹³That same day Noah and Noah's sons, Shem, Ham, and Japheth, went into the ark, with Noah's wife and the three wives of his sons—¹⁴they and all beasts of every kind, all cattle of every kind, all creatures of every kind that creep on the earth, and all birds of every kind, every bird, every winged thing. ¹⁵They came to Noah into the ark, two each of all flesh in which there was breath of life. ¹⁶Thus they that entered comprised male and female of all flesh, as God had commanded him. And the LORD shut him in.

¹⁷The Flood continued forty days on the earth, and the waters increased and raised the ark so that it rose above the earth. ¹⁸**The waters swelled and increased greatly upon the earth, and the ark drifted upon the waters.** ¹⁹**When the waters had swelled much more upon the earth, all the highest mountains everywhere under the sky were covered. ²⁰Fifteen cubits higher did the waters swell, as the mountains were covered. ²¹And all the flesh that stirred on earth perished—birds, cattle, beasts, and all the things that swarmed upon the earth, and all mankind.** ²²All in whose nostrils was the merest breath of life, all that was on dry land, died. ²³All existence on earth was blotted out—man, cattle, creeping things, and birds of the sky; they were blotted out from the earth. Only Noah was left, and those with him in the ark.

CHAPTER 8

²⁴**And when the waters had swelled on the earth one hundred and fifty days,** ¹God remembered Noah and all the beasts and all the cattle that were with

him in the ark, and God caused a wind to blow across the earth, and the waters subsided. [2]**The fountains of the deep and the floodgates of the sky were stopped up,** and the rain from the sky was held back; [3]the waters then receded steadily from the earth. **At the end of one hundred and fifty days the waters diminished,** [4]**so that in the seventh month, on the seventeenth day of the month, the ark came to rest on the mountains of Ararat.** [5]**The waters went on diminishing, until the tenth month; in the tenth month, on the first of the month, the tops of the mountains became visible.**

[6]At the end of forty days, Noah opened the window of the ark that he had made [7]and sent out the raven; it went to and fro until the waters had dried up from the earth. [8]Then he sent out the dove to see whether the waters had decreased from the surface of the ground. [9]But the dove could not find a resting place for its foot, and returned to him to the ark, for there was water over all the earth. So putting out his hand, he took it into the ark with him. [10]He waited another seven days, and again sent out the dove from the ark. [11]The dove came back to him toward evening, and there in its bill was a plucked-off olive leaf! Then Noah knew that the waters had decreased on the earth, [12]He waited another seven days and sent the dove forth; and it did not return to him any more.

[13]**In the six hundred and first year, in the first month, on the first of the month, the waters began to dry from the earth;** and when Noah removed the covering of the ark, he saw that the surface of the ground was drying. [14]And in the second month, on the twenty-seventh day of the month, the earth was dry.

[15]**God spoke to Noah, saying,** [16]**"Come out of the ark, together with your wife, your sons, and your sons' wives.** [17]**Bring out with you every living thing of all flesh that is with you: birds, animals, and everything that creeps on earth; and let them swarm on the earth and be fertile and increase on the earth."** [18]So Noah came out, together with his sons, his wife, and his sons' wives. [19]Every animal, every creeping thing, and every bird, everything that stirs on earth came out of the ark by families.

[20]Then Noah built an altar to the LORD and, taking of every clean animal and of every clean bird, he offered burnt offerings on the altar. [21]The LORD smelled the pleasing odor, and the LORD said to Himself: "Never again will I doom the earth because of man, since the devisings of man's mind are evil from his youth; nor will I ever again destroy every living being, as I have done.

[22]So long as the earth endures,
Seedtime and harvest,
Cold and heat,
Summer and winter,
Day and night
Shall not cease."

CHAPTER 9

[1]**God blessed Noah and his sons, and said to them, "Be fertile and increase, and fill the earth.** [2]**The fear and the dread of you shall be upon all the beasts of the earth and upon all the birds of the sky—everything with which the earth is astir—and upon all the fish of the sea; they are given into your hand.** [3]**Every creature that lives shall be yours to eat; as with the green grasses, I give you all these.** [4]**You must not, however, eat flesh with its life-blood in it.** [5]**But for your own life-blood I will require a reckoning; I will require it of every beast; of man, too, I will require a reckoning of human life, of every man for that of his fellow man!**

[6]Whoever sheds the blood of man,
By man shall his blood be shed;
For in His image
Did God make man.

[7]Be fertile, then, and increase; abound on the earth and increase on it."

[8]And God said to Noah and to his sons with him, [9]"I now establish My covenant with you and your offspring to come, [10]and with every living thing that is with you—birds, cattle, and every wild beast as well—all that have come out of the ark, every living thing on earth. [11]I will maintain My covenant with you: never again shall all flesh be cut off by the waters of a flood, and never again shall there be a flood to destroy the whole earth."

[12]God further said, "This is the signs that I set for the covenant between Me and you, and every living

creature with you, for all ages to come. [13]I have set My bow in the clouds, and it shall serve as a sign of the covenant between Me and the earth. [14]When I bring clouds over the earth, and the bow appears in the clouds, [15]I will remember My covenant between Me and you and every living creature among all flesh, so that the waters shall never again become a flood to destroy all flesh. [16]When the bow is in the clouds, I will see it and remember the everlasting covenant between God and all living creatures, all flesh that is on earth. [17]That," God said to Noah, "shall be the sign of the covenant between Me and all the flesh that is on earth."

[18]The sons of Noah who came out of the ark were Shem, Ham, and Japheth—Ham being the father of Canaan. [19]These three were the sons of Noah, and from these the whole world branched out.

[20]*Noah, the tiller of the soil, was the first to plant a vineyard.* [21]*He drank of the wine and became drunk, and he uncovered himself within his tent.* [22]*Ham, the father of Canaan, saw his father's nakedness and told his two brothers outside.* [23]*But Shem and Japheth took a cloth, placed it against their backs and, walking backward, they covered their father's nakedness; their faces were turned the other way, so that they did not see their father's nakedness.* [24]*When Noah woke up from his wine and learned what his youngest son had done to him,* [25]*he said*

> *"Cursed be Canaan;*
> *The lowest of slaves*
> *Shall he be to his brothers."*

[26]*And he said,*

> *"Blessed be the LORD,*
> *The God of Shem;*
> *Let Canaan be a slave to them.*
> [27]*May God enlarge Japheth,*
> *And let him dwell in the tents of Shem;*
> *And let Canaan be a slave to them.*

[28]Noah lived after the Flood 350 years. [29]And all the days of Noah came to 950 years; then he died.

STUDY QUESTIONS

1. Compare the different readings. How are they similar? How are they different? What picture of human's relationship with God emerges from these passages?
2. Do these passages support the hypothesis that the Bible is a patchwork of many different hands?

3.2. BOOK OF EXODUS: MOSES AND PHARAOH, CHAPTERS 7, 11–12, AND 14

The origins of the Bible remain subject to debate even after three thousand years of intense study. The first books to be composed, scholars agree, were the five books of Torah, which began to appear in various forms around 950 BCE and perhaps a bit later. What makes dating the texts so challenging is that several authors and editors had a hand in the process. Most Biblical scholars hold to the so-called "Documentary Hypothesis," which postulates that the texts as they survive result from the intertwining of several writers' work, writers known by the initials J, E, D, and P. The readings below, from the Book of Exodus, include selections identified with the J author (known as the "Yahwist"), the E author (the "Elohist"), and the P author (the "Priestly Author").

The Jewish Study Bible, *Tanakh*. Published by The Jewish Publication Society.

Note to Reader:

Normal type = J author. *Italic type = E author.*
Bold type = P author.

CHAPTER 7

[1]The LORD replied to Moses, "See, I place you in the role of God to Pharaoh, with your brother Aaron as your prophet. [2]You shall repeat all that I command you, and your brother Aaron shall speak to Pharaoh to let the Israelites depart from his land. [3]But I will harden Pharaoh's heart, that I may multiply My signs and marvels in the land of Egypt. [4]When Pharaoh does not heed you, I will lay My hand upon Egypt and deliver My ranks, My people the Israelites, from the land of Egypt with extraordinary chastisements. [5]And the Egyptians shall know that I am the LORD, when I stretch out My hand over Egypt and bring out the Israelites from their midst." [6]This Moses **and Aaron** did; as the LORD commanded them, so **they** did. [7]Moses was eighty years old **and Aaron was eighty-three**, when **they** made **their** demand on Pharaoh.

[8]**The LORD said to Moses and Aaron,** [9]**"When Pharaoh speaks to you and says, 'Produce your marvel,' you shall say to Aaron, 'Take your rod and cast it down before Pharaoh.' It shall turn into a serpent."** [10]**So Moses and Aaron came before Pharaoh and did just as the LORD had commanded: Aaron cast down his rod in the presence of Pharaoh and his courtiers, and it turned into a serpent.** [11]**Then Pharaoh, for his part, summoned the wise men and the sorcerers; and the Egyptian magicians, in turn, did the same with their spells;** [12]**each cast down his rod, and they turned into serpents. But Aaron's rod swallowed their rods.** [13]**Yet Pharaoh's heart stiffened and he did not heed them, as the LORD had said.**

[14]And the LORD said to Moses, "Pharaoh is stubborn; he refuses to let the people go. [15]Go to Pharaoh in the morning, as he is coming out to the water, and station yourself before him at the edge of the Nile, taking with you the rod that turned into a snake. [16]And say to him, 'The LORD, the God of the Hebrews, sent me to you to say, "Let My people go that they may worship Me in the wilderness." But you have paid Him no heed until now. [17]Thus says the LORD, "By this you shall know that I am the LORD." See, I shall strike the water in the Nile with the rod that is in my hand, and it will be turned into blood, [18]and the fish in the Nile will die. The Nile will stink so that the Egyptians will find it impossible to drink the water of the Nile.'"

[19]**And the LORD said to Moses, "Say to Aaron: 'Take your rod and hold out your arm over the waters of Egypt—its rivers, its canals, its ponds, all its bodies of water—that they may turn to blood; there shall be blood throughout the land of Egypt, even in vessels of wood and stone.'"** [20]**Moses and Aaron did just as the LORD commanded: he lifted up the rod and struck the water in the Nile in the sight of Pharaoh and his courtiers, and all the water in the Nile was turned into blood,** [21]**and the fish in the Nile died. The Nile stank so that the Egyptians could not drink water from the Nile; and there was blood throughout the land of Egypt.** [22]**But when the Egyptian magicians did the same with their spells, Pharaoh's heart stiffened and he did not heed them—as the LORD had spoken.** [23]**Pharaoh turned and went into his palace, paying no regard even to this.** [24]**And all the Egyptians had to dig round about the Nile for drinking water, because they could not drink the water of the Nile.**

[25]When seven days had passed after the LORD struck the Nile, [26]the LORD said to Moses, "Go to Pharaoh and say to him, 'Thus says the LORD: "Let My people go that they may worship Me. [27]If you refuse to let them go, then I will plague your whole country with frogs. [28]The Nile shall swarm with frogs, and they shall come up and enter your palace, your bedchamber and your bed, the houses of your courtiers and your people, and your ovens and your kneading bowls. [29]The frogs shall come up on you and on your people and on all your courtiers.'"

CHAPTER 11

[1]And the LORD said to Moses, "I will bring one more plague upon Pharaoh and upon Egypt; after that he shall let you go from here; indeed, when he lets you go, he will drive you out of here one and all. [2]Tell the people to borrow, each man from his neighbor and each woman from hers, objects of silver and gold."

³**The LORD disposed the Egyptians favorably toward the people. Moreover, Moses himself was much esteemed in the land of Egypt, among Pharaoh's courtiers and among the people.**

⁴Moses said, "Thus says the LORD: 'Toward midnight I will go forth among the Egyptians, ⁵and every first-born in the land of Egypt shall die, from the first-born of Pharaoh who sits on his throne to the first-born of the slave-girl who is behind the millstones; and all the first-born of the cattle. ⁶And there shall be a loud cry in all the land of Egypt, such as has never been or will ever be again; ⁷but not a dog shall snarl at any of the Israelites, at man or beast—in order that you may know that the LORD makes a distinction between Egypt and Israel.' ⁸Then all these courtiers of yours shall come down to me and bow low to me, saying, 'Depart, you and all the people who follow you!' After that I will depart." And he left Pharaoh's presence in hot anger.

⁹Now the LORD had said to Moses, "Pharaoh will not heed you, in order that My marvels may be multiplied in the land of Egypt." ¹⁰**Moses and Aaron had performed all these marvels before Pharaoh, but the Lord had stiffened the heart of Pharaoh so that he would not let the Israelites go from his land.**

CHAPTER 12

¹The LORD said to Moses and Aaron in the land of Egypt: ²"This month shall mark for you the beginning of the months; it shall be the first of the months of the year for you. ³Speak to the whole community of Israel and say that on the tenth of this month each of them shall take a lamb to a family, a lamb to a household. ⁴But if the household is too small for a lamb, let him share one with a neighbor who dwells nearby, in proportion to the number of persons; you shall contribute for the lamb according to what each household will eat. ⁵Your lamb shall be without blemish, a yearling male; you may take it from the sheep or from the goats. ⁶You shall keep watch over it until the fourteenth day of the month; and all the assembled congregation of the Israelites shall slaughter it at twilight. ⁷They shall take some of the blood and put it on the two doorposts and the lintel of the houses in which they are to eat it. ⁸They shall eat the flesh that same night; they shall eat it roasted over the fire, with unleavened bread and with bitter herbs. ⁹Do not eat any of it raw, or cooked in any way with water, but roasted—head, legs, and entrails—over the fire. ¹⁰You shall not leave any of it over until morning; if any of it is left until morning, you shall burn it.

¹¹"This is how you shall eat it: your loins girded, your sandals on your feet, and your staff in your hand; and you shall eat it hurriedly; it is a Passover offering to the LORD. ¹²For that night I will go through the land of Egypt and strike down every first-born in the land of Egypt, both man and beast; and I will mete out punishments to all the gods of Egypt, I the LORD. ¹³And the blood on the houses where you are staying shall be a sign for you: when I see the blood I will pass over you, so that no plague will destroy you when I strike the land of Egypt.

¹⁴"This day shall be to you one of remembrance: you shall celebrate it as a festival to the LORD throughout the ages; you shall celebrate it as an institution for all time. ¹⁵Seven days you shall eat unleavened bread; on the very first day you shall remove leaven from your houses, for whoever eats leavened bread from the first day to the seventh day, that person shall be cut off from Israel.

¹⁶"You shall celebrate a sacred occasion on the first day, and a sacred occasion on the seventh day; no work at all shall be done on them; only what every person is to eat, that alone may be prepared for you. ¹⁷You shall observe the [Feast of] Unleavened Bread, for on this very day I brought your ranks out of the land of Egypt; you shall observe this day throughout the ages as an institution for all time. ¹⁸In the first month, from the fourteenth day of the month at evening, you shall eat unleavened bread until the twenty-first day of the month at evening. ¹⁹No leaven shall be found in your houses for seven days. For whoever eats what is leavened, that person shall be cut off from the community of Israel, whether he is a stranger or a citizen of the country. ²⁰You shall eat nothing leavened; in all your settlements you shall eat unleavened bread."

²¹Moses then summoned all the elders of Israel and said to them, "Go, pick out lambs for your families, and slaughter the Passover offering. ²²Take a bunch of hyssop, dip it in the blood that is in the basin, and apply some of the blood that is in the

basin to the lintel and to the two doorposts. None of you shall go outside the door of his house until morning. ²³For when the LORD goes through to smite the Egyptians, He will see the blood on the lintel and the two doorposts, and the LORD will pass over the door and not let the Destroyer enter and smite your home.

²⁴"You shall observe this as an institution for all time, for you and for your descendants. ²⁵And when you enter the land that the LORD will give you, as He has promised, you shall observe this rite. ²⁶And when your children ask you, 'What do you mean by this rite?' ²⁷you shall say, 'It is the Passover sacrifice to the LORD, because He passed over the houses of the Israelites in Egypt when He smote the Egyptians, but saved our houses.'"

The people then bowed low in homage. ²⁸And the Israelites went and did so; just as the LORD had commanded Moses and Aaron, so they did.

²⁹In the middle of the night the LORD struck down all the first-born in the land of Egypt, from the first-born of Pharaoh who sat on the throne to the first-born of the captive who was in the dungeon, and all the first-born of the cattle. ³⁰And Pharaoh arose in the night, with all his courtiers and all the Egyptians—because there was a loud cry in Egypt; for there was no house where there was not someone dead. ³¹He summoned Moses and Aaron in the night and said, "Up, depart from among my people, you and the Israelites with you! Go, worship the LORD as you said! ³²Take also your flocks and your herds, as you said, and begone! And may you bring a blessing upon me also!"

³³The Egyptians urged the people on, impatient to have them leave the country, for they said, "We shall all be dead." ³⁴So the people took their dough before it was leavened, their kneading bowls wrapped in their cloaks upon their shoulders. ³⁵The Israelites had done Moses' bidding and borrowed from the Egyptians objects of silver and gold, and clothing. ³⁶And the LORD had disposed the Egyptians favorably to the people, and they let them have their request; thus they stripped the Egyptians.

³⁷The Israelites journeyed from Rameses to Succoth, about six hundred thousand men on foot, aside from children. ³⁸Moreover, a mixed multitude went up with them, and very much livestock, both flocks and herds. ³⁹And they baked unleavened cakes of the dough that they had taken out of Egypt, for it was not leavened, since they had been driven out of Egypt and could not delay; nor had they prepared any provisions for themselves.

⁴⁰The length of time that the Israelites lived in Egypt was four hundred and thirty years; ⁴¹at the end of the four hundred and thirtieth year, to the very day, all the ranks of the LORD departed from the land of Egypt. ⁴²That was for the LORD a night of vigil to bring them out of the land of Egypt; that same night is the LORD's, one of vigil for all the children of Israel throughout the ages.

⁴³**The LORD said to Moses and Aaron, "This is the law of the Passover offering: No foreigner shall eat of it. ⁴⁴But any slave a man has bought may eat of it once he has been circumcised. ⁴⁵No bound or hired laborer shall eat of it. ⁴⁶It shall be eaten in one house; you shall not take any part of the flesh outside the house; nor shall you break a bone of it. ⁴⁷The whole community of Israel shall offer it. ⁴⁸If a stranger who dwells with you would offer the Passover to the LORD, all his males must be circumcised; then he shall be admitted to offer it; he shall then be as a citizen of the country. But no uncircumcised person may eat of it. ⁴⁹There shall be one law for the citizen and for the stranger who dwells among you.**

⁵⁰**And all the Israelites did so; as the LORD had commanded Moses and Aaron, so they did.**

⁵¹That very day the LORD freed the Israelites from the land of Egypt, troop by troop.

CHAPTER 14

¹**The LORD said to Moses, ²"Tell the Israelites to turn back and encamp before Pi-hahiroth, between Migdol and the sea, before Baal-zephon; you shall encamp facing it, by the sea. ³Pharaoh will say of the Israelites, 'They are astray in the land; the wilderness has closed in on them.' ⁴Then I will stiffen Pharaoh's heart and he will pursue them, that I may gain glory through Pharaoh and all his host; and the Egyptians shall know that I am the LORD."**

And they did so.

⁵When the king of Egypt was told that the people had fled, Pharaoh and his courtiers had a change of heart about the people and said, "What is this we

have done, releasing Israel from our service?" [6]He ordered his chariot and took his men with him; [7]he took six hundred of his picked chariots, and the rest of the chariots of Egypt, with officers in all of them. [8]**The LORD stiffened the heart of Pharaoh king of Egypt, and he gave chase to the Israelites. As the Israelites were departing defiantly,** [9]**the Egyptians gave chase to them, and all the chariot horses of Pharaoh, his horsemen, and his warriors overtook them encamped by the sea, near Pi-hahiroth, before Baal-zephon.**

[10]As Pharaoh drew near, the Israelites caught sight of the Egyptians advancing upon them. Greatly frightened, the Israelites cried out to the LORD. [11]And they said to Moses, "Was it for want of graves in Egypt that brought us to die in the wilderness? What have you done to us, taking us out of Egypt? [12]Is this not the very thing we told you in Egypt, saying, 'Let us be, and we will serve the Egyptians, for it is better for us to serve the Egyptians than to die in the wilderness'?" [13]But Moses said to the people, "Have no fear! Stand by, and witness the deliverance which the LORD will work for you today; for the Egyptians whom you see today you will never see again. [14]The LORD will battle for you; you hold your peace!"

[15]**Then the LORD said to Moses, "Why do you cry out to me? Tell the Israelites to go forward.** [16]**And you lift up your rod and hold out your arm over the sea and split it, so that the Israelites may march into the sea on dry ground.** [17]**And I will stiffen the hearts of the Egyptians so that they go in after them; and I will gain glory through Pharaoh and all his warriors, his chariots, and his horsemen.** [18]**Let the Egyptians know that I am LORD, when I gain glory through Pharaoh, his chariots, and his horsemen."**

[19]The angel of God, who had been going ahead of the Israelite army, now moved and followed them; and the pillar of cloud shifted from in front of them and took up a place behind them, [20]and it came between the army of the Egyptians and the army of Israel. Thus there was the cloud with the darkness, and it cast a spell upon the night, so that the one could not come near the other all through the night.

[21]**Then Moses held out his arm over the sea** and the LORD drove back the sea with a strong east wind all that night, and turned the sea into dry ground. **The waters were split,** [22]**and the Israelites went into the sea on dry ground, the waters forming a wall for them on their right and on their left.** [23]**The Egyptians came in pursuit after them into the sea, all of Pharaoh's horses, chariots, and horsemen.** [24]At the morning watch, the LORD looked down upon the Egyptian army from a pillar of fire and cloud, and threw the Egyptian army into panic. [25]He locked the wheels of their chariots so that they moved forward with difficulty. And the Egyptians said, "Let us flee from the Israelites, for the LORD is fighting for them against Egypt."

[26]**Then the LORD said to Moses, "Hold out your arm over the sea, that the waters may come back upon the Egyptians and upon their chariots and upon their horsemen."** [27]**Moses held out his arm over the sea,** and at daybreak the sea returned to its normal state, and the Egyptians fled at its approach. But the LORD hurled the Egyptians into the sea. [28]**The waters turned back and covered the chariots and the horsemen—Pharaoh's entire army that followed them into the sea; not one of them remained.** [29]But the Israelites had marched through the sea on dry ground, the waters forming a wall for them on their right and on their left.

[30]Thus the LORD delivered Israel that day from the Egyptians. Israel saw the Egyptians dead on the shore of the sea. [31]And when Israel saw the wondrous power which the LORD had wielded against the Egyptians, the people feared the LORD; they had faith in the LORD and His servant Moses.

STUDY QUESTIONS

1. Compare the different readings. How are they similar? How are they different? How do these passages provide evidence for the Hebrews' belief that they were the Chosen People?
2. In return for God's favor, what special moral and ethical obligations does God ask the Hebrews to follow?

3.3. BOOK OF JEREMIAH, PROPHECY TO ISRAEL, CHAPTERS 7 AND 8, WRITTEN CA. 6TH CENTURY BCE

Jeremiah (late 7th–early 6th century BCE) was a prophet in Jerusalem who warned the Israelites that their sinful behavior would bring God's punishment—an outcome embodied by the destruction of Jerusalem by the Babylonians (586 BCE). Recorded in a poetic style, the message from God preached by Jeremiah threatens desolation for the land and tragedy for its people because they have been disobedient to God's law. In a time of perceived social breakdown, where God's people shed blood and abuse their neighbors, Jeremiah's voice is a reforming force intended to stave off God's punishment.

CHAPTER 7

¹The word which came to Jeremiah from the LORD: ²Stand at the gate of the House of the LORD, and there proclaim this word: Hear the word of the LORD, all you of Judah who enter these gates to worship the LORD!

³Thus said the LORD of the Hosts, the God of Israel: Mend your ways and your actions, and I will let you dwell in this place.

. . .

¹⁶As for you, do not pray for this people, do not raise a cry of prayer on their behalf, do not plead with Me; for I will not listen to you. ¹⁷Don't you see what they are doing in the towns of Judah and in the streets of Jerusalem? ¹⁸The children gather sticks, the fathers build the fire, and the mothers knead dough, to make cakes for the Queen of Heaven, and they pour libations to other gods, to vex Me.

. . .

¹⁹Is it Me they are vexing?—says the LORD. It is rather themselves, to their own disgrace. ²⁰Assuredly, thus said the Lord GOD: My wrath and My fury will be poured out upon this place, on man and on beast, on the trees of the field and the fruit of the soil. It shall burn, with none to quench it.

. . .

²⁷You shall say all these things to them, but they will not listen to you; you shall call to them, but they will not respond to you. ²⁸Then say to them: This is the nation that would not obey the LORD their God, that would not accept rebuke. Faithfulness has perished, vanished from their mouths.

. . .

CHAPTER 8

⁴Say to them: Thus said the LORD:
When men fall do they not get up again?

If they turn aside, do they not turn back?
⁵Why is this people—Jerusalem—rebellious
With a persistent rebellion?
They cling to deceit,

They refuse to return.
⁶I have listened and heard:
They do not speak honestly.

The Jewish Study Bible, *Tanakh*. Published by the Jewish Publication Society.

No one regrets his wickedness
And says, "What have I done!"
They all persist in their wayward course

Like a steed dashing forward in the fray.
    7Even the stork in the sky knows her
        seasons,
And the turtledove, swift, and crane
Keep the time of the coming;
But My people pay no heed
To the law of the LORD.

. . .

For them the smallest to the greatest,
They are all greedy for gain;
Priest and prophet alike,
They all act falsely.
11They offer healing offhand
For the wounds of My poor people,
Saying, "All is well, all is well,"

When nothing is well.
12They have acted shamefully;
They have done abhorrent things—
Yet they do not feel shame,
They cannot be made to blush.

Assuredly, they shall fall among the falling,
They shall stumble at the time of their doom
                        —*said the LORD.*

    13I will make an end of them
                —*declares the LORD*

No grapes left on the vine,
No figs on the fig tree,
The leaves all withered;
Whatever I have given them is gone.
14Why are we sitting by?
Let us gather into the fortified cities
And meet our doom there.
For the LORD our God has doomed us,
He has made us drink a bitter draft,
Because we sinned against the LORD.
15We hoped for good fortune, but no happiness
        came;
For a time of relief—instead there is terror!
16The snorting of their horses was heard from
        Dan;
At the neighing of their steeds
The whole land quaked.
They came and devoured the land and what was
        in it,

The towns and those who dwelt in them.

17Lo, I will send serpents against you,
Adders that cannot be charmed,

And they shall bite you
                        —*declares the LORD.*

18When in grief I would seek comfort,

My heart is sick within me.

STUDY QUESTIONS

1. What forms does disobedience to God take, in Jeremiah's estimation?
2. Remember that the document was read after the destruction of Jerusalem by the Babylonians. Could even more destruction be threatened as a result of future disobedience?

3.4. FIRST BOOK OF KINGS, KING SOLOMON AND THE TEMPLE, CHAPTERS 6–8, CA. 10TH CENTURY BCE

The Book of Kings picks up the story of Israel at the death of King David (970 BCE) and describes the transgressions of his heirs over the course of the next four centuries—creating a justification for the Babylonian Empire's destruction of Israel and Judea in the 6th century BCE. This selection describes—in painstaking detail—the construction of the First Temple of Jerusalem, built by King Solomon (r. 970–931 BCE). After reading the lavish description of this holy site, consider the psychological effect of its complete destruction at the hands of the Babylonian invaders in 586 BCE.

CHAPTER 6

[1]In the four hundred and eightieth year after the Israelites left the land of Egypt, in the month of Ziv—that is, the second month—in the fourth year of his reign over Israel, Solomon began to build the House of the LORD. [2]The House which King Solomon built for the LORD was 60 cubits long, 20 cubits wide, and 30 cubits high. [3]The portico in front of the Great Hall of the House was 20 cubits long—along the width of the House— and 10 cubits deep to the front of the House. [4]He made windows for the House, recessed and latticed. [5]Against the outside wall of the House—the outside walls of the House enclosing the Great Hall and the Shrine—he built a storied structure; and he made side chambers all around. [6]The lowest story was 5 cubits wide, the middle one 6 cubits wide, and the third 7 cubits wide; for he had provided recesses around the outside of the House so as not to penetrate the walls of the House.

[7]When the house was built, only finished stones cut at the quarry were used, so that no hammer or ax or any iron tool was heard in the House while it was being built.

[8]The entrance to the middle [story of] the side chambers was on the right side of the House; and winding stairs led up to the middle chambers, and from the middle chambers to the third story. [9]When he finished building the House, he paneled the House with beams and planks of cedar. [10]He built the storied structure against the entire House—each story 5 cubits high, so that it encased the House with timbers of cedar.

[11]Then the word of the LORD came to Solomon, [12]"With regard to this House you are building—if you follow My laws and observe My rules and faithfully keep My commandments, I will fulfill for you the promise that I gave to your father David: [13]I will abide among the children of Israel, and I will never forsake My people Israel."

[14]When Solomon had completed the construction of the House, [15]he paneled the walls of the House on the inside with planks of cedar.

. . .

. . . [19]In the innermost part of the House, he fixed a Shrine in which to place the Ark of the LORD'S Covenant. [20]The interior of the Shrine was 20 cubits long, 20 cubits wide, and 20 cubits high. He overlaid it with solid gold; he similarly overlaid [its] cedar altar. [21]Solomon overlaid the interior of the House with solid gold; and he inserted golden chains into the door of the Shrine. He overlaid [the Shrine] with gold, [22]so that the entire House was overlaid with gold; he even overlaid with gold the entire altar of the Shrine. And so the entire House was completed.

[23]In the Shrine he made cherubim of olive wood, each 10 cubits high. [24][One] had a wing measuring

The Jewish Study Bible. New York: Oxford University Press, 2004, Tanakh translation by the Jewish Publication Society, pp. 683–693.

5 cubits and another wing measuring 5 cubits, so that the spread from wingtip to wingtip was 10 cubits; ²⁵and the wingspread of the other cherub was also 10 cubits. The two cherubim had the same measurements and proportions: ²⁶the height of the one cherub was 10 cubits, and so was that of the other cherub.

²⁷He placed the cherubim inside the inner chamber. Since the wings of the cherubim were extended, a wing of the one touched one wall and a wing of the other touched the other wall, while their wings in the center of the chamber touched each other. ²⁸He overlaid the cherubim with gold. ²⁹All over the walls of the House, of both the inner area and the outer area, he carved reliefs of cherubim, palms, and calyxes, ³⁰and he overlaid the floor of the House with gold, both the inner and the outer areas.

³¹For the entrance of the Shrine he made doors of olive wood, the pilasters and the doorposts having five sides. ³²The double doors were of olive wood, and on them he carved reliefs of cherubim, palms, and calyxes. He overlaid them with gold, hammering the gold onto the cherubim and the palms. ³³For the entrance of the Great Hall, too, he made doorposts of oleaster wood, having four sides, ³⁴and the double doors of cypress wood, each door consisting of two rounded planks. ³⁵On them he carved cherubim, palms, and calyxes, overlaying them with gold applied evenly over the carvings. ³⁶He built the inner enclosure of three courses of hewn stones and one course of cedar beams.

³⁷In the fourth year, in the month of Ziv, the foundations of the House were laid; ³⁸and in the eleventh year, in the month of Bul—that is, the eighth month—the House was completed according to all its details and all its specifications. It took him seven years to build it.

. . .

⁴⁸And Solomon made all the furnishings that were in the House of the LORD; the altar, of gold; the table for the bread of display, of gold; ⁴⁹the lampstands—five on the right side and five on the left—in front of the Shrine, of solid gold; and the petals, lamps, and tongs, of gold; ⁵⁰the basins, snuffers, sprinkling bowls, ladles, and fire pans, of solid gold; and the hinge sockets for the doors of the innermost part of the House, the Holy of Holies, and for the doors of the Great Hall of the House, of gold.

⁵¹When all the work that King Solomon had done in the House of the LORD was completed, Solomon brought in the sacred donations of his father David—the silver, the gold, and the vessels—and deposited them in the treasury of the House of the LORD.

CHAPTER 8

¹Then Solomon convoked the elders of Israel—all the heads of the tribes and the ancestral chieftains of the Israelites—before King Solomon in Jerusalem, to bring up the Ark of the Covenant of the LORD from the City of David, that is, Zion.

²All the men of Israel gathered before King Solomon at the Feast, in the month of Ethanim—that is, the seventh month. ³When all the elders of Israel had come, the priests lifted the Ark ⁴and carried up the Ark of the LORD. Then the priests and the Levites brought the Tent of Meeting and all the holy vessels that were in the Tent. ⁵Meanwhile, King Solomon and the whole community of Israel, who were assembled with him before the Ark, were sacrificing sheep and oxen in such abundance that they could not be numbered or counted.

⁶The priests brought the Ark of the LORD'S Covenant to its place underneath the wings of the cherubim, in the Shrine of the House, in the Holy of Holies; ⁷for the cherubim had their wings spread out over the place of the Ark, so that the cherubim shielded the Ark and its poles from above. ⁸The poles projected so that the ends of the poles were visible in the sanctuary in front of the Shrine, but they could not be seen outside; and there they remain to this day. ⁹There was nothing inside the Ark but the two tablets of stone which Moses placed there at Horeb, when the LORD made [a covenant] with the Israelites after their departure from the land of Egypt.

¹⁰When the priests came out of the sanctuary—for the cloud had filled the House of the LORD ¹¹and the priests were not able to remain and perform the service because of the cloud, for the Presence of the LORD filled the House of the LORD—¹²then Solomon declared:

The LORD has chosen
To abide in a thick cloud:
¹³I have now built for You
A stately House,
A place where You
May dwell forever.

[14]Then, with the whole congregation of Israel standing, the king faced about and blessed the whole congregation of Israel. [15]He said:

"Praised be the LORD, the God of Israel, who has fulfilled with deeds the promise He made to my father David. For He said, [16]'Ever since I brought My people Israel out of Egypt, I have not chosen a city among all the tribes of Israel for building a House where My name might abide; but I have chosen David to rule My people Israel.'

[17]"Now my father David had intended to build a House of the name of the LORD, the God of Israel. [18]But the LORD said to my father David, 'As regards your intention to build a House for My name, you did right to have that intention. [19]However, you shall not build the House yourself; instead, your son, the issue of your loins, shall build the House for My name.'

[20]And the LORD has fulfilled the promise that He made: I have succeeded my father David and have ascended the throne of Israel, as the LORD promised. I have built the House for the name of the LORD, the God of Israel; [21]and I have set a place there for the Ark, containing the covenant which the LORD made with our fathers when He brought them out from the land of Egypt."

[22]Then Solomon stood before the altar of the LORD in the presence of the whole community of Israel; he spread the palms of his hands toward heaven [23]and said, "O LORD God of Israel, in the heavens above and on the earth below there is no god like You, who keep Your gracious covenant with Your servants when they walk before You in wholehearted devotion; [24]You who have kept the promises You made to Your servant, my father David, fulfilling with deeds the promise You made—as is now the case. [25]And now, O LORD God of Israel, keep the further promise that You made to Your servant, my father David: 'Your line on the throne of Israel shall never end, if only your descendants will look to their way and walk before Me as you have walked before Me.' [26]Now, therefore, O God of Israel, let the promise that You made to Your servant my father David be fulfilled.

[27]"But will God really dwell on earth? Even the heavens to their uttermost reaches cannot contain You, how much less this House that I have built! [28]Yet turn, O LORD my God, to the prayer and supplication of Your servant, and hear the cry and prayer which Your servant offers before You this day. [29]May Your eyes be open day and night toward this House, toward the place of which You have said, 'My name shall abide there'; may You heed the prayers which Your servant will offer toward this place. [30]And when You hear the supplications which Your servant and Your people Israel offer toward this place, give heed in Your heavenly abode—give heed and pardon.

. . .

[54]When Solomon finished offering to the LORD all this prayer and supplication, he rose from where he had been kneeling, in front of the altar of the LORD, his hands spread out toward heaven. [55]He stood, and in a loud voice blessed the whole congregation of Israel:

[56]"Praised be the LORD who has granted a haven to His people Israel, just as He promised; not a single word has failed of all the gracious promises that He made through His servant Moses. [57]May the LORD our God be with us, as He was with our fathers. May He never abandon or forsake us. [57]May He incline our hearts to Him, that we may walk in all His ways and keep the commandments, the laws, and the rules, which He enjoined upon our fathers. [59]And may these words of mine, which I have offered in supplication before the LORD, be close to the LORD our God day and night, that He may provide for His servant and for His people Israel, according to each day's needs—[60]to the end that all the peoples of the earth may know that the LORD alone is God, there is no other. [61]And may you be wholehearted with the LORD our God, to walk in His ways and keep His commandments, even as now."

[62]The king and all Israel with him offered sacrifices before the LORD. [63]Solomon offered 22,000 oxen and 120,000 sheep as sacrifices of well-being to the LORD. Thus the king and all the Israelites dedicated the House of the LORD.

STUDY QUESTIONS

1. What are the terms of God's covenant with Israel, and is there an implied threat if the terms of the contract are broken?
2. Why are the people and their priests advised to worship God and follow his very specific directions?

CHAPTER 4

GREEKS AND PERSIANS

4.1. HESIOD, *WORKS AND DAYS*, LAST THIRD OF 8TH CENTURY BCE

A contemporary of Homer, the Greek author Hesiod produced his two major works, *Theogony* (a genealogical account of the gods) and *Works and Days*, around the last third of the 8th century BCE. *Works and Days* is part letter to his brother Perses, part advice column, and part abstract musings on human righteousness. According to Hesiod, the current Sixth Age of Man, the "race of iron," is consigned to labor; yet this labor is the key to success and happiness. Accordingly, Hesiod provides snippets of advice from farming to the choice of a proper wife.

Now listen closely. If you wish, I will tell you
    another tale—
and tell it well—about how the gods and
    mankind share the same origin.
    The race of men made by the Immortals on
      high Olympus
were made of gold. Kronos then ruled in heaven,
    and mankind lived
like gods themselves, free of worry, toil, and
    sorrow. The misery of age
did not afflict them; from head to foot they
    delighted in feasts,
knew no pains, and died simply by falling asleep.
    They lacked
for nothing. The fertile earth brought forth its
    fruits in plenty,

without any labor on their part; they had only the
    delight of harvesting
as they pleased, happy in their bounty. Since that
    time, when the Earth
closed over that race, they have lived on as spirits,
    by Zeus' design,
to watch over mortal men and bestow them with
    blessings.
Such has been Zeus' reward to them.
    Next came the race of silver to live on high
      Olympus,
a lesser race, sharing neither shape nor spirit with
    those of before.
Their sons lived with their mothers for a hundred
    years, playing

Translation by Clifford Backman.

childish games; but when the years passed and
they reached the age
of young manhood, then their lives were full of
pain and were
cut short on account of their simple-mindedness.
They could not
resist doing harm to one another; they refused to
serve the Immortals
and to make sacrifice on the sacred altars of
the gods (as is demanded of all peoples
everywhere). So Zeus, the son of Kronos, in rage
over their refusal to honor the deities on
Olympus, did away with them.
The earth closed over them, since which time they
are called the
Mortal Blessed below. They have their honor, but
are of second rank.
  Then Father Zeus created a third race of men
out of bronze
—nothing like the silver one—created them out
of ash trees. Terrible
and savage, besotted with the baleful work of
Ares, a violent race.
They did not till the land, their hearts being too
stubborn. Ungainly giants
they were, great in strength with powerful arms
reaching out
from mighty shoulders and torsos. They had
bronze armor and bronze
houses. They worked all manner of things in
bronze since they did not
know iron. Their own violent ways brought them
down, and they
passed to cold Hades, leaving no good names
behind them. Strong
as they were, black death got the better of them,
and they
abandoned the light of the sun; over this race too
the Earth closed.
  Then Kronos' son, Zeus, placed a fourth race
upon the vast and fertile Earth,
a dutiful and noble race of the divine heroes
called demigods,
the predecessors of Man. Brutal war and strife
brought them down,
some of them below the seven gates of Thebes, in
Cadmea,

as they contended for Oedipus' inheritance;
others sailed over the deep sea
to Troy, in the war for fair-haired Helen. There
some were swallowed by Death,
but Father Zeus, Kronos' son, spared others and
set them at far reaches
of the Earth, well away from men, where they live
in bliss
in the Isles of the Blessed near deep-currented
Oceanus:
especially blessed are these heroes, for the fertile
land they inhabit
brings forth its bounty three times a year.
  How much better it would be to have died
before the fifth race
of men, or to be born after their passing! Ours is
an age of iron,
filled with toil and misery that never cease, day or
night. Truly the gods
give our race endless suffering and hardship, even
as they sometimes mix
some joy into our sorrow. Father Zeus will bring
an end to our race too;
the signs will be when we are born with gray
hairs, when fathers and
children have nothing in common, when neither
hosts nor guests will be
hospitable, and friendship between brothers will
cease. Respect for parents
shall end, despite all the warnings of the gods,
and the young will rail harshly
at their elders and fail to support them in their
age. They will rule by force,
attacking each other's cities. They will have no
respect for truthful men,
or the righteous and upright. Evil-doers and
criminals they shall lift up
instead, and might shall make right. Villains will
lie and deceive,
defrauding their betters and breaking sacred
oaths. In their misery
all people will be beset by Envy, the bringer of
misfortune and the shaper
of hate-filled faces. At that time, truly, Decency
and Moral Judgment
will quit the Earth, hiding their faces in white
robes, and return to

High Olympus, abandoning mankind forever and
  taking refuge
with the Immortals. Black suffering shall be
  mankind's fate, with
nothing to help them against evil.

. . .

If your heart desires wealth, do as I say and work.
  Work! And work!
  "When the daughters of Atlas, the
      Seven Sisters, rise in the morning
      sky
    begin the harvest, but plow the fields again
      before they set."
They remain hidden for forty days and forty
  nights, and with the
turning of the year they reappear, at the time for
  the sharpening of iron.
This is the law of the land, for both those who
  dwell near the sea
and those glens and meadows far from it: if you
  would have a fertile land
you must be naked when you drive the oxen,
  naked when you sow,
and naked when you reap—or else Demeter's gifts
  will fail to come
in due season and you will know hunger. You will
  beg for your bread

and earn nothing—just as you have now come to
  me. But I will give
you nothing more. Work, Perses, you fool! Do the
  work laid out for you
and for all by the gods. If not, your fate will be
  suffering—Yes, and for your
wife and children too!—for your neighbors will
  hear your pleas and turn away

. . .

It is wiser to marry a girl who lives near you, and
  to choose her carefully,
or else your neighbors will surely laugh at your
  foolishness. For there
is no blessing greater to a man than a good wife,
  and no curse worse
than a bad one, a scold who needs no hot iron in
  order to brand her man;
be he ever so strong, she will wear him down
  before his time. . . .

Now do as I say: do all that you can to avoid
  becoming the subject of rumor,
for a rumor is a terrible burden—easy to pick up,
  but hard to bear, and nearly impossible
to set down. No rumor ever dies, if enough
  people hear it. In this way, indeed,
a rumor is immortal.

STUDY QUESTIONS

1. What are the causes of toil and misery for people in Hesiod's time?
2. How is work a function of a man's overall reputation in the community?

4.2. HOMER, *THE ILIAD*, 8TH CENTURY BCE

This epic poem retells the ten-year-long siege of the city of "Ilium," or Troy (in modern-day Turkey), by the mighty forces of the Greek brothers Agamemnon and Menelaus. The war, sparked by the abduction of Menelaus's wife Helen by the Trojan prince Alexander (or Paris), quickly

Translation by Clifford Backman.

became a battleground for the gods themselves. The first two selections provide a portrait of the militant posturing and tenuous hierarchy in the Greek camp, after Agamemnon threatens to seize invincible Achilles's slave-girl. The third selection describes the wretched death of Hector, Alexander's brother, at the hands of his mortal foe, Achilles. Homer's use of epithets (concise descriptions designed to remind the audience of character traits while fitting into the poem's meter), like "gleaming-helmeted Hector," bring vibrancy to the elegant poetry.

Agamemnon refuses to release his slave-girl. Apollo's wrath. (Book I, ll. 1–52.)

Anger, O Goddess! Let the dreadful anger of
    Achilles, the son of Peleus,
be your song—an anger that brought countless
    sufferings on the Achaeans,
sent many brave souls to Hades, and left the
    remains of heroes unnumbered
as prey for dogs and vultures. Thus was the will of
    great Zeus carried out.
Start from the moment when [King
    Agamemnon],
the son of Atreus, and god-like Achilles fell out
    with one another.

Which of the gods brought them to quarrel? The
    son of Zeus and Leto—Apollo.
For he was angry at Agamemnon and so sent a
    plague upon the Greeks' camp,
Decimating the people there in return for the
    dishonor the son of Atreus
had done to Chryses—Apollo's own priest.
    Chryses had come
to the Achaeans' ships bearing a great ransom
    with which to free
his daughter Briseis. He carried in his hand the
    golden scepter of Apollo,
wreathed in bands, and begged of all the
    Achaeans—but especially of
Agamemnon [and Menelaus], the two sons of
    Atreus, who commanded them all.

"Sons of Atreus!" he cried, "and all you well-
    armored Achaeans!
May the gods who dwell on Olympus grant that
    you sack Priam's city,
and may they give you a fair wind home!

But release my daughter in return for this ransom,
    out of reverence for Apollo,
the son of Zeus!"

At this, the Achaeans were of a single mind to pay
    due respect to the priest
and accept the ransom he offered, but
    Agamemnon, son of Atreus,
refused outright. He berated the priest, instead,
    and angrily dismissed him.

"Never let me catch you, old man, loitering about
    our ships
or trying to approach me again! If I do catch you,
    your scepter and priestly bands
will do you no good. I will not release your
    daughter! No! She will instead
grow old in Argos, far from her native home,
    working at the loom and in my bed!
Now go, and pester me no more, while you're still
    in one piece!"

Thus he spoke, and the frightened old man
    obeyed. He walked away in silence,
but when he got to the shore of the booming sea
    he prayed to Lord Apollo,
whom beautiful Leto bore:

"Hear me, O Master of the Silver Bow!" he cried,
    "Protector of Cilla
and mighty Ruler of Tenedos! O Sminthian! If
    ever I have pleased you
by building shrines in your honor or burning the
    fat thighbones of cattle
or goats upon your altars—grant this prayer of mine:
Let loose your arrows on the Danaans! Avenge my
    tears!"

Thus he prayed, and Phoebus Apollo heard him.
    With his heart full of anger
the god swooped down from Olympus, bearing
    his bow and quiver.
The arrows on his back rattled from the rage he
    felt as he descended.
His face dark as night, Apollo settled at a distance
    from the Greek ships.
His bow sounded like rolling thunder as he
    rained arrows on the Achaeans.
First he shot their mules and dogs, then quickly
turned upon the soldiers themselves. Funeral
    pyres burned night and day.
For nine days his arrows fell on the Greeks—
and on the tenth day, at last, Achilles call the men
    to assembly.

After being criticized by Achilles, Agamemnon rises in anger to denounce him.
(Book I, ll. 101–20)
And then Agamemnon, the son of Atreus, ruler of
    the plain, rose in wrath.
His heart filled with fury, and his eyes blazed like
    flames.
Glaring first at Calchas he uttered the threat:

"You prophet of doom! Not once have you ever
    prophesied
anything good on my behalf! Catastrophe is what
    you live for—never anything good!
Not a single good word has passed your lips, nor
    a good action follow!
Now you stand among all the Greeks and
    pronounce that the god who afflicts them
does so on account of me, because I refused the
    ransom for Chryses' daughter
so that I could keep her as my own, in my home.
    I admit it! I prefer her
to my own wife Clytemnestra. She loses nothing
    in comparison—
not in beauty or stature, mind or skill.

    Yet still . . . I am willing to give her back, if it
        is better that way.
For I want this army to survive, not perish. In
    return, however,

I demand another prize of honor be given me at
    once. For I, alone of all the Argives,
will not go wanting. That would not be proper.
Every man here can see that my due reward is
    going elsewhere."

When Agamemnon threatens to take Achilles' slave-girl, Briseis, to compensate for the loss of Chryses' daughter, Achilles now lashes out in fury.
(Book I, ll. 148–71)
With glowering eyes swift-footed Achilles frowned
at Agamemnon and said:

"You shameless, greedy, selfish man! Who among
    the Greeks can ever
obey your commands after this, either on march
    or in battle?
I did not come here out of my own quarrel with
    the Trojan spearmen;
they have done no wrong to me. They have stolen
    no cattle or horses of mine,
nor destroyed any of my crops in the rich soil of
    Phthia.
Miles and miles of shadowy mountains and
    roaring seas separate us.
No! It was for you—you cur!—for you that we all
    came, fighting to avenge you
And your brother Menelaus upon the Trojans! But
    you've forgotten this, you dog!
And now you threaten to strip me of my own
    prize-girl,
one for whom I fought hard, and whom all the
    Greeks awarded me.
Not once have I done as well as you,
when the soldiers apportion the plunder from
    any Trojan fortress.
Time and again I have fought more, hand-to-
    hand, than ever you did.
But whenever the time comes for splitting the
    booty, the greater share is always yours,
while I, worn out with fighting, take my smaller
    reward back to my ships.
But this time I shall sail for Phthia!
It would be better for me to return home in my
    curved ships.

I will not stay here, dishonored, to keep piling up
    riches for you!"

**Achilles is persuaded not to set sail, but remains
stubbornly in his tent and refuses to fight.
Without him, the Greeks lose battle after battle
against the Trojans. Eventually the common
soldiers begin to grumble. One of them, named
Thersites, complains to Agamemnon on their
behalf. (Book II, ll. 211–77)**

Gradually, the men sat back down. But one of
    them would not stop.
This fellow, talkative Thersites, whose mind was a
    treasure-chest of trouble,
kept flinging abusive words at Agamemnon and
    the other commanders,
just to entertain the troops. The most intemperate
    man who went to Troy,
he was bow-legged and lame in one foot,
    round-shouldered
and always slumping over his chest. His skull was
    misshapen and
covered with mangy stubble. How much Achilles
    and Odysseus, his two favorite targets,
hated him! This time, however, it was
    Agamemnon at whom he hurled abuse,
the son of Atreus with whom the men were
    already furious.

"What have you got to complain about,
    Agamemnon? What more do you covet?
Your tents are bulging with bronze and beauties—
    after all, we hand over
the best of both to you first of all, whenever we've
    finished taking a stronghold.
Perhaps it's more gold you're after? No doubt
    someone from among the Trojans
will bring you piles of it as ransom for his son—a
    son, by the way, whom
one of us foot-soldiers actually captured.
Or maybe you need a new girl for your bed, one
    kept apart for your sole use?
It is a poor commander who sends common men
    to death for so little."
Thus spoke Thersites, railing at Agamemnon,
    leader of men. But then Odysseus,

glaring at the fellow beneath his deep brow,
    snarled angrily at him:

"Shut up, you loud-mouth! You bag of
    hot air!
How dare you speak thus to your commander!
    I swear that of all the soldiers
who followed the sons of Atreus to Troy, there is
    no wretch worse than you.
You've no right to daydream about going
    home,
or to criticize or protest against kings.
None of us knows how this war will end—
whether we'll sail home in victory or defeat. But
    you blather on and on,
whining about Atreus' son Agamemnon—our
    leader—because our own men
have rewarded him richly. I am telling you now—
    and may these words come to pass:
If I hear your whining voice one more time, may
    my own head
be knocked from my shoulders and may I never
    again be called
the father of Telemachus, if I don't seize you, strip
    off your raiment
and drive you naked through the camp, beating
    you all the way!"

After saying this, Odysseus smacked Thersites
    mightily on his back and
shoulders with his staff. A bloody welt crawled up
    the soldier's back where
the gold-studded staff had landed. A tear welled
    in Thersites' eye,
which he quickly wiped away as he collapsed in
    shame. As for the other soldiers,
angry as they were they could not help laughing,
    and whispered to one another:

"Did you see that? Odysseus has done a thousand
    great feats in this war,
both in council and on the field—but nothing to
    top this! He shut that fool up,
and it'll be a long time, I wager, before that
    no-good braggart dares
to criticize a king again!"

Achilles, rejoining the war after the death of his best friend Patroclus, finally corners the Trojan hero Hector, who had killed him. Their confrontation provides the climactic scene of the poem. Achilles has chased Hector three times around the city walls; at last, ashamed of his fear, Hector turns and faces his certain death. (Book 22, ll. 247–65, 292–372, 395–408.)

When the two men finally squared off and faced
    one another,
Hector was the first to speak, declaring:

"Three times you have chased me around Priam's
    city, but
I will run from you no longer, Achilles, son of
    Peleus.
I was afraid, but now my soul commands me to
    stand and face you,
whether this results in my own death or in your's.
    Come!
Let us call upon the gods—the best guarantors of
    all covenants—
to bear witness to a solemn pact between us. I
    vow
that if Zeus grants me the victory I will do no
    dishonor
to your body, and once I have stripped you of
    your great armor
I will hand your body over to the Greeks. Will you
    grant me the same?"

But swift-footed Achilles glowered at him and
    replied:

"You're mad if you think I'll make a similar
    promise!
There are no 'solemn oaths' between lions and
    their mortal prey,
or between wolves and the lambs they seek—only
    evil thoughts
without end. There is no friendship between us,
no polite truces—only violence until one of us
    lies dead
and the war-god Ares is glutted with his blood."
. . .

Hector saw that the end was near . . . and drew
    the sharp sword that hung
On his left flank—great and mighty it was—and
    gathered his will.
Like an eagle who swoops from on high through
    dark clouds to seize
a young lamb or cowering hare, so did Hector
    swoop down on Achilles,
brandishing his sword.

With wild fury in his heart Achilles drew in to his chest
the beautiful shield Hephaisteus had made for
    him, and lowered his
bright four-horned helmet . . .

Like the evening star that shines first and fairest in
    the heavens
with the fall of night, so shone the glint of
    sunlight off the keen spear
lying poised in Achilles' right hand, as he plotted
    how to do the
most harm to goodly Hector. He surveyed him
    coldly, looking for
the best place to land a blow. But Hector was
    well-armored,
his flesh covered in the bronze gear he had
    stripped from Patroclus
after he slew him. A small opening showed,
    however, where
his collar-bone divided the neck from his
    shoulders—the bare gullet
where the destruction of life comes quickest.

Rushing forward, Achilles drove his spear-point
    into the spot,
clear through Hector's neck. The heavy spear did
    not cut
Hector's windpipe, however, leaving him a chance
    to speak
as he fell to the dust at exulting Achilles' feet.
"Hector!" cried Achilles, "did you really think you
    could kill
Patroclus, steal his armor, and be safe from me?
    Fool!
Though left far behind, by the hollow ships, I still
    remained—

a greater foe in arms than even he—and it is I
who have brought
you to your knees. Know this for certain: while
the Greeks
give Patroclus an honorable burial, your corpse
will lie
as carrion for dogs and vultures!"

Fading fast, gleaming-helmeted Hector spoke:

"I beg you, Achilles, on your soul and those of
your parents—
do not let me be devoured by the dogs in your camp!
Take all the bronze and gold my father and good
mother will offer
in ransom. And let them have my body, so that
our Trojan
Men and women may build me a proper funeral
pyre!"

Swift-footed Achilles shot him an angry glance
and shouted:

"No begging nonsense, you whiney little dog!
No 'By your soul!' and 'The honor of your
parents!'
I wish I had it in me to cut you up and eat you
raw,
so great is the hurt you caused me! There is no
man alive
who can save you from the carrion pack—not even
if ten or twenty times a ransom was laid out
before me,
with promises of even more to follow!
Not even if Priam offered me your own weight in
gold.
No, your mother will make no pyre for you, nor
offer
any funeral-lament for the son she bore. No!
The dogs and vultures will have every scrap of you!"
Then Hector spoke his last:

"Now, at last, I see you clearly, and know what
must be.
Your heart is made of iron, and there's no
persuading you.

But consider this: my end may bring the gods'
wrath upon you,
great as you are, after Paris and Phoebus Apollo
destroy you at the city-gates."

As he spoke, Death enfolded him. Hector's soul
left his body and flew to Hades, bewailing the fate
that
had ended his life in the world as a young man.
Achilles watched him die, and finally said:

"Go ahead and die! I accept my own fate
whenever Zeus and the other gods will it."

As he spoke, Achilles pulled his spear from
Hector's neck,
laid it aside, and stripped the blood-stained
armor from
Hector's shoulders. And as he did so, other Greeks
came
running up to see Hector's noble body and
handsome face—
and each one, as he drew near, gave him another blow.

. . .

Achilles had in mind all manner of foul
treatments for noble
Hector's body. He pierced the tendons behind his
feet, from heel
to ankle, and threaded oxhide cords through each
hole and tied them
to his chariot, letting Hector's head trail in the
dust.
Then he mounted his chariot, raised high the
stripped armor
he had won, and with a flick of the reins drove his
eager team of horses on.
They sped forward and a cloud of dust was kicked
up by
Hector's dragging corpse, his dark hair flowing.
The head that
was once so fair became covered with dirt. Thus
did Zeus
deliver him to his enemy, to be defiled in his own
land.

STUDY QUESTIONS

1. How is the theme of "anger," displayed by both men and gods, developed throughout the epic?
2. How are the reasons for the Trojan War bound up in Agamemnon's need to maintain command of his troops?

4.3. HERODOTUS ON THE EGYPTIANS, FROM *HISTORIES*, CA. 450–420 BCE

The Greek writer Herodotus (ca. 484–425 BCE) is known as the Father of History, because his nine-volume account of four Persian kings is the first major extant work to display a critical use of varied sources, categorized information, and a narrative that supports his historical argument even as it spins off into digressions. Herodotus's major claim is that the Persian method of expansion and conquest ultimately spelled its end in Greece, following the Greek and Persian wars (499–449 BCE). In this passage from Book Two of his *Histories*, Herodotus illustrates his method of ethnographic research. He uses the oral testimony of Egyptian scholars he has met, together with etymological evidence, to posit the ancient origins of groups like the Hebrews.

I am convinced that the names of almost all the Greek gods come from Egypt, for my investigations clearly show that the names are foreign and almost certainly from Egypt because the Egyptians have had gods with the same names ever since their country began. There are exceptions: Poseidon and Dioscuroi, for example, whom I discussed earlier, also Hera, Hestia, the Charites and the Nereïds. I report only what the Egyptians themselves think. As for our gods whose names they do not know, I believe these came from the Pelasgian—again with the exception of Poseidon, about whom the Greeks learned from the Libyans. Only the Libyans have known the name Poseidon and have paid it due honor from the start of their history. It is worth mentioning that the Egyptians do not share our custom of worshipping heroes.

So there are religious customs (plus some other matters that I will get to) that the Greeks certainly adopted from the Egyptians; but other rites have come to us not from the Egyptians but from the Pelasgians—such as making images of Hermes with a phallus. The Athenians were the first Greeks to pick up this custom and they spread it to the rest. Just when the Athenians took a leading role among all the Greeks, the Pelasgians began to dwell in their land; in fact, this is how the Pelasgians came to be regarded as Greeks themselves. Any man who has been initiated in the sacred mysteries of the Cabeiroi—which the people of Samothrace perform, having learned the rites from the Pelasgians—knows what I mean, for the same Pelasgians who lived among the Athenians had previously lived in Samothrace. The Samothracians learned the rites from them. Thus the Athenians were the first Greeks to make images of Hermes with a phallus: they learned it from the Pelasgians, who embellished the practice with a sacred legend that was itself adopted into the sacred rites in Samothrace.

According to what I heard at Dodona, these Pelasgians originally would offer prayers and sacrifices to

---

Translation by Clifford Backman.

all their deities without distinguishing between them either by name or title, on the assumption that they had all played a role in creation and all shared in the offerings presented to them. Much later, however, they learned the names of all the gods from the Egyptians. All the gods, that is, except Dionysius, whose name they never heard until much later. At some point they consulted the oracle at Dodona about the names of the gods (Dodona being the most ancient of all Greek oracles and at that time the only one), and they asked whether or not they should adopt the names they had learned from non-Greeks. The oracle replied that they should do so, and from that time on the Pelasgians performed all their sacrifices using the names, which is how the Greeks came to know them.

About other matters, though—such as how the various gods and goddesses were born, or whether they were all in existence from the very beginning, and what each of them looked like—the Greeks knew nothing until quite recently. It seems to have been, in fact, only since yesterday or the day before, for the poets Hesiod and Homer, who lived no more than four hundred years before my time, were the ones who described the gods' births, gave them titles, associated each with specific qualities and arts, and described their appearance. Other poets [who described such things] who are said to have lived before Hesiod and Homer actually came after them, in my opinion. The priestesses at Dodona passed on all the knowledge I alluded to first, but the ideas about Hesiod and Homer are my own.

In Egypt I heard the following account of the Greek and Libyan oracles. Several priests of the temple to Zeus at Thebes reported that two of their priestesses had been captured and carried off by some Phoenicians, and they had heard that one was sold as a slave in Libya, the other as a slave to some Greeks. These were reportedly the very women who established the oracles I referred to above. When I asked how the Egyptians had learned all of this, they answered that the Theban priests had searched far and wide for the two women, but to no avail. Soon afterward, however, the Egyptians began to hear stories of the two oracles.

I first heard from the priests at Thebes, and the priestesses at Dodona confirmed it, that two black doves flew from Thebes to Egypt; one landed ultimately in Libya but the other returned to Thebes, where it landed in an oak tree and began to speak in human language. It said that a temple to Zeus was to be built on the site, and the people of Thebes reckoned that it was the gods speaking through the bird, and so they built the temple. The dove that flew to Libya, they say, told the Libyans to build a temple to Ammon, which is also Zeus' temple. Three priestesses of Dodona told me all of this: Promeneia was the eldest, Timarete came next, and the youngest being Nicandra. But several others who worked at the temple confirmed their account.

I have an opinion of my own, however. If the Phoenicians did actually abduct the priestesses and sold them, as the story goes, one in Libya and the other in Greece, then the one sold in Greece (which in earlier times was called Pelasgia) must have been sold to the group known as the Thesprotians. Enslaved among that group, she must then have built a temple to Zeus under an actual oak tree. It would only be natural for her, a priestess of Zeus' temple at Thebes, to have brought the cult of Zeus to this new place. Later, once she had learned to speak Greek, she established an oracle, I am guessing, and spread the tale of her sister's enslavement in Libya by the same Phoenicians who had sold her.

More than that, I suspect the people of Dodona called these women "doves" because they were non-Greeks and therefore their speech sounded to them like birdsong. "After some time they spoke with human speech," they said; what else could this mean but that they learned to speak the language the others could understand? A non-Greek tongue sounded to them like birdsong—for really, who ever heard of a bird with human speech? And when they say that the doves were black, they mean only that the women were Egyptian. It is simply a coincidence that the way that oracles speak in Thebes, in Egypt, and at Dodona are similar—same thing for the method of divination.

It is also true that the Egyptians were the first people to establish solemn gatherings who would then process in order and approach their temples. The Greeks learned the practice from them. My evidence: the simple fact that the Egyptians have done this forever, whereas we Greeks have only just begun the practice.

The Egyptians hold solemn assemblies frequently—not just once a year. The assemblies with the greatest energy and excitement are those at the city of Bubastis, for the goddess Artemis, and at Busiris, for Isis. In Busiris, in fact, there stands an enormous temple to Isis. Busiris is in the middle of the Egyptian Delta, and "Isis" is the same as the Greek "Demeter." They also hold a sacred assembly at Saïs for the goddess Athena; another at Heliopolis for Helios, the Sun; yet another at Buto in honor of Leto; and still another at Papremis in honor of Ares.

STUDY QUESTIONS

1. How is Herodotus applying a rational framework to the various stories he has heard?
2. In his opening paragraph Herodotus claims that he is writing history to preserve the "great deeds/wonders (ta thaumata, in Greek)" displayed by "both the Hellenes and the barbarians." Does his analysis primarily display Greek cultural curiosity or cultural chauvinism?

4.4. THUCYDIDES, *PELOPONNESIAN WAR*, EARLY 5TH CENTURY BCE

Thucydides (ca. 460–395 BCE) has been credited with holding Greek historical work to a more scientific standard—divorcing it further from myth as a historical source and retaining a strictly chronological arrangement. His great eight-volume work details the war (431–404 BCE) between Sparta, the polis of military rigor, and Athens, the polis of democracy and philosophy, as well as their allied coalitions. This selection recounts the speech made by the Athenian general Pericles (ca. 495–429 BCE) in honor of the dead from the first year of the Peloponnesian War. Consider how Pericles attempts to renew the spirits of those who mourn fallen Greeks.

During that same winter, and following long-established custom, the people of Athens held a public funeral for the first men to die in the war. This is how the ceremony goes.

Several days before the service they put up a tent in which they lay out the bones of the fallen. This way anyone can bring whatever offerings they like to their own dead. On the day of the funeral they bring in, on wagons, coffins made of cypress (there is a separate coffin for each tribe); then they place the bones in their respective coffins. A single empty bier, suitably adorned, represents all the dead whose bodies have not been found or recovered. Any one who wishes to join the procession may do so, whether foreigner or native, and the women of the dead men's families also attend the funerals and mourn at the

Translation by Clifford Backman.

gravesites. The burials take place in the public cemetery, which is located in the most beautiful suburbs of the city, where they always bury their war-dead. The only exceptions are those who died in the battle of Marathon, whose extraordinary bravery was thought to deserve burial on the field where they fell.

When the coffins have been laid in the earth, a man chosen by the city for his discernment and high reputation delivers a fitting eulogy, and afterwards everyone departs. This, in sum, is how they performed their funerals, and the custom was followed whenever possible throughout the war.

[Editor's note: Pericles was chosen to deliver the eulogy at the first state funeral after the start of the war with Sparta.]

"Before I speak in praise of the dead, let me recount the basic principles by which our community lives and which have made us what we are; and recount also the institutions and qualities that have raised us to greatness. For I think the subject is fitting on the present occasion; moreover, this entire assembly, both foreigners and natives, may gain some benefit from the telling.

"Our ways are not like those of our neighbors. We don't copy others, but are an example to them. Our form of government is called a democracy, for we serve the interest of the many, not the few. While our laws give equal rights to all in private disputes, public preferment recognizes individual distinction. Pride of place in public service thus depends on merit rather than rotation. As for poverty—it is no bar to office. Any man who has the ability, no matter how lowly his rank, can do the city some good. We conduct our public affairs freely and in the open, and we do not judge one another in our private lives. We are not angered when a neighbor pursues his private pleasures, nor do we glare in disapproval (which is a harmless thing, perhaps, but a painful one in its own way). We are obliging in our private doings and we obey the law in our public ones, since fear of offending either our authorities or our laws keeps us from doing wrong. We especially respect the laws that protect the injured, as well as those unspoken laws the breaking of which brings disgrace. . . .

"We value beauty without extravagance, and intellect without loss of manly vigor. We value wealth for the uses to which it can be put, not for show or boasting. We find no disgrace in poverty, only in the failure to avoid it. Our political leaders manage state business as well as their domestic affairs, and even those who are kept busy making a living know something about politics. If a man has no interest at all in public affairs, we alone call his life not quiet but useless. If we are not all involved in creating policy, we are at least good judges of it. We believe action is not hampered by discussion itself but by the failure to discuss policies thoroughly before any action is taken. We differ from other people by our combination of deliberation and action; to others, their blindness results from their ignorance, and they regard discussion as hesitation. True strength of spirit resides in those who have the clearest understanding of life's joys and sorrows, and do not on that account shrink from any danger. . . .

"To sum up, I say that our city, taken all in all, is the teacher of all Greece. Every last one of us seems capable of combining the self-reliance necessary to enjoy life and the ability to adapt with grace and ease to every challenge life presents to us. This is not empty boasting but a verifiable fact, proven by the power our city has won by our character. Athens, alone among today's states, is greater than its reputation; only her enemies, and no one else's, are not ashamed to have suffered defeat at her hands. None of her subjects can complain of being ruled by an undeserving master. Our greatness does not lack for witnesses—there are countless monuments to our power that will make us the wonder of current and future generations. We need no Homer to sing our praises, nor any poet whose fine words will please for a while, only later to fall victim to historical truth. The simple fact is that we have forced open every sea-lane and every nation to our daring and have planted everywhere permanent memorials to our triumphs and failures.

"This, then, is the city for which these men fought and died in their noble determination not to lose. All we who survive should gladly suffer likewise in her service. . . .

"When you consider her greatness, bear in mind that it was the handiwork of valiant men who knew their duty and took pride in doing it, men who, if they ever failed in some enterprise refused to burden the city with a share of their ill-fortune and instead offered up their courage as the best gift they could present her with. All of them alike gave their lives for her and were rewarded with praises that never grow old and with the most worthy of all tombs—not the dust where their bodies lie, but our hearts where the memory of them lives forever and their glory is recalled on every suitable occasion. The whole earth is a tomb for famous men, whose record consists not only of words inscribed on tombstones in their native land but of the unwritten words that live in men's hearts even in foreign lands—the living memory of their spirit rather than their deeds. Strive to emulate these men, understanding full well that happiness is freedom—and that freedom results from courage. You need not fear the dangers of war. . . .

"To the surviving parents of those who lie before us I offer consolation rather than sympathy. For you know that ours is a world of constant and unpredictable change, in which the best fate that can befall us is to attain honor. We commemorate the honorable deaths of our fallen and we commend the honorable grief you now suffer—for it is a blessing indeed to enjoy a life in which honor is attained in the living of it and in the departure from it.

STUDY QUESTIONS

1. In what specific ways does Pericles see Athens as "the school for Hellas"?
2. How does Pericles argue that Athens's cultural achievements result from its democratic political system?

CHAPTER 5

CLASSICAL GREECE AND THE HELLENISTIC WORLD

5.1. BOOK OF EZRA, REBUILDING THE TEMPLE, CHAPTERS 1–3, 5–6, WRITTEN CA. MID-5TH CENTURY BCE

The Book of Ezra picks up the story of the Israelites after the Babylonian Captivity (ca. 586–538 BCE), which ends when the Persian king Cyrus defeats the Babylonians and restores the Israelites to their homeland with permission to rebuild the Temple in Jerusalem. Ezra, in whose name this book is written, was a priest who has been credited with restoring the Torah and its laws to Jerusalem. This selection records King Cyrus's decree; it describes the rebuilding of the Second Temple in Jerusalem, a central spot of worship and symbol of Jewish identity that stood until its destruction by the Romans during the Jewish Revolt in 70 CE.

CHAPTER 1

[1]In the first year of King Cyrus of Persia, when the word of the LORD spoken by Jeremiah was fulfilled, the LORD roused the spirit of King Cyrus of Persia to issue a proclamation throughout his realm by word of mouth and in writing as follows:

[2]Thus said King Cyrus of Persia: The LORD God of Heaven has given me all the kingdoms of the earth and has charged me with building Him a house in Jerusalem, which is in Judah. [3]Anyone of you of all His people—may his God be with him, and let him go up to Jerusalem that is in Judah and build the House of the LORD God of Israel, the God that is in Jerusalem;

[4]and all who stay behind, wherever he may be living, let the people of his place assist him with silver, gold, goods, and livestock, besides the freewill offering to the House of God that is in Jerusalem."

[5]So the chiefs of the clans of Judah and Benjamin, and the priests and Levites, all whose spirit had been roused by God, got ready to go up to build the House of the LORD that is in Jerusalem. [6]All their neighbors supported them with silver vessels, with gold, with goods, with livestock, and with precious objects, besides what had been given as a freewill offering. [7]King Cyrus of Persia released the vessels of the LORD'S house which Nebuchadnezzar had taken away from

From Book of Ezra, Chapters 1–3, 5–6.

Jerusalem and had put in the house of his god. [8]These King Cyrus of Persia released through the office of Mithredath the treasurer, who gave an inventory of them to Sheshbazzar the prince of Judah. [9]This is the inventory: 30 gold basins, 1,000 silver basins, 29 knives, [10]30 gold bowls, 410 silver double bowls, 1,000 other vessels; 11 in all, 5,400 gold and silver vessels. Sheshbazzar brought all these back when the exiles came back from Babylon to Jerusalem.

. . .

CHAPTER 2

[64]The sum of the entire community was 42,360, [65]not counting their male and female servants, those being 7,337; they also had 200 male and female singers. [66]Their horses—736; their mules—245; [67]their camels—435; their asses—6,720.

[68]Some of the chiefs of the clans, on arriving at the House of the LORD in Jerusalem, gave a freewill offering to erect the House of God on its site. [69]In accord with their means, they donated to the treasury of the work: gold—6,100 drachmas, silver—5,000 minas, and priestly robes—100.

[70]The priests, the Levites and some of the people, and the singers, gatekeepers, and the temple servants took up residence in their towns and all Israel in their towns.

CHAPTER 3

[1]When the seventh month arrived—the Israelites being settled in their towns—the entire people assembled as one man in Jerusalem. [2]Then Jeshua son of Jozadak and his brother priests, and Zerubbabel son of Shealtiel and his brothers set to and built the altar of the God of Israel to offer burnt offerings upon it as is written in the Teaching of Moses, the man of God. [3]They set up the altar on its site because they were in fear of the peoples of the land, and they offered burnt offerings on it to the LORD, burnt offerings each morning and evening. [4]Then they celebrated the festival of Tabernacles as is written, with its daily burnt offerings in the proper quantities, on each day as is prescribed for it, [5]followed by the regular burnt offering and the offerings for the new moons and for all the sacred fixed times of the LORD, and whatever

freewill offerings were made to the LORD. [6]From the first day of the seventh month they began to make burnt offerings to the LORD, though the foundation of the Temple of the LORD had not been laid. [7]They paid the hewers and craftsmen with money, and the Sidonians and Tyrians with food, drink, and oil to bring cedarwood from Lebanon by sea to Joppa, in accord with the authorization granted them by King Cyrus of Persia.

[8]In the second year after their arrival at the House of God, at Jerusalem, in the second month, Zerubbabel son of Shealtiel and Jeshua son of Jozadak, and the rest of their brother priests and Levites, and all who had come from the captivity to Jerusalem, as their first step appointed Levites from the age of twenty and upward to supervise the work of the House of the LORD. [9]Jeshua, his sons and brothers, Kadmiel and his sons, the sons of Judah, together were appointed in charge of those who did the work in the House of God; also the sons of Henadad, their sons and brothers Levites.

[10]When the builders had laid the foundation of the Temple of the LORD, priests in their vestments with trumpets, and Levites sons of Asaph with cymbals were stationed to give praise to the LORD, as King David of Israel had ordained. [11]They sang songs extolling and praising the LORD, "For He is good, His steadfast love for Israel is eternal." All the people raised a great shout extolling the LORD because the foundation of the House of the LORD had been laid. [12]Many of the priests and Levites and the chiefs of the clans, the old men who had seen the first house, wept loudly at the sight of the founding of this house. Many others shouted joyously at the top of their voices. [13]The people could not distinguish the shouts of joy from the people's weeping, for the people raised a great shout, the sound of which could be heard from afar.

. . .

CHAPTER 5

[3]At once Tattenai, governor of the province of Beyond the River, Shethar-bozenai, and their colleagues descended upon them and said this to them, "Who issued orders to you to rebuild this house and complete its furnishing?" [4]Then we said to them, "What

are the names of the men who are engaged in the building?" [5]But God watched over the elders of the Jews and they were not stopped while a report went to Darius and a letter was sent back in reply to it.

. . .

CHAPTER 6

[1]Thereupon, at the order of King Darius, they searched the archives where the treasures were stored in Babylon. [2]But it was in the citadel of Ecbatana, in the province of Media, that a scroll was found in which the following was written: "Memorandum: [3]In the first year of King Cyrus, King Cyrus issued an order concerning the House of God in Jerusalem: 'Let the house be rebuilt, a place for offering sacrifices, with a base built up high. Let it be sixty cubits high and sixty cubits wide, [4]with a course of unused timber for each three courses of hewn stone. The expenses shall be paid by the palace. [5]And the gold and silver vessels of the House of God which Nebuchadnezzar had taken away from the temple in Jerusalem and transported to Babylon shall be returned, and let each go back to the temple in Jerusalem where it belongs; you shall deposit it in the House of God.'

[6]"Now you, Tattenai, governor of the province of Beyond the River, Shethar-bozenai and colleagues, the officials of the province of Beyond the River, stay away from that place. [7]Allow the work of this House of God to go on; let the governor of the Jews and the elders of the Jews rebuild this House of God on its site. [8]And I hereby issue an order concerning what you must do to help these elders of the Jews rebuild this House of God: the expenses are to be paid to these men with dispatch out of the resources of the king, derived from the taxes of the province of Beyond the River, so that the work not be stopped. [9]They are to be given daily, without fail, whatever they need of young bulls, rams, or lambs as burnt offerings for the God of Heaven, and wheat, salt, wine, and oil, at the order of the priests in Jerusalem, [10]so that they may offer pleasing sacrifices to the God of Heaven and pray for the life of the king and his sons. [11]I also issue an order that whoever

alters this decree shall have a beam removed from his house, and he shall be impaled on it and his house confiscated. [12]And may the God who established His name there cause the downfall of any king or nation that undertakes to alter or damage that House of God in Jerusalem. I, Darius, have issued the decree; let it be carried out with dispatch."

[13]Then Tattenai, governor of the province of Beyond the River, Shethar-bozenai, and their colleague carried out with dispatch what King Darius had written. [14]So the elders of the Jews progressed in the building, urged on by the prophesying of Haggai the prophet and Zechariah son of Iddo, and they brought the building to completion under the aegis of the God of Israel and by the order of Cyrus and Darius and King Artaxerxes of Persia. [15]The House was finished on the third of the month of Adar in the sixth year of the reign of King Darius. [16]The Israelites, the priests, and the Levites, and all the other exiles celebrated the dedication of the House of God with joy. [17]And they sacrificed for the dedication of this House of God one hundred bulls, two hundred rams, four hundred lambs, and twelve goats as a purification offering for all of Israel, according to the number of the tribes of Israel. [18]They appointed the priests in their courses and the Levites in their divisions for the service of God in Jerusalem, according to the prescription in the Book of Moses.

[19]The returned exiles celebrated the Passover on the fourteenth day of the first month, [20]for the priests and Levites had purified themselves to a man; they were all pure. They slaughtered the Passover offering for all the returned exiles, and for their brother priests and for themselves. [21]The children of Israel who had returned from the exile, together with all who joined them in separating themselves from the uncleanliness of the nations of the lands to worship the LORD God of Israel, ate of it. [22]They joyfully celebrated the Feast of Unleavened Bread for seven days, for the LORD had given them cause for joy by inclining the heart of the Assyrian king toward them so as to give them support in the work of the House of God, the God of Israel.

STUDY QUESTIONS

1. How does the Persian Cyrus come to be enlisted as an agent of the Hebrews' God?
2. What motivates the renewal of the Jews' contract with God after their return from exile?

5.2. AESCHYLUS, *PROMETHEUS BOUND* (UNDATED; 5TH CENTURY)

This drama is attributed to Aeschylus (ca. 525–456 BCE), called the Father of Tragedy. It lyricizes the plight of Prometheus, a Titan, who has been chained to a rock face above the sea, exposed to the elements. Zeus punishes Prometheus for the crime of stealing firebrands from the gods to bring fire—and with it, industry, skill, and enlightenment—to mankind. Prometheus's monologue glorifies and, in a way, justifies his actions. It also enables us to understand what the gods had to fear from Prometheus's disobedience and why the character of "Fire-Bearer" intrigues us to this day.

[PROMETHEUS SPEAKS]
Don't think my silence is the result of pride or a
    stand-offish nature!
My heart is brokenly bitter at the outrageous
    treatment I have received.
As for these new gods and their attributes—who
    gave them to them, if not I?
But I'll hold my tongue; no point in my saying
    what you already know.
Listen instead to what I have to say about human
    suffering.
They were mere children before I gave themMinds
    of their own and the ability to think! I say
    this nowNot in order to reproach them but to
    explain what led meTo gift them so.
When they first looked around, they looked in
    vain;
When listening, they did not truly hear. They were
Like figures in a dream and lived out their lives

Comprehending nothing. They did not know
How to raise brick-walled houses to protect
    themselves
Against the sun, or how to build with wood.
They just scurried about, in dark and dreary caves,
Living underground like ants.
They could not grasp the concepts of winter, or of
Springtime in full flower, or of fruitful summer.
No—they just labored on, without a clue,
Until I showed them the risings and the
    settings
Of the far-off stars.
There's more: that greatest of tools—writing!—
I gave to them. Writing! The boon to memory and
The mother of all arts. And it was I who
Domesticated wild animals for them, taming the
    beasts
To accept harness and saddle, to slave in packs,
    and relieve

Translation by Clifford Backman.

Humans of their heaviest labors.
It was I who tamed horses to pull chariots—one
  of the Delights of prosperity—and none other
  than I
Who discovered how men might be sailors,
  roaming
Over the seas with wings of linen.
But now I am wretched—I, who invented such
  devices
For mankind, am helpless to get myself out of this
Miserable state I'm in.
chorus: Your punishment is indeed shameful.
  Thus driven mad,
You're like a poorly skilled doctor who has fallen
  sick—
Despairing and unable to know the medicine that
  will cure you.
prometheus: When you hear the rest you'll be
  even more amazed
At the clever skills and arts I contrived.
Greatest of all: if someone great fell ill and there
  was
No remedy that could be eaten or drunk, or
  applied as an ointment,
And because of this the victim wasted away—I
  showed men
How to blend soothing remedies that protect
  them
Against all diseases.
I determined how to prophesy, how to interpret

One's dreams after waking, how to read omens in
  off-hand
Comments and in things briefly glimpsed.
I taught them how to read signs in the
  flock-flights
Of taloned birds—which patterns are auspicious,
  and which ones
Foretell of bad news. I taught them too what these
  portents meant
For the various aspects of their lives—their loves
  and hatreds,
And their matings.
I taught them how to read the entrails [of
  sacrificed animals]—
The smoothness and color a gall-bladder must
  have in order
To satisfy the gods, or the required shape of a
  liver, or how
To roast bones with the thighs wrapped in fat.
Thus I taught them divination, the difficult art
Of augury by fire, which had been kept from
  them for so long.
All these things and more I gave, including
Iron, bronze, gold, and silver—all the buried
  blessings of mankind.
Who, other than I, can claim to have bestowed all
  of these?
No one except a lying braggart.
Here is my whole tale in a single phrase:
Prometheus founded all the arts of mankind.

STUDY QUESTIONS

1. In what specific and general ways does Prometheus claim to have benefited mankind?
2. Why was he punished for this assistance by the other gods?

5.3. PLATO, *SYMPOSIUM*, 385–380 BCE

The student of the famed dialectician Socrates and teacher of Aristotle, Plato (ca. 424–ca. 348 BCE) is a crucial link in the development of the Western intellectual chain—redefining philosophy, rhetoric, logic, ethics, and other disciplines according to his idea that the current material world is a mere copy of a perfect spiritual world. This text consists of the dialogue that occurred at a drinking party where each character must deliver a speech in praise of Love. Alcibiades—who drunkenly appears mid-text—delivers a speech on his lover Socrates, who is present at the party. Alcibiades draws a distinction between the value of a gorgeous exterior (as his own) and that of inner brilliance (as that of Socrates).

Suddenly there was a large noise: a large group of people (all of them drunk) jostled the outer door; in the background was a flute-girl they had brought with them. Agathon then shouted to his servants, "Go see who it is. If it's any friends of ours, show them in; if not, tell them the party's over and we're going to bed."

A moment later the voice of Alcibiades—very drunk, very loud—could be heard in the courtyard, wanting to know where Agathon was and demanding to be brought to him. He was half-carried into the house by the flute-girl and some others, but once they got him to the doorway he managed to stand by himself, crowned with an impressive wreath made of ivy and violets from which several ribbons hung down around his head. Alcibiades called out, "Good evening, gentlemen! I'm plastered, but may I join your party? If you say No, then I'll just place my wreath on young Agathon here and leave. That's all I came here to do, anyway. I couldn't make it to the celebration yesterday, but now I'm here to remove this wreath from my own head and put it on Agathon's—such a cute and clever little guy! Oh! You laugh at me because I'm drunk? That's OK, go ahead. But you know I'm right! So tell me, now that you know why I'm here, can I stay? Have a little drink with me?"

Everyone called out and begged him to come in and join us. Agathon asked him to sit right next to him, and so, with a little help from his friends, Alcibiades joined Agathon. He tried to take off his wreath and give it to Agathon but the ribbons were caught in his hair and the whole thing covered his eyes, so he couldn't see that Socrates had made room for him as soon as he had entered. So Alcibiades ended up sitting between Socrates and Agathon. As soon as he was settled, he threw his arms around Agathon, kissed him, and managed to get the wreath on his head.

Agathon ordered his servants to take off Alcibiades' sandals. "Put your feet up! There's room for three on my couch."

"Wonderful idea," replied Alcibiades, "but who's the third?" And turning around as he spoke, he saw Socrates. "Good Lord!" he cried, jumping to his feet. "Socrates! You cornered me again! Always when I least expect it. So, what do you want now, Socrates? How did you just happen to be on this couch, eh? Why aren't you with Aristophanes or someone else we could tease you about? How did you just happen to end up next to the cutest guy in the room?"

"Agathon, protect me!" called Socrates. "You've no idea what it's like to be in love with this man. I fell for him the first time I laid eyes on him—and now he won't let me have two words with another man! And not even two words! If I even look at an attractive man he goes crazy with jealousy. He screams and shouts and seems like he's ready to slap me around. Please get him under control and tell him to forgive me [for lying next to Agathon]. You'll have to rescue

Translation by Clifford Backman.

me, if gets violent. Really, his passion for me is terrifying!"

"I swear I'll never forgive you," cried Alcibiades, "You'll pay for this!" Then he turned to Agathon and said, "But just for now let me have a few of these ribbons, and I'll make a wreath for him too since he has such a lovely old head. Otherwise he'll make a scene and bitch that I made a crown for you, Agathon, for your first victory, but never made one for him despite the fact that he's never lost an argument in his life."

Alcibiades then took a few ribbons and draped them over Socrates' head, then lay back on the couch. Then he suddenly leapt back up again. "Come, come, everyone—you all look entirely too sober, and I won't stand for it. Everyone have a drink! Now, do you remember our agreement? We must have a Master of Ceremonies! But who should that be, I wonder? Until one of you is drunk enough for the job, I appoint myself. Agathon, I want the biggest drinking cup you've got. No, never mind that—tell your servant to bring *that* over here."

He had seen the cooling jar, which he reckoned could hold more than two quarts. He had the servants fill it to the brim with wine, and he drank it all right down. Then he told them to fill it again, but this time for Socrates.

"Not that it'll do any good," said Alcibiades. "We all know, friends, that Socrates will drink anything set in front of him, but none of us has ever seen him drunk."

The servant filled the jar for Socrates, and as he was drinking it Eryximachus called to Alcibiades, "This isn't right! We're not here simply to pour the wine down our throats in silence! Let's have some conversation, or some singing! What you're doing isn't acceptable."

"Ah, Eryximachus," answered Alcibiades, "best of sons of the best and soberest of fathers! How are you?"

"I'm well, thank you," Eryximachus said. "Now, how shall we entertain ourselves?"

"However you like!" said Alcibiades, "I'm yours to command. 'One physician is worth a million men.'[1] Prescribe for us what you think is best."

---

[1] *Iliad* 11.514.

"Listen to this, then," said Eryximachus. "Earlier we decided to spend the evening with each of us, going from left to right, giving the best speech he could in praise of Love. Now, we've all had our say, so you should go next. You certainly have had your share to drink; now that your cup's empty, it's your turn. Once you finish, then you're free to choose a new topic for Socrates, on your right, and when he's done we'll all go round the circle again."

"A splendid idea, Eryximachus! But is it fair to compare the speech of a drunkard with the speeches of men who are still sober? Besides, my friend, you don't really believe a word of what Socrates said just now? The opposite is true! If I ever dare to praise another man—even a god!—in front of him, Socrates lights into me."

"Hold your tongue," warned Socrates.

"Oh, don't try to deny it," shouted Alcibiades. "No! I refuse to speak in praise of anyone in front of Socrates *except* Socrates."

"Well then, go ahead. Do as you wish, and give us a speech in praise of Socrates," said Eryximachus.

"Do you really think I should? Really? Should I just let loose and give him his just desserts in front of everyone?"

"Now wait one minute," interrupted Socrates. "What are you thinking of doing? Mock me with your 'song of praise'?"

"I promise to say nothing but the truth. Is that OK?"

"I'm all in favor of hearing the truth, even from you. Go right ahead," said Socrates.

"All right, I will," said Alcibiades. "But here's what you can do: If I say anything that's not true, stop me and call me a liar. I may make mistakes, but I won't intentionally lie. But don't get upset if I get confused and put things in the wrong order; I shall say things as they come to me. But be patient—even someone who wasn't drunk would find it difficult to describe your extraordinary self."

"Friends, I speak in praise of Socrates! But I find I must use images to do so. You and he may think I am doing this to make fun of him, but isn't so. I am merely aiming at truth.

"Look, doesn't he resemble one of those statues of Silenus you find in so many shops? The kind where he's sitting and holding his pipe or flute, but he's hollow—and when you open him up he's filled with tiny little statues of various gods.

"Look again, doesn't he resemble Marsyas the satyr? Now hold on, Socrates! Even you can't deny that you look just like them. In outer appearance, at least. But you resemble them in other ways too, as you're about to hear.

"For starters, you're a vile, impudent bully. Don't deny it—I'll bring in witnesses if need be. And although you don't play the flute you're quite the player, greater even than Marsyas, who needed an instrument in order to cast spells on others. (So too do any others who play his tunes. Even Olympus played Marsyas' tunes—he learned them directly from him.) No matter who plays his music, from the greatest musician to the simplest flute-girl, his melodies are divine and have the power to cast a spell over men and prepare them to encounter the god and his mysteries. And Socrates, the only difference between you and Marsyas is that you don't need instruments, but can cast your spells by using words alone. Most people hardly ever pay real attention to a speech-giver, even to the greatest orators, but let anyone—man, woman, or child—listen to you speak, or even to a second-hand account of what you've said, and he is both enchanted and possessed.

"If I were to describe the effect his words always have on me, you'd think I'm drunk! I can feel his power even now, even though I'm the one speaking. But I swear to you, whenever he starts to speak my heart races in my chest, tears stream down my cheeks, and I'm a goner. Even the crazy Corybantes seem sane, compared to me, and I'm not the only one.[2] I've listened admiringly to many great orators, including Pericles, but none of them has ever had this effect on me; none has ever touched me so deeply that I began to wonder if my life was any better than that of a wretched slave. Yet that's exactly how this 'Marsyas' here to my right makes me feel all the time—like my life isn't worth living. No, you can't say this isn't true, Socrates! I have no doubt you could have that exact

effect on me at this moment, if I gave you the chance. He traps me into thinking that my life in politics is a waste of time, and that the only things that matter are the things I care least about: namely, my faults, which he says need immediate attention. So I refuse to listen to him. He is like a Siren whose call could hold me captive forever.

"He is the only man in the world who makes me feel ashamed of myself. Surprised to hear I'm capable of that? It's true. I know I'm powerless to prove him wrong, whenever he tells me how I ought to live; but as soon as I'm on my own again, I go right back to my vices. That why my life has become one long struggle to get away and keep away from him! When I run into him again, I instantly feel ashamed of myself again, for I know I've done nothing to better myself even though I promised him I would. Sometimes I think I'd be happier if he were dead. It's true! But I know that if he were to die I would feel even worse. So you see, I can't live with him or without him. What's left to do, therefore?

"That is the effect his satyr's music has on me, and not only on me. Lots of others. So he is like a satyr, and in all kinds of ways. Let me tell you about his powers because they are truly extraordinary. I assure you, none of you understands the truth about him the way I do.

"Since I've started on the topic, let me tell you the truth about him. First of all, he's crazy for pretty boys and stalks them relentlessly, like he's in a trance. Second, he's always saying that he's an ignoramus, one who knows absolutely nothing. Just like Silenus, right? And this is just scratching the surface! Fellow drinkers, I wonder if you have any idea how sober and cautious a man he is on the inside? It turns out, he really doesn't care whether or not a boy is pretty. He doesn't care a bit whether someone is rich, or beautiful, or famous, or any of the things that most people admire. In truth, he regards all these things as beneath contempt, and I'm telling you he feels the same way about us. His whole public life is a sham, one big game of pretending. I doubt if anyone here has ever seen him when he's really serious. One time, though, let me tell you, I caught him when he was opened up like one of those Silenus statues and I saw the small godlike treasures he keeps hidden inside.

---

[2] The Corybantes were fanatical worshippers in the cult of Cybele, known for dancing and chanting themselves into a frenzy.

They were so beautiful, so precious, so amazing, that I lost my will entirely and had to do whatever he asked of me.

"At the time I thought what he wanted most of all was me. What an opportunity! Because I was so confident in my good looks, I really believed that if I simply let him have his way with me, he would teach me everything he knew. He and I had never been alone together, at that point, since I always had one or two of my attendants with me. So I dismissed my attendant and went to meet Socrates alone.

"Now everyone pay close attention, because I want only to say what's true. So if I make a mistake, Socrates, please correct me.

"There I was, at last, alone with him. I assumed that he would start by saying to me whatever words lovers use when they find themselves alone together, and I was enjoying the moment—but then, nothing. Nothing happened at all. Socrates just started talking to me the way he always had done, and at the end of the day he left.

"My next idea was to invite him to come with me to the gymnasium. We exercised together for a while—and I was certain that that would lead to something, especially when no one was around—but he just wrestled with me a few times, nothing more. What else can I say? Nothing happened.

"When I finally admitted to myself that my little plan had failed, I decided on a full frontal assault. No way was I going to withdraw from a battle that I had begun myself! I needed to know just what was going on between us, and so I invited him to dinner—switching roles, as though I was the pursuer and he was the pursued. Now, it took some time before he accepted my invitation, but one day he finally came. He left soon after eating, that first time, and I was too timid to try to stop him, but on our second time I introduced a new conversation topic just as we were finishing our meal—and that kept him talking well into the night. At a certain point he said he needed to get going, but I, using the lateness of the hour as an excuse, persuaded him to spend the night at my house. He laid back down on the couch he had used for eating, the one right next to mine. We were alone.

"So far, you must admit, my story has been rather proper, one I could tell in any company. Were

it not for the truth of an old adage, however—'There is truth in wine, once the servants leave'—you would never have heard the rest of the tale, as I'm about to tell you right now. After all, it wouldn't be fair to Socrates if in offering him a 'song of praise' I failed to mention one of his proudest achievements. Well, then. Have you heard the old saying about snakebites—that once you've received one you'll only talk about it with someone else who's received one, for no one else could understand the pain and how you reacted to it? Let me tell you, what happened to me next hurt more than if a snake has bitten me in my most sensitive organ: my heart! Or maybe my soul, or whatever you call it. Anyway, it was struck and bitten by philosophy. Philosophy, whose grip on the young is as relentless and vicious as a viper's, and makes them do the most remarkable things. Everyone here—you Phaedrus, you Agathon, Eryximachus, Pausanias, Aristodemus, and Aristophanes (I don't need to mention Socrates himself)—all of you have experienced the Bacchic madness of philosophy, and that's why you're entitled to hear the rest of my tale. I know all of you will understand and forgive me for what I did then, and admit now. As for you servants, and for anyone else who overhears me: shut your ears! This tale is not for you!

"So there we were. The lights were put out, the servants had gone. It was the perfect moment, I thought, to speak out and tell him openly what I had in mind. So I shook him, and whispered, 'Socrates, are you asleep?'

"'Not in the least,' he answered.
"'Do you know what I'm thinking?'
"'No, not really.'

"I said, 'You're the only deserving lover I've ever had, but you're so shy! Now here's what I think. I'd be a fool not to give you anything you wanted. You can have me. You can have all that I own. You can even have whatever my friends own! For nothing is so important to me as becoming the best man I can possibly be, and no one can help me achieve that better than you. Given who and what you are—why, I'd be more embarrassed by what some smart people would say if I *didn't* take you as my lover than I would be by what some idiots would say if I *did*.'

"Socrates listened carefully, then replied in that unmistakably ironic tone of his. 'My dear Alcibiades,' he said, 'if everything you say about me is true, then you've already achieved more than you realize. For if it's true that I really could make you a better man, then you must see in me a beauty that is beyond words, one that makes your own handsomeness pale in comparison. So, tell me. Is this really a fair trade you're proposing? You desire more of me than it seems you're entitled to; for you're offering me the mere appearance of beauty in return for the real thing, "like trading gold for bronze."[3] You should think again, my dear boy, for you may be wrong. I might be of no use to you whatsoever. The mind sees most sharply only after our eyes have grown weak with age—and you have a long way to go before you reach that age.'

"When I heard him say all of this, I replied, 'There's nothing more I can say. I've told you exactly what I think. Now it's up to you to say what you think is best, in our mutual interest.'

"'You're right,' Socrates said, 'From this moment on, let's always think as a team. That way we'll always do what is best for both of us.'

"And so, thinking that my words had hit their target and that Socrates was struck by my arrows, I didn't want to give him another chance to start talking, so I jumped to my feet and spread my blanket over him. (It was the middle of winter—but still that's all the clothing he wore!) Then I slipped under the covers and put my arms around this amazing one-of-a-kind man, and spent the night next to him. Socrates, you can't deny a word of this! Despite all my efforts, this fellow turned me down. The arrogant bastard! What a rude thing to do! He rejected my beauty, of which I am so proud! So now, gentlemen of the jury (for that's what you are in this case) you may pass judgment on Socrates' arrogant and outrageous behavior. I swear by all the gods and goddesses, my night with him was as uneventful as if I had spent it with my own father or older brother. And how do you think I felt the next morning? Humiliated, of course!

---
[3] *Iliad* 6.232–236.

But even so I couldn't help but admire his character, his self-control, his resolve. Here was a man whose strength and wisdom was beyond anything I had ever imagined. How could I possibly hate him? I couldn't bear the thought of losing his friendship, but saw no way to persuade him. I knew as well as anyone that he cares even less for money than Ajax cared about what weapons his foes carried, and now the only plan I had been able to hatch to get him had failed. I didn't know what to do and saw no purpose in living any longer. This was true slavery of a kind that no other men were aware.

"Now all of this happened before Athens invaded Potidaea, where we served together in our units and shared the same tents. At first Socrates put up with the hardships of the campaign better than me, and better in fact than any soldier in our army. When our supply lines had been cut, as often happens in war, no one dealt with the lack of food better than he did—even though he is the person who most enjoys a good feast. He accepted the lack of drink too, even though whenever he wants to he can drink anyone under the table. No one in our unit, in fact, ever saw him drunk! (I'll say a bit more about this in a minute.)
. . .

"Would you like to hear what he was like in battle? He really deserves having this story told. Now, you all know that I was decorated for bravery in that battle; but did you know that in that same battle Socrates saved my life? Yes, he did! I was wounded, and he refused to leave me behind, and he rescued me and all my armor! Socrates, you know for a fact that I told the generals right there on the spot that you were the one who deserved a medal. There's no fault in what I said then or in what I say now. The generals, though, cared more about my social standing and so they gave the medal to me, but you know that you were even more excited than they were, for me to get it.

"You ought to have seen him during our miserable retreat from Delium. I rode with the cavalry, while Socrates was with the infantry. The army was scattered everywhere. Socrates was retreating with our friend Laches. By luck I saw them and shouted some words of encouragement. 'I'll never leave you behind!' and that sort of thing. Since I was on horseback I wasn't in any real danger, so I seized the opportunity to watch Socrates—something I hadn't been able to do at Potidaea. The most obvious thing of all was how calm he was, especially compared to Laches. In fact, Aristophanes, some words of yours came to my mind; you see, he was simply meandering along just like he was taking a stroll through the city—even though he was on a battlefield: 'with a conceited gait and a wandering eye'.[4] There he was, observing everything, keeping his eyes out for friends and foes alike. Even at a distance I could see how brave he was and how he would put up a fight against anyone who came at him. That's what saved them both, in fact. For most people put as much distance as possible between themselves and someone like him, on a battlefield. If you want to survive, you chase the ones who run away.

. . .

"Here's something I should have mentioned earlier: Socrates' ideas and arguments, too, are just like those statues of Silenus. When you listen to him argue, everything he says strikes you as ridiculous because he uses words coarser than the hides worn by a satyr. He's always talking about pack mules or blacksmiths, cobblers or tanners; he's always pressing the same old points in the same old ways. If you are an idiot, or maybe just inexperienced, it's impossible to listen to him without laughing. But if we are then when those arguments open up like one of the statues—if you see what's behind their surface—you see right away that nothing else could possibly be true. These are ideas worthy of the gods, filled with little gems of virtue on the inside. They are of great—in fact, the greatest—value to anyone who wishes to become the best man he can be.

"So here ends my song to Socrates. I haven't avoided criticizing him too. I've told you how miserably he treated me. (And he's done the same thing to others: Charmides and Euthydemus, for starters!) He has deceived us all. First he approaches you with an interest, and before you know it you're the one who's in love with him! I'm warning you, Agathon, don't let him trick you! Remember the agony we all have experienced. Be careful. And don't be slow—like the fool in the proverb—to learn from your own mistakes."

Alcibiades' frank speech had made us all laugh like crazy, especially since it was so obvious how much he was still in love with Socrates. Socrates then replied, "Why, you're perfectly sober after all! You must be, or else you wouldn't have been able to conceal your true motive so well; but you let it slip, Alcibiades, at the very end of your speech. Your real motive all along has been to cause trouble between Agathon and me! You want me to love you and you alone—so that you and you alone can then be in love with Agathon. Well, we're not tricked; we see through your little satyr-play. Dear Agathon, let's not let him get away with it. Let no one ever come between us!"

Then Agathon said to Socrates, "You know, you're right! The proof of it is in the fact that he literally came between us here on our couch. Why would he have done that, if not to separate us? But he won't get away with it. I'm coming over to lie next to you right now."

"That's it," said Socrates, "come here and lie on this other side of me."

Alcibiades then shouted, "Dear God! You see how he makes me suffer? He kicks me when I'm down, and never relents. Come, Socrates, don't be so selfish. Let's share him. Have Agathon lie down between us."

"That can't be done," answered Socrates. "You've already delivered your 'song of praise,' so now it's my turn to praise whoever is on my right. But if Agathon were next to you, then he would give a 'song of praise' in my honor again—when in fact I want to now sing a praise to him. Come, come! Don't be so jealous! Let me sing the boy's praises."

"Oh, wonderful!" cried Agathon. "Nothing will make me stay next to you now, Alcibiades. I'm moving, and that's that. I simply have to hear what Socrates has to say about me!"

"There we go again, the same old story," said Alcibiades. "No one can get close to a really good-looking boy whenever Socrates is around! Did you notice how smoothly, how gracefully he got Agathon to lie down next to him?"

At that moment, as Agathon was changing places, a large party of drunks charged into the room and joined our party. The front gate had been left open when someone was leaving. There was noise everywhere, and everyone was drinking, but in no particular order. According to Aristodemus, a bunch of the original

---

[4] Aristophanes, *Clouds*, line 362.

guests made their excuses and left: Eryximachus, Phaedrus, and a few others. Aristodemus himself fell asleep and stayed that way for a long time. (It was winter, the nights were long.) He awoke just as dawn began to break. He could hear roosters crowing, and when he looked around he saw that many others had also fallen asleep, or had simply left.

Only Agathon, Aristophanes, and Socrates were still awake, and they were still drinking out of a large cup they shared, passing it from left to right. Socrates was talking. Aristodemus couldn't remember exactly what they were discussing—he was still half-asleep and had missed the first part of the conversation anyway—but he caught on that Socrates was trying to prove to them that authors should be able to handle tragedy and comedy equally; any tragedian worth his salt should also be a comic poet. Socrates was close to finishing his argument, but in plain fact the others could hardly follow a word he was saying. They were sleepy. Aristophanes in fact had fallen asleep in the middle of Socrates' talk; and it wasn't long before Agathon too drifted off, just as day was breaking.

Once they were asleep, Socrates got up and left, with Aristodemus close behind as usual. He says that Socrates walked straight to the Lyceum, washed, and spent the entire day going about his normal business. Only when the following evening fell did he finally go home to rest.

STUDY QUESTIONS

1. How does the dialogue underscore the importance of self-control, in terms of both drink and sex?
2. Is Socrates attracted to Alcibiades's way of life? Is Alcibiades attracted to Socrates's approach?

5.4. ARISTOTLE, "ON THE ELEMENTS OF TRAGEDY" (*POETICS*, BOOK VI), CA. 335 BCE

The student of Plato and mentor to Alexander the Great, Aristotle (384–322 BCE) reshaped Western philosophy by envisioning a unity among logic, physics, morality, politics, and other studies. This portion from his literary theory text *Poetics* exhibits Aristotle's classic method of deconstructing a concept into its logical, definable, building-block parts.

We will speak later of hexameter-poetry and comedy, so let us turn now to the subject of tragedy. First we must recollect all we have said earlier about it and fashion a formal definition. Tragedy is the representation of an action that is serious and of sufficient magnitude as to be complete in itself; its language consists of every type of literary technique—with each technique being displayed in a discrete part of the play; its form is dramatic, not narrative; and it culminates in an emotional catharsis that transcends pity and fear. Its language incorporates rhythm, harmony, and song—and when I say its techniques are displayed in discrete parts of the play, I mean that some parts are worked out through verse alone, and other parts through song alone.

Since "the representation of tragedy" implies persons acting on a stage, two things obviously follow: first, that elements of spectacle must be part of tragedy; and second, that song and diction must be part of it as well. By "diction" I mean simply the metrical

From Aristotle, *Poetics*, Chapters 6 and 7. Translation by Clifford Backman.

arrangement of the words. "Song," of course, is a term everyone understands.

Tragedy, to repeat, is the representation of action. But action implies agents who possess distinctive qualities of character and thought, for it is from these that we ascribe certain qualities to their actions. Character and thought are the natural causes from which all actions spring, and the success or failure of a tragedy depends on those very actions. The "plot" of a tragedy consists of the arrangement of incidents in the representation of its action. "Character," on the other hand, consists of whatever leads us to ascribe certain qualities to the play's various agents. An agent's "thought" is shown in whatever he says in proving a certain point or expressing a particular truth. Tragedy, therefore, has six distinct parts that determine its quality: plot, character, language, thought, spectacle, and song. Two of these make up the medium of the representation; one comprises the manner of representation; and the other three constitute the objects of the representation. These six elements complete the list. All six, we may confidently state, have been used by every one of our great poets. Every play, in fact, contained the elements of spectacle, character, plot, language, song, and thought.

The most important of the six elements is the arrangement of the incidents that make up the story, for tragedy is more a representation of actions and life than a representation of persons. Life consists of actions, and life's end consists of the nature of the actions we take rather than our qualities. Our character determines our qualities, but it is our actions that make our lives happy—or the opposite. In a tragedy, therefore, people do not act in order to portray characters; they portray the characters in order to present the action. The actions that make up the plot are the whole point of tragedy, and the whole point of anything is to be what it truly is. A tragedy cannot exist without action, but it may exist without character. The tragedies of most of our [contemporary] poets are character-less; the same can be said of poets in general. The same is true in painting—just compare [the works of] Zeuxis and Polygnotus. Polygnotus depicts character very well, but the paintings of Zeuxis are devoid of it. Again: if you string together a series of speeches that depict character, no matter how much skill there is in their style and diction the series will fail to produce the true tragic effect, whereas a play that is lacking in style and diction but has a plot made of well-constructed incidents will have much more success. And by far the most powerful elements of emotional engagement in any tragedy—namely the *peripeteia* [Reversal of Fortune] and the discovery-scene—are essential elements of the plot. A further proof is the fact that novice tragedians master diction and character before they learn to construct an artful plot. This is true of almost all the early dramatists.

We insist, therefore, that plot is the first principle of a tragedy—its heart and soul, one might say. The characters come second. It is the same thing as in painting: for even the most beautiful colors, if laid out without any order or design, will not give the same pleasure as a simple black-and-white sketch of a portrait. Tragedy is the representation of action; it portrays characters only for the sake of advancing the action. Third in order is thought—the power to say whatever can be said, or whatever is appropriate to say, in a situation. In a tragedy's speeches, this is the function of politics and rhetoric. Our older dramatists made their characters speak like statesmen, while our present ones make their characters speak like rhetoricians. Character, in tragedy, is the quality that reveals a person's moral purpose—how he decides upon the things he chooses or avoids. There is no room for character, therefore, in a speech that discusses a subject to which the person is indifferent. Thought, however, is shown in everything one says in arguing for or against something, or in presenting a universal maxim. Fourth among the literary elements of tragedy is diction, by which I mean (as I explained earlier) the expression of individuals' thoughts in words. This is equally true in verse and in prose. In regard to the two remaining elements: song takes precedence over spectacle. Spectacle has undeniable emotional power but it is the least artistic of all the elements, the least poetic. The power of tragedy, after all, can be felt even apart from performance and actors; and besides, the staging of spectacle is more a matter for the set-designer than for the poet.

Now that we have defined the constituent elements of tragedy, let us turn to the proper construction of the plot—the first and most important step. We established that tragedy is a representation of an action that is complete and whole, and of a certain magnitude; whole things exist, after all, that have no magnitude at all. An action that is whole and complete has a beginning, a middle, and an end. A beginning is something that does not necessarily follow from some earlier cause, but which does have something that comes of necessity after it. An end, on the other hand, is something that necessarily follows some earlier thing but has nothing necessarily following after it. A middle, of course, is something that follows some earlier and which leads to something that comes afterward. Any well-constructed tragedy must observe these principles and cannot either begin or end haphazardly. Any beautiful thing, whether it be a living creature or an object made up of various parts, must have an order in the arrangement of its parts, and its must have a certain magnitude. Beauty is a function of order and magnitude. A tiny animal organism cannot be beautiful [to us] since our perception of it cannot help but be limited to an almost imperceptible fraction of time. An immense creature— one that is, say, a thousand miles long—also cannot be beautiful [to us] since we cannot take it all in and therefore lose any sense of its unity and wholeness. In just the same way, then, as living organisms must have a certain degree of magnitude (namely, one that permits us to see its order and wholeness), so too must a plot in a tragedy be of a certain length, one that can be held in the memory. As far as the time-limit of a play goes, that is of no concern to dramatic theory; it is just an issue for the stagers of public performances and for the spectators. At one time it was the rule that plays were timed by a water-clock, but that was because they needed to fit one hundred tragedies [into a single festival]. As far as poetic theory is concerned: the longer the drama the more beautiful it will be, provided it does not violate the perspective of magnitude. As a rule of thumb, a play that allows the tragic hero to pass through a variety of probable or necessary stages, whether from bad fortune to good or from good fortune to bad, will suffice to meet the demand for magnitude.

STUDY QUESTIONS

1. How does Aristotle approach poetic theory? How does he analyze the genre of tragedy?
2. Why, for Aristotle, is plot the most important element of a play?
3. Does Aristotle provide a reasonable explanation of the effects of watching tragedy, in your estimation?
4. How is the audience invited to identify with the tragic hero? Can you think of tragic characters, whether from ancient or more modern plays, that support Aristotle's arguments?

5.5. DIOGENES LAËRTIUS, "LIFE OF ZENO OF CITIUM," *THE LIVES AND OPINIONS OF EMINENT PHILOSOPHERS*, CA. FIRST HALF OF 3RD CENTURY CE

A biographer of the Greek philosophers, Diogenes Laërtius (3rd century CE) has preserved personal information about philosophers whose entire body of work has been lost. Zeno of Citium (ca. 334–ca. 262 BCE), from whose writings only disconnected fragments remain, is known as the Father of Stoicism; most of what we know about his life comes from Laërtius's account. Although

From Diogenes Laertius, *Lives of the Stoics*, from bk. 7. Translation by Clifford Backman his facts are occasionally unreliable, Laërtius jumps energetically from Zeno's appearance to his temper to his writings, embedding excerpts from other writers in his own account. Consider how Laërtius displays Zeno's full expression of the Stoic convictions throughout his daily life—actually living the philosophy.

Zeno was a citizen of Citium on the island of Cyprus. It was a Greek city [at that time] but had been settled originally by the Phoenicians. . . . He studied with Crates, although some sources (like Timocrates in his work *Dion*) assert that he studied also with Stilpo and Xenocrates and also with Polemo. Hecaton says (and in this he is supported by Apollonius of Tyre, in Book One of his work *On Zeno*) that Zeno, when young, consulted an oracle to find out how he could live the best sort of life, and that the divine spirit said he should join his flesh with that of the dead. Grasping the meaning of this right away, Zeno went off to read the works of the ancient writers.

This is how he met Crates. Aboard a merchant vessel sailing from Phoenicia (it had a cargo of purple dye), he was shipwrecked near Piraeus. He travelled then to Athens and sat down next to a bookseller's stall. Zeno was about thirty, at that time. He saw that the bookseller was reading Book Two of Xenophon's *Memorabilia*, a work that Zeno knew and enjoyed. He asked the bookseller where he might find people like [Socrates], and as if by fate at that very moment Crates came walking by. The bookseller pointed and said,

"Follow him." From that very day Zeno studies with Crates. . . .

He use to lay out his arguments while strolling back and forth in the Stoa named after Peisanax but more commonly known as the Painted Stoa—on account of the painting made within it by Polygnotus.[5] Zeno always insisted that the space be cleared of bystanders, for during the rule of the Thirty Tyrants some 1,400 Athenians were massacred there. Nevertheless, people always came to hear him lecture there, and that is how they began to be called Stoics. . . .

Zeno always maintained that opinion was the enemy of knowledge, and that the one thing we need the most is more time. Someone once asked him to define what a friend is. His reply: "Another me." They also say that he once was beating a slave for stealing something, and when the slave cried out "But I was fated to steal!" Zeno answered "Then you were also fated to be beaten!"

---

[5] A stoa was a covered portico, usually surrounding a garden.

STUDY QUESTIONS

1. In what ways does Zeno always appear open to new ideas?
2. Is this form of teaching, from examples and the emulation of great men, an effective one?

CHAPTER 6

EMPIRE OF THE SEA: ROME

6.1. VIRGIL, *AENEID*, BETWEEN 29 AND 19 BCE

Publius Vergilius Maro (70–19 BCE) is the author of three major Latin poems, the most famous of which was his commissioned epic, *The Aeneid*, which recounts the tribulations of the pious hero Aeneas, who fled the Trojan War and wandered the known world until he settled in Italy, symbolic of the founding of Roman civilization. Because Aeneas is the son of the goddess Venus, Virgil also thus creates a divine genealogy for Aeneas's purported descendent: the Roman Emperor Augustus (63 BCE–14 CE). In this way, the enchanting poetry of the epic plays a political role as well. This opening scene begins in medias res and recounts the queen goddess Juno's destruction of the Trojan fleet, showcasing Aeneas's leadership qualities.

I sing of arms and a man—the man driven by fate,
    the man who
first came from the shoals of Troy to Italy, and to
    the Lavinian shore,
buffeted cruelly across land and sea by the will of
    the gods,
by fierce Juno's remorseless rage, and long
    enduring the wreck of war,
until he founded a city and brought his gods to
    Latium,
whence rose the Latin people, the lords of Alba
    Longa,
and the walls of noble Rome. Tell me, Muse, what
    caused it—
Juno's rage—how the queen of heaven was so
    galled
that she drove a man so renowned for virtue to
    endure

such dangers and face so many trials. Can such
    anger
exist in the minds of gods?
    There was an ancient city, Carthage, held by
      Tyrian settlers,
opposite Italy and the distant mouth of the Tiber,
    a city
rich in wealth and the savage arts of war. Juno,
    they say,
loved this one city above all others, more than
    even Samos.
Here she kept her weaponry and her chariot, and
    hoped and strove
that, Fate permitting, the city would gain
    supremacy
over all the world. But she had long ago heard
that descendants of Trojan blood would one day
    overthrow

From Virgil, *Aeneid,* Book 1. Translation by Clifford Backman.

her Tyrian stronghold, and that from them a
        nation would arise
that was wide-ruling and proud in war, and bring
        about
Libya's ruin. The Fates had decreed it. Fearing this,
        and
bearing in mind the long-ago war she had fought
        at Troy
for her dear Argos' sake—
        —and the seed of that anger and its bitter
        sorrow
still had not left the depths of her heart: the
        judgment of Paris,

the injury to her slighted beauty, the people she
        hated,
the honors given to abducted Ganymede—
Juno, the daughter of Saturn, driven farther into
        anger by this,
hurled into the sea those Trojans whom the
        Greeks and pitiless
Achilles had spared, keeping them far from
        Latium.
Driven by Fate from one sea to another, they
        wandered for years:
So hard a task it was, to found the Roman
        people.

STUDY QUESTIONS

1. Why and how are the opening lines of the *Iliad* (Document 4.2) invoked here?
2. How is Virgil grafting Roman history onto the story of the Trojan War and why?

6.2. EPICTETUS, *ENCHIRIDION*, I, V, XIV, RECORDED EARLY 2ND CENTURY

The Greek philosopher Epictetus (55–135 CE) expounded on how Stoic philosophy must be more than an intellectual pursuit—it must direct one's way of life. One must stop struggling against inevitable Fate and accept events with discipline and emotional aloofness. In the early 2nd century, his dictates were recorded by his disciple Arrian in the Enchiridion, or "Handbook." These selections illustrate Epictetus's commitment to the daily application of Stoic values, such as self-control and acceptance of death, to achieve worth and find peace.

Some things we can control, others we cannot. We can control things like our opinions, our interests, our goals, our worries—in a word, our own actions. What we cannot control consists of things like our bodies, our properties, our reputation, our social position—in a word, whatever is not our own doing. . . .

Strive to be able to say to any unfortunate occurrence, "You are just an image [of suffering], not the thing [Suffering] itself," and then think about it with the principles we have taught—and this one most of all: whether the [unfortunate occurrence] pertains to one of the things we can control or to one of the things

Translation by Clifford Backman.

we cannot control. If the latter, then you say that the whole matter means nothing to you. . . .

Worry only about those things that you can control. . . . If you worry about sickness, death, or poverty you will always be miserable. Stop worrying about what you cannot control, and worry about what you can control. Try to suppress your desires, for if you desire what is not in your control, you will live in constant disappointment. . . .

People do not fear specific things but the ideas and notion they associate with those thing. For example, death itself is not frightening, or else it would have appeared so to Socrates. The real terror of death is the frightful notions we have about it. So whenever we are scared, worried, or upset about something, let us not attribute it to the thing that scares, worries, or upsets us—but rather to our ideas about it. It is an ignorant person who blames his unhappiness on something outside of himself; a half-educated person will blame himself; but someone fully knowledgeable will blame neither any thing or himself. . . .

Do not ask for things to happen as you want them to; instead, desire that things happen as they in fact do—that's the way to live. . . .

You are a fool if you wish your wife, children, and friends to live forever, because that is wanting to control what you cannot control, or wanting to possess a power that belongs to another [i.e. God]. Similarly, you are a fool if you want your servant to be not so dishonest, for that is desiring his vice to be not vicious but good. But you can control your longing to have your desires fulfilled. Focus on what you are in fact able to do. . . .

You should live your life as though you are a guest at a dinner-party. Has someone passed a serving platter to you? Then reach out and take a modest portion. If the platter passes you by, don't reach out to stop it. Has the platter not yet come to you? Don't reach for it, but wait for it to come your way. This is how you should act in regard to your children, your wife, public honors, and wealth, and if you do, then you will have earned a place at the feast of the gods. . . .

Remember always that you are an actor in a drama, in the role chosen for you by the Author. Maybe a short role, and maybe a long one. In whatever role He has cast you—a pauper or a cripple, a statesman, or a common person—play it naturally. Your duty is to play the role, not to assign it. . . .

If you wish to be a philosopher, prepare to be laughed at. The crowd will sneer at you and cry out, "Oh, look who's a philosopher all of a sudden?" or "And where does that patronizing look come from, eh?" Be careful not to wear a patronizing look, and keep your mind focused on the matters that God (who made you for philosophy) intends. Remember: if you stay true to your calling, the people who laugh at you now will later admire you. But if you give in to their taunts, you will be doubly a failure. . . .

Keep silence, for the most part, and when you must speak use few words. To engage in a long conversation is certainly allowable, but only when the occasion is appropriate and the conversation has nothing to do with base topics like gladiators, horse races, sports heroes, or feasts. Neither should you care about specific people, whether to blame, praise, or compare them to others. Whenever you can, steer a conversation away from such topics and toward worthy ones. Among strangers, it is best to keep silent. Do not laugh too easily, too frequently, or excessively. Avoid swearing altogether, if you can; if you can't, do it as little as possible. Avoid vulgar public entertainments. . . . Provide for your body's needs, but do not indulge it in the delights of meat, drink, clothing, housing, or even family. Get rid of everything showy and refined. Before you marry, abstain as much as you can from [sexual] contact with women. If you must give in to lust, do it lawfully. But do not sit in judgment and disapproval of those who give themselves sexual liberties—and do not boast of your own abstinence.

When someone tells you that another person has been gossiping about a mistake you have made, do not make excuses for your behavior but simply reply, "He must not know all my other faults, or else he would not have mentioned only that one." . . .

When engaging anyone in conversation, but especially someone of superior station, ask yourself first how Socrates or Zeno would behave in your situation. Then you cannot fail to behave properly. . . .

Men make mistresses of girls as young as fourteen, and these, perceiving that they are valued only for the pleasure they give to men, begin to give themselves over solely to adornment. Instead, we should strive to help them understand that their real value resides in their decency, modesty, and good behavior. . . .

Whatever moral principles you devise for yourself, obey them as though they were divine commands and that you would be guilty of the worst impiety by violating any of them. Pay no attention to what others say of you, for that is no concern of yours. . . . You are no longer a boy, but a grown man . . . so think yourself worthy of living a mature life. Let whatever is the best thing you can do in any situation be your guiding principle. . . .

Finally, keep these three maxims always in mind:

Guide me, Oh Jupiter, and you, Oh Destiny,
to whichever place you have chosen for me.
[Cleanthes]
I follow gladly. If I were wicked and wretched
and did not wish to follow, I still would have to.
The man who accepts his fate is deemed wise
among men,
and knows the laws of heaven. [Euripides]
Crito, if my death pleases the gods, then let it come.
Anytus and Melitus can kill me, but they cannot
hurt me. [Plato]

STUDY QUESTIONS

1. How should the example of Socrates inform the behavior of a wise person?
2. What specific instances does Epictetus give concerning the virtues of moderation?

6.3. TACITUS, *HISTORIES*, BEFORE 117

Gaius Cornelius Tacitus (56–after 117) is perhaps the most renowned Latin historian. As an active statesman, including holding the posts of consul and later governor of Asia, Tacitus had access to the inner workings of imperial Rome under Nero and his successors—which provides the cogent factual and analytical basis of this text. In his other major work, *The Annals*, Tacitus provides one of the earliest references (15.44) to the historical Jesus. The introduction to *Histories* describes Tacitus's view of the state of affairs in his day; his selection on Jewish practices, although he misunderstands them, nonetheless provides some insight into how the Romans viewed this ancient monotheistic religion and culture.

I begin these *Histories* with the year [69 CE] when Servius Galba held the consulship for the second time and Titus Vinius was his partner. Many authors have written of the preceding 820 years, reckoning from the founding of our city, and in describing all the doings of the Roman people they wrote with equal parts of eloquence and liberality. After the battle at Actium, when the only way to preserve peace was for all power to be held by a single man, those great writers passed away. The truthfulness of history took a blow, too, first through men's acquired ignorance of public matters (since they no longer played a role in

Translation by Clifford Backman.

them), and second through the passion to flatter their new masters even though they hated them. Between the people's servile nature, on the one hand, and their hated, on the other, all regard for posterity disappeared. We instinctively recoil from any writer's use of an adulating tone, but we pay rapt attention when he makes snide and spiteful remarks, because a fawning tone implies a dishonorable servility but bitchiness comes across (though falsely) as bold honesty. . . .

I am beginning the history of an era filled with disasters, frightful wars, and bitter civil strife. Even the period's peaceful times had their horrors. Four emperors died by the sword; there were three civil wars and even more foreign ones, and some on the conflicts had both qualities at once. Successes in the east were matched with losses in the west. There was trouble in Illyricum. Gaul's loyalty was never certain. Britain was crushed, but then abandoned. The Suevi and Sarmatiae joined forces to repel us. The Dacians scored a renowned victory over us, then suffered a renowned defeat. And the Parthians were spurred to action by the deceits committed by that fraud, Nero. Italy herself was struck by disasters, some entirely unexpected and others the result of a long build-up. The cities of rich Campania were swallowed whole and buried. Rome itself was beset with riots that consumed some of its most venerable temples; citizens set fire even to the Capitol itself. People profaned our sacred rites; our greatest nobles gave themselves to corruption; the sea was clogged with refugees, its rocks bloodied by violence. Even worse horrors took place in the capital city. Nobility and wealth became causes for political accusations, as did either accepting or declining public office. If one maintained a life of virtue, one was done for. The rewards gained by rumor-mongers were more disgusting than their crimes, for while some snatched up consulships and priestly offices as booty, others grabbed procuratorships and positions of a more personal nature. But they all stole and pillaged in every direction, paying no heed to the hatred and terror they aroused in people. Slaves were bribed to betray their masters, and freedmen to inform on their patrons. Even those without any enemies were brought down—by their own friends.

Bad as it was, the age wasn't so utterly bereft of good qualities that it did not exhibit a few examples of virtuous action. Mothers followed their sons into exile, as wives did for their husbands. Some kinsmen were brave, and some sons-in-law were loyal. Some slaves remained true to their masters even when subjected to torture. Some men of virtue were driven to the ultimate sacrifice [i.e. suicide] and faced it with courage, and their last moments resembled the most fabled deaths of antiquity. Despite the reckless chaos of men's actions, there were divine prodigies to be seen in the skies and on the earth: cautioning rumbles of thunder, for instance, and other signs of things to come, both auspicious and gloomy, doubtful and certain. In sum, at no other time did so many terrible disasters strike the Roman people, nor was there clearer proof that the gods care nothing for our happiness—only for our punishment.

* * *

(5.1–9)

Since I am about to describe the last days of a great and renowned city, it is fitting that I first describe its origins. According to some authorities, the Jews began as exiles from the island of Crete who settled on the northern coast of Africa about the time when Jupiter overthrew Saturn from his throne. The evidence for this resides in their name, since the Idaei were the people who lived by the famous mountain on Crete called Mount Ida, and these Idaei became gradually known as the Judaei by the lengthening of their name in the vernacular. Others maintain the Jews originated in Egypt in the time of Isis, when excess population flowed into neighboring lands under the guidance of the figures Hierosolymus and Judas. Many others claim the Jews began as a race from Ethiopia who were driven out by the loathing of their neighbors to find a new homeland during the time of King Cepheus. A few insist they are Assyrians, a rabble who failed to find land to settle in Mesopotamia and so seized a part of Egypt, but not before establishing a number of cities in what is called Judaea, along the border with Syria. Lastly, some writers hold that the Jews sprang from quite a distinguished root, being none other than the Solymi people celebrated by Homer, who named their most famous city after themselves: Hierosolyma.

Almost all writers, however, agree that at some point in the past a terrible disfiguring disease struck Egypt, for which King Bocchoris turned to the oracle of Hammon to discover the cure. Hammon instructed the king to purify his realm by driving out of the land this detestable race of Jews. The Jews were diligently rounded up and sent into the desert, where they remained, miserable, idle, and forsaken, until one of them, Moyses by name, convinced them to expect no rescue from God or man. They should rely only on themselves, and take for their leader whoever might guide them out of their present misery. . . .

Wanting to secure his own position of authority, Moyses gave the Jews a unique form of worship, one that runs counter to everything practiced by all other nations. What is sacred to us is worthless to them, and they allow themselves what is forbidden to us. In their temple they have consecrated an image of the animal who guided them during their long, parched wandering. They slay rams, in derision of Hammon, and sacrifice oxen, to mock the Egyptian worship of Apis. They refuse to eat pork, which they associate in memory with leprosy. (Swine are vulnerable to the disease.) They commemorate the long hunger of their wanderings by performing regular fasts, eating only an unleavened bread in honor of what they had grabbed, in their haste, when entering exile. . . .

Among themselves the Jews are unfailingly honest and compassionate, but they regard all other nations as their hated enemies. They sit apart from other peoples at meals and will not sleep under the roof of a non-Jew. As a race they are almost uniquely prone to lust, yet they will not couple with foreign women. . . . They practice circumcision as a way to distinguish themselves from others; anyone who joins their religion must submit to the custom. They despise all the gods of other nations. . . . The Jews have only a mental image of their God as a single essence, and regard representations of God in human form, made out of perishable materials, as profanations. They believe only the essence of things to be supreme and eternal. . . . and do not allow any images to be put up in their cities—not even to flatter their own kings or to pay respect to our emperor. . . .

Their country is bounded by Arabia to the east, Egypt to the south, Phoenicia and the Mediterranean to the west. To the north it commands a sweeping view of Syria. As a people the Jews are healthy and do not tire easily. Rain is uncommon in Judaea but the soil there is fertile. . . . Judaea consists largely of scattered villages but it does have some cities. Jerusalem is the capital where once stood a temple of immense grandeur. . . . Only a Jew was allowed to approach its gates, and only their priests were permitted to cross the threshold. . . .

Pompey was the first Roman to subdue the Jews, and availing himself of the right of conquest he entered their temple. That is how it became known that it was empty, with no image of their God inside and their shrine possessing no secret knowledge. The walls of Jerusalem were subsequently destroyed, but the temple was left standing. . . . Under the emperor Tiberius everything remained quiet. When Caligula, however, ordered his own statue to be set up in the temple, the Jews opted for war.

STUDY QUESTIONS

1. What was the effect, in Tacitus's opinion, of one-man rule on the entire state's moral character?
2. How does Tacitus relate the exclusivity of Jewish culture to the resentment of Jews by others?

6.4. FROM SUETONIUS, *LIVES OF THE TWELVE CAESARS: CALIGULA; CLAUDIUS*, CA. 119 CE

A friend of Pliny the Younger, Suetonius (69–122 CE) also kept company with the Roman emperors Trajan and Hadrian, whose secretary he became. Although his *Lives of the Caesars* (from Julius Caesar to Domitian) has often been accused of being gossipy and melodramatic, Suetonius made use of the senatorial archives that he accessed as an imperial secretary to bolster his accounts with documentary evidence. Suetonius's lives of Caligula and Claudius display different reigns by these arguably brilliant leaders—the first driven by megalomania and the second by scholarly interests.

[Caligula]

So much for Caligula the emperor; now we speak of Caligula the monster. . . . Almost as though he wore a royal diadem, he turned the image of the Principate into that of an absolute monarchy. Since his lackeys told him he surpassed all other princes and kings, he started to claim divine power for himself, even to the point of sending to Greece for the most beautiful and sacred of all its statues of the gods (even those of Jupiter on Mount Olympus), and ordered their heads to be removed and replaced with likenesses of his own. . . . He put up a special shrine to himself as a god, complete with a staff of priests, the finest animals for sacrifices, and a life-sized statue of himself made of gold, which was dressed each day in clothes identical to whatever he was wearing that day. . . .

He ordered his own brother Tiberius Gemellus to be killed by a military tribune without warning, and he likewise forced his father-in-law Silanus to slash his own throat with a razor. . . . He spared his uncle Claudius simply so that he could make fun of him. . . . He made a habit of fornicating regularly with all three of his sisters, seating them just below him at banquets while his wife lay just above. It is widely reported that he took Drusilla's virginity when she was still a child; his grandmother Antonia, it is said, caught them in bed together. . . . When Drusilla died [38 CE] he proclaimed a period of public mourning; during this time he regarded it a capital crime if anyone laughed, bathed, or dined with their families. . . .

His gift for cruelty is shown by the following episodes. When the price of beef, for feeding the wild beasts that fought in his gladiatorial shows, was deemed too high, he ordered criminals to be fed to them instead. He looked out at a group of elderly convicts from a colonnade, and without bothering to read out the charges against them simply ordered them all to be led away, "one bald head after another." He condemned a number of men of high rank to be branded like cattle with a hot iron and sent to work in the mines or at road-building; others were caged like animals or thrown to the wild beasts. A few had their bodies sawn through.

[Claudius]

. . . Claudius became emperor at the age of fifty [41 CE] . . . . He was a modest, unpretentious man who refused to take the title of imperator. . . . He always sought the Senate's approval before recalling anyone from exile, and asked that the commander of the Praetorian Guard and military tribunes might accompany him to his house as a gracious favor of the Senate. He also made sure to seek the permission of the consuls before scheduling any fairs to be held on his private estates. . . . As a consequence, it took

Translation by Clifford Backman.

no time at all for his behavior to win him the respect and devotion of the people. So great was their affection for him that when a rumor spread that he had been attacked and killed on a visit to Ostia, the people were horrified. Crowds quickly surrounded soldiers and senators everywhere, calling them traitors and assassins, and did not relent until several magistrates brought forth a number of witnesses to swear that Claudius was in fact quite safe and making his way peaceably back to the capital.

STUDY QUESTIONS

1. How might Caligula's cruelty have resulted from his unrivalled control of Rome?
2. Was Claudius's seeming respect for the Senate merely a fraud?

6.5A. MARCUS AURELIUS, *MEDITATIONS*, CA. 170–180 CE

Written while Marcus Aurelius (121–180 CE) was on campaign in land that includes modern-day Hungary and Austria, these compiled cogitations (written in Greek) reveal the Roman emperor's Stoic beliefs. Intended as a type of personal guide or reflective exercise, the *Meditations* touch on mortality, morality, social cares, and self-control, among other themes. Consider the Roman emperor's elegant tone as well as his modest views of the transience of life, which contrast with his supreme political status.

Begin every morning by saying to yourself, "Today I will encounter meddling, ingratitude, arrogance, deceit, envy, and selfishness, and all of these things will be due to their offenders' ignorance of the difference between Good and Evil. But I myself have long recognized the nature and magnificence of the Good, and the nature and meanness of Evil; the nature, too, of the one who does wrong, for he is my brother (not in the physical sense of blood and seed, but as a fellow-creature endowed with intellect and a share of the divine). Therefore none of those things can harm me, for no one can implicate me with what is base. Neither can I be angry with my brother, nor hate him, for we were created to work together, like a man's two feet or hands, two eyelids, or two rows of teeth, upper and lower. To oppose each other, therefore, is against Nature. Anger and aversion are obstructions.

* * *

Bear in mind always that as a Roman and a man you should perform your duties well and with dignity and in a spirit of kindness, liberality, and justice. In so doing you free yourself of the burden of all cares; and you will be successful in this so long as you approach every deed as if it were the last action of your life, setting aside inattentiveness and the desire to avoid the dictates of reason, hypocrisy, self-regard, and complaint about what life has doled out to you. You can see how little a man needs in order to lead a

From Marcus Aurelius, *Meditations* 6.1. Translation by Clifford Backman.

quiet life—which is a divine life. The gods themselves will require nothing more from a man who lives this way.

* * *

Even if he were to live for three thousand years or as many as ten thousand, every man has but one life to live and to lose—this one, and no other. Remember this, for all lives, the longest and the shortest, come to the same end. The present moment is the same to everyone, although that which perishes [at any moment] is not the same; that is why that which is lost appears to be only a mere moment. A man, after all, cannot lose either the past or the future, for how can anyone take from him what he does not possess? So remember these two things: first, that all eternal things are similar and come round in a circle, and it makes no difference at all whether one sees the same things for a hundred years or two hundred or for however so great a time; second, the man who lives the longest and the one who lives the briefest life both lose the same thing. The present moment is the only thing that one can lose, for it is all that one possesses—and you can only lose what you possess.

* * *

A man's soul does violence to itself when it turns into a canker or tumor upon the universe, to the extent that that is possible. To be irritated at anything that happens is to cut oneself off from Nature, since Nature consists of the natures of all things combined. The soul also does violence to itself when it turns away from any person or advances upon any with the intent to harm—such are the souls of the wrathful.

The soul does a third kind of violence to itself when it surrenders itself to pleasure or pain, a fourth kind when it dissembles and does or says something insincerely or falsely. And a fifth kind of violence when it allows itself any act or movement that is without purpose or does anything thoughtlessly and without a care to its correctness. For it is right that even the smallest actions be done for a reason. The whole point of being a rational creature, after all, is to follow the dictates of reason and the law of the most ancient city and state.

The span of a human life is a mere point, its substance is in constant flux, its perception ever dim, the makeup of the body given to decay, its soul is a whirl, its destiny hard to determine, and its fame a matter without any meaning. In a word, everything that makes up a human body is a moving stream, what makes up the soul is a dream and vapor; life is a battle, a journey by a stranger, and what comes afterward is oblivion. What, then, is the one sure guide for a man in life? Philosophy. But Philosophy requires that a man keep his spirit free from violence and harm, above all pains and pleasures; that he does nothing without a purpose nor anything falsely and hypocritically; that he act without feeling that a duty should be left to another man's care; and that he accept everything that happens, everything that is fated—for everything comes from the place from which he himself comes. Finally, he accepts death with a calm mind, since death is nothing more than the dissolving of the particles of which every living being is made. If no harm comes to the elements themselves as they continually rearrange themselves in new being, why should a man fear the change the dissolving represents? For it is part of Nature, and nothing in Nature is evil.

STUDY QUESTIONS

1. How is Marcus Aurelius emulating the advice of Epictetus (Document 6.2), and would this have been more difficult for an emperor to follow?
2. Why would accepting the transience of life lead to calmness in the face of death?

6.5B. THE THIRD-CENTURY IMPERIAL-SUCCESSION CRISIS

The massive and chaotic mess of Rome's civil war is made clear by this simple list of the individuals who held, however briefly, the imperial title in the 3rd century. Almost all were generals. As you can see, only five died of natural causes.

Emperor	Reign	Manner of death
Commodus	180–192	Murdered
Pertinax	193	Murdered
Didius Julianus	193	Murdered
Pescennius Niger	193–194	Killed in battle
Clodius Albinus	193–197	Killed in battle
Septimus Severus	193–211	Natural death (!)
Caracalla	211–217	Murdered
Geta	211	Murdered
Macrinus	217–218	Murdered
Diadumenianus	218	Murdered
Elagabalus	218–222	Murdered
Seleucus	218–222	Probably murdered
Uranius	218–222	Probably murdered
Gellius Maximus	218–222	Murdered
Verus	218–222	Murdered
Severus Alexander	222–235	Murdered
Sallustius	225–227	Murdered
Taurinus	225–227	Suicide
Maximinus Thrax	235–238	Murdered
Magnus	235–238	Killed in battle
Quartinus	235–238	Killed in battle
Gordian I	238	Suicide
Gordian II	238	Killed in battle
Pupienus	238	Murdered
Balbinus	238	Murdered
Gordian III	238–244	Killed in battle
Sabinianus	240	Killed in battle
Philippus Arabus	244–249	Killed in battle
Pacatianus	248	Murdered
Iotapianus	248	Murdered
Silbannacus	249	Killed in battle
Sponsianus	249	Killed in battle
Philippus Iunior	249	Murdered
Decius	249–251	Killed in battle
Priscus	250	Murdered

Emperor	Reign	Manner of death
Licinianus	250	Murdered
Henerrius	251	Killed in battle
Hostilian	251	Plague
Trebonianus Gallus	251–253	Murdered
Volusianus	251–253	Murdered
Aemilianus	253	Murdered
Valerian	253–260	Murdered
Mareades	259	Murdered
Gallienus	253–268	Murdered
Ingenuus	260	Suicide
Regalianus	260	Murdered
Macrianus I	260–261	Natural death (!)
Macrianus II	260–261	Murdered
Quietus	260–261	Murdered
Postumus	260–269	Murdered
Piso	261	Murdered
Valens	261	Murdered
Ballista	261	Murdered
Mussius Aemilianus	261	Murdered
Memor	261	Murdered
Aureolus	262	Murdered
Celsus	267	Murdered
Saturninus	267	Murdered
Claudius II	268–270	Plague
Censorinus	268–270	Murdered
Laelianus	269	Murdered
Marius	269	Murdered
Victorinus	269–270	Murdered
Quintilius	270	Suicide
Aurelian	270–275	Murdered
Domitianus	271–272	Murdered
Urbanus	271–272	Murdered
Septimius	271–272	Murdered
Tetricus I	271–274	Natural death (!)
Tetricus II	273–274	Natural death (!)
Firmus	273	Killed in battle
Felicissimus	271	Killed in battle
Faustinus	274	Probably murdered
Tacitus	275–276	Murdered
Florianus	276	Murdered
Probus	276–282	Murdered
Bonosus	280	Suicide
Proculus	280–281	Murdered
Saturninus	281	Murdered
Carus	282–283	Struck by lightning
Numerian	283–284	Murdered
Carinus	283–285	Murdered
Diocletian	288–305	Natural death (!)

CHAPTER 7

THE RISE OF CHRISTIANITY IN A ROMAN WORLD

7.1. JOSEPHUS, *THE JEWISH WAR*, CA. 75 CE

Titus Flavius Josephus (37–ca. 100) was a Roman citizen and Jewish historian. His contemporary work (written in Greek) chronicles the Jewish War (66–70 CE)—a bitter revolt against the Roman occupation of Judea, which resulted in the destruction of the Second Temple in 70 CE. This selection details the Roman invasion of Jerusalem and its gruesome aftermath. In writing about the Jewish religion in the 1st century, Josephus also provides a window into burgeoning Christianity—including references to the historical Jesus and John the Baptist.

CHAPTER 1

The suffering in Jerusalem grew worse every day, and the leaders of the rebellion, who were themselves already in agony, were made even more miserable by the effects of the famine on the general populace. The number of corpses that lay in piles everywhere was indeed a horrible sight, and produced such a noxious stench that it hindered the movement of those who attempted to march forth from the city to fight the Romans. Even so, once the soldiers were suited up and in formation they marched without fear even though they sometimes had to step on the bodies. They did not consider this an offense to the dead or any sort of ill-omen for themselves, for they already bore the guilty stain of killing ten thousand of their own people, and as they moved against the Romans they acted as though they reproached God Himself—

for being too slow in punishing them. They continued fighting, but without any hope of victory. . . .

When the Romans finished building their ramparts, the battlements struck fear in the Romans and the Jews alike. The Jews saw that their city would certainly fall if they could not destroy the ramparts by fire, and the Romans feared that they would not be able to replace them, if the Jews managed to burn them down, since the surrounding area was then so deforested and their men so exhausted by labor. . . . What discouraged the Romans the most was the fact that the Jews' courage was stronger than the sufferings they had had to endure. . . .

CHAPTERS 3–4

The rebels in the temple struggled every day to drive the Roman soldiers from their battlements. One

Translation by Clifford Backman.

day—it was the twenty-seventh day of Tamuz—they devised a plan. They stuffed the entire western portico with dry materials, bitumen, and pitch, all the way to the beams that supported the roof, and then made a show of sloughing off in a state of exhaustion. This inspired the most rash of the Romans to get excited and attempt to pursue them. They set the ladders against the portico and climbed atop it. That was when the more prudent Romans understood what was happening and stopped their climb. But by this time the roof was full of soldiers—and the Jews immediately set the whole trap on fire. Flames flew everywhere in an instant. The Romans who had halted their climb were anguished by the fate of their fellows, who cried out in distress. Seeing themselves surrounded by flames, they threw themselves headlong from the roof, some into the city streets and some into the temple courtyard itself, right in the midst of their enemies. . . . Among the Romans was a young man named Longus, who deserves to be remembered—so let him serve as a monument to all those who were slain. The Jews admired this Longus very much on account of his courage, and very much wanted him dead. They promised him no harm, if he would surrender himself to them. His brother Cornelius, however, told him not to hand himself over, since to do so would tarnish his honor and that of the whole Roman army. And so Longus lifted his sword and killed himself. . . .

The number of Jews who died of famine in the city was prodigious, their sufferings unspeakable. If so little as a morsel of any kind of food was found, violence broke out and even best friends would take arms against each other in order to get it. . . . People ran about in a daze, stumbling and staggering like mad dogs, reeling against doors like drunkards. . . . Their hunger was so great that they put anything at all into their mouths, even things that the vilest animals would not touch: belts and sandals, the leather that they stripped from their shields, husks of straw. . . . But why should I go on listing the shameful level that famine drove people to? Especially when I have a story to tell unlike any story in any book of history. . . .

There was a woman named Mary, the daughter of Eleazar, who came from the village of Bethezob

(which means "house of hyssop" in Hebrew) beyond the Jordan River. Of good family and wealth, she had fled to Jerusalem like everyone else and was there when the Roman siege began. Everything she possessed that she had brought with her had been snatched away, including whatever food she had managed to save, by the rapacious guardsmen who burst into her house every day in search of something to eat. This drove her half-crazed and prompted her to hurl abuse and threats at the rebels, who, though they grew very angry at her, refrained from ending her misery by killing her. . . . When the famine grew so bad that it pierced her very bowels, she was driven to a point of madness. . . . and snatching up her infant son, she said to him, "Poor child! How can I save you from this war, this famine, these rebels? As for the Romans, if we survive the war they will make us slaves. The famine will kill us, though, before our enslavement begins. And these rebels are a worse scourge than the other two. So come, dear child. Be my food, be a curse upon the rebels, and a warning to the whole world. Your death completes the sufferings of the Jews." Having said these words, she killed her son and roasted him. After she had eaten half of his body, she took the other half and put it away, and at this very moment the rebels returned to her home. Despite the horrible scent they warned her that they would cut her throat on the spot if she did not hand over whatever she had been cooking. Mary then replied that she had a nice portion for each of them and took the covering off what was left of her son. The men were filled with horror and revulsion as they looked at the sight. "Come and eat!" she said. "This is my son. I did this myself. Eat, here's food for you; I've already had some. No? Don't pretend that you're more delicate than a woman, or that you have more compassion for him than I do. But if you're going to be so fussy, and reject my sacrificial offering, leave the second half for me too." Hearing this, the men withdrew with a shudder. Nothing had ever shaken them so, yet they found it difficult to leave the boy's remains with the mother. Soon the whole city had learned of this dreadful occurrence and everyone shuddered to picture the scene to themselves. Fearing that they too could be driven to such an extreme, many prayed for death and regarded those who had already perished as fortunate not to have survived to hear of such wretchedness. . . .

When two of the legions had finished building their ramparts, on the eighth day of the month of Ab, Titus ordered his battering rams to be brought forward and set against the western wall of the inner temple. Prior to this, a variety of smaller siege engines had blasted the wall non-stop for six days without making a crack in it. . . . But by this time some soldiers had already set fire to the gates, the silver-plating on which failed to stop the flames from reaching the wood underneath. The fire spread quickly then, and in no time reached the cloisters. When the Jews saw the flames engulfing more and more of the temple their spirits broke and they collapsed to the ground so horror-struck that hardly any of them ran to quench the fire or to flee; instead they watched in stunned silence. . . .

Titus sought his commanders' opinions about what should be done about the temple. Some of them advocated following the rules of warfare and demolishing it, since the Jews would never cease their rebellions against Rome so long as the temple stood. Others recommended that Titus save the building for the Jews on condition that they abandon it, remove all their weaponry from it, and surrender—but if the Jews refused, they urged, then Titus should let the flames consume it, since in that case the building could be regarded as more of a military base than a sacred dwelling. In such a case, they urged, the impiety of burning a sacred site would belong not with the Romans but with the rebels whose actions had led to this result. . . . [In the end] Titus ordered a company of volunteers to make their way through the ruins and put out the fire. . . . But when Titus retired for the night several Jews who had been laying in wait leapt out at the Romans once more, attacking those who were attempting to quench the fire in the inner temple. The Romans drove off their attackers and proceeded all the way to the innermost sanctum of the temple, whereupon one of the soldiers, unbidden and unconcerned for the consequences of his rash act, snatched a burning timber and set fire to a gilt-edged window, through which ran a passageway that extended to all the rooms on the north side of the temple. The flames quickly spread even further, and

the Jews let out a great cry . . . for it was then certain that their entire holy house would perish.

CHAPTERS 8–10

Then one of the temple priests—Jesus, the son of Thebuthus—came forward, having received Caesar's grant of safe-passage, bringing various treasures that had been deposited in the temple. He handed over to Caesar a treasure of candlesticks, tables, cisterns and vials, all made of solid gold and very heavy. He surrendered a number of veils and garments too, each studded with precious stones, and a great number of other precious vessels that they had used in their worship. Phineas, the temple's treasurer, also brought forth a wealth of purple and scarlet cloaks and priestly vestments, such as were worn in the Holy of Holies, along with vast quantities of cinnamon, cassia, and other sweet spices which they regularly used to mix together and offer as incense to God. . . .

Caesar, seeing so great a multitude of Jews in the city, but aware that his own men were exhausted from killing, ordered that no more Jews should be killed except those who had taken arms against Rome; all the rest were to be taken alive. . . . The number of captives was ninety-seven thousand, and the number of the dead was one million and one hundred thousand—the majority of whom were Jews who did not live in Jerusalem itself but had come up to the city for the feast of unleavened bread. . . . The number of those who perished exceeded those ever destroyed before by man or God, anywhere in the world. To consider only the publicly-known accounts, the Romans killed some, carried over others as captives, and even searched underground for more. Finding many of these latter ones, the Romans broke open the ground and killed everyone they found. They also found some two thousand Jews who had already killed themselves underground, and some who had died of famine. The stench of these corpses was so great that most of the Romans had to withdraw. Some others, though, were greedy, climbed over and picked through the heaps of dead bodies. The Jews had hidden much treasure in these caverns, enough to make many Romans think any way of acquiring it was unlawful. . . .

Thus was Jerusalem taken, in the second year of the reign of Vespasian, on the eighth day of the month of Elul. . . . From the time of King David, the first Jew to rule from there, to that of Titus' destruction of the temple were one thousand, one hundred, and seventy-nine years. But from the building of the city to its end were two thousand, one hundred, and seventy-seven years. Neither its antiquity, nor its riches, neither the spread of its people over all the earth, nor the extraordinary veneration given to it as a holy site, could save it from destruction. Thus ended the siege of Jerusalem.

STUDY QUESTIONS

1. What were, according to Josephus, the Romans' reasons for burning down the Temple?
2. How did the Romans display humane qualities in the midst of the siege and sack of Jerusalem? Could these descriptions have resulted from Josephus's overall motives in writing?

7.2. PLINY THE YOUNGER, LETTERS, 97–112 CE

The nephew of the naturalist Pliny the Elder, Gaius Plinius Caecilius Secundus, called Pliny the Younger (61–112), passed through the cursus honorum under the emperors Domitian and Trajan. A friend of Tacitus (author of Document 6.3) and employer of Suetonius (author of Document 6.4), Pliny the Younger also wove his personal experiences of imperial Rome into his works. In his "Letter to Tacitus," Pliny poignantly describes his uncle's death in the eruption of Mount Vesuvius (79); in his "Letter to Trajan," he recounts his understanding of early Christianity in the Roman Empire.

To Tacitus

You asked me to send you an account of my uncle's death, so that you may describe it accurately in your writings. I am honored by your request—for if this disaster is recorded by you, I am sure that it will live forever in memory. . . .

On the 24th of August, in early afternoon, my mother asked my uncle to take a look at a cloud of unusual size and shape. . . . He rose from his books and mounted a small hill nearby, from which he could get a better view of the uncommon sight. It was not clear at first which mountain the cloud was surrounding, but we later learned, of course, that it was Mount Vesuvius. The cloud, as it rose up from the mountain, was shaped rather like a pine tree and shot up to a tremendous height. . . . It appeared bright in some places, and dark and mottled in others, because of the dirt and ashes cast up in it. . . . My uncle ordered his small boat to be readied, and climbed on board. . . . He steered his course directly at the danger, the better to see what was happening and to dictate his observations of the whole dreadful scene [to his secretary] . . . . He got so close to the mountain that cinders, pumice-stones, and blackened bits of burning rock were falling into his boat, getting thicker and hotter the closer he drew. . . . Wide tongues of flame burst from the sides of Vesuvius, showing bright and clear. . . .

Translation by Clifford Backman.

[After landing and advancing to the villages and towns under the mountain] he witnessed houses rocking from side to side as though shaken from their foundations by repeated blows. In the open fields burning rocks and cinders fell in profusion. . . . forcing them to tie pillows to their heads with table napkins as their only defense against the storm of stones. . . . They thought it best to return to the shore and see if they could embark, but the waves were extremely high and roiling. My uncle lay down on a sailcloth that his servants had spread out for him, and called twice for some water to drink. He drank, but as he did so a wall of sulphurous flames came so close that they had to rise and leave. Helped by two servants, my uncle stood—and instantly fell over, dead. I suppose he suffocated on the noxious fumes.

To Trajan

I always turn to you, my lord, when in doubt—for there is no one I trust better to guide me when I am uncertain and to teach me when I am ignorant of any matter. I have never had anything to do with a trial of Christians, and don't know what charges are made against them, or how they are investigated, and what degree of bother to go through in the effort. I am more than a little uncertain about whether to treat them all the same or to make concessions to the young and the aged among them. Are they to be pardoned if they express contrition? If a man used to be a Christian but has since ceased to be one, is he to be free of punishment? If one is a Christian but has otherwise committed no offense, should he be charged [with a crime]? Or do we prosecute only those Christians who commit additional offenses?

In dealing with the Christians who have been brought before me, I have done as follows. First I questioned them as to whether or not they were Christians. Those who acknowledged it I then questioned a second and third time, threatening them with punishment. Those who persisted in their ways, I had executed. Whatever the nature of their beliefs, I decided, they deserved punishment simply for being so stubborn and obstinate. There were some among them who were Roman citizens, and I signed orders for them to be transferred to Rome.

Accusations against others then spread, as so often happens, and several things followed. An anonymous

affidavit was published that listed the names of many people who were believed to be Christians. Those who denied that they were or had ever been Christians I put to the test; I had them invoke the Roman gods, offer prayer and incense and wine to your image (which I had ordered to be brought together for this specific purpose—along with statues of the gods), and curse Christ. It is said that no true Christian can be forced to do any one of these things—and so those who passed the test I ordered to be released. Others named by the anonymous tipster swore oaths that they were Christians—but then they denied it, saying that they used to be Christians but had long since ceased to be, anywhere from three to twenty-five years ago. These too all worshiped your image, sacrificed to the statues of the gods, and cursed Christ.

They testified, though, that the extent of their former error had been limited to meeting with other Christians on a fixed day, before dawn, and singing responsively a hymn to Christ as their god, and that they swore simply not to commit fraud, theft, or adultery, not to bear false witness, and not to refuse to return anything that had been entrusted to them. Having done this, they said, they usually separated but reassembled later [and somewhere else] in order to share a meal. A simple, regular meal, I should add. But they insisted that they had ceased even this limited participation after, in accordance with your instruction, I had released an edict forbidding political associations. Naturally, I thought it prudent to find out if this was really true by torturing two slave-women whom the Christians call "deaconesses." All that I learned from this, though, was disgusting and gross superstition.

That is when I stopped my investigation and hurried to consult you. The matter strikes me as warranting this appeal because of the number of people involved. There are many lives at stake—of every age and rank, and both sexes. This superstition is spreading like a contagion and is now to be found not only in the cities but also in villages and on farms; nevertheless, it is possible to stop it and cure it. It is abundantly clear that our temples, which for a time had been almost deserted, have once again begun to be frequented; that the established rites, so long neglected, are being resumed; and that sacrificial animals are coming in from everywhere—animals for which not too long ago hardly a single purchaser could be found.

This is why I think it easy to imagine multitudes of people returning [to Roman ways] if an opportunity for amnesty is offered.

[Trajan responded to Pliny with a brief letter of his own.]

You did well, Pliny, in sifting through the cases of the people charged with being Christians. It is not possible to lay down a single rule to serve as a fixed guide. Christians should not be sought out, but if any are accused and brought before you, and if you find them guilty, they should be punished. There is one exception to this rule. Anyone who denies being a Christian and proves it by worshipping our gods should be granted amnesty even if he was under suspicion in the past. Anonymous public accusations should have no place in our justice—for it would establish a dangerous precedent to accept such accusations, and it would be against the spirit of our age.

STUDY QUESTIONS

1. How did Pliny the Elder's scientific curiosity lead to his death in 79 CE?
2. Were Pliny's goals and methods in dealing with the Christians brought before him reasonable? Were the Christians merely stubborn?

7.3. CELSUS/ORIGEN, *CONTRA CELSUS*,[1] BOOK I, CHAPTERS 6, 28; BOOK III, CHAPTER 62; BOOK IV, CHAPTER 73; BOOK VIII, CHAPTERS 41, 49, 55; CA. 177 CE

The Greek philosopher Celsus (2nd century) wrote a treatise against early Christians entitled *On the True Doctrine*. Although this work has not survived on its own, it was incorporated into the treatise *Against Celsus* by Origen (ca. 184–ca. 253), a theologian and Church Father who responded to Celsus's accusations, claim by claim. In this way, scholars could recreate Celsus's original text. The portions included here reveal Celsus's accusations of doctrine (such as the virgin birth), historical points (Jesus's affiliation with the lowest classes), and the relationship between Christians and their God.

It is by invoking the names of demons and reciting incantations that the Christians seem to possess [miraculous] power. That was how [Jesus] accomplished his marvels—by sorcery—and since he understood that others would eventually learn the same skills and do the same things as he, and that they would boast of doing them "by the power of the Lord," he therefore denied them admittance to his kingdom.

But if he excludes sorcerers for doing the same things he had done, then he is wicked. And if he is not wicked for what he did, then neither are those who do the same. [1.6]

Translation by Clifford Backman.

[1] Halsall: http://www.bluffton.edu/~humanities/1/celsus.htm/ or http://web.archive.org/web/20060201230403/http://duke.usask.ca/~niallm/252/Celstop.htm/. Celsus's words appear in regular type; Origen's interpolations are in italics.

Celsus describes the case of the Jew who disputed with Jesus and defeated Him (or so he thought) on a variety of points. In the first place, he accuses Christ of having invented the story of His virgin birth, *and reproaches Him for having been* born in a Jewish village to a poor rustic who made her living by spinning and was denounced by her carpenter-husband because of her adultery. Rejected by her husband, she wandered aimlessly for a while until, in her shame, she gave birth to the bastard Jesus. This Jesus, being poor, eventually found work as a servant in Egypt—where he learned some of the magical powers that the Egyptians pride themselves on knowing. It was then that he returned to his homeland, full of himself because of his new knowledge, and by means of these powers proclaimed himself a God. [1.28]

I charge the Christians with nothing more than the truth, as you can see by the following. In other cults, anyone who wishes to invite [an outsider] to participate in its mysteries always says, "Anyone with clean hands and a pure tongue, [enter]," or "Whoever is without pollution, whose spirit knows no evil, and who has lived a just and upright life, [enter]." These are the invitations used by those who promise to purify people of sin. But who do these Christians invite? Every sinner! Everyone devoid of understanding! Whoever is a child! In a word, any miserable person at all! That's who they say will be received in the kingdom of God. But is a thief not a sinner? A cad? A burglar? A poisoner? One guilty of sacrilege? A grave-robber? Who wouldn't a man invite [into a cult], if he would invite such criminals as these? [3.59]

The Christians say that it was specifically to sinners that God was sent. But why was he not sent to those who were without sin? What is wrong with not being sinful? It seems that God will welcome the unrighteous man who repents his wickedness but not the righteous man who approaches God with virtue from the very beginning! [3.62]

Isn't it ridiculous to think that the same God who, in his righteous fury, threatened the Jews, then killed them all (including their infants), and destroyed their city by fire, would send his own son among them, to endure the sufferings this Jesus endured? [4.73]

You may mock and scorn the statues of our divinities—but if you were to insult Bacchus or Hercules face-to-face you would feel the consequence of it. But those who crucified your God when He was living among you suffered nothing, neither then nor later. And what has happened since his death to make anyone believe that he wasn't a fake, this "Son of God"? So: the God who sent his own son to earth with teachings meant for all mankind let his son be treated abominably, and let his teachings vanish—and all without showing a single sign of concern? What father was ever so cruel? Now, you can say that he suffered so much because he wanted to, that it was his desire to endure all that came at him. But then you have to allow that the same could be true of those [pagan] gods you revile and reject—that they too want to be reviled, and that they are therefore now bearing it all patiently. You have to play fair on both sides. But [watch out]: our gods always punish those who scorn them. Get ready to run and hide, or be caught and perish! [8.41]

Do you not see the absurd contradiction in making so much of the human body as you do—to look expectantly for it to rise from the dead—as if it were the single most precious part of us, and yet, on the other hand, to treat it with such scorn that you willingly expose it to torture? Any person who values the body yet can think such things, is someone who doesn't deserve to be reasoned with. Instead, he exposes himself as a gross being, polluted, and determined to reject common sense for no reason at all. I wish to converse with people who hope to enjoy eternal life with God by means of their spirit or mind—whether they want to call it a "spiritual substance," or a "spirit of holy and blessed intelligence," or a "living soul," or a "heavenly and eternal offspring of a divine spiritual nature," or any other name they wish. For these are the people who are right—the ones who understand that those who live upright lives shall be blessed, and those who are unjust shall receive eternal torment—and who never waver from this truth. [8.49]

[The Christians] have to make a choice. If they want to refuse to render due service to the [pagan] gods and respect to those men who preside over their cults, then let them not grow to manhood, take wives, or have children; let them take no part in the business of life; and let them leave this world with all possible speed and leave no one behind them, so that their whole hateful race may disappear from the face of the earth. On the other hand, though, if they wish to marry and raise children, to taste the fruits of the earth and to partake of all of life's blessings and its appointed sorrows (for Nature has decreed a portion of sorrows to all men, since sorrows must exist—and earth is the only place for them), then they must accept the duties of life until they are released from its bonds, and they must pay the honor due to those gods who control the affairs of this life—unless, that is, they want to appear ungrateful. But it would be gross injustice, if they wish to receive the blessings that the gods bestow, but pay them nothing in return. [8.55]

STUDY QUESTIONS

1. Could Celsus's criticisms be used to recreate Christian beliefs, even central ones, in the period he was writing (late 2nd century)?
2. In what ways are the charges of injustice and immorality applied to Christians, and were such charges deserved?

7.4A. THE NICENE CREED, TWO VERSIONS

This creed was recorded at the Council of Nicaea (325 CE) to clarify early Christian beliefs as they were confronted with Arian heresy. The heretic Arius (ca. 250–336) held that although Jesus was the divine Son of God, he was also created, meaning that he was not eternal alongside God the Father. This posed problems for the orthodox Christian belief in a Trinity that was made of three distinct persons (Father, Son, and Holy Spirit) who were also one being—thus threatening the Son's eternal nature also threatened this unity. These versions of the Nicene Creed reveal how doctrine changed over time to accommodate and clarify changing Christian realities.

THE FIRST VERSION OF THE NICENE CREED

We believe in one God, the Father Almighty,
    Maker of all things seen and unseen.

We believe in one Lord, Jesus Christ, the Son of
    God,

The only-begotten of the Father, God
    of God, Light of Light,
true God of true God, begotten—not
    made—
one in substance with the Father.
Through Him all things were made,
    both those in heaven and those
    on earth.

Translation by Clifford Backman.

For us men and for our salvation He
came down from Heaven, was
incarnate, and was made man.
He suffered [death] and rose again on
the third day. He ascended
into Heaven and He shall
come again to judge the quick
and the dead.
We believe in the Holy Spirit.

And anyone who says that there was a time when
the Son of God was not, or that before
He was begotten He was not, or that He
was made of things that were not, or
that He is of different substance or
essence [from the Father], or that He is
created, subject to change, or to
conversion—the Catholic and
Apostolic Church anathematizes him.

THE FINAL VERSION OF THE NICENE CREED

We believe in one God, the Father Almighty,
maker of heaven and earth, and of all
that is, seen and unseen.

We believe in one Lord, Jesus Christ, the only
Son of God.
eternally begotten of the Father, God
from God, Light from Light,
true God from true God, begotten—not
made—

one in Being with the Father.
Through Him all things were made.
For us men and for our salvation He
came down from heaven; by
the power of the Holy Spirit he
was born of the Virgin Mary,
and became man.
For our sake He was crucified under
Pontius Pilate; He suffered,
died, and was buried. On the
third day He rose again in
accordance with the Scriptures;
He ascended into Heaven and
is seated at the right hand of
the Father. He will come again
in glory to judge the living and
the dead, and His kingdom will
have no end.

We believe in the Holy Spirit, the Lord, the
giver
of life, who proceeds from the Father
and the Son. With the Father and the
Son he is worshipped and glorified. He
has spoken through the prophets.

We believe in one holy Catholic and apostolic
Church. We acknowledge one baptism
for the forgiveness of sins. We look for
the resurrection of the dead and the life
of the world to come. Amen.

STUDY QUESTIONS

1. What caused a need for a document of this type, and how was it designed to be used?
2. How do both versions of the Creed deal with the specific, if thorny, issue of the Christian Trinity?

7.4B. MINUCIUS FELIX, *OCTAVIUS*, CHAPTER 30, "RITUAL CANNIBALISM CHARGE AGAINST CHRISTIANS," 3RD CENTURY CE

Although little is known of Minucius Felix's personal information, his work *Octavius* provides many telling details about early understandings of the Christian faith. *Octavius* is staged as a discussion between a pagan, Caecilius Natalis, and a Christian, Octavius Januarius, where Minucius Felix plays the peacekeeper. In this way, the author is able to correct misunderstandings and assumptions about Christian faith and practice.

I would like to meet the man who thinks or says that we engage in the blood-sacrifice of babies! Who can possibly believe anyone could injure an infant, so small, so tender, to draw blood from it and drain its life away before it even has a chance to live? The only person capable of doing such a thing is the one capable of thinking such a thing! Romans, I have seen you abandon your children to wild beasts and birds of prey! I have seen you crush them and strangle them! O, what miserable deaths. You have women who drink potent potions to end the lives that have begun in their wombs—murder before birth. And all these things you have learned from your gods. Saturn not only exposed his children—he devoured them. Parents in parts of Africa have been known to kiss and caress their bawling babies, soothing them so that Saturn not be given a sacrifice who was in tears. Both the Tauri of Pontus and the Busiri of Egypt immolate their own house-guests as a sacred rite. The Gauls inhumanely offer human sacrifices to Mercury. Roman priests have been known to bury Greek men and women alive—yes, and Gallic ones too! To this very day you worship Jupiter Latiaris with murder—a suitable sacrifice, actually, for a son of Saturn, gorged as he is with the blood of evil criminals. I believe it was Saturn himself taught Catiline how to swear a blood-oath to a political conspiracy; who taught Bellona to bathe her sacred rites in human gore; and who taught men to treat epilepsy by drinking human blood—a "cure" worse than the disease itself. Good followers of Saturn are those who eat the wild beasts in the arena, wet and dripping with the blood of their victims, and fattened with the flesh and entrails of men. No! To we Christians it is unlawful to see or permit murder. And not only do we shrink from human blood, we won't even use the blood of animals in our food.

Our devilish attackers have spread another lie about us too—namely, that we engage in incestuous orgies; our detractors' goal is to stoke popular loathing against us, staining the glory of our modesty with an outrageous charge, so that people will hate us before they even have a chance to learn the truth. That is what your hatchet-man Fronto did. He levied a charge at us but offered no evidence, only some random rhetorical accusations. Other peoples, however, are the founders of this vile horror. Among the Persians son and mother are permitted promiscuous relations. Men marry their own sisters in Egypt as well as in Greece. Your legends and stage-tragedies—which you both read and hear with such pleasure—are filled with tales of incest. You worship incestuous gods who have intercourse with their own mothers, sisters, and daughters. Is it any wonder that you permit and indulge in incest yourselves? Wretches! You probably even engage in it without knowing it, gratifying your lust, as you do, constantly, and fathering children everywhere. But in your wanderings you expose your children at home to the lusts of others. Is

Translation by Clifford Backman.

it any wonder, then, that all of you eventually return to your own seed? Thus you continue the stain of incest without knowing it.

We [Christians], however, preserve our modesty—not only in our appearance but in our hearts, living as we do, gladly, within the bonds of faithful marriage. We each approach our one and only wife, if we desire to procreate, or we approach no one at all. At our banquets the only thing we share is our food, and our banquets are modest and sober. We do not indulge in entertainments and long bouts of drinking. We temper our joy with gravity and chaste conversation. Our bodies too are chaste—and more than chaste, since many of us choose lives of sworn celibacy; we delight in our chastity but make no boast of it. So far are we, in fact, from incestuous indulgence that many of us cannot even hear of normal sexual relations between men and women without blushing.

STUDY QUESTIONS

1. From what specific practices of the Christians did the charges of incest and cannibalism ultimately, if mistakenly, derive?
2. How does Octavius turn these charges against non-Christians?

7.5. GOSPEL OF THOMAS, 4TH CENTURY?

Discovered in 1945, the Gospel of Thomas numbers among the fifty-two writings preserved in a cave in Egypt. Written in Coptic, the Gospel of Thomas—the disciple of Jesus—is an extra-Biblical text read by Gnostics. Although it was never accepted in the canonical Bible, the Gospel of Thomas was popular in certain geographical regions like Syria, where Thomas converted Christians after Jesus's death. The 114 sayings in this "Gospel" partly reflect the familiar sayings from the four synoptic Gospels and partly emerge from Gnostic understandings of early Christian tenets.

Jesus said, "If you do not abstain from the world, you will not find the kingdom of God. And if you do not keep the Sabbath, you will not see the Father." [1.4–11]

Jesus also said, "I stood amidst the world and appeared to the people in the flesh. I found everyone satiated, and no one thirsty. My heart worries about the children of man because they are blind in their hearts and they do not see." [1.11–21]

Jesus also said, "Wherever there are three, they are without God; but where there is only one, I say that I am with him. Lift the stone and there you will find me. Split the wood, and I am there." [1.23–30]

And Jesus said, "A prophet is not accepted in his own land, nor does a physician heal those who know him." [1.30–5]

Jesus also said, "A city set on the summit of a high mountain can neither fall nor be hidden." [1.36–41]

From the Oxyrhynchus Papyri, no. 1, 654, and 655; translation by Clifford Backman.

These are the hidden sayings that Jesus spoke when alive and that Judas, also called Thomas, wrote down. And he said, "Whoever understands how to interpret these sayings will not taste death." [654.1–5]

"Let the seeker not stop seeking until he finds [what he seeks]; and when he finds it, he will marvel. When he marvels, he will have authority; and when he has authority, he will know peace." [654.5–9]

Jesus also said, "If those leading you say 'The kingdom [of God] is in the sky,' then the birds of the sky will guide you. If they say 'The kingdom is below ground,' then the fish of the sea will lead you. The kingdom of God is within you, and without you. Whoever knows himself will find this out. And when you know yourself, you will know that you are the children of the living Father. But if you do not know yourself, you live in poverty and you are poor." [654.9–21]

Jesus also said, "A person old in years will not hesitate to ask a child—even if he is only seven days old—about his place in life. . . . For many who are first will be last, and many who are last will be first. [654.21–7]

Jesus also said, "Know what is in front of your face, and that which is hidden from you will be revealed. For there is nothing hidden that will not be made clear, and nothing buried that will not be raised again." [654.27–31]

His disciples said to Jesus, "When will we be visible? When will we be able to see you?" And Jesus answered, "When you are naked and not ashamed." [655i.17–23]

STUDY QUESTIONS

1. Is a collection of sayings like this one more useful than the narrative basis of the canonical Gospels (Matthew, Mark, Luke, and John)?
2. How does the document reveal the effect of "secret" knowledge imparted among Gnostic Christians?

7.6. AUGUSTINE OF HIPPO, SEVENTH DISCOURSE ON THE GOSPEL OF JOHN

The bishop of Hippo (in modern Algeria), Saint Augustine (354–430) shaped the theology and philosophy of Christianity on the brink of the end of the Roman Empire. Originally a "heretical" Manichee, Augustine experienced a personal conversion and entered into study with Saint Ambrose (ca. 330–397). Augustine's major works include *City of God*, a treatise on the eternal world beyond Earth, and the autobiographical *Confessions*. Although he wrote many memorable texts on large, definitive issues—from the doctrine of original sin to the just war theory—Augustine also devoted himself to pastoral care. This sermon, preached to his congregation while a pagan festival temptingly occurred outside the church, reveals a more personal side of Augustine's understanding of man's relationship to God.

Translation by Clifford Backman.

No one has ever seen God. Yet, if we love one another, God remains in us, and his love is brought to perfection in us. This is how we know that we remain in him and he in us, that he has given us of his Spirit. Moreover, we have seen and testify that the Father sent his Son as savior of the world. Whoever acknowledges that Jesus is the Son of God, God remains in him and he in God. We have come to know and to believe in the love God has for us. God is love, and whoever remains in love remains in God and God in him.

Love is a sweet word, but sweeter still is the deed. We cannot be always speaking of it, for we have so many things to do and our daily business pulls us in different directions. It's not that we don't have nothing better to talk about—we just don't have the time to sit around and talk about love. But although we cannot be always talking about it, we may always be loving. Just as with the "Alleluia" that we sing daily this time of year—are we in fact always singing it? Of course not. We don't sing "Alleluia" for an hour, by which I mean not only that we don't sing it for an entire hour but that we don't even sing it for a single minute out of every hour. We're too busy with other things.

"Alleluia," as you know, means "Praise the Lord." The person who praises God aloud cannot always be doing it, but the one who praises God by the way he lives his life, can do so always. Acts of mercy and love, the holiness of piety, chastity, and sobriety—all these are things we can practice all the time, in public or at home, with others or alone in our rooms, while conversing or keeping quiet, when busy or at leisure. And we should practice them always, because all of these are internal virtues. . . .

Dear brothers, you heard earlier in the Gospel reading (at least if you were listening not only with your ears but with your heart), "Take care not to perform righteous deeds in order that people may see them." [Matt 6.1] Now, did Jesus mean by this, that we should hide from the eyes of others the good things we do, out of fear of being seen? But if we fear spectators, then we will never have imitators—and so we ought to be seen doing good, but we should not do good in order to be seen doing it. . . . Do good not to win praise for yourself but for the God who has given you the ability to do good. . . . I tell you, my

brothers, and in fact I would not let this go unsaid: Take up good works whenever you can, regardless of the season, the day, and the hour. . . . What you can, when you can. . . . Let your charity never cease or be interrupted. Love always, in every season. As it is written, "Let mutual love continue." [Heb 13.1]

Some of you have probably been wondering, while I've been talking about this epistle of St. John, why it is "brotherly" love he emphasizes so much. . . . He speaks over and over again of this love—and yet he seldom mentions the love we should have for God. (He does mention love for God, of course.) Similarly, he says hardly a word about loving our enemies. He extols and preaches charity with the greatest energy, but tells us only to love one another rather than to love our enemies. But we just heard, in our Gospel reading, "For if you love those who love you, what recompense will you have? Do not the tax collectors do the same?" [Matt 5.46] . . . . Love is like fire: it touches first what is nearest before extending to what is further away. A beloved person is closer to you than a stranger, and a benign stranger is closer to you than a sworn enemy. So give your love to those who are closest to you . . . then extend it to strangers who have done you no ill, and then extend it again to your enemies. This is what the Lord requires of us—and it explains why John here says nothing about loving an enemy. . . .

All love—both common human love (for which we use the word *amor*) and spiritual love (the love we have for what we aspire to, and for which we use the word *dilectio*)—involves desiring the well-being of the one loved. Whether we mean *dilectio* or *amor* (the latter being the word Christ used when He asked, "Peter, do you love me?" [John 21.17]), we do not mean that we love others in the way, say, that a glutton loves fowl—for he loves fowl in order to kill them and eat them; his love desires the end of their existence. We love food in order to consume it and be strengthened by it—but that is not how we love people. That love is benevolent and springs from a desire to do good for others. If there is no good we can do for someone, the desire for it alone suffices to prove our love. We certainly don't wish someone to be wretched, so that we can extend mercy to him! Feed the hungry, certainly; but how much better it would be if no one knew hunger and we had no one to give bread to. Clothe the naked, but oh, that all were clothed and need did not exist! We bury the dead, but how we look forward to the time when life is eternal and no one dies! We reconcile those who are in disagreement, yet how much we hope for the eternal peace of Jerusalem, where everyone shall live in harmony! . . .

Dear brothers, I've spoken at some length here, because the importance of the love we give to others requires it. If there be no love in us, then my words are useless; but if we have that love, then my words will be like oil cast upon a flame. To one without a feeling of love, perhaps my words may kindle it; to one with flame already let, perhaps my words will fuel it. . . ." If we love one another, God remains in us, and his love is brought to perfection in us." [1 John 4.12] Begin to love, and be perfected—for God has thereby begun to dwell within you, and his in-dwelling will make you perfect. "This is how we know that we remain in him and he in us, that he has given us of his Spirit." [1 John 4.13] Thanks be to God! . . .

So much do I love to speak about love that I almost wish this epistle had no end. No other text is so impassioned in calling us to love; there is no message more sweet that can be preached to us, nor more healthful for us to imbibe—but only if we acknowledge God's gift by living in love. Let us not forget to be thankful for such a great and gracious gift. God had only one Son, but desires that He be not an only child. He wishes us to be His brothers, adopted by Him into eternal life.

STUDY QUESTIONS

1. How does Augustine describe the feeling of "love" in terms of actual deeds?
2. What is the style of this sermon, and how might it have appealed to an audience?

CHAPTER 8

THE EARLY MIDDLE AGES

8.1. GILDAS, *ON THE RUIN AND CONQUEST OF BRITAIN*, CA. 525–CA. 540 CE

Gildas (500–570) was a British cleric living when the last of Roman rule in Britain was snuffed out by Germanic invaders (the era that gave birth to the Arthurian legends). As the primary contemporary account of British events in the 6th century, Gildas's three-part sermon offers his explanation of why the situation had become so dire: because of the sins and corruption of the British kings, people, and clergy. The work is modeled on the Biblical prophets who descry the state of the world and warn civilization that it must change, before it is too late.

[1.3–4] The island of Britain sits almost at the edge of the world, off to the west and northwest, where it plays its part in what is called the divine balance that sustains the entire world. From its southwestern tip it stretches some eight hundred miles to the north and another two hundred across, not counting several promontories that reach out from curved bays. It is protected by broad, impassable seas on all sides except for the straits on the southern coast, where ships cross to Belgian Gaul. It benefits from the estuaries of two great rivers—the Thames and the Severn—along which valuable goods from other lands came via ships. There are also many smaller streams, twenty-eight cities, numerous strongholds, and some other major, if unremarkable, monuments—walls, fortified towers, gates, and houses whose roofs are firmly built even though they appear dangerously high. Britain is rich with widespread plains, well-situated hills that

are amenable to cultivation, and mountains that provide convenient pasturage for cattle. Colorful flowers line the paths along these highlands, giving them a beautiful appearance like that of a bride adorned with bright jewels. The land is fed by many clear springs, whose flowing waters bring a cascade of snow-white gravel; by many bright rivers that move with a gentle murmur, offering to those relaxing on their banks a promise of sweet sleep; and by many lakes that overflow with cool streams of living water.

The history of this island, so proud and resilient from its origins, is one of ungrateful rebellion—rebellion against God, against its fellow men, and sometimes against distant kings and their peoples. Of all that reckless men are capable of doing, what vileness and unrighteousness can be worse than to deny God the fear that is owed Him, to deny charity to one's fellow man, and to deny honor to those in

Translation by Clifford Backman.

positions of authority over them? What can do greater harm to our faith than to violate heavenly and human desires, or, having already violated these, to give oneself over to lusts and selfishness?

I pass over in silence the ancient sins by which the whole human race was held in bondage before the coming of Christ; neither will I bother to narrate the most hellish horrors (surpassing in number even those of the Egyptians) of my native land. True, some of these exist even today, to disfigure our land everywhere according to their savage custom. . . . The only evils I wish to publicize are those our island has suffered, and has at times inflicted on others, since the time of the Roman emperors. I will do this to the best of my ability. No native writings or records can assist me, since these (if they even existed!) have been destroyed by fires or carted off in ships carrying our exiled leaders. Instead, I have to rely on foreign writers whose accounts are far from clear, since they contain so many gaps.

[1.23–26] In stout ships of war under full sail came the cries of a brood of fierce cubs born of a savage lioness—the Saxons—whose cries came to us as omens and auguries. A prophecy had foretold that they would occupy for three hundred years the country toward which they directed their prows, half of that time (that is, 150 years) spent in ravaging the land. They sailed under the command of their brutish leader and sank their deadly talons in the eastern shore of our island, and their homeland, seeing the success of this first contingent, sent out another ship, and another, to join their bastard companions. Thus were the seed of iniquity and the root of bitterness planted in our soil, until the poisonous plant grew and developed strong branches and full foliage. Having gained a foothold, the Saxons negotiated to have us supply them with provisions, as though they were our defenders preparing to endure great hardship on our account. For a time our provisions closed the dog's maw, to use an expression; but soon enough they complained that our monthly offerings were insufficient and declared that if we did not increase their volume they would break our treaty with them and lay waste the whole island. They did not wait long to turn their threats into deeds.

Because of our earlier sins, the fire of divine vengeance blazed across our land from coast to coast, stoked continually by the wretches from the east. This fire devoured all the scattered settlements and lands, and did not stop until it had consumed nearly the entire island, licking the western ocean with its red and savage tongue. The catastrophe bears comparison with that of the Assyrians upon Judaea, for there was fulfilled among us, as among the Jews, the prophet's lament, "They have set your sanctuary on fire, profaned your name's abode by razing it to the ground," [Ps 74.7] and again, "O God, the nations have invaded your inheritance; they have defiled your holy temple." [Ps 79.1] All our settlements were brought low with the repeated blows of battering rams. Our people were cut down everywhere by gleaming swords and raging fires, including the priests and bishops. Sadly, the streets of our villages are filled with the ruins of once-high towers that have been pulled to the ground, with stones pried from fences or left over from the smashing of sacred altars, with dismembered pieces of human bodies that are so covered with lurid clots of blood that they look as though the people had been run through a wine-press, and whose only chance for any kind of burial is to rot in the ruins of collapsed homes; all the rest will simply fill the stomachs of ravenous beasts and birds. . . .

Some surviving wretches were apprehended in the mountains and killed in heaps; others were so overcome by hunger that they surrendered themselves to their enemies, to be enslaved forever. . . . Eventually the barbaric raiders returned to their homeland, and what was left of our people came together from all around, as bees rush to their hive when a storm is brewing, and prayed as one to God with their whole hearts. As the phrase goes, "burdening the air with unnumbered prayers" they begged not to be destroyed. Rather, they took up arms and elected to challenge their conquerors in battle under the leadership of Ambrosius Aurelianus, a man of modest character. Alone of all the Romans, he had managed to survive the tumultuous times (his parents, being clothed in imperial purple, had been killed), and his descendants in my own time are fallen far from his ancient nobility. Nevertheless, these people gained a victory, with God's help.

Since that time, our people won some more victories and so did our enemy. Indeed, the Lord is testing our nation—the Israel of today—and the depth of its love for Him. The struggle continued up to the time of the battle of Badon Hill, the last great slaughter inflicted upon us. This was in the year of my birth, one month less than forty-four years ago, and to this very day not one of our villages is what it used to be. Instead, all lie desolate, routed, and ruined. . . .

Britain has kings, but they are nothing but tyrants. Britain has judges, but they are wicked men who engage in non-stop plunder and pillage of helpless commoners, to the delight and benefit of criminals and thieves everywhere. [Our rulers] have innumerable wives—harlots and adulteresses all. They swear oaths only to perjure themselves and to lie every time they make a vow. They fight wars, but evil ones against their own subjects. And while they pursue simple thieves relentlessly throughout the entire country, the robbers who sit with them at their noble tables are not only esteemed but rewarded. . . .

[108] But why mince words? . . . I will say what I mean. . . . You are not priests of God but enemies to Him, not bishops but practiced sinners! Not ministers of Christ, but traitors to the holy apostles whom you supposedly succeed! You may have heard the words of the apostle Paul but you have not absorbed them and you do not feel their weight. Like stone idols which can neither see nor hear, you stood at the altar while his words came pouring down like thunder at you! "Brethren," he said, "this saying is trustworthy and deserves full acceptance." [1 Tim 1.15] He spoke of trustworthiness and deserving. "Whoever aspires to the office of bishop desires a noble task." [1 Tim 3.1] But you seek the bishops' offices out of covetousness, without even pretending it involves spiritual worthiness; you certainly put no store in good works. "Therefore a bishop must be irreproachable, married only once, temperate, self-controlled, decent, hospitable, able to teach, not a drunkard, not aggressive, but gentle, not contentious, not a lover of money." [1 Tim 3.2–3] This calls for tears, not more words. . . . How horribly things have changed, to see the commands of heaven crushed under foot. The lot of you arm yourselves with deeds and words in order to attack these teachings, to destroy them. Teachings that one ought to suffer for and lay down one's life for!

[110] Priests! Not a single one of you should flatter yourself on the purity of your body. The souls of your flock . . . will be asked on the Day of Judgment, and they will denounce you as murderers of souls! . . .

May Almighty God, the God of all consolation and mercy, preserve His very few good priests from all evil, and make them citizens of His city the Heavenly Jerusalem, where is the assembly of all saints. In the name of the Father, Son, and Holy Spirit, to whom be honor and glory for ever and ever. Amen.

STUDY QUESTIONS

1. How is the idea of a contract between the Britons and God introduced here, and what hope is there that God will protect against the invaders?
2. What considerations might have prompted the Romans to withdraw from Britain in the 5th century?

8.2. GREGORY OF TOURS, *HISTORY OF THE FRANKS*

Gregory served as bishop of Tours from 573 until his death in 594. He wrote many hagiographies, which he collected into three volumes: the *Lives of the Fathers*, the *Glory of the Confessors*, and the *Glory of the Martyrs*. He is best remembered, however, for his lengthy and rambling *History of the Franks*, which covers the period from St. Martin of Tours (d. 397) to the year 591. Switching back and forth between the family of Clovis and the various bishops of northern France, he tries to present the Merovingian era as a chapter in God's plan for Christianizing western Europe. In the two passages below, he describes the last four years of Clovis's life (r. 481–511) (Bk. II, ch. 35–42) and Gregory's own encounter with a Jew in the court of King Chilperic (r. 561–584) (Bk. VI, ch. 5).

CLOVIS' LAST YEARS (BK. II, CH. 35–42)

[II, 35] King Alaric II of the Visigoths, seeing that Clovis was overrunning one nation after another, sent ambassadors to him, saying, "Dear brother, it would be wise for us to meet—if you are interested, and God willing." Clovis agreed and rode to meet Alaric. They convened just outside the village of Amboise, which is on an island in the Loire river, in the diocese of Tours. They negotiated and settled upon a treaty of eternal friendship, which they celebrated with a shared feast, after which they both rode home in peace. At that time there were countless people in Gaul eager for Frankish rule.

[36] One consequence of this treaty, however, was that Bishop Quintinianus of Rodez fell from favor and was driven out by the people of his own city, who had long criticized him, saying, "If it were up to you, the Franks would be our lords!" It did not take long for their resentment to burst into open quarrel with the bishop, for the Visigoths who lived in the city were suspicious of Quintinianus' loyalties, and the rest of the townsmen went so far as to accuse him publicly of wanting to hand the city over to the Franks. And so a plot was hatched to assassinate him. Quintinianus found out about it and fled one night, together with his most trusted attendants, to Clermont, where he was kindly received by St. Eufrasius, the bishop who

had succeeded Aprunculus. Eufrasius was a native of Dijon. He gave Quintinianus fine lodgings amid fields and vineyards, insisting that "This diocese has ample resources to support us both—for the charity preached by the blessed Apostle [St. Martin] must be carried on by all of God's ministers." The bishop of Lyons also gave Quintinianus some property that he administered in Clermont. For more details regarding St. Quintinianus, the wrongs done to him, and the miracles performed by God through him, see the pertinent chapter in my *Lives of the Fathers*.

[37] "I cannot bear seeing Arians living in Gaul," Clovis announced one day to his ministers. "We're going to attack them, and with God's help we'll crush them and take over all their land." Everyone agreed with this idea, and so Clovis assembled his army and marched on Poitiers. Along the way, some of his troops passed through the diocese of Tours, so Clovis gave an order that, out of respect for St. Martin, none of his men should requisition anything in the region except fodder and water. It happened that one soldier came upon some hay belonging to an elderly, poor farmer, and the soldier said to him, "The king says we cannot take anything but fodder, right? Well, this hay is fodder; we won't be going against orders if we take it." Then he knocked the old man down and took his hay. When

---

Translation by Clifford Backman.

this was reported to Clovis, he pulled out his sword and executed the soldier on the spot. "We can give up any hope of winning this campaign if we offend St. Martin!" he declared. Thus he made his point, and the rest of the army took nothing in the region after that. Then Clovis sent messengers loaded with gifts to the church of St. Martin, saying, "Go, and bring me back good tidings from God's house." And then he prayed, "O Lord, if you are on my side and wish to deliver into my hands the wretched [Arian] heretics who have shown themselves so hostile to you, then give us a sign as these messengers enter St. Martin's church, a sign that shows clearly your support for me, your servant Clovis."

The messengers set out, and as they had been commanded they soon arrived at Tours; they entered the church exactly when the choir's soloist was singing the antiphon:

You girded me with valor for war,
     subjugated my opponents beneath me.
You made my foes expose their necks to me;
     those who hated me I silenced. [Ps. 18.39–40]

When the messengers heard this, they gave thanks to God, made their vows to St. Martin, and returned gladly to report to the king.

When Clovis and his army reached Vienne, they could find no way to cross the river since it was swollen from heavy rains, and so he prayed that night that God would show him a way across. The next morning, as it happened, a large doe appeared and entered the river. Everyone recognized that this was a heavenly sign, and that they could follow the doe across the river. Once on the other side, Clovis marched toward Poitiers. They made camp one evening and saw a pillar of fire rise from the local church of St. Hilary and advance toward them. To everyone this appeared a clear sign that that blessed saint was adding his support to Clovis' campaign to rout the heretics, against whom St. Hilary had himself done battle in defense of the faith. Clovis instantly gave orders forbidding any looting by his men as they passed through the region—and indeed no one took from anyone.

On the outskirts of Poitiers at that time there lived a saintly and God-fearing man named Maxentius, who, although the abbot, lived in seclusion from the rest of his monastery. It would be pointless to mention the name of the monastery at that time, for it is now known only as the Cell of St. Maxentius. When the monks there saw the approach of some Frankish soldiers they hurried to their abbot and begged him to come out and bless them. He took such a long time in coming out of his cell that the monks grew frightened and forced his door open; then they pushed him out into the open. Maxentius walked fearlessly up to the troops, presumably to ask them not to harm the monastery, when all of a sudden a soldier drew his sword and swung it at Maxentius' head—but his arm froze in mid-air, right by the abbot's ear, and the sword clattered to the ground. The soldier instantly threw himself at the saint's feet and begged forgiveness. His companions, seeing all of this, raced back to the main army filled with dread that they would have to pay with their lives for such an offense. The saint, meanwhile, rubbed the soldier's arm with holy oil and made the sign of the Cross over him, and instantly the man recovered. Thus, thanks to Maxentius, the monastery escaped unharmed. Maxentius performed many more miracles in his lifetime, as any reader who is interested may find in my *Life of Maxentius*. But this particular event occurred in the fifteenth year of Clovis' reign.

Soon thereafter, Clovis met King Alaric [II] and his army of Visigoths on the battlefield at Vouillé, about ten miles from Poitiers. After several volleys of javelins, the soldiers fought hand to hand; in the end the Visigoths fled (as they so often did), giving the victory to Clovis, who had God on his side. (One of Clovis' allies in this fight was Chloderic, the son of Sigibert the Lame. Sigibert had been lame ever since being wounded in the knee in a battle against the Alamanni at their fortress at Zülpich.) Clovis killed Alaric. Just as the Goths were fleeing, however, two of them turned and rushed suddenly at Clovis, one on each side, and struck him with their spears. Fortunately, thanks to his stout leather corselet and his speedy horse, Clovis escaped—but he very nearly died.

A large contingent from Auvergne, under the jurisdiction of Apollinaris, took part in this battle but their commanders (all of senatorial rank) were all killed. Alaric's son, Amalaric, escaped and made it all the way to Spain, where he ruled wisely for many years. Clovis, meanwhile, sent his own son, Theuderic, to Clermont, passing through Albi and Rodez on the way. Theuderic brought every place he passed by under his father's rule, and thus all the lands between the Visigoths and the Burgundians came to belong to Clovis. Alaric II had been king for twelve years. Clovis spent the winter in Bordeaux, seized all of Alaric's treasure at Toulouse, and then advanced to Angoulême—where God showed him such favor that the city's walls collapsed of their own weight when Clovis merely looked at them. Clovis drove the Visigoths from the city and took command. This was the culmination of his victorious campaign, and afterward he returned to Tours where he bestowed countless gifts upon the church of St. Martin.

[38] One day some letters arrived for Clovis from the [Byzantine] emperor Anastasius I [r. 491–518], conferring the title of consul on him. There was a ceremony in St. Martin's, where Clovis stood and assumed a purple tunic and the military robes [of the empire], and crowned himself with a diadem. Then he mounted his horse and rode among the people, showering them with gold and silver coins, as he progressed from the doorway of St. Martin's to the cathedral at Tours. From that day forward he was addressed either as "consul" or "augustus." After Tours he went on to Paris, which he made the seat of his government. His son Theuderic accompanied him.

[39] After Bishop Eustochius of Tours died, Licinius was ordained his successor—the eighth bishop after St. Martin himself. The war I described just above took place during Licinius' episcopacy, and it was in his time too that Clovis came to Tours. Licinius is reported to have spent time in the east and even to have visited the Holy Land; some say he went all the way to Jerusalem and saw the very site of Our Lord's death and resurrection, about which we have read in the gospels.

[40] While living in Paris Clovis sent a secret message to Sigibert's son, Chloderic. He wrote, "Your father is old and lame in one leg. When he dies his kingdom will pass, rightfully, to you—and my alliance will come with it." Chloderic was thus tempted by a lust for power and began to plot his own father's death.

One day Sigibert exited the city of Cologne and crossed the Rhine river, since he wanted to walk in the forest at Buchau. In the middle of the day he took a nap in his tent, which is when Chloderic loosed assassins on him. Having murdered his father, Chloderic then took possession of the realm. But by God's judgment, Sigibert's killer fell into the very trap he had laid for his father. He dispatched messengers to Clovis to announce Sigibert's death—"My father is

dead," he wrote, "and I have seized both his kingdom and his treasure. Send messengers of your own to me, and I will gladly bestow upon you anything you desire from this treasure." To this Clovis replied, "Thank you for your good will. Please do show your treasure to my messengers—but you may keep it all."

When the messengers arrived, they examined all the treasure that Chloderic was eager to show them. "This was the chest in which my father kept all his gold coins," boasted Chloderic.

Clovis' men replied, "Plunge your hand down to the bottom of the chest, so we can see how much is there." And as soon as Chloderic leaned forward to do so, one of the Frankish envoys raised his double-sided axe and split his skull with it. Thus did the wretch Chloderic shared his father's fate.

After Clovis heard that both Sigibert and Chloderic were dead he traveled to Cologne himself and ordered all the town's inhabitants to assemble. "While I was boating down the Scheldt river, Chloderic, the son of your king, conspired against his own father and spread a rumor that I was the one who wanted him dead. Sigibert fled through the forest at Buchau, but Chloderic's assassins caught up with him and killed him. Then when Chloderic was showing off his father's treasure, he too was murdered—by whom, I don't know. I am not responsible in any way. I have no interest to murder any of my fellow kings, for regicide is a terrible crime. But things have happened in this way, I advise you to make the best of the situation by turning to me and putting yourself freely under my authority."

The people, hearing him, pounded their shields and roared their approval, then they raised Clovis up on a shield and acclaimed him their king. This is how he acquired Sigibert's kingship, treasure, and people. With every passing day God inspired more and more people to submit themselves to Clovis, who consequently grew enormously in power—for he always walked before God with an upright heart and did whatever was pleasing in His sight.

[41] Clovis' next victim was Chararic. This fellow had been asked to help Clovis during his struggles with Syagrius, but he had remained neutral. He gave aid to neither side, preferring to wait to see who would win before declaring allegiance, and this is why Clovis now moved against him. He cleverly trapped Chararic and threw him in prison. He

ordered both Chararic and his son to be tied up, then had their hair cut off, with the subsequent order that they be ordained as priest and deacon, accordingly. At this, Chararic burst into tears and cried out, "All you have done is cut leaves from a tree that is still green and thriving; they'll soon grow back, larger than ever! Death to the man who has done this to me!" Clovis heard about this, and so he had their heads cut off too, and after they were both dead he seized their kingdom, treasure, and people too.

[42] The king at Cambrai at that time was Ragnachar, a man so lost to lechery that he could not even leave the women of his own family alone. He had a counselor named Farro who defiled himself with the same filthy habit. It was said of this man that whenever Ragnachar had anything—whether food, gift, or anything else—placed before him, he would proclaim "It's good enough for me and Farro!" This put all the Franks in their retinue in a great rage. And so Clovis bribed Ragnachar's bodyguards with armbands and sword-belts that looked like gold but were really just cleverly gilded bronze, and with these he hoped to turn Ragnachar's men against him. Clovis then sent his army against Ragnachar; and when Ragnachar dispatched spies to bring back information on the invaders and asked them upon their return, how strong the attackers were, they replied: "They're good enough for you and Farro!" Clovis himself finally arrived and arranged his soldiers for battle. Ragnachar watched as his army was crushed and tried to sneak away, but his own soldiers captured him, tied his hands behind his back, and brought him—together with Ragnachar's brother, Ricchar—before Clovis.

"Why have you disgraced our Frankish people by allowing yourself to be tied up?" asked Clovis. "It would have been better for you if you had died in battle." And with that, he lifted his axe and split Ragnachar's skull. Then he turned to his brother Ricchar and said, "And as for you, if you had stood by your brother's side he would not have been bound in this way." And he struck Ricchar with another blow of his axe and killed him. When these two were dead, the bodyguards who had betrayed them discovered that the golden gifts they had received from Clovis were fake. It is said that when they complained of this to Clovis he answered, "That is all the gold a man should

expect when he willingly lures his own ruler to death," adding that they should be grateful for escaping with their lives instead of being tortured to death for having betrayed their masters. Hearing this, the men begged for mercy, asking only for their lives.

Now both of these kings, Ragnachar and Ricchar, were relatives of Clovis; so was their brother Rignomer, whom Clovis had put to death at Le Mans. Then, having killed all three, Clovis took over their kingdoms and their treasuries. He carried out the killing of many other kings and blood-relations in the same way—of anyone, really, whom he suspected of plotting against his realm—and in so doing he gradually extended his control over the whole of Gaul. One day he summoned an assembly of all his subjects, at which he is reported to have remarked about all the relatives he had destroyed, "How sad it is for me to live as a stranger among strangers, without any of my family here to help me when disaster happens!" But he said this not out of any genuine grief for their deaths, but only because he hoped somehow to flush out another relative whom he could kill.

GREGORY AND THE JEW (BK. VI, CH. 5)

King Chilperic, who was then still at Nogent-sur-Marne, sent his baggage train ahead while he made the rest of his plans to travel to Paris. I had gone to pay my respects before he left, and while I was visiting him a Jew named Priscus came in. This fellow was on familiar terms with the king, having been an agent on his behalf in some commercial ventures. Chilperic placed his hand on the Jew's head, in a gentle manner, and said to me, "Come, bishop! You lay your hand on him too!" Instantly the Jew pulled away. "'O faithless and perverse generation!'" the king quoted [Matthew 17.17], "why can't you accept what was promised to you by your own prophets? Can't you see that the mysteries of the Church were foretold by the sacrifices of your own people?"

The Jew answered, "God has no need of a son! He never had a son, and He does not have any partner in His kingdom! Indeed, He Himself said, through Moses, 'See now that I, I alone, am he, and there is no god besides me. It is I who bring both death and life, I who inflict wounds and heal them.'" [Deut. 32.39]

The king responded, "But God brought forth, by His Spirit, His own eternal Son from a womb—a Son no younger than Himself in time, and no lesser than Himself in power. For God said, 'From the womb of the morning-star have I begotten you' [Psalm 110.3]. This Son, born at the beginning of time, He later sent to heal the world. Your own prophet has declared, 'He sent His word and healed them.' And as for your other claim, that God never had a Son, listen to another of your prophets, who put these words in His mouth: 'Shall I bring a mother to the point of birth, and yet not let her child be born?' He said this in regard to the people born in Him by faith."

The Jew answered, "How is it possible that God should be made man, or be born of a woman, or submit to lashing, or be condemned to death?"

At this point the king grew silent, so I took up the debate myself. "God's becoming man, as the Son of God," I said, "was the result of our needs, not His— for if He had not become man, then He could not have saved us from the prison of sin and servitude to the Devil. And now, as in the story we've both read of David slaying Goliath, I'll run you through with your own sword, pulling my proof not from the Gospels or the writings of any apostle (none of which you would accept) but from your own Scriptures. Listen to this, one of your own prophets prophesying:

He is both God and man, and who has known him?
"And also by the same:

Such is our God;
and no other is to be compared to him
He has uncovered the whole way of
    understanding,
and has given her to Jacob, his servant,
to Israel, His beloved.
Afterwards did He show Himself upon earth,
And conversed with mortals. [Baruch 3.37–38]
"And here is proof that He was born of a Virgin,
    from another of your prophets:
    Behold, a virgin shall conceive and bear a son,
    And shall call him Emmanuel, "God is with
        us." [Isaiah 7.14]
"Still another prophet showed beyond doubt that
    He would submit to being lashed:
    They pierced my hands and feet, and divided
        my garments among them. [Psalms 22.17]

"In another place this same prophet says:
    They gave me poison for my food;
    And for my thirst they gave me vinegar to
        drink. [Psalms 69.22]
"And finally, to show that it would be through
    the Cross that He would restore the world
    (long lost to Satan) to His Kingdom, the
    same prophet David says:
    The Lord reigns from a tree. [Psalms 96.10]

"But this doesn't mean that He did not reign before [the Crucifixion], together with the Father. Instead it means that He accepted a new and unprecedented dominion over the people whom He delivered from slavery to Satan."

The Jew then replied, "But why would God need to suffer these things?"

"I have already answered you," I said. "Mankind was innocent at Creation, but was tricked by the Serpent's guile and led to break God's commandment. Thus he was cast out of Paradise and condemned to suffer on the earth. It was only by the death of Christ, God's True and Only Son, that man was reconciled to God."

The Jew asked, "But couldn't God have sent more prophets or messengers to call mankind back to the path of salvation? Why did He Himself have to be humbled in the flesh?"

I retorted, "Mankind was inclined to sin from the very beginning of time. The Great Flood, the destruction of Sodom, the plagues on Egypt, the miracle of the parting of the sea and the river Jordan—none of these were enough to frighten mankind into obedience. He kept on resisting God's word and refusing to believe the prophets. More than that, he even killed the prophets who were preaching repentance! No, if God Himself had not come down from heaven, man's salvation would never have happened. We were reborn by Christ's baptism, cured by His wounds, raised up by His Resurrection, and glorified by His Ascension. Your own prophet declares the necessity of God's coming to heal us:

He bore the punishment that makes us whole,
    and by his wounds we were healed. [Isaiah 54.5]
"and he continues:

He bore the sins of many and interceded for the
    transgressors. [Isaiah 53.12]
"and:

Like a lamb led to slaughter,
    Or a sheep silent before shearers
    He did not open his mouth.
Seized and condemned, he was taken away.
Who would have thought any more of his destiny?
"and:
    The Lord of Hosts is his name. [Isaiah 54.5]

"This is the One of Whom Jacob speaks—the very
Jacob whom you proudly claim as your ancestor—
when he blesses his son, Judah; for in addressing
Judah it is as though he is addressing Christ, the Son
of God, in person:

You, Judah, shall your brothers praise
    —your hand on the neck of your enemies;
the sons of your father shall bow down to you.
Judah is a lion's cub,
You have grown up on prey, my son.
He crouches, lies down like a lion,
Like a lioness—who would dare rouse him? . . .
His eyes are darker than wine,
And his teeth are whiter than milk. [Genesis
    49.8–9, 12]

"And even though Christ Himself said, 'No one takes
[My life] from me, but I lay it down on my own,' the
apostle Paul wrote, 'If you confess with your mouth
that Jesus is Lord and believe in your heart that God
raised him from the dead, you will be saved.'"

In spite of all my proofs, this wretched Jew was
unyielding and showed no sign at all of believing me;
instead, he just stood there in silence. King Chilperic
recognized that he would never be made to feel remorse, no matter what we said, and so he turned to
me and said that he had to leave but wanted my blessing first. "Bishop," he said, "I will say to you the words
Jacob said to the angel: 'I will not let you go unless
you bless me.'" [Genesis 32.26] And as he said this he
ordered water to be brought to him. We both washed
our hands, and I said a prayer. Then I took some
bread, gave thanks to God for it, and received it along
with the king. We drank some wine, and wished each
other Farewell as we departed. Chilperic mounted his
horse and set off for Paris, together with his wife,
children, and all the members of his household.[1]

---

[1] Compare the biblical passages as translated by the Jewish
Publication Society, noting first that the book of Baruch
is not accepted in the Jewish canon.
Isaiah 7.14: "Assuredly, my Lord will give you a sign of His
own accord! Look, the young woman is with child and
about to give birth to a son. Let her name him
'Immanuel.'"
Psalm 22.17: "Dogs surround me; a pack of evil ones closes
in on me, like lions [they maul] my hands and feet."
Psalm 69.22: "They give me gall for food, vinegar to quench
my thirst."
Psalm 96.10: "Declare among the nations, 'The Lord is
king!' The world stands firm; it cannot be shaken; He
judges the people with equity."Isaiah 54.5: "For He
who made you will espouse you—His name is 'Lord of
Hosts.' The Holy One of Israel will redeem you—He is
called 'God of all the Earth.'"
Isaiah 53.12: "Whereas he bore the guilt of many and made
intercession for sinners."
Genesis 49.8–9, 12: "You, O Judah, your brothers shall
praise; Your hand shall be on the nape of your foes;
Your father's sons shall bow low to you. Judah is a lion's
whelp; On prey, my son, have you grown. He crouches,
lies down like a lion, Like the king of beasts—who dare
rouse him? . . . His eyes are darker than wine; His teeth
are whiter than milk."

STUDY QUESTIONS

1. Gregory of Tours was an accomplished hagiographer, a person who wrote biographies of
   saints, martyrs, and other holy people. What elements from this excerpt of his life of Clovis
   resemble a hagiography? How does Gregory portray Clovis?
2. In the High and Later Middle Ages, disputations were formal debates between Christian and
   Jewish theologians. Although Gregory's encounter with a Jew in the court of King Chilperic
   occurs centuries before the first recorded disputations, how is it a type of disputation? How is
   the Jew portrayed? Who wins the debate?

8.3. GREGORY THE GREAT, "LIFE OF ST. BENEDICT," 593 CE

As a revered pope and saint, Gregory (540–604) is best known for his reforms of Christian life, from revising the liturgy to his "Rule for Pastors" for improving care of Christians. This selection is taken from Gregory's "Life of St. Benedict," an account of St. Benedict of Nursia (ca. 480–563), Father of Western monasticism and founder of the Benedictine Order. Although St. Benedict's organization of a monastic community was highly practical, Gregory depicts him here predominantly as a miracle-worker and visionary, thus highlighting his mystical side.

---

[1] There once was a man who led a most venerable life, blessed by grace and in name, for he was called Benedict. Even as a youth he possessed the mind of a mature man. He was always younger in years than he was in virtue, and although he lived in the world and had opportunity to enjoy all the delights it has to offer, he always despised vain pleasure. The world's vanities he regarded as worthless nothings. Born to noble parents in the district of Nursia, Benedict was raised in Rome where he had the opportunity to study the human arts, but since he saw so many people, similarly situated, fall into dissolute and base ways, he stepped back from the world he knew. He feared becoming too well acquainted with lewdness, which would end only in a headlong fall into a dangerous and godless existence. Therefore he gave up his studies and renounced his claim to his father's house and wealth, and wanting nothing more than to serve God, he went out in search of a place where he could pursue his longing for a holy purpose in life. He went forth, armed with a simple wisdom that took the place of his learned but ignorant scholarship.

I was unable to unearth all the marvelous things he did in his life, but I did manage to learn any number of things about him (which I know record) from four of his disciples: Constantinus, an exceptional and pious man who succeeded Benedict as abbot; Valentinianus, who was in charge of the Lateran Abbey for many years; Simplicius, the third minister-general of Benedict's order; and Honoratus, who is currently the abbot of the monastery where Benedict began his sanctified life.

[2] One day when Benedict was alone, temptation came to him in the form of a blackbird that flew so closely about his face that, if he could, the holy man might have grabbed it with his hand. Instead, he simply blessed himself by making the sign of the cross—and the bird flew away. He was beset, however, by a terrible bout of temptation of the flesh such as he had never experienced before.

He had once happened to see a particular woman, and the spirit of temptation burned her memory into his mind, and the image of her now inflamed him with lust so powerfully that for a moment the servant of God nearly was overcome with it. The thought of abandoning his wilderness life came upon him, but with God's grace he came to his senses. Seeing a thick patch of briar- and nettle-bushes growing nearby, Benedict threw off his clothing and leapt headlong into them, rolling back and forth so long that by the time he stood up his flesh was covered with the most pitiful lacerations. The wounds to his body cured the wounds to his soul by turning its pleasure into pain, and by the searing hurt to his outer form, he quenched the raging fire of lustful thought within his soul. One fire replaced another, and he overcame his sin.

He would often tell his disciples in later years that this episode so reduced any temptation of the

Translation by Clifford Backman.

flesh in him that he scarcely ever felt it anymore. Many people soon began to abandon the world too, in the hope of becoming one of his disciples—for having freed himself from temptation he turned himself into a man of masterful virtue. In the book of Exodus, recall, Moses commands the Levites that while men may serve as priests from the age of twenty-five, only those aged fifty and above may be ordained as keepers of the holy vessels. [Num 8.24–6]

[11] Another time a group of monks were working on an extension to a certain wall when the Old Enemy [Satan] appeared to Benedict, that man of God, as he was praying in his cell, and jeered at him, saying that he was going to cause trouble with the monks. Benedict's spirit then rushed to the monks' aid, telling them to be careful for the devil was at hand. No sooner had Benedict's voice spoken than the Evil Spirit knocked down the wall on which the monks had been working, and killed a young monk—a boy, really, the son of a certain nobleman. This pitiful occurrence drove everyone into a profound grief, not for the wall but for the death of their little brother. The monks wasted no time in bringing the sad news to Benedict, who quickly ordered them to bring him the lad's body. Being so mangled and maimed, the body had to be delivered in a sack since the stones of the wall had not only broken the boy's limbs but had crushed his very bones.

Benedict had the monks lay the boy on the floor in his cell, on the precise spot where he always knelt when in prayer. Then he sent the monks away, closed his cell door, and fell immediately began to pray. What a marvel then occurred! Within the space of an hour Benedict's prayers had healed the boy, who stood up as lively as ever and returned to his work, helping the monks repair the wall. The Old Serpent had thought he could insult Benedict, but Benedict emerged triumphant.

[38] The cave [at Subiaco] where Benedict first took up his solitary vigil even to this day continues to work miracles, if those who pray there are in need of them. What I am about to tell you happened only recently. A certain woman had so lost the use of reason that she became insane and spent days and night on end walking up and down and back and forth, in mountains, in valleys, through woods and fields, and rested only when she collapsed from exhaustion, wherever that happened to occur. It happened one day that, wandering again at random, she chanced to arrive at Blessed Benedict's cave. Not knowing anything about the site, she entered the cave and spent the night. The following morning she awoke fully healed, her mind and wits as sound as they had ever been, and to the day she died she lived a healthy existence, as though her madness had never happened. . . .

There can be no doubt that the saints perform countless miracles at the spot where they lie buried. . . . Since simple-minded people might doubt whether or not a particular saint is actually present to hear their prayers, he or she works an even greater miracle at the site [than elsewhere] to compensate for the weakness of the visitors' souls. But he whose mind is firmly fixed on God has a stronger faith, and he knows that the saint is there in spirit to hear his prayer even though he may not be there in body. For as Our Savior himself said, "If I do not go, the Advocate will not come to you." [John 16.7]

STUDY QUESTIONS

1. Benedict's renunciation of the world took what specific forms?
2. How does Benedict's goal of a solitary life relate to those of the "desert fathers" of the Church?

8.4. BEDE, *ECCLESIASTICAL HISTORY OF ENGLISH PEOPLE*, COMPLETED CA. 731 CE

The Venerable Bede (ca. 673–735), as he is known, is also called the Father of English History not only because of the wide scope of his account, but also because he applied historical inquiry to his work—interviewing living witnesses to events, interpreting, and moving beyond the hagiographies used by his fellow writers. As the title indicates, Bede is a source for the particular development of the "insular" church—that is, of the British Isles—in contrast with the church of continental Europe. The first portion of this selection recounts the arrival of St. Augustine of Canterbury, who was sent by Pope Gregory the Great to establish an English church and convert the pagan locals; the second portion memorializes Pope Gregory.

[1.25] Encouraged by the kind words of the blessed father Gregory, Augustine and his fellow-servants of Christ resumed their work in God's name and soon arrived in Britain. The most powerful of the kings at that time was Ethelbert of Kent, whose realm extended northward to the river Humber, which marks the boundary of the northern and southern Angles. To the east lay the island of Thanet, which the English reckon as six hundred hides from end to end. A waterway of roughly three furlongs, called the Wantsum, separates Thanet from the mainland and can be crossed at only two places. This is where Augustine and his companions—reported to have numbered forty—landed. Following Pope Gregory's instructions, the missionaries had brought Frankish interpreters with them, and they sent them to Ethelbert to deliver the news that they had come from Rome and that anyone who heard their message would undoubtedly receive the joy of eternal life in the kingdom of heaven with the one, true and living God. Ethelbert listened to what the interpreters had to say, and sent back the message that Augustine and his companions were to stay on the island; the king would provide for them all until he had decided what course of action to take. He was already familiar with Christianity, since his wife Bertha—a member of the Frankish royal house—was a Christian. Indeed, her

family had consented to the marriage only on the condition that she should remain free to hold and practice her faith without any hindrance, and to this end they had assigned a bishop, Liuthard, to accompany her as a spiritual guide.

Several days later King Ethelbert came to Thanet and summoned Augustine and his companions to an open-air audience. He was careful not to meet them inside any house, for he maintained the ancient English superstition about practicers of magic, that they work their spells of deception and control best when indoors. The monks, though, were empowered by God, not the Devil, and they duly approached Ethelbert while carrying a silver cross as a standard and a wooden placard on which they had painted a likeness of Our Lord and Savior. They began by singing a litany for their own eternal salvation and for those on whose account they had come this far. The king then commanded them to sit and bade them to preach the "Word of Life" to him and his court. When they had done so, Ethelbert replied, "Fair words and fair promises. But their content is new to us, and seems doubtful. I cannot accept them, if that means abandoning the ancient beliefs by which I and the whole English nation have lived. But you have travelled far, and I can see the honest sincerity of your desire to share with us what you find to be true and worthy. We

Translation by Clifford Backman.

will not harm you, but instead extend our hospitality to you. We do not forbid you to preach to our people and to convert however many you can; in fact, we will provide you with all the supplies you need."

The king awarded them a residence in the city of Canterbury, which was his capital, and remained true to his word, granting the missionaries full provisions and not restricting their freedom to preach. According to tradition, the monks approached the city while carrying aloft the holy cross and the painted likeness of Our Lord and King Jesus Christ, and, as was their custom, singing aloud, "We pray to you, O Lord, in all your mercy, that although we are all sinners, you turn your wrath away from this city and from your holy house. Amen."

[1.26] As soon as they had settled into the house given them by the king, the missionaries started to emulate the life of the apostles and the early Church: constant prayer; fasting and keeping vigils; and preaching the Word of Life to any who would listen. Material things meant little to them, and they would accept gifts of food and other necessities only from those to whom they preached. They gladly endured any hardship, even death, for the sake of the truth they proclaimed, and as a consequence, after a brief time, a number of the heathens, who admired the simplicity of their holy lives and the promise of their heavenly message, converted and were baptized. On the eastern side of the city there stood an old church consecrated to Saint Martin that had been built during Roman times; this was where the Christian queen mentioned above came to pray. The missionaries and their converts congregated there to sing psalms, pray, celebrate Mass, preach, and baptize, until King Ethelbert's own conversion gave them even more freedom to preach and to build or restore churches throughout the realm.

Eventually the king and others [in his court], guided by the holy example of the missionaries' lives and moved by their promises of salvation (the truth of which was confirmed by many miracles that they performed), also converted and were baptized. From that point on, large crowds gathered daily to hear God's Holy Word, and they too abandoned their pagan rites and entered the unity of Christ's Holy Church as full-fledged believers. Ethelbert was pleased by their conversions and faithfulness, but he

still refused to compel anyone to accept Christianity, for he had learned well from his teachers and spiritual guides that service to Christ must be freely undertaken and never the result of force. Before long he gave his teachers at Canterbury another residence, one appropriate to their station, and a variety of landholdings to provide for their needs.

[2.1] Gregory was born a Roman, the son of Gordian and a descendant of many noble and devout ancestors, among whom was Felix, the former bishop of that see [of Rome] and a man of great distinction in Christ's Church, and Gregory dutifully maintained the family tradition by the nobility and devotion of his own religious life. With God's help he took his natural gifts for worldly success and dedicated them entirely to attaining heavenly glory—for he withdrew from secular life and sought admission to monastic life. There he lived a life of such perfection in grace that in later years he would weep at the memory of how firmly his mind was then set on high things, soaring above everything transient, and how completely he dedicated himself to thoughts of heaven. It was as though, while rooted in his body, he could transcend its bounds in contemplation. He even looked forward to death—something most men regard as a punishment—as the entry to a new life and the reward for all his labors. Whenever he mentioned this, he did so not to call attention to his superior virtue then, but to lament what he regarded as the decline in his virtue as a result of his pastoral work. Once, conversing intimately with his deacon Peter about his earlier life in the spirit, Gregory said sadly, "Pastoral work requires me to deal with worldly men. And compared to the cloudless beauty of my former life, my spirit now feels polluted with the muck and mire of worldly affairs. After being wasted in attending to the mundane matters of countless people, my soul tries to meditate on purely spiritual matters, but can't help but do so with diminished energy. Comparing what I have to put up with now, with what I have lost, I can't help feeling that the burden is great—greater than ever. . . ."

From the day he was called from his monastic life, was ordained to priestly life, and was sent to Constantinople as the representative of the Holy See, Gregory never gave up his spiritual exercises, even amid the maelstrom of earthly politics. Some of his fellow monks had accompanied him to the imperial city, out of devotion to him, and he always maintained a regular religious observance with them. This served as an anchor for him, holding him fast to the peaceful shore of prayer-life even while his daily life tossed on the endless waves of worldly affairs; studying with them always refreshed his mind after it was worn down by mundane things. . . .

Here I must stop to tell a story handed down by our forebears that explains the origins of Gregory's deep desire for the salvation of our [English] nation. The story goes, that one day some merchants, recently arrived in Rome, put their goods on display in the market-square when Gregory happened to be among the crowd who gathered around. His eye fell upon some boy-slaves who were for sale—fair-skinned, fine-cut features, and with beautiful hair. Intrigued by them, he asked where in the world they had come from.

"They are from Britain," he was told; "everyone there looks like this."

He asked next if the Britons were Christians or still ignorant heathens.

"They are pagans," came the answer.

"Oh, how sad!" Gregory sighed, "How sad that such bright-faced people are still in the clutches of the Author of Darkness, and that such graceful features conceal minds ignorant of God's grace! Tell me, what is the name of these people?"

"They're called 'Angles,'" someone said.

"The name suits them," Gregory replied, "for their faces are angelic. It would be a good thing if they shared in the inheritance of the angels in heaven. Tell me, what is the name of the province they come from?"

"Deira," came the answer.

"That's good," said Gregory. "They will one day be rescued from the wrath [*de ira*] of God and called to the mercy of Christ. And what is the name of their king?"

"Aelle," he was told.

To which Gregory replied one last time, making a play on the king's name, "Then it is fitting that their land shall one day echo with the praise of God, our Creator, with the 'Alleluia.'"

STUDY QUESTIONS

1. Why does the king endorse the Christian mission in his territories, even before he himself converts?
2. How are the needs of the spirit and the body contrasted throughout Gregory's life?

8.5. DHUODA, *HANDBOOK FOR WILLIAM*, 841/843 CE

A strikingly rare example of a well-versed female author in the Carolingian period, the noblewoman Dhuoda (ca. 803–ca. 843) recorded a list of courtly guidelines for her son William, who was retained as a hostage by King Charles the Bald to ensure the loyalty of Dhuoda's husband. In a world of belligerent conflict between the heirs of Charlemagne, Dhuoda, right before her death, instructs William in how to become a loyal vassal, a useful member of court, and, above all, a good Christian. In the genre of a "mirror" or "handbook," this work expresses a mother's sense of loss blended with pride and hope for her distant son.

Translation by Clifford Backman.

In the name of the Holy Trinity, here begins the hand-book which Dhuoda, his mother, sent to her son William.

I know very well how most women rejoice to be with their children in this world, but I, Dhuoda, live far away from you, William, am anxious and want to do something special for you—so I am sending you with little book of mine, written down [by a scribe] in my name. Read it and learn from it, keeping it as a mirror, so to speak. I rejoice in the hope that it may remind you, when you are reading it, of how you should behave—for my sake.

[Pr 1.1] For we humans, attaining perfection requires great and persistent effort. We combat evil things by applying the medicines that counteract them. We must struggle not only against worldly people who burn in the maw of Envy but also, as the Apostle [Paul] says, we must combat "the evil spirits in the heavens." [Eph 6.12] Why? Because there are people who, despite their worldly success and material wealth and out of some secret malice, still are jealous of others and plot against them as much as they can, even while feigning friendship.

[Pr 1.4] You have many books at hand—and you will receive more—in which to read and excite your curiosity, to ponder and scrutinize, and to contemplate; you also have (and will receive more) learned men who can teach you and by whose example you can most easily learn how to behave in both aspects of your life. Consider how it is with doves—who keep watch for herons and falcons, their predators, even when drinking clear-flowing waters, lest they be captured—they fly away, laughing, and escape to wherever their pleasure takes them. You will do likewise if you, in your reading, look to the words of the orthodox saints and those Fathers who went before us, and if you observe how the greatest magnates and court figures faithfully obey the commands of God and their earthly lords. Follow their examples, if you can, and you will not only avoid the hidden snares set by those of evil spirit, but you will also elude the clutches of those who are your open enemies. Then you will increase in spiritual and physical strength and, with Christ's help, succeed. Read and consider closely what is written in Solomon's book, "I will now praise the godly, our ancestors, in their own time." [Sira 44.1]

[Pr 1.5] Although we are merely unimportant exiles who do not number among the great magnates, yet we bear within ourselves the faults of this world and are thus always pulled downward rather than lifted up toward heaven. But according to the warning given in the Old Testament, we ought to bear the names of the twelve patriarchs on our foreheads, just as the Holy Scripture commands us, according to the vision granted to Ezechiel, to take as our examples the creatures with six wings and eyes in both the front and the back of their heads. And so I offer this to you as a guiding principle: detest the wicked, flee from the immoral, the sluggish, and the proud; and in all that you do, avoid those who are sick in their souls. Why? Because they lay snares, like mousetraps, to deceive people. They never give up paving the way to scandal and wickedness—even if they themselves tumble in order to bring others down with them. This has happened in the past; I exhort you to avoid it in the present and future. May God permit that your fate be in no way joined to theirs.

[Pr 1.6] Inquire into, hold close, and observe faithfully the examples of those men of great worth in the past, present, and future who have proven their faithfulness to God and have persevered in this world. That is the meaning of the Scripture verse that commands us to holds the written names of the twelve patriarchs in our hands and to wear them on our foreheads, and to keep our eyes looking both forward and behind. These are virtues! When these twelve men were in this world they were constantly aiming toward heaven, growing and flourishing toward God. Wise in faith and soul, theirs was a happy path as they set themselves to worthy ends in thought and deed, and they left behind for us an example, so that in seeking that same path, we may do as they did. . . .

[Pr 6.1] If by chance your heart suffers harm, perhaps at the instigation of the devil, by the temptation to fornicate, or any other goading of the flesh, resist it with chastity, and keep in mind the purity of the blessed patriarch Joseph, and of Daniel, and of those others who maintained the purity of their bodies and souls by faith as regarded their masters and neighbors. They deserved to be saved and given high honor, and to be gathered up by the Lord among the number of His saints. For as the Apostle says, "God will judge the immoral and adulterers;" [Heb 13.4] and the Psalmist relates that those who fornicate will perish far from you. And the Apostle likewise says, among other things, "Every other sin a person commits is outside the body, but the immoral person sins against his own body." [1 Cor 6.18]

[Pr 6.2] Therefore, son, avoid fornication and keep your mind turned away from prostitutes. It is written, "Do not let your passions be your guide, but keep your desires in check." [Sira 18.30] Do not let your soul fly away in pursuit of evil desires. For if you do risk giving in to one of these ills, then certainly they will make you fall upon your sword or into the hands of your enemies. They will say with the prophet [Isaiah], "Bow down, that we may walk over you." [Isa 51.23] May this never happen to you! . . . By seeking God's help, you may escape the thrill of such embraces and such tempestuous turmoil. It is indeed the eyes in your head that ignite the flesh to carnal desire, yet the struggle against these evils is an interior one. . . ." Death has come up through our windows," [Jer 9.20] and "Everyone who looks at a woman with lust has already committed adultery with her in his heart." [Matt 5.28]

[Pr 6.3] But for those who maintain continence and suppress all carnal desires, you will find it written, "The lamp of the body is the eye. If your eye is sound, your whole body will be filled with light." [Matt 6.22] . . . Learned teachers do not deny sanctified marriage to the union of flesh, but they do strive to root out filthy and wrongful fornication. Enoch was chaste, along with Noah, Abraham, Isaac, Jacob, Joseph, and Moses, and all those others who struggled to keep their hearts pure in Christ through the institution of marriage. What more can I say?

[Pr 6.4] And so, my son, whether you keep your body in the splendid gift of virginity, or in the chastity of the marriage-union, you will be free from starting this great sin. Your mind will rest secure and be in that peace that comes through the eight beatitudes. And there will be fulfilled in you, along with other worthies, as it is written, the worthy praise offered by many: "Blessed are the clean of heart, for they will see God." [Matt 5.8]

STUDY QUESTIONS

1. Why does Dhuoda see sexuality as a particular temptation to young men?
2. What is suggested by Dhuoda's frequent allusions to the Bible in her arguments?

8.6. FROM TROTULA, 13TH CENTURY CE

Originally associated with a female physician named Trotula of Salerno (11th–12th century), this compendium of medical care for women deals with infertility, childbirth, and birth control methods, as well as cosmetics, beautification techniques, and dietary advice. These selections pinpoint a handful of concerns that medieval women had, from family planning to aesthetics.

Translation by Clifford Backman.

Here begins the *Book on the Maladies of Women* according to Trotula.

When God, the Creator of the universe, first established the world, He distinguished between the individual natures of things—each according to its kind—and He endowed human nature with a single dignity above all other things: He gave humans freedom of reason and intellect. This gift set mankind above the condition of all animals. And God, in wanting to sustain human generation in perpetuity, carefully and providentially created males and females, thus establishing the foundation for the production of offspring. And He created them in such a way, to ensure the arrival of fertile offspring, that their natures formed a pleasing interlocking mixture; for the males He constitutes a hot and dry nature, to which He opposed the cool and wet nature of the females. Thus, should a man overflow with an excess of one of his qualities, the woman could contain it. In this way the stronger qualities of heat and dryness dominate the man, who is the stronger and more worthy of the sexes, while the weaker qualities of coolness and wetness dominate the woman, who is the weaker and less worthy sex. God did this so that the male, in his strength, might pour out his essence into the woman just as seed is sown in a field, and that the female, in her weakness a natural subject to the man, might receive the seed provided by Nature.

But because women are weaker than men and frequently experience childbirth, maladies often abound in them, especially in the organs dedicated to Nature's work; and whether because of their fragile nature, shame, or embarrassment, they seldom reveal their sufferings and illnesses (which occur in such a private area) to any physician. Their general misfortune is pitiable, and this fact, together with the prompting of a certain specific woman stirring my heart, has led me to give clear explanations about their maladies and how to restore them to health. With God's help I have worked diligently to collect passages from the better parts of the works of Galen and Hippocrates, to the end that I might discuss and explain the causes, symptoms, and cures of women's diseases.

[74] Some women are incapable of conception, either because they are too skinny and lean, or because they are too fat and the flesh of the womb-orifice shuts out the man's seed and does not let it enter. Other women's wombs are smooth and slick, which means that the man's seed, once received, cannot be kept inside. This also happens sometimes because the man's seed is too watery; once it enters the womb, its excessive fluidity causes it to flow outside. Some men, too, have very cold and dry testicles, and they rarely generate, if ever, because their seed is incapable of the task.

[75] Treatment. If a woman is barren either on account of her own difficulty or her man's, let the following treatment be attempted. Take two pots and place some wheat bran in each one; add some of the man's urine to one of the pots, and add some of the woman's urine to the other. Let the pots sit for nine or ten days. If the barrenness is the woman's fault, you will find many worms in her pot and the bran will stink; you will find the same thing in the man's pot if the barrenness is his fault. If you find this in neither of the pots, then neither of them is at fault and they should be able to conceive if aided by certain medicines.

[83] If a woman chooses not to conceive, she should wear against her naked flesh the uterus of a goat that has never had offspring.

[86] Another method would be to take a weasel and remove its testicles without killing it. The woman should then wrap them in the skin of a goose or of some other animal, and wear them against her naked bosom. Then she will not conceive.

[87] If a woman has previously been badly torn in childbirth and fears ever getting pregnant again, she should put into her afterbirth as many grains of barley or spurge as the number of years she wishes to remain barren. If she wishes to remain barren forever, she should put in a whole handful.

[126] A wet nurse should be young and have good coloring—a woman who mixes a little red with white, who is neither too close to, nor too far removed from, her last birth, who is unblemished, whose breasts are not too flabby nor too swollen but who has a healthy, ample chest, and who is moderately fat.

[127] Diet. A wet nurse should avoid eating salty, spicy, and acidic foods, and anything in which the heat is strong; also astringent foods like leeks and

onions; and any of those spices that are added to give food more flavor, such as pepper, garlic, or rocket—but especially garlic. She should avoid stress and be careful not to induce her menses. If her milk runs low, she should eat porridge made of bean-flour or rice; she should also have wheat bread mixed with milk, sugar, and perhaps some fennel—for these things increase the milk supply. If her milk becomes too thick, let her nourishment be cut back, and compel her to work. One could also give her a vinegary syrup or light wine. If her milk becomes too thin, on the other hand, her foods should be thick and strong, and she should get extra sleep. If the child's bowels are loose, the wet nurse should eat whatever makes her constipated.

[245] There is an ointment used by noble women that removes hairs, refines the skin, and removes blemishes. Take the juice from the moist leaves of a cucumber and mix them with almond milk in a bowl. Add quicklime and orpiment; then add some gum resin that has been beaten together with a little wine. Let the mixture rest for a day and a night. Then cook. Once it has been well cooked, remove the gum resin and add a little oil or wine, plus some quicksilver. Remove the concoction from the heat, and add a powder made of the following herbs: mastic, frankincense, cinnamon, nutmeg, and clove, all in equal amounts. The ointment thus produced has a sweet smell and gently softens the skin. Noblewomen in Salerno regularly use this as a depilatory.

[246] Once a woman has rubbed herself all over with this ointment, she should sit in very hot steam—but she should not further massage her skin or else it will become chapped. Once in the steam, she should simply pull out her pubic hairs. If they do not come out easily, she should pour hot water over herself and wash herself thoroughly, though drawing her hand gently over her skin. If she scrubs too vigorously when her skin is tender, she will be quickly excoriated by the ointment. Having done all this, let her enter a lukewarm bath and be washed well. She should then exit the bath, take a paste made of bran and hot water, strained, and pour it over her body, for this cleanses and smoothes the skin. Then she should wash again in warm water, and stand to let her skin dry a little. Then she should take a mixture of henna and egg whites, and rub this all over her body. This too smoothes the flesh, and removes any inflammation that may have resulted from the depilatory. Let her remain thus anointed for a while, then rinse herself with warm water, wrap herself in a very white linen cloth, and go to bed.

[250] If a woman desires long black hair, she should take a green lizard, remove its head and tail, and cook it in regular cooking oil. Then rub the oil into her hair. It will make the hair long and black.

[251] A method acquired from the Saracens. Take the rind of an extremely sweet pomegranate and grind it, then boil it in vinegar or water, and strain it. Add to the residue a large amount of powder made from apples or alum, until it reaches the texture of a poultice. Wrap this, like dough, around the entire head. Afterward, mix some bran with oil in a pot and heat it until the bran is burnt. Then sprinkle the bran-ash on the head. She should then wet her hair thoroughly, then wrap her head a second time in the method described. Leave it on overnight, for best results. Then wash the hair, and it will be completely black.

STUDY QUESTIONS

1. How are male and female bodies distinguished in "scientific" terms, especially in respect to degree of heat and moisture?
2. Was it dangerous for Trotula to include information drawn from "pagan" and Muslim sources (and perhaps from direct observation by women such as midwives)?

CHAPTER 9

THE EXPANSIVE REALM OF ISLAM

9.1. EXCERPTS FROM THE QUR'AN, 7TH CENTURY CE

The Holy Qur'an was revealed to Prophet Muhammad over the course of twenty-two years, from 610 to 632. The *surat* ("chapter") that follows came early, while Muhammad was still living in Mecca. It describes the ranks of the good and the evil, from the angels in heaven to the earthly prophets (and those who rejected them). It is interesting to compare these verses with the corresponding passages in the Hebrew Bible. Note, for instance, that here Abraham offers his son Ismail (born of his servant-woman Hagar), rather than Isaac (born of his wife Sarah), as a sacrifice to God. Words and phrases in square brackets are added to complete the sense of the sentence and do not appear in the Arabic.

SURAT 37. AS-SAFFAT: THOSE RANGED IN RANKS

In the name of Allah, Most Gracious, Most Merciful.

[VV. 1—21]

> By those who range themselves in ranks,
> those who so are strong in repelling [evil],
> those who thus proclaim the Message [of Allah]!
> Verily, verily, your God is One!
> Lord of the heavens and of the earth,
> and all between them, and Lord of every point at
>   the rising of the sun!
> We have indeed decked the lower heaven with
>   beauty
> [in] the stars,—
> [for beauty] and for guard against all obstinate
>   rebellious Satans.

> [So] they should not listen their ears in the
>   direction
> of the Exalted Assembly and they are cast away
>   from every side,
> repulsed. And for them is a perpetual
>   chastisement,
> except such as snatch away something by stealth,
>   and they
> are pursued by a flaming fire, of piercing
>   brightness.
> Just ask their opinion: Are they the more difficult
> To create, or the [other] beings We have created?
> Them have We created out of a sticky clay!
> Truly dost thou marvel while they ridicule,
> And when they are admonished, pay no heed,—
> And, when they see a Sign, turn it to mockery,
> And say, "This is nothing but evident sorcery!
> What! When we die, and become dust and bones,

Shall we [then] be raised up [again]?
And also our fathers of old?"
Say thou: "Yea, and ye shall then be humiliated
[on account of your evil],
then it will be a single [compelling] cry;
and behold, they will begin to see!
They will say, 'Ah! Woe to us! This is the Day of
    Judgment!'
[A voice will say,] 'This is the Day
of sorting out, whose truth ye [once] denied!'"

[VV. 22–74]

"Bring ye up," it shall be said, "the wrong-doers
and their wives, and the things they worshipped—
besides Allah, and lead them to the Way, to the
    [Fierce] Fire!
But stop them, for they must be asked:
'What is the matter with you, that ye help not
    each other?'"
Nay, but that day they shall submit [to Judgment],
And they will turn to one another,
And question one another.
They will say: "It was ye who used to come to us
From the right hand."
They will reply: "Nay, ye yourselves had no faith!
Nor had we any authority over you. Nay, it was
ye who were a people in obstinate rebellion!"
"So now has been proved true, against us, the
    Word
of our Lord that we shall indeed [have to] taste
[the punishment for our sins]:
We led you astray: for truly we were ourselves
    astray."
Truly, that Day, they will [all] share in the
    Chastisement.
Verily, that is how We shall deal with Sinners.
For they, when they were told that there is
no god except Allah, would puff themselves up
    with Pride,
and say: "What! Shall we give up our gods
For the sake of a Poet possessed?"
Nay! He has come with the [very] Truth,
And he confirms [the Message of] the messengers
    [before him].
Ye shall indeed taste of the Grievous
    Chastisement;—

And you are requited naught save what ye did.
But the chosen servants of Allah,—
For them is a Sustenance determined,
Fruits; and they [shall enjoy] honour and dignity,
In Gardens of delight.
Facing each other on raised couches,
Round will be passed to them a Cup
From a clear-flowing fountain,
Crystal-white, of a taste
Delicious to those who drink [thereof],
Free from headiness;
Nor will they suffer intoxication therefrom.
And besides them will be chaste women;
    restraining
Their glances, with big eyes [of wonder and
    beauty].
As if they were [delicate] eggs closely guarded.
Then they will turn to one another and question
    one another.
One of them will say:
"I had an intimate companion [on the earth],
who used to say, 'Do you really believe?
When we die and become dust and bones, shall
    we
Indeed receive rewards and punishments?'"
He said: "Would you like to look down?"
He looked down and saw him in the midst of the
    Fire.
He said: "By Allah! Thou wast little short
Of bringing me to perdition!
Had it not been for the Grace of my Lord,
I should certainly have been among those
    brought [there]!
Is it [the case] that we shall not die,
Except our first death, and that we shall not be
    punished?"
Verily this is the supreme triumph,
For the like of this let all strive, who wish to strive.
Is that the better entertainment or the Tree of
    Zaqqum?
For We have truly made it [as] a trial
For the wrong-doers.
For it is a tree that springs out of the bottom of
    Hell-fire:
The shoots of its fruit-stalks
Are like the heads of devils:

Truly they will eat thereof and fill their bellies
    therewith.
Then on top of that they will be given
A mixture made of boiling water.
Then shall their return be to the [Blazing] Fire.
Truly they found their fathers on the wrong Path;
So they [too] were rushed down on their
    footsteps!
And truly before them, many of the ancients went
    astray;—
But We sent aforetime among them, warners.
Then see what was the End of those who were
    warned
Except the chosen servants of Allah.

[VV. 75–113]

[In the days of old] Noah cried to Us,
and We are the Best to hear prayer.
And We delivered him and his people from the
    great Calamity,
and made his progeny to endure [on this earth];
and we left [this blessing] for him among
    generations
to come in later times:
"Peace and salutation to Noah among the
    nations!"
Thus indeed do We reward those who do right.
For he was one of Our believing Servants.
Then the rest We overwhelmed in the Flood.
Verily from his party was Abraham.
Behold, he approached his Lord with a sound heart.
Behold, he said to his father and to his people,
    "What
is that which ye worship?
Is it a Falsehood—gods other than Allah that ye
    desire?
Then what is your idea about the Lord of the
    Worlds?"
Then did he cast a glance at the Stars,
and he said: "I am indeed sick [at heart]!"
So they turned away from him, and departed.
Then did he turn to their gods and said,
"Will ye not eat [of the offerings before you]?
What is the matter with you that ye speak not?"
Then did he turn upon them, striking [them] with
    the right hand.

Then came [the worshippers] with hurried steps
    to him.
He said: "Worship ye that which ye have
    [yourselves] carved?
But Allah has created you and your handiwork!"
They said: "Build him a furnace, and throw him
    into the blazing fire!"
[This failing], they then plotted against him,
but We made them the ones most humiliated!
He said: "I will go to my Lord! He will surely
    guide me!
O my Lord! Grant me a righteous [son]!"
So We gave him the good news of a forbearing son.
Then, when [the son] reached [the age of
serious] work with him, he said: "O my son!
I have seen in a dream that I offer thee in sacrifice.
Now I see what is thy view!" The son said:
"O my father! Do as thou art commanded:
Thou will find me, if Allah so wills one of the
    steadfast."
So when they had both submitted [to Allah],
and he had laid him prostrate on his forehead
    [for sacrifice],
We called out to him, "O Abraham!
Thou hast already fulfilled the dream!"—thus
    indeed
do We reward those who do right.
For this was a clear trial—
and We ransomed him with a monstrous sacrifice:
And We left for him among generations [to come]
    in later times:
"Peace and salutation to Abraham!"
This indeed do We reward those who do right
for he was one of Our believing Servants.
And We gave him the good news
of Isaac—a prophet—one of the Righteous.
We blessed him and Isaac: but of their progeny
are [some] that do right, and [some] that
    obviously
do wrong, to themselves.

[VV. 114–138]

Again, [of old] We bestowed Our favour on Moses
    and Aaron,
and We delivered them and their people from
    [their] Great distress,

and We helped them, so they were victorious;

and We gave them the Book which helps to make
    things clear;

and We guided them to the Straight Way.

And We left for them among generations [to
    come] in later times:

"Peace and salutation to Moses and Aaron!"

Thus indeed do We reward those who do right.

For they were two of Our believing Servants.

So also was Elias among those sent [by Us].

Behold, he said to his people,

"Will ye not fear [Allah]? Will ye call upon Baal

and forsake the Best of Creators,—

Allah, your Lord and Cherisher,

and the Lord and Cherisher of your fathers of old?"

But they rejected him, and they will certainly

be called up [for punishment],

except the chosen Servants of Allah [among
    them].

And We left for him among generations
[to come] in later times:

"Peace and salutation to such as Elias!"

Thus indeed do We reward those who do right.

For he was one of Our believing Servants.

So also was Lüt among those sent [by Us].

Behold, We delivered him and his adherents, all

except an old woman who was among those who
    lagged behind:

Then We destroyed the rest.

Verily, ye pass by their [sites] by day—

and by night: Will ye not understand?

[VV. 139–182]

So also was Jonah among those sent [by Us].

When he ran away [like a slave from captivity]
to the ship [fully] laden,

he [agreed to] cast lots, and he was of the
    rebutted:

Then the big Fish did swallow him,

and when he had done acts worthy of blame.

Had it not been that he [repented and] glorified
    Allah,

he would certainly have remained inside the Fish
till the Day of Resurrection.

But We cast him forth on the naked shore in a
    state of sickness,

and We caused to grow, over him, a spreading
    plant
of the Gourd kind.

And We sent him [on a mission]
to a hundred thousand [men] or more.

And they believed; so We permitted them
to enjoy [their life] for a while.

Now ask them their opinion: Is it that thy Lord
has [only] daughters, and they have sons?—

Or that We created the angels female, and they
are witnesses [thereto]?

Behold, they say, out of their own invention,

"Allah has begotten children"? But they are liars!

Did He [then] choose daughters rather than sons?

What is the matter with you? How judge ye?

Will ye not then receive admonition?

Or have ye an authority manifest?

Then bring ye your Book [of authority] if ye be
    Truthful!

And they have invented a kinship

between Him and the Jinns: But the Jinns know

[quite well] that they will be brought before Him.

Glory to Allah! [He is free] from the things they
    ascribe [to Him]!

Not [so do] the Servants of Allah, the chosen
    ones.

For, verily, neither ye nor those ye worship

can lead [any] into temptation concerning Allah,

except such as are [themselves] going to the
    blazing Fire!

[The angels] "Not one of us but has a place
    appointed;

And we are verily ranged in ranks [for service],

and we are verily those who declare [Allah's]
    glory!"

And there were those who said,

"If only we had had before us a Message
from those of old,

we should certainly have been Servants of Allah,
sincere [and devoted]!"

But [now that the Qur'an has come], they reject it:
But soon will they know!

Already has Our Word been passed before [this]
to Our Servants sent [by Us],

that they would certainly be assisted,

and that Our forces,—they surely must conquer.

So turn thou away from them for a little while, and watch them [how they fare], and they soon shall see [how thou farest]! Do they wish [indeed] to hurry on our Punishment? But when it descends upon their courtyards before them, Evil will be the morning for those who were warned [and heeded not]!	So turn thou away from them for a little while, and watch [how they fare] and they shall soon see [how thou farest]! Glory to thy Lord, the Lord of Honour and Power! [He is free] from what they ascribe [to Him]! And Peace on the messengers! And Praise to Allah, the Lord and Cherisher of the Worlds.

STUDY QUESTIONS

1. How do these verses from the Qur'an compare with corresponding passages in the Hebrew Bible?
2. Culturally, what is the significance of the Qur'an's depiction of Abraham offering his son Ishmail as a sacrifice rather than Isaac? How would this important difference shape Arab and Muslim identity?

9.2. IBN ISHAQ, *THE LIFE OF MUHAMMAD*

Ibn Ishaq (704–770) is one of the earliest of the Prophet's biographers. The original text of his biography does not survive; it was edited, separately, by two of his pupils, and only one of those recensions (made by Ibn Hisham) survives. Below are two passages—one depicting the famous "night journey" of the Prophet's spirit to Jerusalem and its vision of paradise, and the other a narrative of the fate of the Jewish community at Medina, the Banu Qurayza. Some scholars reject this (long) section of Ibn Ishaq's work, arguing that it cannot be trusted since it derives only from the recollections of Jewish converts to Islam.

THE NIGHT JOURNEY

I have heard the traditions that were passed on by Abdullah b. Mas'ud, Abu Sa'id al-Khudri, the Prophet's wife Aisha, Mu'awiya b. Abu Sufyan, al-Hasan b. Abu'l-Hasan al-Basri, Ibn Shihab al-Zuhri, Qatada, and Umm Hani d. Abu Talib. Each person passed on what he or she was told about what happened when the Prophet went on his Night Journey, and I have

placed their information together in what follows. The question of the *masra* of the Journey, and the details surrounding it, is so complicated that only the power and authority of Allah Himself can understand it—a lesson for us all who would learn, and a blessing and mercy for all who believe. But surely it was by the will of Allah that He took the Prophet by night and showed him all that He wished him to see, proving to

---

Translation by Clifford Backman.

the Prophet the mighty authority and power by which Allah accomplishes whatever He wants.

The traditions I have heard assert that Abdullah b. Mas'd reported that al-Buraq—the winged animal whose stride reached as far as a man can see, and on whom all earlier prophets rode—was brought to Muhammad, who mounted it. The Prophet's Companion [Gabriel] flew with him, and together they saw all the wonders of heaven and earth before landing, at last, at the temple in Jerusalem. There they saw the friends of God—Abraham, Moses, and Jesus—standing with a group of prophets. The Apostle prayed with them, after which someone brought him three jars, one of milk, one of wine, one of water. The Apostle [later] said, "When these jars were brought forward I heard a voice, saying 'If he chooses the water, he and his people will drown; if he chooses the wine, he and his people will lose their way; but if he chooses the milk, he and his people will be rightly guided.' I chose the one with milk, and drank it, and then Gabriel said to me, 'You and your people will be rightly guided, O Muhammad.'"

* * * * *

A member of Abu Bakr's family told me that the Prophet's wife Aisha used to say, "The Apostle remained with me, but Allah took his spirit, that night."

Ya'qub b. Utba b. al-Mughira b. al-Akhnas reported to me what Mu'awiya b. Abu Sufyan replied, when someone asked him about the Night Journey of the Prophet: "It was truly a vision from Allah." This report does not disagree with the report of al-Hasan, since it was Allah Himself who said, "I have shown you this vision as a test for mankind." Neither does it disagree with Allah's word in the story of Abraham and his son, when Abraham said, "O son! I have seen in a dream that I am to make a sacrifice of you," and then acted upon it. In my opinion, Allah's revelation comes to His prophets whether they are awake or asleep.

I have heard, too, that the Apostle used to say, "My eyes may sleep, but my heart stays awake." Allah alone knows the truth of revelation, and how it was that Muhammad saw his vision. Asleep or awake, it all truly happened.

Now al-Zuhri claimed to have heard from Sa'id b. al-Musayyab that the Prophet once described Abraham, Moses, and Jesus to some of his companions, in talking about that night, and supposedly said, "I never saw a man who resembled me as much as Abraham did. Moses had a red face, was tall and thin, had curly hair and a hooked nose, like a member of the Shanu'a tribe. Jesus, the son of Mary, was of medium height, and he also had ruddy skin, but he had many freckles on his face and had long straight hair, like one who has just emerged from a bath. It is possible that his hair was dripping with water, but there was no water visible on it. The one among you who looks most like Jesus is Urwa b. Mas'ud al-Thaqafi."

* * * * *

One in whom I trust reported to me, on the authority of Abu Sa'id al-Khudri: "I once heard Allah's Apostle say, 'When I was finished in Jerusalem, a ladder appeared before me—the finest I have ever seen. It was the ladder that all men see, when Death approaches them. My companion [Gabriel] climbed it with me. When we reached the Gate of the Watchers we beheld an angel, Isma'il, who was its guard. He had twelve thousand angels under his authority, each one of whom had another twelve thousand under its command.' Whenever the Apostle told this story, he always added, *No one but Allah knows the strength of His army.* [Sura 74.31] When Gabriel brought me forward, Isma'il asked me who I was, and when I told him that I was Muhammad he asked me if I had been entrusted with a mission. When I replied that I had, he wished me well."

Another witness, one who heard it from someone who had heard it directly from Allah's Apostle, reported that Muhammad said: "When I entered the lowest heaven, all the angels smiled and welcomed me, and they all wished me well—except for one. This one spoke along with the others but he did not smile or show any joy. I asked Gabriel the reason for that one's behavior, and he answered that [that angel] has never smiled and never will—but if by chance he ever were to smile, he would smile at me; and the reason he never smiles is because he is Malik, the Keeper of Hell. I said to Gabriel . . . 'Would you tell him to show me Hell?' 'Certainly,' answered Gabriel, adding, 'O Malik, show Muhammad Hell.' Then Malik raised the lid that covers Hell. Flames shot so high into the sky that I feared they would devour everything, and so I begged Gabriel to order Malik to send the flames back to where they had come from—which he did. The feeling of [the flames'] return to Hell was like the descent of a shadow. Once the flames were back in place, Malik replaced the lid."

Abu Sa'id al-Khudri relates that the Apostle said: "When I entered the lowest heaven I saw a man sitting in judgment of the spirits who passed before him. To some he would say, 'A good soul in a good body!' while to others he would frown and say, 'An evil spirit in an evil body!' I asked Gabriel who this was, and he replied that it was our ancestor Adam, reviewing all the souls of his descendants. The souls of all believers gave him great delight, but the souls of unbelievers filled him with disgust, as I described.

"Then I saw some men with distended lips, like those of a camel; they held in their hands flaming coals. They would thrust these down their throats, and the burning coals would then emerge from their anus. Gabriel told me these were the damned who [in life] had stolen and consumed the wealth belonging to orphans.

"Then I saw some other men, suffering like the family of Pharaoh. They had enormous bellies, so large that they trampled over their own stomachs like a herd of camels maddened by thirst. Having been cast into Hell, they constantly tramped themselves ever deeper, unable to get out of their own way. These were those guilty of usury.

"Then I saw sitting men sitting at a table, with piles of good fat meat in from of them, but also piles of stringy, stinking meat. They were eating only the rancid meat. These were the damned who forsook the women whom Allah had permitted to them [i.e., their wives] and pursued only the women denied them [i.e., mistresses].

"Then I saw women hanging from their breasts. These were the women who had given their husbands bastard children."

I heard from Ja'far b. 'Amr, who heard it from al-Qasim b. Muhammad, that the Apostle said: "Allah's wrath is great against any woman who brings a bastard into her family. Bastards deprive legitimate sons of their inheritance-portion, and learn private things they have no right to know."

As related by Sa'id al-Khudri, "the Messenger of God said: 'Next I was lifted up to the second heaven, where I encountered the cousins Jesus, the son of Mary, and John, the son of Zakariah. In the third heaven there was a man with a face like a full moon—Joseph, the son of Jacob. In the fourth heaven I saw a man named Idris—and We raised him to a lofty station [Sura 19.57]. In the fifth heaven I saw a man with long white hair and beard, more handsome than any man I have ever met. This was Aaron, son of Imran, beloved by his people. In the sixth heaven I saw a man with dark skin and a hooked nose, like those of the Shanu'a tribe. This was my brother Moses, son of Imran. Then in the seventh heaven I saw a man sitting on a throne, beside the gate that led to the immortal abode [i.e., Paradise]. Every day seventy thousand angels went in, never to emerge until the Day of Resurrection. I have never seen a man more like me—this was Abraham, my father. Abraham himself took me, then, into Paradise, where I saw a woman with ruby-red lips. I asked her whose woman she was, for she was very pleasing to me. She answered, "Zayd b. Haritha."' Later, the Apostle of Allah told this story to Zayd, and made him very happy."

THE MASSACRE OF THE BANU QURAYZA

Muhammad issued an order that no one was to perform the afternoon prayer until after he had reached Banu Qurayza, and he sent Ali ahead of him, bearing the Apostle's banner. The soldiers rallied when they saw it, and Ali advanced as far as the town's fortifications. While camped outside the town, Ali heard some Jews say insulting things about Muhammad, which prompted him to turn quickly and rush to meet the Apostle on the road. He told him that he did not need to come any closer or deal with the miserable Jews.

"Why not?" Muhammad asked. "Did you hear them slandering me?" And after Ali replied that he had done exactly that, the Prophet went on, "Once they see me they will stop."

Then the Apostle approached the Jews' fortifications and cried out, "Listen, you animals! God has rejected you and brings His vengeance upon you!" . . .

The Prophet stopped by one of the Jews' wells near Banu Qurayza, at a place called the Well of Ana. His men joined him. Some of them arrived after the evening prayer, but they had skipped the afternoon prayer because of what the Prophet had said about not praying the afternoon prayer until he had arrived at Banu Qurayza. These men had kept busy instead with a multitude of preparations for battle, in the time for afternoon prayer, and they prayed the afternoon prayer after the evening prayer, as the Prophet had instructed them. Allah did not blame them in His Book, and neither did the Prophet reproach them. . . .

[The Muslim army besieged Banu Qurayza for 25 days. Finally the Jews asked the Prophet to send an emissary with whom they could discuss the terms of surrender.]

Then the Jews sent a message to the Apostle, saying, "Send us Abu Lubaba . . . so that we may negotiate." Muhammad agreed and sent him. The Jews rose to meet him, and suddenly the [Jewish] women and children raced up to him with tears in their eyes, crying "O, Abu Lubaba! What should we do? Should we surrender to Muhammad?"

"Yes," replied Abu Lubaba, and as he spoke he drew his finger across his throat, indicating that otherwise they would be slaughtered. He felt sorry for them; nevertheless, he afterwards reported, "I knew before I had taken a single step that I had been disloyal to Allah and His Messenger [in warning the Jews of their fate]." He left Banu Qurayza—only he did not return to Muhammad. Instead he shackled himself to a column in the [nearby] mosque and vowed, "I will not leave this place until Allah forgives me for what I have done!" He further swore that he would not return to Banu Qurayza nor allow himself to be seen anywhere in the town where he had been disloyal to Allah and His Apostle.

Muhammad, meanwhile, waited a long time for Abu Lubaba to return, and when he heard what his emissary had done, he said, "If Abu Lubaba had come to me, I would have asked Allah to forgive him. But since he has sworn his oath I will not let him leave the mosque until Allah forgives him."

(I later heard from Yazid b. Abdullah b. Qusayt how the Apostle of God learned of Allah's forgiveness of Abu Lubaba. It happened one morning while the Prophet was at home with Umm Salama. She said to me, "One morning at sunrise I heard the Apostle laugh. 'Why are you laughing?' I asked him. He answered, 'Because Abu Lubaba has been forgiven.' 'May I tell him?' I asked. When the Messenger agreed, Yazid hurried to the mosque and stood in the doorway of the women's quarter—this was before the wearing of veils was required of women—and announced, 'Rejoice, Abu Lubaba! Allah has forgiven you!' Several men then rushed forward to release him from his shackles, but he said, 'No! Not until the Prophet himself frees me by his own hand!' Soon the Apostle himself came by as he was going to morning prayer, and he set Abu Lubaba free.")

[After the Jews surrendered, Muhammad decided their fate.]

And so the Jews surrendered. Muhammad confined them in Medina in the vicinity of d. al-Harith, a woman of al-Najjar, and walked to the marketplace (which is the site of today's market, still, in Medina) and had several trenches dug. Afterwards he gave orders for the Jews to be brought to him in small groups, and he cut off their heads. Two whom he singled out were Huyayy b. Akhtab (that enemy of Allah!) and the Jewish leader, Ka'b b. Asad. Altogether he killed between six hundred and seven hundred of them, although some sources claim a number as high as eight hundred or even nine hundred. All of them, as they were brought forward to Muhammad, asked Ka'b what was going to happen to them. He replied, "Death, by God! What do you expect? Can't you see that he [Muhammad] never stops summoning, and that no one ever returns?"

It went on like this until the Apostle had put an end to all of them. At the last, Huyayy b. Akhtab himself was brought forward. He wore an elaborate robe in which he had torn countless holes, by sticking his fingers through the fabric, in order to ruin its value as booty. His hands were tied with a rope that hung his neck. When he saw the Apostle of Allah he declared,

"I swear by our God that I do not regret opposing you! Anyone who forsakes God will be forsaken!" And then he turned to his men and said, "God's command is just—for He has called in His Book for a massacre of the sons of Israel." Then he sat down and his head was cut off. . . .

(I learned from Muhammad b. Ja'far b. al-Zubayr (who had heard it from Urwa b. al-Zubayr) that the Prophet's wife Aisha once said, "Only one Jewish woman was killed. She had been standing with me and talking. All of a sudden she started to laugh loudly; this is when the Apostle of Allah was beheading her [peoples'] men in the marketplace. A voice came out of nowhere and called her name. 'By heaven, what is happening?' I asked. 'I am to be killed,' was her reply. 'But why?' I asked. 'Because something I once did,' she answered. Then she was taken away and beheaded." Afterwards Aisha used to say sometimes, "I will always marvel at her good spirit and her laughter when she knew she was going to die.")

. . . Then the Apostle divided the spoils of Banu Qurayza—the property, the women, and the children—among the Muslims after taking out a one-fifth portion. He decreed the amount of shares to each person: each horseman received three shares (two for the horse, one for its rider); each foot-soldier received one share. On the day of the battle against Banu Qurayza, there were thirty-six horsemen. It was the first time that booty was distributed, after taking out a one-fifth portion, and it was the precedent used by the Prophet for dividing the spoils from all future raids.

After this the Messenger of Allah sent Sa'id b. Zayd al-Ansari (the brother of b. Abdul-Ashhal) with a number of the Jewish women of Banu Qurayza to Najd, where he sold them for weapons and horses.

The Apostle had chosen one of the Jewish women for himself. She was Rayhana d. Amr b. Khunafa, a woman of the Banu Amr b. Qurayza. She remained with him until she died. The Apostle proposed to marry her and place the veil on her, but she said, "No. Keep me for yourself, if you will, but do not marry me. That will be better for both of us." So the Apostle left her and put her away in anger at the fact that she had shown disdain for Islam, once she was captured, and clung to her Judaism. But one day the Prophet was sitting with his companions when he heard the approach of sandaled feet behind him. He announced, "I hear Tha'laba b. Sa'ya coming! She is bringing good news: Rayhana has accepted Islam!" This gave him great pleasure.

STUDY QUESTIONS

1. Ibn Ishaq's biography of the Prophet Muhammad is an important document for understanding the history of the early Muslim community. Reading this excerpt from the "night journey," what impact do you think the Prophet's vision of paradise would have on believers?

2. A very different side of the Prophet Muhammad is portrayed in the narrative of the massacre at Banu Qurayza. What are the historical consequences of the Prophet Muhammad serving as both a military and a spiritual leader of the Muslim community? Compare the depiction of the Jews of Banu Qurayza with Gregory of Tour's depiction of the Jew in the court of King Chilperic. What are the similarities? What are the differences?

9.3. AL-GHAZALI, *THE DELIVERER FROM ERROR*

Abu Hamid al-Ghazali (1058–1111) is widely regarded as medieval Islam's greatest thinker, a Muslim counterpart to Christianity's St. Augustine. Born in the Khurasan province in today's Iran, he was a precocious youth who quickly showed extraordinary intellectual ability. He studied Islamic law, *kalam* (a kind of elementary theology), philosophy, and the sciences, excelling in all. At the early age of thirty-four he was appointed professor of Islamic sciences at the Nizamiyah *madrasa* in Baghdad, perhaps the most prestigious academic position in the caliphate. A few years later, however, he went through a spiritual crisis that resulted in his loss of belief in religious rationalism and his embrace of the mystical Sufi tradition. He spent several years in travel and meditation and then reemerged in public life and devoted his last years to teaching Sufism. His memoir *al-Munqidh min al-dalal* (*The Deliverer from Error*) describes his spiritual journey. Below is a passage recounting his discovery of Sufism.

Having had my fill of these types of teachings, I turned my mind instead to the Way of the Sufis, which I understood as a discovery that can be made not by the intellect but by action. Sufi wisdom consists of a kind of carving away, ridding oneself of bad habits and vicious sentiments—for these are spiritual stumbling blocks—in order to empty one's heart of everything except the thought and remembrance of Allah. I soon found that the theory was easier than the practice. I began studying Sufi teachings by reading their books . . . until I had learned all that I could, of their teachings. Gradually, however, it became clear to me that the essence of their wisdom cannot be acquired through study; it can only be attained by tasting it, by ecstatic release, by transformative experience. Consider how great is the difference between knowing the definitions, causes, and symptoms of health and stability, and actually being healthy and stable. . . . In a similar way, there is a difference between knowing the definition, causes, and symptoms of mystical rapture and actually experiencing it—and consequently longing to rid oneself of the things of this world. . . .

I had already clearly learned that my only hope of achieving eternal blessedness lay in pious living and denying my heart its passions, and that the necessary way to begin was to detach my heart from the world, to withdraw utterly from this place of illusion, and to devote myself solely to Allah, the Most High, and His eternal realm. I understood that I could achieve this only by turning my back on fame and fortune, and to flee from all my activities and relationships. I focused on the reality of my existence and beheld the extent to which I was consumed on all sides. My daily actions—even the most noble of them, being engaged in public and private teaching—were devoted to sciences that mattered nothing to my journey to the realm of paradise. My public teaching was not intended, as it should have been, to glorify Allah but was geared and driven by my desire for fame and honor. I saw that I was standing on the edge of a cliff that was giving way, about to fall into the Endless Fire, unless I changed my ways.

I meditated endlessly on this, wanting to do something about my life while I still had the ability. One day I would be determined to quit Baghdad and cut myself off from all responsibilities—but then the next day I would change my mind. One step forward, then one step back. In the morning I might long only for the things of the afterlife, but by evening my baser desires would come to the fore. Earthly concerns held me in

Translation by Clifford Backman.

chains, while spiritual longing cried out, "Get away! Get away! A long journey awaits you, and time is running out. All the [intellectual] trappings that engulf you are nothing but trickery and nonsense. When will you prepare for the afterlife, if not now? If you will not cut yourself away from earthly concerns now, when will you ever?" Then my spirit would revive and I would be determined, absolutely determined, to take off and flee; but Satan was quick to respond. . . .

When I realized how powerless I was to make up my mind, how totally paralyzed I was, how lost I was with no idea how to proceed, I turned to Allah the Most High, and He "Who listens to the distressed when he calls on Him" [Qur'an 27.62] answered me. He guided my heart away from fame and fortune, away from family, children, and friends. I announced publically my decision to leave for Mecca, even though I secretly intended to go instead to Syria, since I feared the caliph and my colleagues learning of my plan to reside in Damascus. I was crafty and careful in my arrangement about leaving Baghdad, just as I was rock-steady in my resolve never to return. All the religious leaders in Iraq talked about me incessantly, since none of them could imagine that my departure had a spiritual motive. My position among them, after all, they regarded as the pinnacle of status. "That is their attainment of knowledge." [Qur'an 53.30] . . .

I left Baghdad after distributing whatever wealth I had accumulated, setting aside only as much as I needed to survive and to support my children. I explained to everyone that my Iraqi fortune was intended to support the people, being my pious alms [zakat]. Truly this is the best of all possible arrangements available to a scholar, to support his family. Then I went to Damascus, where I lived for two years. I devoted myself entirely to ascetic withdrawal, solitude, and spiritual disciple, in order to purify my soul, to increase in virtue, and to clean my heart and keep it focused always on Allah the Most High—all as I had been taught by the writings of the Sufi masters. I often prayed all day in the mosque, all alone, isolated high up in the minaret. I went from Damascus to Jerusalem, shutting myself daily in the Dome of the Rock. Eventually I felt called to make the hajj, to receive the blessings of Mecca and Medina, and to visit the tomb of the Prophet of Allah (May Allah's peace and blessing be upon him!), after first visiting the tomb of Ibrahim the Friend of Allah (May Allah's peace and blessing be upon him!). So I set out for the Hijaz.

Just then, however, certain problems and pleas from my children drew me back to Baghdad, even though I had been utterly resolved never to return there. But even while back in Baghdad I chose to live apart, desiring not to disturb the purification of my heart or my constant mindfulness of Allah. Local events, family issues, and the daily need for sustenance pressed in upon me, however, and marred my peaceful solitude. The state of spiritual ecstasy came to me only seldom, although I never stopped pursuing it. Obstacles always appeared in my way, but I never gave up the pursuit.

I lived this way for ten years. It is impossible to describe in detail the things that were revealed to me in those ecstasies that did come, but I can say this much—in the hope that it may be of some use: The Sufis are without a doubt the ones who most perfectly follow the ways of Allah the Most High, who live the best of all lives, the most holy, and the most pure. Not even if one combined all the knowledge of the scholars, all the wisdom of the sages, and all the teachings of the theologians, the total still would not equal even a single aspect of Sufi conduct and belief— for everything a Sufi does and meditates upon, whether in public or in private, is inspired by the light of prophecy, and no light on earth shines brighter than the light of prophecy.

How else to describe it? The first requirement of Sufism is purity, the total purification of the heart from everything other than Allah the Most High. It is the complete absorption of the heart by mindfulness of Allah, reminiscent of the prayer *Allahu al-akhbar*. The goal is to dissolve oneself into Allah. . . .

As soon as one sets upon the Sufi path, visions reveal themselves. Even when wide awake, a Sufi may see angels or the spirits of the prophets, and may hear their voices teaching him. One's spirit can ascend beyond seeing visions of forms and likenesses, to reach a stage that is beyond words. To even attempt to describe this stage is to commit an error that one must be careful to avoid. In only a most general way, the ascent is a closeness to Allah that some call absorption, or identification, or union—all these words fail.

STUDY QUESTIONS

1. How is Al-Ghazali's story of how he embraced Sufism similar to other stories of religious conversion and spiritual awakening?
2. Comparing Al-Ghazali with Ibn Rushd, how is Sufism a different form of Islam? How are they compatible?

9.4. *ONE THOUSAND AND ONE NIGHTS*, 12TH CENTURY

Also known as Arabian Nights, the multiauthored, massive work *One Thousand and One Nights* brings together centuries of tales and legends from Persian, Arabic, Indian, and Mesopotamian traditions. The first Arabic version dates to 12th-century Cairo, Egypt. This composite work is held together by the story of Scheherazade, a Persian queen who stays the moment of her execution by engaging Shahryar, a king who beheaded each virginal wife the day after their marriage, in intriguing cliffhanger stories. The most famous selections from this work are the tales of Aladdin and Sinbad; this selection reveals a comical, irreverent side of Scheherazade's voice and hints at mutual views of contemporary Muslims, Jews, and Christians sharing a common public space.

"This tale, however, is not more wonderful than the story of what happened in the case of the tailor, the hunchback, the Jew, the inspector and the Christian." "What was that?" asked the king, AND SHAHRAZAD EXPLAINED:

I have heard, O fortunate king, that once upon a time, in the old days, in the city of China there lived a tailor, an open-handed man with a liking for pleasure and entertainment. He used to go out with his wife from time to time to see the sights. One afternoon, the two of them went early and came back home towards the evening. On their way home, they found a hunchback whose strange appearance would raise a laugh even from a man who had been cheated in a bargain and which would dispel the grief of the sad. The tailor and his wife went over to look at him, and they invited

him to come home with them to keep them company that night. He agreed and accompanied them.

Night had now fallen and the tailor went off to the market, where he bought a fried fish, together with bread, lemons and a milky dessert. On returning, he set the fish before the hunchback and they ate. His wife then took a large bit of fish and crammed it into her guest's mouth, which she covered with her hand, telling him that he had to swallow it in one gulp. "And I shall not allow you to chew it." The hunchback did swallow it, but it contained a solid bone which stuck in his throat and, his allotted span having come to an end, he died.

Morning now dawned and Shahrazad broke off from what she had been allowed to say. Then, when it was the twenty-fifth night, SHE CONTINUED:

From Robert Irwin, *The Arabian Nights: Tales of 1001 Nights*, volume I: *Nights to I to 294*, translated by Malcolm C. Lyons with Ursula Lyons. London: Penguin, 2010, pp. 172–8.

I have heard, O auspicious king, that when the tailor's wife gave the hunchback a mouthful of fish to eat, as his allotted span had ended, he died instantly. "There is no might and no power except with God," exclaimed the tailor. "Poor man, that he should die like this at our hands!" "Why are you wasting time?" said his wife. "Haven't you heard what the poet says:

Why do I try to console myself with the impossible,
When I have never met a friend who bears my sorrows?
How can one sit on a fire before it is put out?
To sit on fire brings harm."

"What am I to do?" asked her husband. "Get up," she said. "Carry the man in your arms and spread a silk covering over him. We must do this tonight, and I shall go in front, with you following behind. You are to say: 'This is my son and this is his mother, and we are taking him to see the doctor.'" On hearing this, the tailor got up and carried the hunchback in his arms, while his wife kept saying: "My son, may you recover; what is paining you and where are the symptoms of smallpox showing?" Everyone who saw them said: "These people have a child with smallpox." They continued on their way, asking for the doctor's house, until they were directed to the house of a Jewish physician. They knocked on the door and down came a black slave girl, who opened it. When she saw a man carrying a child and accompanied by a woman, she asked: "What's the matter?" The tailor's wife replied: "We have a child with us and we would like the doctor to have a look at him. Take this quarter dinar, give it to your master, and let him come down to see my sick son." The girl went up and the tailor's wife came through the door and said to her husband: "Leave the hunchback here and then let's make our escape." The tailor agreed, and propping the hunchback against the wall, he and his wife made off.

The slave girl went to the Jew and told him: "There is someone at the door with a sick person. His wife is with him and he has handed me a quarter dinar for you to go down to look at him and to prescribe something suitable." The Jew, delighted to see the money, got up quickly and went off in the dark, but as soon as he put his foot down, he stumbled over the corpse. "O Ezra!" he cried. "O Moses and the Ten Commandments! O Aaron and Joshua, son of Nun! I seem to have stumbled over this sick man and he has fallen down the stairs and died. How can I get the corpse out of my house? He carried it inside and told his wife what had happened. She said: "Why are you sitting there? If you wait until daybreak, then both you and I will lose our lives. We have to take him up to the roof and drop him onto the house of our neighbor, the Muslim. As he is an inspector in charge of the king's kitchens, if he is left there overnight, the dogs will come down from the roofs and drag it off, for they do a great deal of damage to all the stuff that he brings home."

So the Jew and his wife went up to their roof, carrying the hunchback, and they lowered him to the ground by his arms and legs, leaving him by the wall, before going off. No sooner had they done this than the inspector came home, opened the door and went up, carrying a lighted candle. He noticed a man standing in the corner under the ventilation shaft. "By God!" he exclaimed. "This is a fine thing! It must have been a man who has been stealing my stores!" Turning to the corpse, he said: "It was you who has been stealing the meat and the fat, when I thought it was the cats and dogs of the neighbourhood. I have put myself in the wrong by killing them, when all the time it was you, coming down from the roof." He took up a large hammer and, brandishing it, he went up to the corpse and struck it on the breast. When he found that the man was dead, he was moved with grief, and, fearing for his own life, he exclaimed: "There is no might and no power except with God Almighty! May God curse the fat and the sheep's tail!" He then added: "How was it that I brought this man's life to an end with my own hand?" The inspector looked at his victim and found that he was a hunchback. "Wasn't it enough for you to be a hunchback," he asked, "that you had to become a thief and steal meat and fat? O God, the Shelterer, cloak me with Your gracious covering." He then hoisted the corpse on to his shoulders as the night was ending and took it out of his house. He continued to carry it until he reached the edge of the market, where he propped it up at the side of a shop at the head of an alley. He then left the corpse and made off.

A Christian, the king's broker, was the next to appear on the scene. He was drunk and had come out to go to the baths, realizing in his drunkenness, that is was nearly time for matins. He went on, staggering as he walked, until, when he was near the corpse, he squatted down to urinate. Then, casting a sideways glance, he saw someone standing there. As it happened, at the beginning of that night his turban had been stolen and when he saw the hunchback leaning against the wall, he imagined the man meant to steal the one that he now had on. So he balled his fist and struck the hunchback on the neck, felling him to the ground. He called to the market watchman, and then, in the excess of his drunkenness, he set about belabouring the corpse and trying to strangle it. The watchman came up and found the Christian kneeling on the Muslim and hitting him. "What has he done?" he asked. The Christian said: "He wanted to steal my turban." "Get away from him," ordered the watchman, and when the Christian had got up, he went to the hunchback and found him dead. "By God," he said, "this is a fine thing—a Christian killing a Muslim," and after having tied the Christian's hands, he took him to the house of the *wali*. All the while the Christian was saying to himself: "O Messiah, O Holy Virgin, how could I have killed this man and how quickly he died from a single blow!" Drunkenness vanished, to be replaced by care, and the Christian together with the hunchback spent the rest of the night until morning in the *wali*'s house.

In the morning, the *wali* sentenced "the killer" to be hanged. The executioner was ordered to proclaim his crime; a gallows was set up under which the Christian was made to stand, and the executioner came and put a rope around his neck. He was on the point of hanging him when the inspector made his way through the crowd. When he saw the Christian about to be hanged, he cleared a way for himself and then said: "Don't do it; it was I who killed him." "Why did you do that?" asked the *wali*. "I came home last night," he said, "and found that he had come down through the ventilation shaft and had stolen my goods, so I struck him on the chest with a hammer and he died. I carried him off to the market and propped him up in a lane nearby." He added: "It is not enough for me to have killed a Muslim that I should kill a Christian as well? I am the one to be hanged." On hearing this, the *wali* freed the Christian and told the executioner to hang the inspector on his own confession. The executioner took the rope from the neck of the king's broker and put it round that of the inspector, who was made to stand under the gallows.

He was about to be hanged when, all of a sudden, the Jewish doctor came through the crowd, shouting to them and to the executioner: "Don't do it! It was I and I alone who killed him. I was at home last night when a man and a woman knocked at my door bringing with them this hunchback, who was sick. They gave my servant girl a quarter of a dinar. She told me about them and handed me the money, but it turned out that the pair had brought the hunchback into the house, left him on the stairs and gone off. I came down to look at him, but in the darkness I tripped over him and he fell down to the bottom of the stairs, killing himself on the spot. My wife and I carried him up to the roof and lowered him into the ventilation shaft of this inspector, who lives next door to us. The man was dead, but when the inspector came and found him in his house, he took him for a thief and struck him with a hammer so that he fell to the ground, leaving the inspector to think he had killed him. Isn't it enough for me to have unknowingly killed one Muslim that I should knowingly be responsible for the death of another?"

When the *wali* heard this, he told the executioner to release the inspector and to hang the Jew. The executioner took him and put the rope round his neck, but at that the tailor came through the crowd and told him to stop: "It was I and I alone who killed the man. Yesterday I went out to see the sights, and in the evening I met this hunchback, drunk and singing at the top of his voice to his tambourine. I invited him home and bought a fish, which we sat down to eat. My wife took a piece of it and making it into a mouthful, she crammed it into his gullet where a bit of it stuck, killing him instantly. Then my wife and I took him to the Jew's house. The servant girl came down and opened the door for us, and I told her to tell her master that a woman and a man were at the door with a sick person and to ask him to come and look at him. I gave her a quarter of a dinar and while she went up to her master, I carried the hunchback to the head of the stairs and propped him up there, after which my wife and I went away. The Jew came down and tripped over the hunchback and thought that he had killed him. Is that right?" he asked the Jew. "Yes," said the Jew, at which the tailor turned to the *wali* and said: "Release the Jew and hang me."

When the *wali* heard what he had to say, he was astonished by the whole affair, which he said should be recorded in books. Then he told the executioner to release the Jew and to hang the tailor on his own confession. "I'm tired of this," complained the executioner. "I bring one man forward and put another one back and no one gets hanged." Then he put the rope round the tailor's neck.

So much for these people, but as for the hunchback, the story goes that he was the king's fool and that the king could not bear to be parted from him. After getting drunk, he had left the king and had been away all night. As he was still not back by midday the next day, the king asked some of his courtiers about him, and they replied: "Master, his dead body was brought to the *wali*, who ordered his killer to be hanged. Then a second and third person arrived, each of them claiming to have killed him and each telling the *wali* the reason for it." When the king heard this, he called to his chamberlain, telling him to go to the *wali* and to fetch him all those concerned.

When the chamberlain went there, he found the executioner about to hang the tailor. "Don't do it!" he shouted, and he told the *wali* what the king had said. He then brought everyone, the *wali*, the tailor, the Jew, and the Christian and the inspector, and had the corpse of the hunchback carried along with them. When the *wali* stood before the king, he kissed the ground and told him what had happened to each of them—but there is nothing to be gained from repetition. The king himself was filled with amazement and delight at the story, and gave orders that it should be recorded in letters of gold. He then asked those present whether they had ever heard anything more astonishing than the story of that hunchback.

At that, the Christian came forward and said: "Your majesty, if you give me leave, I will tell you of something that happened to me which was more remarkable, stranger and more entertaining than the story of the hunchback." When the king told him to produce his story, HE SAID: . . .

STUDY QUESTIONS

1. How does the story particularly satirize Jews and Christians living among Muslims?
2. How does the story suggest that it is human nature to cover up one's mistakes and come to erroneous conclusions?

9.5. MAIMONIDES, *LETTER TO YEMEN*, 1172 CE

R. Moshe b. Maimon (1135–1204) was the greatest Jewish scholar of the Middle Ages. Born in Cordoba, during the regime of the Almoravids, he studied Torah and Talmud with his father, who was also a rabbi, and read Greek philosophy in the Arabic translations then circulating in Spain. He became a physician, which is how he supported his family after they (along with many other Jews) went into exile after the brutal Almohad regime replaced the relatively benign Almoravids in 1148. Maimonides lived in Morocco for many years before settling in Fustat, Egypt. An extraordinarily prolific writer, Maimonides composed his *Letter to Yemen* in 1172, in response to a request for guidance from the Jewish community there, which was experiencing persecution from two sources—the local Islamic ruler and a Jewish reformer who had declared himself the Messiah and announced the approaching End of Days.

Translation by Clifford Backman.

. . . Remember always that ours is the true, divine, authentic religion, as revealed to us by Moses, who is pre-eminent among all the prophets from beginning to end. It is through this faith that the Holy One has set us apart from the rest of mankind. The Holy Scripture says: "Yet it was to your fathers that the Lord was drawn in His love for them, so that He chose you, their lineal descendants, from among all peoples—as is now the case" [Deut. 10.15]. This is not owing to our merits, though. It was the will of the Holy One, because our forefathers knew Him and submitted to Him. We read: "It is not because you are the most numerous of peoples that the Lord set His heart on you and chose you—indeed, you are the smallest of peoples; but it was because the Lord favored you and kept the oath He made to your fathers that the Lord freed you with a mighty hand and rescued you from the house of bondage, from the power of Pharaoh king of Egypt" [Deut. 7.7–8]. The Holy One has set us apart with His laws and teachings, and our unique status is the consequence of those commandments and statutes. The Scripture says of His mercies to us: "Or what great nation has laws and rules as perfect as all this Teaching that I set before you this day?" [Deut. 4.8]. This is why all the nations on the earth rise up against us, out of their envy and malice. This is why all the kings of the earth persecute us, out of their hatred and injustice. All have wanted to impede the Lord, but in vain. From tyrant to slave, everyone who has ever lived since the time of the Covenant and has sought dominion on earth, if he was violent and crude, has tried from start to finish to destroy our Law and obliterate our religion. Whether by sword, murder, or riot, all have done so—Amalek, Sisera, Sennacherib, Nebuchadnezzar, Titus, Hadrian, and others. May their bones be ground into dust! And they are only the first of two types of men who have tried to impede the Lord's will.

The second type consists of the most civilized and sophisticated of peoples—the Syrians, the Persians, and the Greeks. These too have tried to destroy our Law and obliterate our religion, but they have done so with crafty arguments and the controversies their thinking has stirred up. They try to undermine the Law with their argumentative writings, to obliterate it with words just as the tyrants attempt to do with swords. Neither of them, however, will ever succeed,

for we possess the Holy One's promise, through Isaiah, that He will destroy all who seek to weaken the Law or demolish it with armies. The Holy One will destroy them—but this must be understood as a metaphor only, a way of saying that any enemy's attempts will be wholly frustrated. . . .

And after [the Syrians, Persians, and Greeks] there came a new sect that combined their methods into one, both conquest and controversy, thinking thus they could wipe out the entire Jewish nation and religion. This sect claimed the power of prophecy and established a new religion, contrary to our own. They claimed an equally divine revelation, in the hope of raising doubt and creating confusion. . . . The first to do so was Jesus the Nazarene. May his bones be ground into dust! He was a Jew, having a Jewish mother, but his father was a Gentile, for our Law states that a child born of a Jewish mother and Gentile father (or, of course, of a Jewish mother and a slave) is a true Jew. Thus one can only call Jesus a non-Jew in an indirect manner of speaking, for he led his followers to believe he was a prophet sent by the Lord to explain the Law, and to believe that he was the Messiah anticipated by all. But his teaching of the Law was faulty and opened the way to its total annulment, the undoing of its commandments, and the breaking of its prohibitions. Our sages of blessed memory rendered a fitting punishment on him, after learning of his reputation and teachings. . . .

Another sect arose not long afterwards, a sect based on Jesus and taught by one whose lineage was of Esau. He [Paul] did not set out to create an entirely new religion. He was not an offense to Israel, and he stirred up no antagonism [toward the Jews] among his followers. The faults of his teachings, however, were obvious to everyone, and his activity ceased when we caught him. His fate is well known.

After [Paul] came the Madman [Muhammad], who followed the path laid out for him by his predecessor. The Madman, however, had ambition to rule others and subject them to his power, and so he invented his well-known religion [Islam].

All of these men presumed to compare their ravings with our divine religion, but only an idiot would set human inventions alongside divine revelations. Our religion differs from theirs as much as a living person differs from a statue of marble, wood, bronze, or silver, no matter how elegantly carved. . . .

Only someone who knows nothing at all about the Holy Scriptures' hidden meanings and the Law's deeper truths could possibly think our religion has anything in common with any other he compares it to. Only such an imbecile would equate the fact that our Law contains commandments and prohibitions, and that other religions also detail permitted and not-permitted actions; or that both contain systems of required rituals, positive and negative commands, and apportion rewards and punishments thereby. Only if one grasps the inner meanings of the Law, can one appreciate the fact that the essence of our true religion rests on the deep, hidden meanings of its commandments and prohibitions—every single one of which will benefit anyone straining after perfection, by removing every impediment that stands between him and his goal. . . . The teachings of those religions that outwardly resemble our own, however, have no deeper meaning. They are mere imitations of ours. Their supporters have copied our faith in order to give themselves honor by pretending to be like us. Their fakery is obvious to those who know, which makes them laughing-stocks and fools; one laughs at them just as one laughs when seeing apes imitate the actions of men.

This foolishness was prophesied by Daniel, when he predicted that arrival of someone who would proclaim a religion supposedly like ours, with its own Scriptures and oral traditions, and would be arrogant enough to proclaim a special revelation from the Lord and to have spoken with Him, among other extraordinary things. Here we see Daniel prophesying the rise of the Arabs after the destruction of Rome, with his declaration of the appearance of the Madman who would destroy Rome, Persia, and Byzantium. . . . Bear in mind that the Holy One told Daniel that He would destroy the Madman despite his successes and endurance, and destroy also the followers of his predecessors [Jesus and Paul]. All those who have persecuted us will perish in the end—those who sought to destroy us with the sword, those who used argument, and those who now mimic us. . . .

You write that there is a man in one of your cities who claims to be the Messiah. I am not surprised, neither at him nor his followers. No doubt the man is mad, and as a sick person he is not to be condemned or rebuked; an illness is not the fault of the sufferer. As for his followers, I suspect they fell under his sway because of the wretchedness of their lives and their failure to understand the true meaning and importance of the Messiah. They probably are confusing the Messiah for the son of their anticipated Mahdi. But I am surprised that you, an enlightened man who has read the teachings of the rabbis, are tempted to believe in him. Don't you know, my brother, that the Messiah will be a prophet more luminous than any who has come in Moses' wake, and that a willfully false prophet deserves capital punishment. . . .

Remember, the Christians falsely attribute prophetic power to Jesus the Nazarene—may his bones be ground into dust!—and believe he rose from the dead and performed other miracles. Even if (just for the sake of argument) these claims were true, there still would be no reason to believe Jesus is the Messiah. I could show you a thousand proofs from the Holy Scriptures to contradict their claim.

In the end, who would ever claim Messiahship except one who wishes to make a public fool of himself? If this man you mention acts out of pride or spite, I would say he deserves death, but it appears to me instead that he has a melancholy and confused mind, and so I advise you—for your own good as well as for his—to put him in chains and detain him until the Gentiles learn that he is insane. Once you have broadcast loudly the news of this man and his illness, you can then release him without putting him at risk. If the Gentiles learn of him after you have incarcerated him, they will examine him and declare him mad, and you will be left unmolested. But if you do nothing about him until after the Gentiles have learned of him, then you will incur their wrath.

Remember, my brother: the Holy One has thrown us among the Arabs who now persecute us so severely. The Scriptures warned us of the unfair laws they would raise against us: "Our enemies themselves shall judge us" [Deut. 32.31] Never did any nation abuse, belittle, demean and hate us, the way they do. . . .

1. How does Maimonides describe the defects of both Christianity and Islam?
2. Maimonides lived in Cordoba, Spain, at the same as Ibn Rushd. What does this say about Spanish culture during the Middle Ages?

9.6. USAMAH IBN MUNQIDH, *MEMOIRS*, 1183

A Muslim knight, diplomat, and poet, Usamah ibn Munqidh (1095–1188) provides a distinctive account of living on the receiving end of the Latin Crusades. Usamah served the Muslim leaders Zengi, Nur al-Din, and finally Saladin—to whom he dedicated his work—but had Crusader friends, too. Written in Arabic, Usamah's *Memoirs* are a string of anecdotes and morality tales that reveal how the Muslims and Christians managed to live side by side in Syria. Interspersed among the hostilities are genuine moments of entertainment and camaraderie, such as the section reprinted here in which the Templars defend Usamah at prayer; or his exaggerated disbelief that a woman would cast aside a Muslim nobleman in favor of a Frankish shoemaker.

A leopard jumps from a church window and kills a Frank.—In the church of Hunāk was a window forty cubits high. Every day at noontime a leopard would come and jump to the window, where it would sleep until the end of the day, at which time it would jump down and go away. At that time, Hunāk was held as a fief by a Frankish knight named Sir Adam, one of the devils of the Franks. Sir Adam was told the story of the leopard and he said, "As soon as ye see it, let me know." The leopard came as it was wont to do and jumped into the window. One of the peasants came and told Sir Adam about it. The latter put on his coat of mail, mounted his horse, took his shield and lance and came to the church, which was all in ruins with the exception of one wall which was standing and in which the window was. As soon as the leopard saw him, it jumped from the window upon him while he was on his horse, broke his back and killed him. It then went away. The peasants of Hunāk used to call that leopard, "the leopard that takes part in the holy war" [*al-namir al-mujāhid*].

One of the characteristics of the leopard is that in case it wounds a man and a mouse urinates on the wound, the man dies. It is very difficult to keep the mouse away from one wounded by a leopard. In fact, they sometimes go so far as to fix a bed for him in the midst of water and tie cats all around him for fear of the mice.

. . .

Prefers to be a Frankish shoemaker's wife to life in a Moslem castle.—A number of maids taken captive from the Franks were brought into the home of my father (may Allah's mercy rest upon his soul!). The Franks (may Allah's curse be upon them!) are an accursed race, the members of which do not assimilate except with their own kin. My father saw among them a pretty maid who was in the prime of youth, and said to his housekeeper, "Introduce this woman

From Philip Hitti, *An Arab-Syrian Gentleman and Warrior in the Period of the Crusades: Memoirs of Usāmah Ibn-Munqidh.* Princeton, N.J.: Princeton University Press.

into the bath, repair her clothing and prepare her for a journey." This she did. He then delivered the maid to a servant of his and sent her to al-Amīr Shihāb-al-Dīn Mālik ibn-Sālim, the lord of the Castle of Ja'bar, who was a friend of his. He also wrote him a letter saying, "We have won some booty from the Franks, from which I am sending thee a share." The maid suited Shihāb-al-Dīn, and he was pleased with her. He took her to himself and she bore him a boy, whom he called Badrān. [80] Badrān's father named him his heir apparent, and he became of age. On his father's death, Badrān became the governor of the town and its people, his mother being the real power. She entered into conspiracy with a band of men and let herself down from the castle by a rope. The band took her to Sarūj, which belonged at that time to the Franks. There she married a Frankish shoemaker, while her son was the lord of the Castle of Ja'bar.

. . .

Newly arrived Franks are especially rough: One insists that Usāmah should pray eastward.—Everyone who is a fresh emigrant from the Frankish lands is ruder in character than those who have become acclimatized and have held long association with the Moslems. Here is an illustration of their rude character.

Whenever I visited Jerusalem I always entered the Aqsa Mosque, beside which stood a small mosque which the Franks had converted into a church. When I sued to enter the Aqsa Mosque, which was occupied by the Templars [*al-dāwiyyah*], who were my friends, the Templars would evacuate the little adjoining mosque so that I might pray in it. One day I entered this mosque, repeated the first formula, "Allah is great," "and stood up in the act of praying, upon which one of the Franks rushed on me, got hold of me and turned my face eastward saying, "This is the way thou shouldest pray!" A group of Templars hastened to him, seized him and repelled him from me. I resumed my prayer. The same man, while the others were otherwise busy, rushed once more on me and turned my face eastward, saying, "This is the way thou shouldest pray!" The Templars again came in to him and expelled him. They apologized to me, saying, "This is a stranger who has only recently arrived from the land of the Franks and has never before seen anyone praying except eastward."

Thereupon I said to myself, "I have had enough prayer." So I went out and have been surprised at the conduct of this devil of a man, at the change in the color of his face, his trembling and his sentiment at the sight of one praying toward the *qiblah*.

. . .

Their judicial trials.—I attended one day a duel in Nāblus between two Franks. The reason for this was that certain Moslem thieves took by surprise one of the villages of Nāblus. One of the peasants of that village was charged with having acted as a guide for the thieves when they fell upon the village. So he fled away. The king sent and arrested his children. The peasant thereupon came back to the king and said, "Let justice be done in my case. I challenge to a duel the man who claimed that I guided the thieves to the village." The king then said to the tenant who held the village in the fief, "Bring forth someone to fight the duel with him." The tenant went to his village, where a blacksmith lived, took hold of him and ordered him to fight the duel. The tenant became thus sure of the safety of his own peasants, none of whom would be killed and his estate ruined.

I saw the blacksmith. He was a physically strong young man, but his heart failed him. He would walk a few steps and then sit down and ask for a drink. The one who had made the challenge was an old man, but he was strong in spirit and he would rub the nail of his thumb against that of the forefinger in defiance, as if he was not worrying over the duel. Then came the viscount [*al-bishkund*], i.e., the seignior of the town, and gave each one of the two contestants a cudgel and a shield and arranged the people in a circle around them.

The two met. The old man would press the blacksmith backward until he would get him as far as the circle, then he would come back to the middle of the arena. They went on exchanging blows until they looked like pillars smeared with blood. The contest was prolonged and the viscount began to urge them to hurry, saying, "Hurry on." The fact that the smith was given to the use of the hammer proved now a great advantage to him. The old man was worn out and the smith gave him a blow which made him fall. His cudgel fell under his back. The smith knelt down over him and tried to stick his fingers into the eyes of the adversary, but could not do it because of the great quantity of blood flowing out. Then he rose up and hit his head with the cudgel until he killed him. They then fastened a rope around the neck of the dead person, dragged him away and hanged him. The lord who brought the smith now came, gave the smith his own mantle, made him mount the horse behind him and rode off with him. This case illustrates the kind of jurisprudence [85] and legal decisions the Franks have—may Allah's curse be upon them!

. . .

Reflections of Usāmah on old age.—Little did I realize at that time that the disease of senility is universal, infecting everyone whom death has neglected. But now that I have climbed to the summit of my ninetieth year, worn out by the succession of days and years, I have become myself like Jawād, the fodder dealer, and not like the generous man [*al-jawād*] who can dissipate his money. Feebleness has bent me down to the ground, and old age has made one part of my body enter through another, so much so that I can now hardly recognize myself; and I

continually bemoan my past. Here is what I have said in describing my own condition:

When I attained in life a high stage
For which I had always yearned, I wished for death.
Longevity has left me no energy
By which I could meet the vicissitudes of time
    when hostile to me.
[98] My strength has been rendered weakness,
    and my two confidants,
My sight and my hearing, have betrayed me, since
    I attained this height.
When I rise, I feel as if laden
With a mountain; and when I walk, as though I
    were bound with chains.
I creep with a cane in my hand which is wont
To carry in warfare a lance and a sword.
My nights I spend in my soft bed, unable to sleep
And wide awake as though I lay on solid rock.
Man is reversed in life: the moment
He attains perfection and completion, then he
    reverts to the condition from which he started.

STUDY QUESTIONS

1. What proof does Usamah offer of the uncivilized nature of the French invaders of the Middle East?
2. How does he demonstrate Islamic cultural, if not always military, superiority in his account?

9.7. IBN RUSHD, *ON THE HARMONY OF RELIGIOUS LAW AND PHILOSOPHY*

Ibn Rushd (full name: Abu al-Walid Muhammad b. Ahmad b. Muhammad b. Rushd) was born in Cordoba, the grand capital city of Islamic Spain, in 1126. His family was a prominent one, made up of distinguished religious jurists and physicians, and he received a sound classical Islamic education. He later served as a qadi and physician, but his greatest intellectual love was for philosophy. His most important works, apart from his commentaries of Aristotle, were *On the Harmony of*

Translation by Clifford Backman.

Religious Law and Philosophy, The Methods of Proof in Regard to Religious Doctrine, and *The Incoherence of the Incoherence.* The last book was a response to *The Incoherence of the Philosophers* by al-Ghazali—hence the odd title. Translated below is an abridged version of the third chapter of *On the Harmony of Religious Law and Philosophy;* it treats the issues of fate and predestination. Ibn Rushd died in Marrakesh, Morocco, in 1198.

The question of fate and predestination is one of the most complicated questions in all religion, because the traditional teachings on this problem, when closely viewed, are seen to be contradictory. But this is also true of rational efforts to address it. The first contradictions appear in the Qur'an and the hadith. Many verses in the Qur'an proclaim as universal truth that all things are predestined, and that man is fated to do all that he does; but many other verses say, to the contrary, that man's actions are freely chosen and not fated at all.

These are some verses that say everything is determined and inevitable (many others could be cited as well):

"Say: 'Yes, those of old and those of later times, all will certainly be gathered together for the meeting appointed for a Day Well-Known." [Qur'an 56.49]

"Allah doth know what every female [womb] doth bear, but how much the wombs fall short [of their time or number] or do exceed. Every single thing is with Him in [due] proportion. He knoweth the Unseen and that which is open: He is the Great, the Most High." [Qur'an 13.8–9]

"No misfortune can happen on earth or in your souls but is recorded in a Book before We bring it into existence: That is truly easy for Allah." [Qur'an 57.22]

As for verses that state that man's actions are the result of his free will, or that proclaimed things are possibly and not necessarily going to happen:

"Whatever misfortune happens to you, is because of the things your hands have wrought, and for many [a sin] He grants forgiveness." [Qur'an 42.31]

"But those who have earned evil will have a reward of like evil." [Qur'an 10.27]

"Those who believe, and do deeds of righteousness, and establish regular prayers and give zakat, will have their reward with their Lord: on them shall be no fear, nor shall they grieve." [Qur'an 2.277]

Sometimes contrary statements even appear within a single passage:

"It is part of the Mercy of Allah that thou dost deal gently with them. Wert thou severe or harsh hearted they would have broken away from about thee: so pass over [their faults], and ask for [Allah's] forgiveness for them; and consult them in affairs [of moment]. Then, when thou hast taken a decision, put thy trust in Allah. For Allah loves those who put their trust [in Him]. If Allah helps you, none can overcome you. If He forsakes you, who is there, after that, that can help you? In Allah, then, let believers put their trust." [Qur'an 3.159–160]

or

"Whatever good, [O man!] happens to thee, is from Allah; but whatever evil happens to thee, is from thyself and We have sent thee as a Messenger to [instruct] mankind. And enough is Allah for a witness. He who obeys the Messenger, obeys Allah: but if any turn away, We have not sent thee to watch over them." [Qur'an 4.80–81]

We can see this also in the Prophet's *hadith.* On one occasion he said, "Every child is born in the true religion [Islam]. It is his parents who later turn him into a Jew or a Christian." But on another occasion he said, "Some people were created for Hell and live lives fit for it; others were created for Heaven and live lives fit for it." Clearly the first teaching states that the situation one is born into is the cause of disbelief, since true belief is natural to all, but the second teaching says that evil and disbelief are set by Allah and man is fated to follow them.

Because of this, Muslims have split into two factions. The first are the Mutazilites, who believe that one's goodness or wickedness result from one's own action—and that one will be rewarded or punished accordingly. The Jabarites hold the opposite view, asserting that one is fated to do whatever one does in life.

The Asharites are a group that has tried to follow a compromise between these two extremes. They maintain that one chooses one's actions, but the power to perform the actions is the creation of Allah—and only in this sense one can say that Allah creates the actions themselves. This, however, makes no sense, for if an action and the power to perform it are both created by Allah, then the man is logically compelled to perform it. This is only one reason for the confused split over this problem. . . .

It may be asked, therefore, how is the contradiction between tradition and reason to be reconciled—which surely is the role of religion, not to keep divided what ought to be reconciled by pursuing a middle course? It is clear, first of all, that Allah created the power we possess to perform deeds that are contradictory. But our actions are not brought to fulfillment except from outside of us, by Allah's intention for us, which removes the obstacles to our doing them; therefore our actions are only effected when our will and ability are in alignment with Allah's intent. In this way our completed actions result from our own will and from the fitness of our will with Allah's design for us, from the outside, and this alignment is what we call predestination. Allah's design therefore neither impels our actions nor hinders them, but it is the cause of our willing the actions. Our intentions are produced either by our imagination or by our desire to effect something that is not in our power but is in the power of something outside of us. For example: if we see something good, we admire it and desire to acquire it even though it is not in our power to achieve. Similarly, if we see something bad, we turn from it instinctively. Our intention, our will, depends on causes outside ourselves. . . .

To understand causes is to understand the secret knowledge of the essence of a thing before it comes into existence. But since it is the arrangement of causes that brings something into existence at a particular time, the knowledge of a thing must exist prior to the thing itself. To understand all causation, therefore, is to know what exists and what does not exist at any given moment. Praised be Allah, Who

has complete understanding of all creation and all causation! This is what the words "Keys of the secret" mean in the verse "With Him are the keys of the Unseen, the treasures that none knoweth but He. He knoweth whatever there is on the earth and in the sea. Not a leaf doth fall but with His knowledge: There is not a grain in the darkness [or depths] of the earth, nor anything fresh or dry [green or withered], but is [inscribed] in a Record Clear [to those who can read]." [Qur'an 6.59]

If this argument is true, then it should now be clear how we freely choose our own actions even while they are predetermined by fate. This reconciliation is the true purpose of religion, and of those Qur'anic verses and *hadith* that appeared contradictory. In defining those passages' universal nature in this way, all contradictions disappear—and so do all doubts raised by the apparent contradictions. Everything that comes into existence by means of our will is brought to fulfillment by the combination of our will and the causes that lie outside us. Doubts arise when we take in account only one aspect of agency. . . .

[Al-Ghazali] writes that a man who asserts any cause to be co-existent with Allah is like a man who equates the role of a pen, in writing, with the work of the scribe who uses it. In other words, the pen and the man are both to be called scribes, because the word *writing* can be applied to both. That word, however, is the only thing they share; apart from it, they have nothing in common. Such is the case with the word *creator*, when we apply it to Allah and to causation. But I argue back that his example is faulty, because Allah is the creator of the essences of everything that affects causation, whereas in al-Ghazali's example the scribe is not the creator of the essence of the pen, and of the act of writing, and of the words written. This is why I say that there is no creator but Allah—a statement that harmonizes our perceptions, our reason, and our religion. . . .

So praises to "the Wise, the All-Knowing!" [Qur'an 67.14] Allah has shown us the truth in His Book, "And what will explain to thee what is the Day of Sorting Out?" [Qur'an 77.14] And again, "He has made subject to you the Night and the Day; the Sun and the Moon; and the Stars are in subjection by His command: verily in this are Signs for men who are wise." [Qur'an 16.12]

And again, "And He is Allah: there is no god but He. To Him be praise, at the first and at the last." [Qur'an 28.70] He also says, "This is [true] guidance: And for those who reject the Signs of their Lord is a grievous chastisement of abomination." [Qur'an 45.11] There are many other verses that I could cite on this matter. If there were no wisdom in the messages with which Allah has favored us, we would not possess the blessings that we have and for which we are ever grateful to Him.

STUDY QUESTIONS

1. How does Ibn Rushd present the contradictions in the Qur'an and in traditional teaching concerning predestination and free will? What arguments does Ibn Rushd put forward to reconcile the seemingly irreconcilable contradictions between faith and reason?
2. Compare Ibn Rushd's approach to Islamic doctrine with that of Al-Ghazali's in *The Deliverer from Error*. How are they different? How are they similar?

9.8. MAIMONIDES, *GUIDE FOR THE PERPLEXED*, 12TH CENTURY

The famed rabbi Moses Maimonides (1135–1204) lived a wandering life as a philosopher and physician in North Africa, since he left Spain in exile after the harsh Almohad invasion of the Iberian Peninsula (1148). Fascinated with Greek philosophy and Islamic scientific knowledge, Maimonides traveled to Morocco, the Holy Land, and Egypt. He consolidated Jewish law from the Torah in his great fourteen-volume work, the Mishneh Torah (completed ca. 1180), which lays out all rules of Jewish observance. The *Guide for the Perplexed*, written in the form of a letter to a questioning student, reveals Maimonides's philosophical contributions rather than his thoughts on Jewish theology and law.

CHAPTER V

WHEN the chief of philosophers (Aristotle) was about to inquire into some very profound subjects, and to establish his theory by proofs, he commenced his treatise with an apology, and requested the reader to attribute the author's inquiries not to presumption, vanity, egotism, or arrogance, as though he were interfering with things of which he had no knowledge, but rather to his zeal and his desire to discover and establish true doctrines, as far as lay in human power. We take the same position, and think that a man, when he commences to speculate, ought not to embark at once on a subject so vast and important; he should previously adapt himself to the study of the several branches of science and knowledge, should most thoroughly refine his moral character and subdue his passions and desires, the offspring of his imagination; when, in addition, he has obtained a knowledge of the true fundamental propositions, a

Moses Maimonides, *Guide for the Perplexed*, translated by Friedländer (1904). http://www.sacred-texts.com/jud/gfp/gfp019.htm.

comprehension of the several methods of inference and proof, and the capacity of guarding against fallacies, then he may approach the investigation of this subject. He must, however, not decide any question by the first idea that suggests itself to his mind, or at once direct his thoughts and force them to obtain a knowledge of the Creator, but he must wait modestly and patiently, and advance step by step.

In this sense we must understand the words "And Moses hid his face, for he was afraid to look upon God" (Exod. iii. 6), though retaining also the literal meaning of the passage, that Moses was afraid to gaze at the light which appeared to his eye; but it must on no account be assumed that the Being which is exalted far above every imperfection can be perceived by the eye. This act of Moses was highly commended by God, who bestowed on him a well deserved portion of His goodness, as it is said: "And the similitude of the Lord shall he behold" (Num. xii. 8). This, say our Sages, was the reward for having previously hidden his face, lest he should gaze at the Eternal. (*Talm. B. Berakot Fa.*)

But "the nobles of the Children of Israel" were impetuous, and allowed their thoughts to go unrestrained: what they perceived was but imperfect. Therefore it is said of them, "And they saw the God of Israel, and there was under his feet," etc. (Exod. xxiv. 10); and not merely, "and they saw the God of Israel"; the purpose of the whole passage is to criticize their act of seeing and not to describe it. They are blamed for the nature of their perception, which was to a certain extent corporeal—a result which necessarily followed, from the fact that they ventured too far before being perfectly prepared. They deserved to perish, but at the intercession of Moses this fate was averted by God for the time. They were afterwards burnt at Taberah, except Nadab and Abihu, who were burnt in the Tabernacle of the congregation, according to what is stated by authentic tradition. (*Midr. Rabba ad locum.*)

If such was the case with them, how much more is it incumbent on us who are inferior, and on those who are below us, to persevere in perfecting our knowledge of the elements, and in rightly understanding the preliminaries which purify the mind from the defilement of error: then we may enter the holy and divine camp in order to gaze: as the Bible says, "And let the priests

also, which come near to the Lord, sanctify themselves, lest the Lord break forth upon them" (Exod. xix. 22). Solomon, also, has cautioned all who endeavour to attain this high degree of knowledge in the following figurative terms, "Keep thy foot when thou goest to the house of God" (Eccles. iv. 17).

I will now return to complete what I commenced to explain. The nobles of the Children of Israel, besides erring in their perception, were, through this cause, also misled in their actions: for in consequence of their confused perception, they gave way to bodily cravings. This is meant by the words, "Also they saw God and did eat and drink" (Exod. xxiv. 11). The principal part of that passage, viz., "And there was under his feet as it were a paved work of a sapphire stone" (Exod. xxiv. 10), will be further explained in the course of the present treatise (ch. XXVIII). All we here intend to say is, that wherever in a similar connection any one of the three verbs mentioned above occurs, it has reference to intellectual perception, not to the sensation of sight by the eye: for God is not a being to be perceived by the eye.

It will do no harm, however, if those who are unable to comprehend what we here endeavour to explain should refer all the words in question to sensuous perception, to seeing lights created [for the purpose], angels, or similar beings.

CHAPTER VI

THE two Hebrew nouns *ish* and *ishshah* were originally employed to designate the "male and female" of human beings, but were afterwards applied to the "male and female" of the other species of the animal creation. For instance, we read, "Of every clean beast thou shalt take to thee by sevens," *ish ve-ishto* (Gen. vii. 2), in the same sense as *ish ve-ishshah*, "male and female." The term *zakar u-nekebah* was afterwards applied to anything designed and prepared for union with another object. Thus we read, "The five curtains shall be coupled together, one (*ishshah*) to the other" (*aḥotah*) (Exod. xxvi. 3).

It will easily be seen that the Hebrew equivalents for "brother and sister" are likewise treated as homonyms, and used, in a figurative sense, like *ish* and *ishshah*.

CHAPTER VII

IT is well known that the verb yalad means "to bear," "they have born (*ve-yaledu*) him children" (Deut. xxi. 15). The word was next used in a figurative sense with reference to various objects in nature, meaning, "to create," e.g., "before the mountains were created" (*yulladu*) (Ps. xc. 2); also, "to produce," in reference to that which the earth causes to come forth as if by birth, e.g., "He will cause her to bear (*holidah*) and bring forth" (Isa. Iv. 10). The verb further denotes, "to bring forth," said of changes in the process of time, as though they were things which were born, e.g., "for thou knowest not what a day may bring forth" (*yeled*) (Prov. xxvii. 1). Another figurative use of the word is its application to the formation of thoughts and ideas, or of opinions resulting from them: comp. "and brought forth (*ve-yalad*) falsehood" (Ps. vii. 14); also, "and they please themselves in the children (*yalde*) of strangers" (Isa. ii. 6), i.e., "they delight in the opinions of strangers." Jonathan the son of Uzziel paraphrases this passage, "they walk in the customs of other nations."

A man who has instructed another in any subject, and has improved his knowledge, may in like manner be regarded as the parent of the person taught, because he is the author of that knowledge: and thus the pupils of the prophets are called "sons of the prophets," as I shall explain when treating of the homonymity of *ben* (son). In this figurative sense, the verb *yalad* (to bear) is employed when it is said of Adam, "And Adam lived a hundred and thirty years, and begat (*va-yoled*) a son in his own likeness, in his form" (Gen. V. 3). As regards the words, "the form of Adam, and his likeness," we have already stated (ch. 1) their meaning. Those sons of Adam who were born before that time were not human in the true sense of the word, they had not "the form of man." With reference to Seth who had been instructed, enlightened and brought to human perfection, it could rightly be said, "he (Adam) begat a son in his likeness, in his form." It is acknowledged that a man who does not possess this "form" (the nature of which has just been explained) is not human, but a mere animal in human shape and form. Yet such a creature has the power of causing harm and injury, a power which does not belong to other creatures. For those gifts of intelligence and judgment with which he has been endowed for the purpose of acquiring perfection, but which he has failed to apply to their proper aim, are used by him for wicked and mischievous ends; he begets evil things, as though he merely resembled man, or simulated his outward appearance. Such was the condition of those sons of Adam who preceded Seth. In reference to this subject the Midrash says: "During the 130 years when Adam was under rebuke he begat spirits," i.e., demons; when, however, he was again restored to divine favour "he begat in his likeness, in his form." This is the sense of the passage, "Adam lived one hundred and thirty years, and he begat in his likeness, in his form" (Gen. v. 3).

CHAPTER VIII

ORIGINALLY the Hebrew term *makom* (place) applied both to a particular spot and to space in general; subsequently it received a wider signification and denoted "position," or "degree," as regards the perfection of man in certain things. We say, e.g., this man occupies a certain place in such and such a subject. In this sense this term, as is well known, is frequently used by authors, e.g., "He fills his ancestors' place (*makom*) in point of wisdom and piety"; "the dispute still remains in its place" (*makom*), i.e., *in statu quo* [*ante*]. In the verse, "Blessed be the glory of the Lord from His place" (*mekomo*) (Ezek. iii. 12), *makom* has this figurative meaning, and the verse may be paraphrased "Blessed be the Lord according to the exalted nature of His existence," and wherever *makom* is applied to God, it expresses the same idea, namely, the distinguished position of His existence, to which nothing is equal or comparable, as will be shown below (ch. LVI).

It should be observed that when we treat in this work of any homonym, we do not desire you to confine yourself to that which is stated in that particular chapter; but we open for you a portal and direct your attention to those significations of the word which are suited to our purpose, though they may not be complete from a philological point of view. You should examine the prophetical books and other works composed by men of science, notice the meaning of every word which occurs in them, and take homonyms in that sense which is in harmony with the context. What I say in a particular passage is a key for the comprehension of all similar passages. For example, we have explained here *makom* in the sentence "Blessed be the glory of the Lord from His place" (*mekomo*); but you must understand that the word makom has the same signification in the passage "Behold, a place (*makom*) is with me" (Exod. xxxiii. 26), viz., a certain degree of contemplation and intellectual intuition (not of ocular inspection), in addition to its literal meaning "a place," viz., the mountain which was pointed out to Moses for seclusion and for the attainment of perfection.

CHAPTER IX

THE original meaning of the word *kisse*, "throne," requires no comment. Since men of greatness and authority, as, e.g., kings, use the throne as a seat, and "the throne" thus indicates the rank, dignity, and position of the person for whom it is made, the Sanctuary has been styled "the throne," inasmuch as it likewise indicates the superiority of Him who manifests Himself, and causes His light and glory to dwell therein. Compare "A glorious throne on high from the beginning is the place of our sanctuary" (Jer. xvii. 12). For the same reason the heavens are called "throne," for to the mind of him who observes them with intelligence they suggest the Omnipotence of the Being which has called them into existence, regulates their motions, and governs the sublunary world by their beneficial influence: as we read, "Thus saith the Lord, The heavens are my throne and the earth my footstool" (Isa. lxvi. 1); i.e., they testify to my Existence, my Essence, and my Omnipotence, as the throne testifies to the greatness of him who is worthy to occupy it.

This is the idea which true believers should entertain; not, however, that the Omnipotent, Supreme God is supported by any material object; for God is incorporeal, as we shall prove further on; how, then, can He be said to occupy any space, or rest on a body? The fact which I wish to point out is this: every place distinguished by the Almighty, and chosen to receive His light and splendour, as, for instance, the Sanctuary or the Heavens, is termed "throne"; and, taken in a wider sense, as in the passage "For my hand is upon the throne of God" (Exod. xvii. 16), "the throne" denotes here the Essence and Greatness of God. These, however (the Essence and Greatness of God) need not be considered as something separate from the God Himself or as part of the Creation, so that God would appear to have existed both without the throne, and with the throne: such a belief would be undoubtedly heretical. It is distinctly stated, "Thou, O Lord, remainest for ever; Thy throne from generation to generation" (Lam. v. 19). By "Thy throne" we must, therefore, understand something inseparable from God. On that account, both here and in all similar passages, the word "throne" denotes God's Greatness and Essence, which are inseparable from His Being.

Our opinion will be further elucidated in the course of this Treatise.

STUDY QUESTIONS

1. Does Maimonides's *Guide* suggest there are potential dangers in inquiring too closely into philosophical matters?
2. Is there a contradiction between his characterization of Aristotle as "chief of philosophers" and his close reading of Hebrew scripture?

CHAPTER 10

REFORM AND RENEWAL IN THE GREATER WEST

10.1. EINHARD, *LIFE OF CHARLEMAGNE,* WRITTEN CA. 817–833

Einhard (ca. 775–840) was a longtime scholar and companion in the Carolingian court during the reigns of Charlemagne and his son, Louis the Pious. In a short, charming work perhaps modeled on Suetonius's *Lives of the Twelve Caesars* (Document 6.4), Einhard provides a glimpse into the daily life of Charlemagne—his likes and dislikes, his accomplishments and shortcomings. Although history remembers Charlemagne as a man of insatiable ambition and tireless political work, Einhard tempers this protodivine view with the reminder that Charlemagne, for all his imperial titles, also loved the company of his family and friends.

X. Charles also subdued the Bretons, who live on the sea coast, in the extreme western part of Gaul. When they refused to obey him, he sent an army against them, and compelled them to give hostages, and to promise to do his bidding. He afterwards entered Italy in person with his army, and passed through Rome to Capua, a city in Campania, where he pitched his camp and threatened the Beneventans with hostilities unless they should submit themselves to him. Their duke, Aragis, escaped the danger by sending his two sons, Rumold and Grimold, with a great sum of money to meet the King, begging him to accept them as hostages, and promising for himself and his people compliance with all the King's commands, on the single condition that his personal attendance should not be required. The King took the welfare of the people into account rather than the stubborn disposition of the Duke, accepted the proffered hostages, and released him from the obligation to appear before him in consideration of his handsome gift. He retained the younger son only as a hostage, and sent the elder back to his father, and returned to Rome, leaving commissioners with Aragis to exact the oath of allegiance, and administer it to the Beneventans. He stayed in Rome several days in order to pay his devotions at the holy places, and then came back to Gaul.

XI. At this time, on a sudden, the Bavarian war broke out, but came to a speedy end. It was due to the arrogance and folly of Duke Tassilo. His wife, a

From Einhard, *The Life of Charlemagne*. Ann Arbor: University of Michigan Press, 1961, pp. 34–7, 39–43.

daughter of King Desiderius, was desirous of avenging her father's banishment through the agency of her husband, and accordingly induced him to make a treaty with the Huns, the neighbors of the Bavarians on the east, and not only to leave the King's commands unfulfilled, but to challenge him to war. Charles' high spirit could not brook Tassilo's insubordination, for it seemed to him to pass all bounds; accordingly he straightway summoned his troops from all sides for a campaign against Bavaria, and appeared in person with a great army on the river Lech, which forms the boundary between the Bavarians and the Alemanni. After pitching his camp upon its banks, he determined to put the Duke's disposition to the test by an embassy before entering the province. Tassilo did not think it was for his own or his people's good to persist, so he surrendered himself to the King, gave them the hostages demanded, among them his own son Theodo, and promised by oath not to give ear to any one who should attempt to turn him from his allegiance; so this war, which bade fair to be very grievous, came very quickly to an end. Tassilo, however, was afterward summoned to the King's presence, and not suffered to depart, and the government of the province that he had had in charge was no longer entrusted to a duke, but to counts.

XII. After these uprisings had been thus quelled, war was declared against the Slavs who are commonly known among us as Wilzi, but properly, that is to say in their own tongue, are called Welatabians. The Saxons served in this campaign as auxilliaries among the tribes that followed the King's standard at his summons, but their obedience lacked sincerity and devotion. War was declared because the Slavs kept harassing the Adodriti, old allies of the Franks, by continual raids, in spite of all commands to the contrary. A gulf of unknown length, but nowhere more than a hundred miles wide, and in many parts narrower, stretches off towards the east from the Western Ocean. Many tribes have settlements on its shores; the Danes and Swedes, whom we call Northmen, on the northern shore and all the adjacent islands; but the southern shore is inhabited by the Slavs and Aïsti, and various other tribes. The Welatabians, against whom the King now made war, were the chief of these; but in a single campaign, which he conducted in person, he so crushed and subdued them that they did not think it advisable thereafter to refused obedience to his commands.

. . .

XIV. The Saxon War next came to an end as successful as the struggle had been long. The Bohemian and Linonian wars that next broke out could not last long; both were quickly carried out under the leadership of the younger Charles. The last of these wars was the one declared against the Northmen called Danes. They began their career as pirates, but afterward took to laying waste the coasts of Gaul and Germany with their large fleet. Their King Godfred was so puffed with vain aspirations that he counted on gaining empire over all Germany, and looked upon Saxony and Frisia as his provinces. He had already subdued his neighbors the Adodriti, and made them tributary, and boasted that he would shortly appear with a great army before Aix-la-Chapelle, where the King held his court. Some faith was put in his words, empty as they sound, and it is supposed that he would have attempted something of the sort of he had not been prevented by a premature death. He was murdered by one of his own bodyguard, and so ended at once his life and the war that he had begun.

XV. Such are the wars, most skillfully planned and successfully fought, which this most powerful king waged during the forty-seven years of his reign. He so largely increased the Frank kingdom, which was already great and strong when he received it at his father's hands, that more than double its former territory was added to it. The authority of the Franks was formerly confined to that part of Gaul included between the Rhine and the Loire, the Ocean and the Balearic Sea; to the part of Germany which is inhabited by the so-called Eastern Franks, and is bounded by Saxony and the Danube, the Rhine and the Saale—this stream separates the Thuringians from the Sorabians; and to the country of the Alemanni and Bavarians. By the wars above mentioned he first made tributary Aquitania, Gascony, and the whole of the region of the Pyrenees as far as the River Ebro, which rises in the land of the Navarrese, flows through the most fertile districts of Spain, and empties into the Balearic Sea, beneath the walls of the city of Tortosa. He next reduced and made tributary all Italy from Aosta to Lower Calabria, where the boundary line runs between the Beneventans and the Greeks, a territory more than a thousand miles long; then Saxony, which constitutes no small part of Germany, and is reckoned to be twice as wide as the country inhabited by the Franks, while about equal to it in length; in addition, both Pannonias, Dacia beyond the Danube, and Istria, Liburnia, and Dalmatia, except the cities on the coast, which he left to the Greek Emperor for friendship's sake, and because of the treaty that he had made with him. In fine, he vanquished and made tributary all the wild and barbarous tribes dwelling in Germany between the Rhine and the Vistula, the Ocean and the Danube, all of which speak very much the same language, but differ widely from one another in customs and dress. The chief among them are the Welatabians, the Sorabians, the Abodriti, and the Bohemians, and he had to make war upon these; but the rest, by far the larger number, submitted to him of their own accord.

XVI. He added to the glory of his reign by gaining the good will of several kings and nations; so close, indeed, was the alliance that he contracted with Alfonso, King of Galicia and Asturias, that the latter, when sending letters of ambassadors to Charles, invariably styled himself his man. His munificence won the kings of the Scots also to pay such deference to his wishes that they never gave him any other title than lord, or themselves than subjects and slaves: there are letters from them extant in which these feelings in his regard are expressed. His relations with Aaron, King of the Persians, who rules over almost the whole of the East, India excepted, were so friendly that this prince preferred his favor to that of all the kings and potentates of the earth, and considered that to him alone marks of honor and munificence were due. Accordingly, when the ambassadors sent by Charles to visit the most holy sepulcher and place of resurrection of our Lord and Savior presented themselves before him with gifts, and made known their master's wishes, he not only granted what was asked, but gave possession of that holy and blessed spot. When they returned, he dispatched his ambassadors with them, and sent magnificent gifts, besides, stuffs, perfumes, and other rich products of the Eastern lands. A few years before this, Charles had asked him for an elephant, and he sent the only one that he had. The Emperors of Constantinople, Nicephotus, Muchael, and Leo, made advances to Charles, and sought friendship and alliance with him by several embassies; and even when the Greeks suspected him of designing to wrest the empire from them, because of his assumption of the title Emperor, they made a close alliance with him, that he might have no cause of offense. In fact, the power of the Franks was always viewed by the Greeks and Romans with a jealous eye, whence the Greek proverb "Have the Frank for your friend, but not for your neighbor."

STUDY QUESTIONS

1. How does the document reinforce Charlemagne's status as a Christian warrior, particularly in his use of oaths and relics?
2. What does the exchange of gifts reveal about the scope and purpose of international relations in the period?

10.2. POPE GREGORY VII, *LETTERS*

Gregory VII (r. 1073–1085) was the most zealous and radical of the reforming popes, so much so that the Church Reform is widely named after him. Although he certainly was a forceful figure, it would be a mistake to consider him only as a Machiavellian pursuer of power for its own sake. The following sampler from his collected letters shows his personality from a variety of angles.

LETTER TO THE BISHOP OF LINCOLN, REGARDING A PRIEST SENT TO ROME TO ONFESS HIS GUILT IN KILLING A MAN (1073)

Bishop Gregory, servant of the servants of God, to Bishop Remedius of Lincoln, in England, sends greetings and apostolic blessing.

The bearer of this letter—the priest whom you charged, in your letter to me, with the crime of murder—cannot ever be permitted to serve the sacred altar in future, by any sanction of the holy fathers. Neither can I consent to his restitution [to holy orders], for that (Heaven forbid!) would go against canon law.

However, if you, in your compassion, find that he displays before God sufficient penance for the crime he committed, then as an act of charity you should see to it that he is granted some means of support from the Church, lest he be crushed by poverty and led to ungodly living. While he may never, under any condition, merit a return to priestly life, he may justifiably receive some provision from the Apostolic See.

On the other matter for which you wrote—namely, your request that I absolve you of your own sins by the authority of the chief Apostles, Sts. Peter and Paul, in whose place I, however unworthy, serve—I hereby do so, so long as you do all you can to preserve the purity of your body as a temple before God.

And as for your final request, that I command your best services on my behalf, I hereby issue this particular demand—that you strengthen me with your prayers, so that we may together be worthy of eternal joy.

LETTER TO THE BISHOP OF CHALON-SUR-SAÔNE, REGARDING REPORTS OF SIMONY AND OTHER ABUSES COMMITTED BY KING PHILIP I OF FRANCE (1073)

I have learned from several trusted sources that among the rulers of our time who have brought ruin to God's Church by greedily putting it up for sale. . . . King Philip of France so greatly oppresses the French churches that he seems to have become the epitome of this hateful sin. His actions are even more offensive since they occur in a realm widely known for its good judgment, piety, strength, and its steadfast devotion to the Roman Church. I am particularly outraged (that is, not simply as a matter of fulfilling my duties as pope) by his actual destruction of churches. We need to condemn much more severely such audacious attacks on our very religion. Through his chamberlain Alberic, the king gave us every assurance that he would respect our position, reform his personal life, and set the churches of France in good order.

For these reasons I wish now to test the value of his promise in regard to the church of Mâcon, which has long lacked a bishop and has been reduced practically to rubble, and therefore it is my desire that he permit the archdeacon of Autun, unanimously elected by the clergy and people there and (I am told) approved by the king, to be installed as the new bishop of Mâcon—and that this installation take place, as of course it ought, without any payment of

Translation by Clifford Backman.

money. If Philip refuses, let him know without any doubt that I will not permit such ruination of the Church, but will attack his stubborn persistence in disobedience with all the canonical severity I possess, by the authority of the Blessed Apostles Sts. Peter and Paul. Either the king will abandon his evil commerce in the heresy of simony and freely allow worthy people to be installed in the leadership of the Church, or the people of France will be cut down by the sword of a general anathema. Unless they intend to reject the Christian faith altogether, the people will refuse to obey him in future.

I go to the trouble of entrusting this letter to you, my ever-watchful and loving brother [in Christ], so that you will convey it to King Philip and make every possible effort—in writing, speech, or action—to persuade him to allow the church of Mâcon, and every French church, to be provided with pastors according to canon law. I have laid this duty upon you because I know you to be of sound judgment and to be close to the king. If I have overlooked anything, please supply it by your own keen intelligence. May you carry out this purpose in such a way that you win God's favor and my good will.

AN EARLY CALL TO CRUSADE (1074)

Bishop Gregory, servant of the servants of God, to all who are willing to defend the Christian faith, sends greetings and apostolic blessing.

You should know that the person bearing this letter, returning from across the sea, came to Rome and met with me, in which meeting he repeated the news we have already heard from so many others—namely, that a pagan people have vanquished the Christians [in the East] and with unimaginable cruelty have laid waste to all the lands almost to the very walls of Constantinople; that these conquered territories they are now ruling with tyrannical violence; and that they have slain untold thousands of Christians as though they were so many sheep. Out of our love for God and our wish to be recognized as Christians, we ought to be overwhelmed with grief at the wound done to this great [Byzantine] empire and the murder of so many faithful Christians, and yet we are called to more than grief alone. The example of Our

Redeemer and the bonds of brotherly love summon us to offer our lives in order to liberate them: "Because He has laid down His life for us, and we ought to lay down our lives for our brothers" [1 John 3.16].

You should therefore know that, trusting in God's mercy and the power of His might, we are now doing all that we can to prepare to bring aid to the Christian [Byzantine] Empire as soon as possible, and therefore we beseech and admonish you, by the faith in which you are united through Christ in caring for all the sons of God, and by the authority of St. Peter, the Prince of the Apostles, to feel compassion for the wounds and blood of your brethren and the threat now confronting the aforesaid empire. For the sake of Christ we beg you to join in the difficult task of bringing aid to our brothers. Send us your messengers at once, informing us of what God inspires you to do in this matter.

LETTER TO THE DIOCESE OF CONSTANCE (1075)

Gregory, bishop and servant of the servants of God, to all the clergy and laity, both great and small, in the diocese of Constance who love Christian law, greetings and an apostolic blessing.

We sent to our brother Otto, your bishop, a most earnest letter in which (as our office requires) we ordered him, by our apostolic authority, to root out the heresy of Simony from his church and to uphold by zealous preaching the requirement of chastity among the clergy, and to enforce its steadfast maintenance by episcopal visitation. The words of the Gospels and the letters of the apostles, not to mention the decrees of authoritative council and the teachings of our most honored doctors have all commended it, and so we cannot disregard the issue or neglect it without risking great injury to our soul and the souls of all the people of Christ. Your bishop, however, has been inspired neither by reverence for St. Peter's command nor by the duty of his office—for we have discovered that he has not made any efforts to carry out our fatherly instructions. Instead, we have heard that he has openly permitted his clergy to act in ways repugnant to our (indeed, St. Peter's) command—which turns his guilt of disobedience into one of rebellion.

For he has not only allowed clergy who already had women to keep them, but has even permitted those who did not have women the unlawful shamelessness of taking them!

Having learned of this, we were deeply angered and sent him a second letter that made the depth of our indignation quite clear and enjoined him even more sharply to obey our command. At the same time we summoned him to appear at the Roman Synod called for the first week of the next season of Lent, to give an account of himself and to explain to the entire assembly the reasons (if there can possibly be any) for his disobedience.

Dearest sons, we bring all of this to your attention in order to help save your souls. For if he remains determined to be openly hostile and belligerent to St. Peter and the Holy and Apostolic See, then it is clearly shown that a man who does not honor his mother and father has no right to expect or ask their faithful children to give obedience to him. It is unseemly for a man who submits to no master to lord it over disciples of his own. Therefore by our apostolic authority, as already stated, we charge all of you, both great and small, who stand on the side of God and St. Peter to show [Bishop Otto] neither respect nor obedience while he continues in his determined obstinacy; you need not fear endangering your souls on this account. For if he remains determined to resist our commands, as we have already stated, then by the authority of St. Peter we absolve all of you from every necessity to obey him; even if you are bound to him by a sacred oath, as long as he is a rebel against God and the Apostolic See you shall owe him no loyalty at all—for a man should obey no one before his Creator, Who has pride of place over all others. We are obliged to resist anyone who is self-proud against God, so that he may, in the face of this resistance, learn to turn back to the path of righteousness.

What a dangerous thing it is, and how far removed from Christian law, to refuse to be obedient, especially to the Holy See—as you can learn from the words of the blessed prophet Samuel (the very words that Pope Gregory [I] took care to expound in the last book of his *Moralia*). We set them in writing now, so that we may keep them before us; in this way you will know beyond doubt that this is no new teaching we are speaking of. We are merely rehearsing the ancient teaching of the holy fathers: "But Samuel said, 'Obedience is better than sacrifice, to listen, better than the fat of rams. For a sin of divination is rebellion, and arrogance, the crime of idolatry.'" [1 Sam 15.22–23] It is right that obedience be valued more than sacrifices, because in sacrifice we kill flesh that is not our own, but in obedience we kill our own will. How much more readily a man pleases God to the extent he overcomes his own willful pride and sacrifices himself before God's eyes by the sword of His command! Disobedience, though, is likened to the sin of witchcraft in order to show by contrast how great is the virtue of obedience; the contrast makes it clear how much we should praise the latter. For if rebellion is like the sin of witchcraft, and stubbornness like the crime of idolatry, then only obedience brings the reward of faith—for without obedience a man can appear to be faithful while actually being the opposite.

TO THE ALMORAVID RULER OF MAURETANIA, THANKING HIM FOR HIS RECENT GIFTS AND THE RELEASE OF SOME PRISONERS (1076)

God, Who created the universe and without Whom we can neither do nor even think anything good, has inspired you, in your heart, to this act of kindness; and as He enlightens all who come into this world, He has enlightened your mind to this end. The Almighty God, Who desires that all people be saved and none perish, mercifully urges us, above all, that apart from loving Him we love one another, desiring to do nothing to another that we would not want done to ourselves. For this reason, we—that is, you and I—are especially obliged to show to the nations an example of this loving kindness, for we believe and confess the same One God, although in different ways, and we praise and worship Him daily as the Creator of all things and the Ruler of this world. As the Apostle [Paul] says: "He is our peace, Who has made us both one." [Eph. 2.14] Many of our leading figures here in Rome, when I informed them of your gracious act in the name of God, expressed admiration and approval of your good will and virtue. . . .

The Lord knows that we extend to you our love, for His honor, and that we hope for your salvation and glory, both in this life and in the next; and we pray in our heart and with our lips that God will lead you to the Abode of Happiness, the bosom of the holy patriarch Abraham, after many years of life here on earth.

TO ABBOT PETER OF FUCECCHIO AND PRIOR RUDOLF OF CAMALDOLI (1081?)

Gregory, bishop and servant of the servants of God, to Abbot Peter of Fucecchio and Prior Rudolf of Camaldoli, greetings and an apostolic blessing.

You requested that I absolve Ughiccio the son of Bulgarelli even though he has neither confessed his sin nor repented of it. As you know, before he sinned so grievously I held him dear and loved him more than any of his fellow-princes in Tuscany, because, like his father before him, he worked diligently to defend the good and to establish true religion in his lands. That is why, if it were at all possible to agree to your request, I would gladly grant him absolution on account of his own former goodness and his wife's current prayers, along with your own request. But neither reason nor the custom of the Holy Church permits this; neither does the example of the Holy Fathers offer a precedent for absolving someone who has been properly and canonically excommunicated, refuses to admit his fault, and does not seek forgiveness with his whole heart. Unless a man repents with his whole heart and confesses his sin, any absolution offered him would be without effect and could only be regarded as a lie.

But since Count Ughiccio continues to defend his wickedness by insisting his excommunication was unjust and done in order to win political points elsewhere, he should himself investigate and ponder the writings of the Holy Fathers on such matters. He should remember that he took part in a sacrilegious conspiracy by the citizens of Lucca and not make matters worse for himself by defending his actions. On top of this, he brought down the sword of anathema on himself for a second and no less serious failing: he allowed, and even encouraged, the lawfully and canonically installed bishop of Lucca to be driven from his church.

In all honesty, I would not wish to excommunicate anyone against the dictates of justice, not even if I knew that I myself would have to suffer going into exile or risk injury on that account; for every person, even the most insignificant, is someone for whom Christ shed His blood. But in order to persuade Count Ughiccio to repent his crime in a fitting, Christian way, I would gladly risk any harm or danger that might come to me, and therefore I urge you and plead with you to remember him in your daily prayers, imploring God's mercy to visit, soften, and turn to penitence Ughiccio's heart and mind—so that through sincere penance, tears, and pleas for forgiveness for his sins Ughiccio may some day be counted again, by his performance of good works, among the members of the Holy Church.

STUDY QUESTIONS

1. What sort of pope emerges from the letters of Gregory VII? How would you describe his political outlook?
2. What picture of the second half of the 11th century emerges from Gregory's correspondence? Is it a connected world?

10.3. GUIBERT DE NOGENT, *GESTA DEI*, 1107–1108

The French monk Guibert of Nogent (ca. 1055–1124) entered the church at around the age of twelve, but his firsthand knowledge of knights and, most importantly, crusaders, gives his *God's Deeds* through the Franks a particularly personalized account of the curiosities of the First Crusade (1096–1099). Guibert also wrote a protoautobiography—the first major example since Augustine's *Confessions* in the 5th century—that reveals his interior mode of thought. These selections from *God's Deeds* vividly describe crusader events: a battle between the Turks and the crusaders, a false miracle, the experience of viewing the city of Antioch for the first time, and the difficulties and curiosities of war.

BOOK IV

After the count of Saint-Gilles heard that the Turks, who usually supplied the garrison for the city of Antioch, had left the stronghold, he sent part of his army ahead to take possession of the city and to maintain control of it. He chose four men from among the leaders of his army, of whom three had the same name, that is, Peter, and the fourth was called William of Montpellier, a man well known among us for his feats of arms, and he gave them 500 knights to lead. And so, not far from the above-mentioned city, they entered a valley and in that valley found a fort, and there they heard that the Turks, with a large army, were in control of the city of Antioch, and in addition they learned that the Turks were making great preparations of men and arms, to defend themselves against the French, in case they attacked. Therefore one of those Peters we named above, whose surname had been derived from a place called Roaix, separating himself from his companions, entered a valley of a town named Rugia, [151] where he found Turks and Saracens, with whom he fought. After killing many of them, he pursued the others. The Armenians took notice of this and, pleased with the man's bravery, and impressed by his unusual boldness against the Turks, surrendered voluntarily to his command.

Quickly thereafter he was given control of a city named Rusa [152] when its inhabitants capitulated, and several other forts surrendered to him. The rest of the army departed from Coxon, the city we mentioned, and marched through high mountains along incredibly rocky paths so narrow that no one could pass the man in front of him, but each man had to proceed one step at a time, stepping carefully, in single file. A deep gulley lay beneath the narrow, rough path, so that if a horse happened to push up against another horse, he would fall to instant death. There you would have seen armed men, who, having just been converted by the hardship and starvation of the journey from knights into foot-soldiers, were suffering wretchedly, smashing their fists, tearing their hair, begging for the relief of death, selling their shields, helmets, and all of their arms, regardless of their true worth, for three or four, perhaps five cents. When they could find no buyer, they threw their shields and other fine equipment into the gulley, to disencumber their weakened, endangered bodies. When they finally emerged from these rocks and precipices, after unbearable suffering, they entered a town called Marasim, [153] whose inhabitants came forth joyfully to meet them, bringing abundant supplies to sell to the soldiers. The rich earth replenished

Guibert de Nogent, *The Deeds of God through the Franks.* http://www.gutenberg.org/cache/epub/4370/pg4370.html/.

the exhausted men, until the presence of their leader Bohemund, who was following those who were waiting for him there, was restored to them.

Finally they arrived in the plains where the renowned city of Antioch was situated, whose particular glories, beyond those by means of which she flourished in this world, are those which grew out of her Christian fame. Pharphar was the name of the river on which she was located. When our men had reached a place near the bridge over that river, some of them, who had been assigned the task of forming the vanguard of the army, met up with a large force of Turks, who were well supplied with provisions, and were hurrying to bring aid to the besieged. When our men saw them, they charged with Frankish ferocity, and almost instantly defeated them and scattered them in all directions. Like charging rams, they tore them to pieces, and the Turks threw away the arms that only moments before had been able to inspire terror. The mass of foot-soldiers fled through their own lines, in their haste and confusion wounding and crushing their own allies. The madness of pride now felt humiliation, and the man who anticipated taking pleasure in heaping up destruction upon us was now happy if he could get himself out alive, even though dishonored. Those who had come to bring aid to the besieged were turned into instant, filthy piles of cadavers. The Almighty mercifully converted what they had brought to aid the besieged into gifts for the besiegers. Thus after they had been destroyed, like grain crushed by hail, great quantities of grain and wine fell into our hands, and the foot-soldiers acquired the valuable horses, camels, mules, and asses that remained. And so our men built camps on the shore of the above-mentioned river. Bohemund, together with 4000 of his best men, undertook blockade of the city's gate, and remained on guard all that night to prevent anyone from getting in or out. The next day, the twelfth calends of November, [154] the fourth day of the week, in the middle of the day, the army arrived, set up camp, and began a blockade of three of the city's gates; the fourth gate was left free, since it was inaccessible to the besiegers because of the great height of the surrounding mountains, and the narrowness of its paths. However, not only the inhabitants, but the Turks themselves who were inside the city were so frightened by us that none of them came out to fight us. No one put up any resistance, but instead they behaved as though we had come to the market, and this pretense of peace continued, as though a truce had been declared, for fifteen days. The city was surrounded by signs that augured well for beginning this siege; fresh abundance of everything necessary to sustain life was vividly present; I am surprised that at that time the crusaders found abundant grapes hanging on the vines everywhere, wheat shut up not in granaries, but in ditches and underground pits. The trees had plenty of apples, and whatever made their lives more comfortable was supplied by an extremely fertile soil. The Armenians and the Syrians, who formed the entire population of the city (except for the Turks, who, as I mentioned earlier, were not permanent residents), since they inhabited the city itself, and were titular Christians, visited us in great numbers, and told them whatever they had learned among us. They enticed the Franks with their deceptive, repeated lies, and, whispering in their ears, using the most flattering terms, they claimed that they shunned the Turks, although they did not allow their own wives to go beyond the city limits; when they left the Franks, and were back in the city, they reported to the Turks whatever news they had been able to gather about the weaknesses of the Christian side. Thus, informed by the Syrians about our plans, the Turks from time to time rushed out from the city to sneak up upon our men and attack them as they were searching for food, and they covered over the most used paths and made unexpected attacks upon them as they sought the mountains and the sea, never permitting them to rest from ambush or open attack. Not far off was a fort named Harenc [155] in which they had placed a garrison of the fiercest Turkish warriors, who made frequent raids upon the Franks when they were unprepared. Our leaders, unwilling to suffer such affronts, sent a large force of cavalry and infantry to find out where those who were doing so much harm to their men were concealing themselves. When they found their hiding place, they at first attacked them, but then, cleverly simulating flight, they permitted themselves to be brought to a position where they knew that Bohemund was waiting in ambush. At that point, two of our men died in pursuit of the Turks. Coming out of his hiding-place, Bohemund fell upon the enemy, leading the group who appeared to have turned their backs, delivering the punishment they deserved by attacking the Turks with all his forces. He killed many of them, made others prisoners, and brought those he had captured back to the gate of the city, where, to terrify the citizens who were watching, he ordered that they be decapitated. Some of the citizens, however, climbed to the top of this gate and wore out our men by discharging so many arrows that a cloud of missiles flowed in the midst of Bohemund's camp, and one woman died when struck by one of the arrows. Finally the leaders consulted with each other, and decided to set up a fort at the top of a mountain which they called Malregard, and which, as a formidable stronghold, might serve to drive away the Turks. Thus the fort was being constructed, and there you would have seen the greatest princes laboring at carrying rocks. There no poor man might complain that he had to endure hardships inflicted upon him by the power of great men, since those who were in charge would permit themselves no rest in bringing the work to completion. For they knew by the instinct of pious nature, even if they had not read it, what Marius, according to Sallust, said, "If you behave gently, but rule the army firmly, you will be a master, not an general." [156] And when the fort was built, the leaders took turns guarding it. Christmas was near, and the grain and other food for the body began to diminish severely, and throughout the army everything that was for sale was expensive. There was no energy to go even a moderate distance to seek food; within the territory held by those who called themselves Christians almost nothing to eat could be found; no one could go into the Saracen region without large military force. Therefore, compelled by hunger, the leaders held a meeting to discuss how to deal with the danger of such a large group of men starving unless something were done for them. Finally they decided to send part of the army to search everywhere for supplies, while the others maintained the siege they had undertaken. Bohemund then said, "If, O powerful soldiers, it seems prudent to you, I, with the support of the army of the count of Flanders, shall devote myself to the effort of procuring food."

The offer was accepted gratefully by the younger men, since they were worn out by greater thirst and more urgent need for food. The day after the Lord's Nativity, which was the second day of the week, had been celebrated, with what emotion and energy they could muster, the two princes just mentioned, together with 20,000 foot-soldiers and cavalry, set out as swiftly and as energetically as they could to attack the Saracen provinces. Meanwhile the Turks, Arabs, Saracens, and other Gentiles, who had assembled from Jerusalem, Damascus, Aleph, [157] and other places, with one purpose in mind, to bring aid, hastened to Antioch in large numbers. They had heard that the Christians were coming into their own lands, to gather food and other supplies; as dusk fell, they moved in formation towards the place where they had learned our men were, with an eagerness that would soon be turned to grief. They divided themselves into two lines of battle, setting the first in front of us, and moving to position the other behind us. But the count of Flanders, trusting in divine power, with the sign of the Cross fixed to his heart and body, relying confidently on the excellent count Bohemund, attacked the enemy with the courage to be expected of such men. The battle began, but from the first moment of contact, the enemy turned in flight. The battle turned into victory, and many a sharp spear shattered in the bodies of those who had turned their backs to flee. The enemy's shields were battered by long ashwood lances that were struck with such force that they dwindled into slivers. No helmet prevented a head struck by the edges of the Crusaders' swords from being wounded; and they found the stitching of their so-called impenetrable cuirasses too fragile. Armor protected no part of the body; whatever the barbarians thought firm was weak; whatever the Franks touched shattered. The field was covered with innumerable corpses, and the thick pile of dead men disturbed the evenness of the grassy field. Everywhere the earth, sprinkled with the hateful blood of Gentiles, grew dark. Those who survived the carnage we inflicted saved their lives by their speed afoot, and were pleased to unburden themselves of their spoils, not out of generosity towards us, but to increase their speed. Our state of mind changed utterly: fear changed into courage, battle into victory, mourning into joy, hunger into plenty. He who was naked now had clothing, those who were on foot now had chariots, the poor man had money, the man who had been cast out now danced with gratitude and joy. While these things were going on, the fact that Bohemund and the count of Flanders were not present at the siege was not hidden from the Turks who were in control of Antioch. Made more confident by their absence, they came out, though cautiously, to challenge us in battle more often, trying to find out where the besiegers were weakest. Finally, seeing day, the third day of the week, that seemed apt for trying their courage, they made a sudden assault, and killed many of our foot-soldiers and knights, who were caught unaware. The magnificent bishop of Puy lost a mainstay of his court, the man who was his standard-bearer, who was among those who perished. Had not the river upon whose banks their camp was pitched separated them, the carnage among the Christians would have been very great. Meanwhile, Bohemund was on his way back, having pillaged the Saracen provinces; he was traveling through the mountainous area in which Tancred was staying, thinking that there he might be able to find something to help the men besieging Antioch. Although some of our men had carried off whatever they could see, many found nothing at all, and returned empty-handed, that is, without anything that could be eaten. Bohemund, however, never without a plan, when he saw them wandering about unsuccessfully, spoke these words, "If you are looking for material with which to sustain life, if you want to provide adequately for the bodily needs dictated by hunger, then while you search for food do not risk your lives. Stop scurrying through the pathless mountains, since you know that your enemies are preparing hidden traps for you in these horrible, desolate places. Let the army move forward united, for each is made stronger by the presence of the other, so that if one part is attacked violently, the other may offer assistance. For even as a sheep, if it escapes from the shepherd's grasp, is exposed to the wolf's jaws, so the knight, if he wanders forth alone from the tents of his companions, invariably becomes a plaything for plunderers. Therefore remain together with each other and with your men, and rather eat very little food than feed upon rare delicacies in permanent captivity. To go out and come back together, to take pleasure in being together, to do nothing rash, these are the things that sensible men do; anyone who wanders away wishes to die." He spoke, and returned to his companions, without enriching the besiegers in no way by his return. But the clever Armenians and Syrians, when they saw that the army's food was running out, and there was nothing left to buy, traveled about among all the places that they knew, bought grain, and brought it back to the army that was suffering from a lack of supplies. They sold the grain at inordinate prices, so that the amount of grain a single ass could carry brought eight of their besants, which they called "purpled," approximately 120 sous. Clearly those who could not possibly pay such a price were in great danger of succumbing to a terrible crisis of hunger. And if the leaders were already becoming hard pressed to pay such price, what could he do who, for all his previous wealth, was now all but a pauper?

STUDY QUESTIONS

1. What is the role of the Christian God in this battle?
2. What does the document reveal about Western Christians' prejudices against non-Catholic Christians in the Greater West?

10.4. PETER ABELARD, *SIC ET NON*

Peter Abelard was an early proponent of the new learning of the 12th-century Renaissance. A rascally student and later a brilliant teacher, he made a name for himself with his first important book, *Sic et Non* (*Yes and No*), which was a compilation of contradictory passages from patristic sources and Church councils. Abelard's purpose was to highlight the fact that ecclesiastical tradition alone is insufficient to lead the faithful to truth. A critical intelligence and the application of logic was required—precisely the tools offered by the new learning. The preface to the book is printed below. The ellipses [. . .] consist mostly of examples he quotes to illustrate his points.

If some of the writings of the saints not only differ from one another but actually contradict each other, we ought not to rush to judgment (given the sheer multitude of their written words) about those great figures by whom the world itself is to be judged—for as the Scriptures say, "The saints shall judge the nations" [Wisdom 3.7–8], and also, "You will also sit as a judge" [Matthew 19.28]. So let us not presume to dismiss as liars, or condemn as mistaken, those men of whom the Lord Himself said, "Whoever listens to you, listens to Me; and whoever rejects you, rejects Me" [Luke 10.16]. Remembering our own weakness of mind, let us be more sure of our lack of understanding than of their inability to write, for they are the ones of whom He Who is Truth Itself once said, "For it is not you who are speaking, but the Spirit of your Father Who speaks through you" [Matthew 10.20]. Is it any wonder, then, since we lack the Spirit through Which these things were written, spoken, and revealed to the saints, that we should also lack the means to understand their teachings? Especially given the fact that each of those writers is as overflowing in wisdom as in words. As Cicero pointed out, sameness in everything destroys the appetite and causes one to feel queasy; and so it is fitting that the writings of our forefathers vary on issue after issue and that they are not cheapened by the use of low, common language. As St. Augustine observed, ideas should not be reviled simply because they are obscure; indeed, they should be more highly valued, the more difficult they are to investigate and understand. Considering the great diversity of the people we are talking about, it is to be expected that their writings are an assortment. The precise meaning of any of their words might be unknown or unfamiliar to many readers. And if we are going to use these texts for considering matters of doctrine, we ought to pay more attention to how they have been understood [down the centuries] than how their specific wording functions, as no less an expert on language than the great grammarian Priscian has taught us. . . .

Whenever we confront writings of the saints that appear to contradict truth, we ought to be especially careful not to be misled by false attributions of authorship or corruptions in the text, for there are many apocryphal works in circulation that have saints' names attached to them in order to give them greater authority, and even the texts of the Holy Scriptures are sometimes corrupted by scribal errors. This is what St. Jerome, the most trustworthy author and reliable translator of all, warned of in his letter to Laeta, concerning her daughter's education: "Let her be wary of all apocryphal writings. Even if she wants to read them not for their dogmatic truth but only to enjoy their miracle stories, she should know that they were not written by the men listed as their authors. It takes a great deal of discernment to find any gold hidden in such mud." . . . [Jerome also found scribal errors in the Holy Gospels:] "We find another

Translation by Clifford Backman.

instance in the gospel of Matthew, where it says 'then he gave back the thirty pieces of silver, as it is written in the book of the prophet Jeremiah' [Matthew 27.9]. Only we do not find this phrase in Jeremiah; it is in Zechariah [Zechariah 11.13]. Behold—an error, just like any other." Is it any wonder, then, since scribes in their ignorance have even introduced errors into the gospels, if we see mistakes creeping into the writings of the later Church Fathers, which are far less authoritative? Therefore, when we encounter anything in the books of the saints that seems to be contradictory to truth, the pious, humble, and charitable thing to do . . . is to assume that at that specific point the text may have been corrupted or incorrectly translated, or else to acknowledge that we do not understand it.

No less important is it to consider whether such passages come from writings by the saints that they themselves later retracted or corrected once they had discovered the truth. St. Augustine did this many times. Or perhaps they were writing to cite the opinion of someone else rather to express than their own view—as Ecclesiastes often did, introducing many unsound statements into the Scriptures. He wanted to be understood, not to stir up confusion. . . .

It is an element of everyday speech to describe the existence of things according to the perceptions of our senses. For example, we know that no truly empty space exists anywhere in the world—that is, a space that utterly lacks air or any other type of matter—and yet we straightforwardly call a box or chest "empty" because that is how our sense of sight perceives it. We judge things by the evidence of our eyes: thus sometimes we speak of the starry heavens, and sometimes not; sometimes we say the sun is hot, and other times not; sometimes we say the moon is more or less bright, and sometimes not so much. Similarly, we sometimes say that things will remain the same forever, when it is clear to us that they will not. Why is it so surprising, therefore, if we occasionally find ideas expressed by the Holy Fathers in their writings that are their own opinions rather than the actual truth? Whenever contradictory things are said about a single issue, we must be careful to distinguish statements offered with the force of a command, from those offered with a measure of indulgence, and from those offered as exhortations to perfection.

Only by considering the intentions behind such passages, can we hope to find a remedy for statements that oppose one another.

If a statement is a direct command, we must decide if it is general or specific—that is, one applicable to everyone in general, or to certain individuals alone. We need to take into account when certain statements were made, or the reasons for their being made, because it often happens that what one time-period permitted, another one forbade, and what is often commanded with great insistence is sometimes tempered with flexibility. It is especially necessary to make these distinctions when dealing with the Church's decrees and canons. It will be easy to resolve many controversies if we can be on our guard for different authors using the same words but for different purposes.

Any reader who cares to resolve conflicts in the writings of the saints will pay attention to all these matters. If a conflict is so great that it cannot be resolved by reasoning, then the authorities must be weighed against one another, and whichever side has stronger evidence and more likelihood [of being correct] should be retained above all. Thus did St. Isidore say to the bishop of Massio: "To close this letter of mine, let me add that whenever opposing opinions are found in the acts of Church council, more weight should be given to the view that is of greater and more ancient authority."

Indeed, it has happened that various prophets have lacked, at times, the grace of prophecy, but being in the habit of prophesying have offered false statements of their own making, believing as they made them that the spirit of prophesy was truly upon them. God allowed the errors to occur as a means of keeping the prophets humble—that they might recognize more clearly what things come from the Spirit of God, and what comes from their own spirits; and know that when they possess the spirit of prophecy they have it as a gift from the Holy Spirit, Who can neither lie nor be mistaken. For when this Spirit is upon one, just as it does not bestow all its gifts on one person, so does it not enlighten the mind of the prophet regarding everything; instead, it reveals a bit here, and a bit there, and whenever it clarifies one thing it conceals another. St. Gregory said as much in his first homily on Ezechiel, using clear examples. And even St. Peter, the prince of the apostles, shimmering with miracles and the gifts of divine grace after the extraordinary pouring out of the Holy Spirit, promised by God, and who taught his disciples nothing but the truth, was not ashamed to abandon a pernicious untruth [he had asserted] about the practice of circumcision and various other ancient rites, after he was publicly and soundly corrected (although in a friendly way) by the Apostle Paul.

When it becomes clear that even the prophets and apostles were no strangers to error, what is the surprise in finding some mistakes in the numerous writings of the holy fathers, or in their scribal transmission? Just as these saints should not be accused of lying, if at one time or another they have said something contrary to the truth, for they were acting out of simple ignorance rather than duplicity—so too, and in the same way, one ought not impute to presumption or sinfulness something that someone says out of love and in order to teach. For as all know, God distinguishes between actions on the basis of the intentions that lay behind them, as it says in Matthew, "If your eye is sound, your whole body will be full of light" [Matthew 6.22]. And in the treatise *On Ecclesiastical Discipline* by St. Augustine: "Have charity, and do what you can." . . . For it is one thing to lie, quite another to make an error when speaking—so long as one falls away from the truth by mistake rather than out of malice. If God allows this to happen even to His holy saints, as we have pointed out, in situations where no harm is done to the faith, then it does not fail to bear fruit for those very saints, who undertake all things for the sake of the good. Even the Doctors of the Church—who are so diligently attentive— believe that there exist errors in their writings that need correction; this is why they grant to posterity the license to emend those texts or simply not to follow them, if they themselves did not have the time to retract or correct their works. . . .

One ought to read literature not with the requirement of believing it but with the freedom to judge it. And in order that the room for this freedom be not lost, and that the healthy work of treating difficult questions and translating their language and style is not denied to later authors, the excellence of the canonical authority of the Old and New Testaments has been set apart from the books of later authors. If anything there strikes the reader as absurd, he cannot say that the author of this or that book did not possess the truth. Either the manuscript is corrupt, or the translator made a mistake, or the reader has failed to understand. . . .

[St. Augustine] calls the canonical writings of the Old and New Testaments texts about which it is heresy to say that something in them contradicts truth. In this regard he wrote, in his fourth letter to St. Jerome: "In commenting on the Letter of Paul to the Galatians I came across something that distressed me terribly. But if something in the Holy Scriptures is, or can be shown to be, a lie (even a "white lie") then what authority will the text have thereafter? How can anyone pass judgment on the Scriptures? Who is so shameless as to crush them under the heavy weight of falsehood?" And in another letter on the same issues: "It seems to me to be an exceedingly dangerous thing to regard anything in holy books as a lie—that is, to think that the men through whom the Scriptures were written and passed on to us would have lied about anything in their books. For if a single lie, even the smallest one, is acknowledged to exist in so lofty an authority, then not a single particle of the books will remain, which someone will not explain away as the invention or imagining of the author's mind, using this incredibly dangerous excuse whenever someone comes across something difficult to practice or hard to believe." . . .

With these points now made, may it please you that I have here endeavored to gather various passages from the holy fathers that stand out in my memory on account of their apparently differing opinions on various issues. May these passages inspire young readers to strenuous exercise in seeking out the truth, and may the search make them sharper readers in the end. The first key to wisdom is defined, of course, as determined and frequent questioning. Aristotle, the most insightful philosopher of them all, urged his students to embrace the act of questioning with their whole hearts; in his preface "Ad aliquid" he wrote: "Perhaps it is difficult to declare confidently on matters of this sort, unless one does it often and in great detail; but it would not be useless to doubt a number of specific points." For indeed, by doubting we come to questioning, and by questioning we discover the truth. "Seek, and you will find," said the One Who is Truth Itself; "knock, and the door will be opened for you." He taught us with His own moral example. Sitting at age twelve amidst His teachers and inquiring into those things He wanted to discover, He showed us by His questions the way to be a student rather than the way to be a teacher by exposition, even though the full and complete wisdom of God was present in Him. Therefore, when certain passages of Scripture are laid before us, the authority of those very Scriptures is commended the more they excite the reader and spur him to seek out their truth.

For this reason it pleased me, in this current book, to compile into a single volume numerous passages from the writings of the saints, following the decree of Pope Gelasius regarding the books that are held to be authentic. Thus it is assured that I have introduced nothing from apocryphal writings. I have appended excerpts from the *Retractations* of St. Augustine, from which it will be clear that I have quoted nothing that he himself later retracted or corrected.

STUDY QUESTIONS

1. How does Abelard construct his argument that ecclesiastical tradition alone is insufficient to lead the faithful to truth? What evidence does he provide to support his case?
2. What are the characteristics of Abelard's argument that make it representative of the new rationale approach to understanding that emerged in the 12th century?

10.5. OTTO OF FREISING, *THE TWO CITIES*

Bishop Otto of Freising (1115–1158) is one of our best sources for the German empire from the 10th to 12th centuries. His book *The Two Cities* is an example of a "universal history": in eight books it proceeds from the creation of the world and the story of Adam and Eve to Otto's own time. The goal of "universal history" was to view contemporary events in a broader context, in the effort to see God's hand at work in the world. In this passage from Book Six (ch. 27–33), Otto relates the German leaders' role in spreading Latin Christianity into eastern Europe, among the Poles and Hungarians.

[27] In the year 1001 from the Incarnation of Our Lord, the emperor Otto [III] died without an heir, and Duke Henry of Bavaria, the son of Hezilo, was elected to succeed him by all the nobles. He was the eighty-seventh ruler in line from Augustus. Henry waged many wars—bravely, successfully—throughout Germany, Bohemia, Italy, and Apulia until God finally granted him his rest, and being so devout in his Christian faith, he established the renowned bishopric of Bamberg and endowed it with the many lands and honors we see in our own lifetime. Moreover, he gave his sister Gisela in marriage to Stephen, the king

Translation by Clifford Backman.

of the Hungarians, in return for having Stephen and all his people convert to the true faith. The Hungarians, to this day a most pious Christian people, regard Stephen as the founder of their faith and even revere him as a saint. But the pious emperor Henry departed from the world in his twenty-fourth year as duke (the eleventh of his years as emperor) and was buried in the cathedral church at Bamberg, where, as is well known, his tomb is today renowned for the miracles performed at it.

[28] In the year 1025 from the Incarnation of Our Lord, Conrad, a Frank, was unanimously elected to succeed Henry, who had died without an heir and had personally recommended Conrad, even though Conrad had not been a royal favorite during Henry's time on the throne. Conrad thus became the eighty-eighth in line from Augustus. On his father's side, Conrad was descended from Duke Conrad of Worms, who had died in Otto [III's] wars against the Hungarians; on his mother's side, his ancestors included the most illustrious princes of Gaul, descended from the ancient race of Trojans, and baptized in the faith by the Blessed Remigius. Conrad's wife was also named Gisela, who sprang from the ancient and glorious blood of the Carolingians. As one writer put it:

> When one adds four generations to the ten already shown,
> From Charlemagne's line comes Gisela, for her wisdom renowned.

She had previously been married to Duke Ernest of Swabia, the brother of Margrave Albert of Upper Pannonia, and have given him two children, Ernest and Herman; it was after her husband's death that she married the Conrad we are discussing.

As king, Conrad was energetic in war, wise in counsel, tactful, sagacious, utterly devoted to the Christian faith, and was filled with the humility that is so becoming in a king. Early in his reign, Duke Boleslaw, the Polish noble recently defeated in battle by Conrad's predecessor Henry, plotted to break away from the empire and establish a kingdom of his own, but he died unexpectedly and was succeeded by his son Mieszko. This Mieszko planned to follow his father's intentions, and towards that end he drove his own brother Otto from his principality, and so King

Conrad led his army into Poland in order to restore Otto to his rightful place and punish Mieszko for the harm he had caused. Mieszko proved unable to repulse the king's attack, and so, having taken a few shards of Germany, he fled to Duke Udalrich of Bohemia, who had already set himself up as an enemy of the kingdom.

Udalrich, however, hoped to get back into Conrad's good graces by handing Mieszko over to him, only to find that Conrad, being so chivalrous by nature, refused to receive an enemy from the hands of a traitor. Meanwhile Otto had taken possession of the Polish duchy and sent to Conrad the crown that his and Mieszko's father had unlawfully and disgracefully fashioned for himself. Otto made a further point of subjecting himself to Conrad in all things. Not long after this, Otto died at the hands of a treacherous armorer, and Mieszko—now an exile instead of a king—went to Conrad to beg forgiveness. Thanks to the intercession of Queen Gisela, Conrad restored to Mieszko a one-third part of what he had previously held entire, and it is well known that that smaller province has remained subject to the German kings ever since and has paid tribute to them.

Around the same time two kinsmen of Conrad's—the duke of Worms, also named Conrad, and Ernest, the duke of Swabia and the Alemanni (who was also King Conrad's stepson)—rose up in rebellion, just when the king had departed for Italy, first naming his infant son Henry as his successor. Queen Gisela, Duke Ernest's mother, advised him quickly to travel to Italy to reconcile with the king and offer him aid. Conrad's military train celebrated the start of Easter at Vercelli, where he met with Margrave Rainier and the citizens of Lucca; once these had submitted to him, he marched on to Rome.

[29] In the year 1027 from the Incarnation of the Lord, Conrad was crowned in Rome by Pope John on the very day of the Easter Festival. He entered the coronation ceremony walking in the position of honor between King Canute of England and Duke Rudolph of Burgundy—Queen Gisela's uncle; and from the people of Rome he received the titles *emperor* and *augustus*. At some point during the week a riot broke out between the local citizens and the emperor's troops, and a terrible battle ensued, in which

many Romans fell or fled and the emperor emerged victorious. He promptly made peace with the citizens, however, and withdrew his troops from the city. He also captured a notorious local bandit named Tahselgart and hanged him. But as he was returning to France by way of the Pyrenees, Conrad learned that his stepson, Duke Ernest, had once again rebelled against him, having been so advised by Count Werner [of Kiburg]. Conrad then rendered a most solemn judgment against him, and by the authority of his royal majesty he banned Ernest from land and sea, compelling him to go into exile in the forest—where he was subsequently killed by some of the king's loyal followers. Ernest's brother, Herman, succeeded to the dukedom.

[30] Around the same time King Rudolph of Burgundy (also known as Gallia Lugdunensis) died. In his will he bequeathed his crown to his nephew Henry, who was Conrad's son. . . .

[31] When Rudolph made this bequest, Count Odo of Gallia Celtica (the son of Rudolph's sister) advanced the unreasonable claim that the kingdom belonged by right to him instead of Henry, and he led his army into it just when the emperor Conrad was busy subjecting the Poles, as mentioned earlier. When the emperor heard of Odo's action, he marshaled his own army to invade Burgundy. This was around Christmas-time, however, and so it was too cold for his men to march all the way there, and so they waited until the following summer. In three weeks they had reduced all of Odo's land to dust and ashes, forcing him to plead for mercy, and only after Odo gave assurance under a solemn vow that he would not further trouble Burgundy did Conrad return home.

The next year Conrad ventured into Burgundy once more and accepted the submission of all the princes there, including the Metropolitan of Lyons; taking several of them as hostages-to-the-court he returned to Germany in peace. Not too much later he ventured into Italy to squash a rebellion by a rabble of insolent commoners who had nearly unseated their noble masters. He celebrated Christmas at Verona, then traveled by way of Brescia and Cremona to Milan, where he arrested the bishop for having joined a conspiracy against him, and handed him over to the Poppo, the Patriarch of Aquileia. The

bishop eventually escaped, unnoticed, and fled, which prompted Conrad, after celebrating Easter Day at Ravenna that spring, to lay waste to the district surrounding Milan, conquering and demolishing many strongholds while receiving the submission of many others. Then he marched on to Cremona, where he met with the pope, whom he received most graciously and treated with the utmost respect. After he sent the pope on his way [back to Rome], Conrad journeyed to the mountain districts [to the north] in order to avoid the summertime heat.

But while these events were taking place in Italy, Count Odo once again broke his vow and rose up against Conrad one more time, in Gaul. He died in disgrace, however, for when he was besieging a certain stronghold called Bar-le-Duc, he was killed by Duke Gozelo of Lorraine and some other troops loyal to the king, who then sent his standard to Italy as a token of their victory that was sure to please the emperor. Also at that time the bishops of Piacenza, Vercelli, and Cremona were convicted of treason and sent into exile, although this was and still is a controversial matter. Soon thereafter the emperor was celebrating Christmas at Parma when a riot broke out in which Conrad's chamberlain was killed. The emperor was enraged by this and attacked the city most bitterly. The citizens defended themselves bravely, but in the end too many of them fell to ward off Conrad's attack. The city was put to the torch.

Around this time the pope in Rome excommunicated the archbishop of Milan, who had also rebelled against Conrad. The emperor was then on the other side of the Apennines, having brought all of the eastern portion of Italy under his control, and was entering Apulia. (Queen Gisela, in the meantime, had gone on pilgrimage to Rome and would rejoin him later.) He passed through Capua, Benevento, and a great many other cities of that region, and planned to return home by way of the Adriatic coastline' but the district was suffering from a contagion that made the air unhealthy to breathe, and many of his leading nobles and other soldiers died, including Duke Hermann, the son of Queen Gunnhild (who was, in her turn, the bride of Conrad's son), and Duke Conrad of Franconia. These catastrophic losses inspired a poet to compose some verses on the fragility of human life; their style is simple but tragically expressive. They begin with the lines:

> Let him with a voice both clear and strong
> Gather all around him to hear this song.

Not much later, but after he had returned from Italy, the emperor took ill in the middle of the Feast of Pentecost, which he was celebrating in Frisia, in the city of Utrecht, and died. It was the seventeenth year of his reign as duke and the fourteenth of his reign as emperor. They buried his heart and other vital organs there in Utrecht and transported the rest of his body to Speyer, where it was laid to rest in the Marienkirche.

[32] In the year 1040 from the Incarnation of Our Lord, Henry III, the son of the aforesaid Queen Gisela, began his sole reign as the eighty-ninth emperor in line from Augustus—having already started to govern while his father was still alive. With Henry the imperial title finally returned to someone born of the ancient and noble stock of Charlemagne. Henry equaled his father in all respects and even surpassed him in the best qualities. He governed with moderation, although he made a rash mistake at the very start of his reign when he launched a campaign against the Bohemians, who were opposed to his rule, and lost many men in the dense forests there. These losses fueled his righteous indignation, however, and prompted him to inflict far greater damages on the people of Bohemia until their duke finally submitted to him. He also made frequent war on the Hungarians. When, instigated by the rebel leader Obo, they treacherously drove their own king, Peter, into exile, however, Henry gave him refuge. At the urging of Margrave Albert (whose brother-in-law he was), Henry marched into Pannonia with an army that, though small in number, won a great victory against a large Hungarian force; thus did Henry restore Peter to his throne—a victory that inspired Herman the Lame to compose the poem that begins:

> This voice of mine must sing a lay.

Henry married Agnes, the daughter of the most illustrious nobleman in Gaul, Duke William of Poitou and Aquitaine. At the wedding celebration, which was held, according to custom, at Ingelheim, he gave to all the poor in the region the money that would otherwise have gone to the jesters and actors (those limbs of Satan!) who attended but went away empty-handed. Sadness accompanied the celebrations, though, since young Leopold, the most illustrious son of Margrave Albert, was carried off by an early death. Mourned by all, he was buried in the city of Trèves by his uncle Poppo, who was archbishop there. This was the Leopold who, together with his father, seized the Eastern March from the Hungarians and defeated, against tremendous odds, the huge army led by the traitor Obo, who was harassing his border. It was a dangerous undertaking, even for one as brave as Leopold.

About the same time a shameful state of confusion beset the Church in Rome, for three men (one of whom was called Benedict) usurped the papal throne all at once, dividing between them the office and its revenues. One sat in St. Peter's Cathedral, the second in the church of Santa Maria Maggiore, and the third (Benedict) in the Lateran Palace. I have heard from eyewitnesses that all three lived a dissolute life. A certain priest named Gratian, a devout man filled with compassion for Mother Church on account of the wretched state. She had fallen into, approached the three usurpers and by the zeal of his piety persuaded them, with money, to vacate their seats. Benedict, the most stubborn person of the group, insisted on keeping the revenues from England. The people of Rome proclaimed this priest as the great liberator of the Church and chose him to be the new pope, Gregory VII. When King Henry heard about this he summoned his army and marched into Italy. Gratian met him at Sutri and reportedly offered the king a precious crown, to assuage his anger. Henry initially received him with fitting honors but later assembled a synod of bishops, who, together with the king, persuaded him to withdraw from the papacy because he had disgraced himself with simony; in Gratian's place they appointed Bishop Suitger of Bamberg, who took the name Clement, and the whole Church consented to his appointment. According to tradition, Hildebrand had followed Gratian across the Alps and into Italy, and later, when he himself was made pope, he took the name Gregory out of love for him. Gratian's name has since been removed from the list of popes. As Lucan once wrote:

> The gods upheld the victorious cause, Cato the defeated one

And this is true of Hildebrand, who was much the most zealous and unyielding supporter of the Church, and the most vigorous opponent of the opinions of the emperor and the German bishops [regarding lay investiture] that ultimately carried the day.

The Roman Church, in our opinion, has been so weakened in the canonical election of popes that Clement and the four men who succeeded him, were included in the list of popes only because the emperor decided to place their names on it. I shall describe later how the Church regained Her freedom, through the tireless exertions of Hildebrand, then Leo, and then Alexander—all of which I learned from the testimony of men I trust.[1]

[33] In the year 1047 from the Incarnation of Our Lord, the victorious King Henry III was crowned emperor and augustus at Rome by Pope Clement on Christmas Day, the ninetieth ruler in line from Augustus. Upon leaving Rome Henry led his army through Apulia before returning home to Germany. In the same year Suitger—that is, Pope Clement—died and was succeeded by Poppo, the patriarch of Aquileia [who took the name Damasus II].[2] A short time later King Peter of Hungary lost his eyesight and his kingship at the hands of a courtier named Andrew. When Poppo/Damasus died, Bishop Bruno of Toul

succeeded him as head of the Church and took the name Leo IX. He came from a noble Frankish family and was King Henry's own choice to succeed to the throne of St. Peter. According to one report Henry was traveling through Gaul shortly after becoming emperor and visited the monastery of Cluny—where the aforementioned Hildebrand happened to hold the office of prior. Hildebrand [accompanied Henry to Rome and] boldly rebuked Leo for having risen to the papacy with the aid of a layman, saying with pious zeal that it was an unlawful seizure by force of the government of the Church. Hildebrand then urged Leo to trust him, promising that he could manipulate things in such a way that the Church's liberty to hold a free election would be restored, and that King Henry would not be roused to anger. Leo agreed, took off his papal robe, and put on again a pilgrim's garb. Then Leo and Hildebrand set off together for Rome, where, with Hildebrand's help, Leo was elected as supreme pontiff by the clergy and people of the city. Thus did the Church regain the right to free election.

Henry, in the meantime, invaded Lorraine and forced Duke Godfrey and Duke Baldwin to capitulate. After this, a synod was held at Mainz in the presence of Pope Leo and Henry. The king once again invaded Pannonia to put down Lord Andrew, who had arrogantly deposed King Peter and usurped the Hungarian throne. The Hungarians, though, fled from the German army and either hid or destroyed the stocks of food they had; with no way to keep his soldiers fed or supplied, Henry therefore laid waste the whole countryside, and then returned home. The next year he invaded Pannonia yet again, taking Pope Leo with him.

Then the Normans—a restless people—invaded Apulia. Led by Duke Robert Guiscard, a man of common birth but uncommon energy, they inflicted every type of misery on the people there, using guile and violence in equal measure. Pope Leo, after returning to Rome with an army, wanted to bring the Normans to heel, making them subject to the Church and the German Empire. He marched against the Normans, and a great battle ensued. Many died, and Leo was forced to flee to Benevento. So many died, in fact, that to this day the people of Benevento point to a hill that they insist is made of the piled-up bones of all those killed that day. Leo died one year later and is

---

1 Otto should not have been quite so trusting of his interviewees, since the account he gives in ch. 32 is filled with errors. The priest Gratian was actually one of the three usurper-popes, under the name Gregory VI. His meeting with Henry III took place at Piacenza, not Sutri. Henry's synod did take place at Sutri (December 1046), but it ousted only Gratian/Gregory and the second pope, Sylvester III; the third pope, Benedict IX, had remained in Rome and refused to recognize the synod. His pseudo-pontificate ended only with his death in 1048.

2 Another mistake—Damasus II was not Poppo of Aquileia, but Poppo, bishop of Brixen, another German. He died within a year.

buried in St. Peter's in Rome; his tomb is renowned for the miracles it performs. Gebhardt of Eichstätt succeeded him, taking the name Victor, and then another German succeeded him, taking the name of Stephen.

The next time Henry went to Italy he returned to Germany with his kinswoman Beatrice, the mother of Mathilda. Beatrice's husband, Margrave Boniface, had just died. Henry himself took ill not long afterwards at a place called Bodfeld, which is on the border of Saxony and Thuringia. He performed a public confession of his sins, and died. It was the seventeenth year of his reign as duke and the eleventh of his reign as emperor. He is buried next to his father. Herman the Lame has thoroughly described his deeds and virtues, as well as those of his father, in a short book.

STUDY QUESTIONS

1. What about Otto's history makes it a "universal history"? How is time viewed in Otto's history of the Holy Roman Empire? Why does Otto infuse his account with references from classical antiquity?
2. How does Otto characterize the popes?

10.6. FROM "SONG OF ROLAND,"
CA. 1140–CA. 1170

This chanson de geste was passed down orally for several generations and recorded between 1140 and 1170. The oldest existing work of vernacular French literature, it recounts the story of the brave count Roland, a kinsman of the emperor Charlemagne, who led the rear guard of the Frankish army into Spain on a mission to liberate Christian cities from Saracen, or Muslim, rule. Historically, the devastating battle described in this story occurs in 778 in a mountain pass in the Pyrenees, called Roncevaux—but between the Frankish forces and local Basque tribes, not Muslims as depicted in this story. A troubadour would have sung this tale; allegedly, it was performed for the army of William the Conqueror while waiting on the Norman beach to cross the English Channel. Consider how this tale might have appealed to aristocratic, warrior audiences.

91
Roland has made his way to the Spanish pass,
Riding Veillantif, his good, swift horse.
The arms he bears become him well.
. . .
But he brandishes his spear,   1155
And turn its point towards the sky,
A pure white pennon fixed upon its tip,

And its golden streamers fluttering down upon
   his hands.
His body is noble, his face fair and smiling;
His companion follows closely behind   1160
And the Franks hail him as their protector.
Towards the Saracens he looks fiercely
And humbly and tenderly towards the Franks.
And he addressed them in a courtly fashion:

"The Song of Roland," trans. Glyn Burgess (New York: Penguin, 1990).

"My lord barons, gently, not too fast!   1165
These pagans are heading for great slaughter;
Today our spoils will be fine and noble.
No king of France has ever had such wealth."
At these words the armies come together.

· · ·

111

The battle is awesome and intense.
Oliver and Roland strike mighty blows;
The archbishop deals more than a thousand.
The twelve peers do not hold back   1415
And the Franks strike in unison.
The pagans die in their hundreds and thousands;
Those who do not flee have no escape from death.
Whether they like it or not, they meet their end.
The Franks lose their best defenders;   1420
They will not see their fathers and kinsmen again,
Nor Charlemagne who awaits them in the pass.
In France there is a most terrible storm,
A tempest with thunder and strong winds,
Rain and hail in great quantity.
Lightning strikes again and again
And the whole earth, in truth, begins to quake.
From Saint Michel del Peril to Seinz,
From Besançon to the port of Wissant,
There is no house whose walls do not
    collapse.   1430
At high noon a great darkness gathers;
There is light only when the sky is rent.
No one could see it without a feeling of dread.
Many say: "It is all over with us;
The end of the world is upon us."   1435
They do not know it, but their words are wrong;
It is the great sorrow for the death of Roland.

· · ·

115

The archbishop is first to start the battle.
He sits astride the horse he took from Grossaille,
A king whom he killed in Denmark.
The horse is mettlesome and fleet of foot;
Its hooves are hollowed out and its legs flat.
It is short in the haunches and broad in the
    crupper,
Long in the flank and high along its back;
Its tail is white and its mane yellow,
Its ears small and its head tawny.   1495

There is no beast which can match it for pace.
The archbishop spurs on with great valour;
He will not miss this chance to attack Abisme.
He goes to deal him a prodigious blow to the
    shield
With its precious stones, amethyst and
    topaz,   1500
Esterminals and blazing carbuncles.
A devil gave this shield to him in Val Metas
And it was presented to him by the emir Galafres.
Turpin strikes it and in no way spares it;
After his blow it is not, I think, worth a penny
    piece.   1505
He slices him through from one side to the other,
Flinging him dead in an empty spot.
The Franks say: "This is an act of great valour;
In the archbishop's hands the crozier is truly safe."

· · ·

134

Count Roland with pain and distress
Sounds his Oliphant in great agony.
The clear blood gushes forth from his mouth
And in his skull the temple bursts.
The sound of the horn which he holds carries
    far;   1765
Charles hears it, as he makes his way through the
    pass.
Duke Naimes heard it and the Franks listen to it.
The king said: "I can hear Roland's horn;
He would never have blown it, if he were not in
    a fight."
Ganelon replies: "There is no battle;   1770
You are old, hoary and white-haired.
Such words make you seem like a child;
You are well aware of Roland's great pride.
It is a wonder that God has stood for it so long.

· · ·

171

Roland feels that he has lost his sight;
He rises to his feet, exerting all his strength.
All the colour has drained from his face.
Before him lies a dark-hued stone;   2300
On it he strikes ten blows in sorrow and
    bitterness.
The steel grates, but does not break or become
    notched;

"O, Holy Mary," said the count, "help me!
O, my good sword Durendal, what a fate you
    have suffered!
Now that I am dying, I have no more need of
    you;   2305
With you I have won so many battles in the field
And conquered so many vast lands,
Which Charles with the hoary-white beard now
    holds.
May you never be owned by a man who flees in
    battle!
A very fine vassal has held you for so long   2310
There will never be such a man in blessed
    France."

172

Roland struck the sardonyx stone;
The steel grates, but does not shatter or become
    notched.
When he saw that he could not break it,
He begins to lament over it to himself: 2315
"O, Durendal, how fair and clear and white you
    are!
How you shimmer and sparkle in the sun!
Charles was in the Sales of Maurienne,
When through his angel God on high told him
To give you a captain to count.   2320
Then the noble and mighty king girded it on me.
With it I conquered Anjou and Brittany
And with it I conquered Poitou and Maine;
With it I conquered Normandy the free
And with it I conquered Provence and
    Aquitaine   2325
And Lombardy and all Romagna.
With it I conquered Bavaria and all Flanders
And Burgundy and all Apulia.
And Constantinople, which rendered homage to
    him.
In Saxony his commands are obeyed.   2330
With it I conquered Scotland and Ireland
And England, which became his domain;
With it I have conquered so many lands and
    countries
Which Charles with the white beard now holds.
For this sword I grieve and sorrow;   2335
I should rather die than leave it in pagan hands.
God, our Father, spare France this disgrace!"

173

Roland struck upon the dark-hued stone;
He hacks away more of it than I can tell.
The sword grates, but neither breaks nor
    shatters;   2340
It rebounds towards heaven.
When the count sees that he cannot break it,
He lamented over it to himself very softly:
"O, Durendal, how fair and sacred you are!
In the golden hilt there are many relics: 2345
Saint Peter's tooth and some of Saint Basil's
    blood;
Some hair from the head of my lord Saint Denis
And part of the raiment of the Blessed Virgin.
It is not right for pagans to possess you;
You must be wielded by Christians.   2350
May no coward ever have you!
With you I have conquered vast lands.
Charles with the hoary-white beard now holds
    them;
They have made the emperor mighty and rich.
. . .

176

Count Roland lay down beneath a pine
    tree;   2375
He has turned his face towards Spain.
Many things began to pass through his mind:
All the lands which he conquered as a warrior,
The fair land of France, the men of his lineage,
Charlemagne, his lord, who raised him.   2380
He cannot help weeping and heaving great sighs;
But he does not wish to be unmindful of himself.
He confesses his sins and prays for the grace of
    God:
"True Father, who has never lied,
You who brought back Lazarus from the
    dead   2385
And rescued Daniel from the lions,
Protect my soul from every peril
And from the sins which I have committed in
    my life."
He proffered his right glove to God;
Saint Gabriel took it from his hand.   2390
Roland laid his head down over his arm;
With his hands joined he went to his end.
God sent down his angel Cherubin

And with him Saint Michael of the Peril.
With them both came Saint Gabriel.   2395
They bear the count's soul to paradise.

177

Roland is dead, God has his soul in heaven.
The emperor arrives at Rencesvals;
There is no road or path there,
No open space, no yard or foot,   2400
Not covered with either Franks or pagans.
Charles cries out: "Where are you, fair nephew?
Where is the archbishop and Count Oliver?
Where is Gerin and his companion Gerer?
Where is Oton and Count Berenger,   2405

Yvon and Yvoire, whom I loved so dearly?
What has become of the Gascon Engeler,
Duke Samson and Anseis the brave?
Where is Gerard of Roussillon, the old,
And the twelve peers whom I had left
    behind?"   2410
To what avail, when no one could reply?
"O God," said the king, "what great sorrow
That I was not here when battle commenced."
He tugs at his beard like a man beset
    with grief;
His brave knights shed tears.   2415
Twenty thousand fall to the ground in a faint;

STUDY QUESTIONS

1. What does the document reveal about codes of "courtesy" in feudal culture?
2. How is Christianity offered as a justification for violence against the enemy, in the warriors' words and actions?

CHAPTER 11

WORLDS BROUGHT DOWN

11.1. DANTE ALIGHIERI, THREE SPEECHES FROM *THE DIVINE COMEDY*

Translated below are three famous speeches from *The Divine Comedy*, one each from the *Inferno*, the *Purgatorio*, and the *Paradiso*. In the first, Dante encounters Odysseus, who suffers in the eighth circle of Hell and relates how he arrived there. In the second passage, Dante's guide, the Roman poet Virgil, bids Dante goodbye after leading him through Hell and Purgatory; as a non-Christian, he can ascend no higher. The third speech consists of the hymn to the Virgin Mary that Dante here places in St. Bernard of Clairvaux's mouth, as he begs her assistance in leading Dante to the great climax of the epic: the vision of God. All of the music of Dante's language is lost in translation, of course, but here are my best efforts.

INFERNO 26.90–142

When I finally left Circe, who had held me,
    beguiled,
for more than a year near Gaeta (before it was
    styled
as such by Aeneas), neither love for my child,

nor pity for my father—then bent with age—
nor my love for Penelope—the source of
    her joy—
could overcome my longing for another stage

where I could experience the richness of life
and learn all I could of a world that was rife
with the vices and virtues of men.

That is why I set out for the open sea
with only one ship and a small company
of those by whom I never deserted would be.

From one shore to the next, I went as far as
    España,
and the land of Morocco, and the isle of Sardinia,
and all the other islands that are bathed by the sea.

I and my comrades had already grown
old and slow when we finally reached the place
where Hercules set up his guard of stone

to block anyone from venturing beyond.
On our right was Seville, on our left was Ceuta,
but I sailed on. "O brothers!" I shouted,

Translation by Clifford Backman.

"You have seen already many dangers,
a hundred thousand of them, so you're no
    strangers
to risk as you've come here, the far west.

You must not now deny yourselves the challenge
of going yet further west, and range
beyond the sun, and explore the unpeopled
    world.

Remember your lineage, the seed that gave you
    birth!
You were not made to live here on Earth
like brutes. You must pursue knowledge and true
    worth!"

I so inspired my comrades with this little speech
to continue our journey, they pushed forward
    with a screech
and it took all my strength to hold them back,
    within reach.

So turning our ship, with the stern toward
    morning,
we pulled on our oars; it was as though they were
    wings
and we flew, always somewhat to the left
    inclining.

In the sky at night I beheld the strange stars
of the South Pole. The familiar stars, the ones that
    were ours,
had fallen from the sky and lay below the
    horizon.

Five times did the light from the moon come
    down,
and brighten, and fail, after we had left familiar
    ground
and to that hard passage we ourselves had bound,

when suddenly a mountain, distant and dark,
rose before us, high over our barque—
the highest mountain I'd ever seen, grim and
    stark.

We were glad at first, but our joy turned to
    sorrow
when from that place a fierce whirlwind did
    blow
that hammered at our ship and crushed the prow.

Three times the whirlwind whipped us around,
and then a fourth time the cyclone wound
and flipped us, stern skyward, our prow pointing
    down.

And as though Someone desired it: the ship sank,
    and we drowned.

PURGATORIO 27.115–142

"Today your hungering will be put
to peaceful rest through the sweet fruit
that all mortals seek among life's branches."

Thus did Virgil speak, and to his solemn words
nothing ever spoken to me before
could compare, for the delight they offered.

Urge upon urge to climb ever higher
came upon me, and with every new step
I felt the strength of wings lifting me up.

When the whole staircase lay beneath us
and we stood at last on the highest step,
Virgil fixed his eyes on me, and said:

"My son, you have now seen the passing
and the eternal fires, and have reached the place
beyond which I cannot go.

I have brought you to this point through wit and
    art;
but now let joyfulness be your guide.
You have passed steeps and narrows. Now, the
    other side!

Behold the sun that shines upon your brow!
See there! Grasses and flowers and shrubs
that the Earth produces, all on its own.

You can rest here now, or stroll a while
until you behold the glad and lovely eyes
that once, full of tears, sent me to your side.
Expect no other word or signal from me.
Your will is now strong and healthy and free;
to act against it would be a mistake.

I crown and miter you, lord of yourself."

PARADISO 33.1–21

Oh Virgin Mother, daughter of your own son,
most humble and exalted of all creatures,
fixed goal of all in God's eternal plan,

it was you who so ennobled human nature
so greatly that He Who created us did not
    disdain,
to make Himself man, one with His creation.

Within your womb was rekindled the love
that provided the warmth needed for this
    flower
to come to bloom within this everlasting peace.
For all here in Paradise you are the noon-time
    torch
of charity—and down on earth, for mortal men,
you are the living spring of hope.

Lady, you are so great and so powerful,
that anyone who seeks grace without turning to
    you
is like one wishing to fly without wings.

Not only does your loving kindness race
to anyone who asks for it, but it often times
flows freely even before the asking.

In you is compassion, in you is pity,
in you generosity—in you is brought together
everything that is good in creation.

Here is a man, who from the lowest depth
of the universe up to this high place
has witnessed, one by one, the lives of souls;

he begs you to grant him through your grace
the power to lift his vision higher still,
to witness the goal of salvation.

And I, who never burned for my own vision
more than I burn for his, offer you all my
    prayers—
and I pray they are enough—

that you, through your own prayers, may
    disperse
the cloud of his mortality, that he might have
the Sum of All Joy revealed to his eyes.

I pray you also, O Queen who can achieve
whatever you wish, keep his affections sound
once he has had his vision, and returns.
May you protect him from the stirrings of the
    flesh.
Behold!—Beatrice, with all the saints,
clasp their hands in prayer, to win your assent!"

STUDY QUESTIONS

1. What vision of the cosmos is conveyed by these three speeches?
2. Why is Odysseus condemned to the inferno? What does Virgil represent? Why can he not ascend any higher than Purgatory? How is Bernard of Clairvaux's hymn to the Virgin representative of the cult of Mary?

11.2. DANTE ALIGHIERI, *THE DIVINE COMEDY*, "PAOLO AND FRANCESCO IN HELL"

Dante's great epic tells of his journey through Hell, Purgatory, and Heaven, guided at first by the Roman poet Virgil, then by his beloved Beatrice. Hell consists of a deep, terraced pit, each level representing a different sin, where the souls of the lost receive their fitting punishments. After passing through Limbo (where dwell the souls of the virtuous non-Christians—Homer, Plato, Aristotle, Caesar, Cicero, Averroës, Avicenna, and Saladin among them), they enter the circle of the Lustful. Dante sees many famous lovers, but spends most of his time visiting with two contemporaries of his, Francesca da Rimini and her lover Paolo Malatesta, who was also her brother-in-law.

After I heard my Master recite the names
  Of all these lovers—knights and dames—
I was dazed with pity, confused, and ashamed.
I said, "With all my heart, dear Poet, I wish to
  speak
  With those two there, who move with such
    mystique,
  Gliding lightly on the winds, both strong and
    weak."
And he said, "You will see, when they draw near,
  That if you ask them, in the name of their
    love so dear,
  To tell their tale, they will comply. Soon you
    will hear."
Then a gusty blast drove the pair beside us
  And I called over the wind, "If it not be
    denied us,
  O battered souls, come and tell us your tale.
    Oblige us."
Like doves who, driven by desire and will,
  Stretch out their wings and soar high until
  They reach their nest, ready to take their fill
Of their love, so did these two fly from the throng
  there
  That surrounded Dido, toward us, through
    the malignant air,

So strongly did my tender call affect the pair.
"O gracious creature, O one so good,
  Who through even this foul atmosphere
    would
  Come visit us, who stained the world with
    blood!
Were it in our power to be friends with the
  Universal King
  We would ask Him to grant you peace, for
    you bring
  A spirit of generous pity for the pain we're
    suffering.
Whatever you wish to say, to ask, or to know,
  Is our pleasure to help your understanding to
    grow,
  Especially here where the mighty wind has
    ceased to blow.
The land where I was born lies on the shore
  Where the Po River and the waters that feed
    it, both great and poor,
  Flow to where they flow no more.
Love, which quickly can seize the most gentle
  heart,
  Gripped this man here—he lusted for my
    body's art
  In a way that still tears my soul apart.

Translation by Clifford Backman.

Then Love, which spares no beloved from love's
ration,
Gripped me as well with such a lusty passion
That, as you see, it binds us still, in a fashion.
And Love then caused us both to die;
Cain's Hell awaits our killer!—That is our
cry!"
Such were the words the air carried, like a
sigh.
When those guilty souls had finished their tale
I bowed my head in sadness at their betrayal.
My Poet asked, "What do you think of
suffering on that scale?"
At length I spoke: "Master, I cannot explain:
All those sweet thoughts of love, and desire's
strain,
Brought these two lovers so much pain!"
Then I turned to the pair and tried to speak.
"Francesca," I began, "the torment you suffer
is so bleak
That my eyes fill with tears that roll down my
cheek.
But please, I beg you: In your blissful hours—
How, by what signs, did Love's great powers
Allow the two of you to know each other's
desires?"
"There is no pain that is greater," she began, "(if
I may),
Than to remember, here, on this grim-bleak
day,

The happiness we had then. Your Guide
knows, and can say
As much! But if you truly wish to know
How such a love as ours did grow,
I'll tell you—my words and tears both shall
flow.
One day we sat reading, to pass the time,
Of Sir Lancelot's [and Guinevere's] passionate
crime.
We were alone, and innocent, and in our
prime.
Over and over again, as we read, our eyes
Met, and our faces flushed, and with tender
sighs
We yielded—at the moment when with
passionate cries
Those two lovers brought together their trembling
lips.
Imagining that he was, like Lancelot, in the
grips
Of like love, this one here, who forever trips
By my side, gently kissed me. I doubt not whether
It was that book which brought us together;
And yet all that day we read no further."
As she spoke these lines, poor Guido wept
So fully and movingly that pity swept
Over me. Dazed and swooning, I then
stepped
To one side, and fell near-dead to Hell's stony
floor.

STUDY QUESTIONS

1. How do Francesca and Paolo embody the code of chivalry? How do they transgress the code?
    What is the meaning of the reference to Lancelot?
2. What attitude does Dante take toward Paolo and Francesca?

11.3. BOCCACCIO, "THE GREAT PLAGUE"

The Decameron is Giovanni Boccaccio's (1313–1375) literary masterpiece, a tapestry of one hundred short stories told by a group of friends who fled Florence at the outbreak of the Black Death; to amuse themselves, each tells a story—one each day for ten days. Boccaccio prefaced the collection with a famous prologue that sets the scene; it is one of the most powerful surviving contemporary descriptions of the plague that hit Europe at the very end of 1347. Boccaccio lost his father to the plague, a fact that probably inspired the somber description he offers below.

I tell you, then, that in the 1348th year from the Blessed Incarnation of the Son of God there appeared in Florence, the fairest of all Italian cities, the deadly plague. Whether it was spread by the influence of the celestial bodies, or came upon us men through the just wrath of the Lord as punishment for our sins, it had originated many years earlier in the East, where it annihilated innumerable people, propagating itself relentlessly from place to place until it came at last, calamitously, to the West.

In Florence, in the early spring of the aforesaid year, the wretched effects of the disease appeared for the first time, with symptoms that were beyond belief—and despite all that human ingenuity and care could think of to avert it: the whole city cleansed of pollutants by officials appointed especially for the purpose, the refusal to admit entry into the town by anyone appearing ill, and the adoption of countless other precautions to maintain good health. Despite too all the humble prayers addressed to God, and chanted repeatedly in public processions, by the devout.

The symptoms of the sick differed from those in the East, where a nosebleed was the first visible hint of the inevitable approach of death. Among the men and women in Florence alike, the first sign of the pestilence was the appearance of certain tumors in the groin or the armpits. These swellings usually grew to the size of an apple or of an egg; sometimes, larger, sometimes smaller. The common folk called these tumors *gavoccioli*. From the groins and armpits these *gavoccioli* spread quickly and randomly in every direction. Once the spreading had begun, a second symptom appeared: livid black spots along the arms and thighs. Sometimes these spots were few in number but large in size; sometimes they were just the opposite—many but small. The spots were as certain a sign of the victim's approaching death as were the *gavoccioli*. Every effort by physicians, whether in technique or medicine, proved no match for either the symptoms or the sickness itself. Whether because the plague was fundamentally untreatable or because our physicians were simply not up to the challenge, hardly anyone contracted the disease and recovered; instead, most victims were dead within three days of the first visible symptom and usually without showing a fever or any other accompanying symptom. Apart from the actual physicians, a horde of men and women without the least bit of medical knowledge tried to care for the sick, but in their ignorance they applied all the wrong remedies.

The viciousness of the plague was made even worse by every type of human contact, which passed the disease from one person to another just as a raging fire devours every flammable thing brought in contact with it. But this proved even worse, for a person did not need to touch or converse with an inflicted sufferer in order to place himself in immediate and deadly peril; anyone who even touched the clothes of the sick, or anything else that the sufferer had used or touched, was apt to contract the disease.

Translation by Clifford Backman.

What I am about to say seems unbelievable, and if many so people—myself included—had not witnessed it directly, I would hardly dare to write it down; a single witness would never suffice.

So virulent and unstoppable was the pestilence that it was propagated not only from person to person but, even more startling, it was observed many times to spread from objects belonging to one of the sick or newly dead to some animal (that is, not a human being at all) and to cause not merely the animal's sickening but its almost instantaneous death. Let me describe for you something I once saw with my own eyes. The rags of a poor beggar who had succumbed to the plague were left lying it a street; two hogs approached and rooted their snouts around in them and then, taking them in their teeth, slapped the rags back and forth with shakes of their heads, and then all of a sudden they convulsed once or twice and dropped to the ground dead, as though poisoned. They fell on the very rags they had been unlucky enough to disturb.

These happenings, plus countless others that were similar in nature or even worse, caused a host of fears and wild beliefs to take root among those who survived, with the result that they settled on a single and cruel precaution—namely, they all sought to preserve their own health by avoiding or running away from anyone who was sick and from anything that belonged to them. . . .

In the face of so much suffering and misery, all respect for law—whether divine or human—broke down and virtually disappeared, because the administrators and executors of the laws were, like everyone else, either dead or ill, and they had too few subordinate officials available to carry out any of their duties. The result? Everyone was free to do whatever they wanted. Most people steered a middle course between the extremes of either fasting obsessively (like some did) or indulging themselves in drinking and wantonness (as many others did). Instead, they simply took care to meet their needs and satisfy their appetites. Instead of locking themselves away, they walked about freely—although usually with a posy of flowers in their hands, or a bundle of fragrant herbs or a packet of different spices, which they continually pressed to their noses, thinking to comfort their brains against the stench of corpses, sick bodies, and medicine that filled the air. Others pursued the more selfish but probably safer alternative of simply running away, believing that the best and most effective measure against the disease was distance. Convinced of this, and caring for no one but themselves, vast numbers of men and women abandoned the city, their homes, their relatives, their estates and belongings altogether and fled to the countryside or even further, as if God in His wrath would use this plague to punish mankind for its sins on the basis of where they happened to be, and attack only those who happened to be within city walls. Perhaps they thought that the entire urban population would be annihilated, that the city's last hour had finally arrived.

Not all the people in any particular group died; nor did all the people in any particular group survive. To the contrary, many fell ill in each and every camp. But having established themselves as examples to the healthy, those who survived languished away with virtually no one to care for them, abandoned by everyone. Not only did one town-dweller avoid another, neighbor avoid neighbor, or relative avoid relative, everyone communicating only at great distance, but the plague had so struck people's hearts that brothers abandoned brothers, uncles their nephews, sisters their brothers, and even wives their husbands. Worst of all, and almost beyond belief, mothers and fathers deserted their own children and refused to care for them, abandoning them like strangers. . . .

Many people died, therefore, who might have survived if they had received any help. That is why, apart from the natural virulence of the plague itself, the number of deaths reported day and night was so enormous that it dumbfounded everyone who heard it, to say nothing of the people who witnessed it directly. And that is why a number of new customs arose among those who survived, customs altogether contrary to established ways of doing things. . . .

Among the city's common folk, the burghers for the most part, a pathetic spectacle appeared. Whether immobilized by hopelessness or unable to leave because of concern for their property, they remained in the city and so fell ill by the thousands every day, and lacking anyone to care for them or help them, they almost inevitably died without exception. Many dropped dead right in the streets, day and night; others, who died in their homes, were only discovered when the stench of their rotting corpses caught their neighbors' attention. As a result, dead bodies lay everywhere. People soon fell into a regular routine, more out of fear of contamination by the corpses than out of respect or affection for the dead: acting alone or with the help of others, they would take the bodies of the newly deceased out of their homes and leave them lying outside their front doors. Anyone who came down the street, especially early in the morning, thus saw countless corpses every day. Funeral biers were then sent for, and if there were none of these available, workers carrying mere planks of wood would cart the bodies away. It was not uncommon to see a single bier that had two or even three corpses on it—a husband and wife, perhaps, or a group of siblings, or a father and his son, or some other clutch of relatives. It would be impossible to count the number of times when two priests, carrying a cross in front of a bier on the way to a burial, would suddenly have three or four other biers fall in line behind them; thinking themselves on their way to conduct a single burial, they would find by the time they reached the churchyard that they were six, seven, or eight more to perform. Even so, no tears or candles or mourners were involved, to honor the dead. Conditions were so bad that most people showed no more care for the human dead than nowadays they show for a dead goat, for it was quite clear that death—the one thing that, in normal times, no wise man ever accepted with patience (even though it happened relatively rarely and unobtrusively)—had been brought home to even the most feeble-minded; the problem was that the catastrophe was so unimaginably great that no one was really able to care. There were so many corpses arriving at all the churches every day, and almost by the hour, that in no time at all they ran out of consecrated ground, especially if, as by ancient custom, they were to grant a separate burial plot for each person. So when all the graves were filled up, they dug huge pits in the churchyard, into which they placed newly arrived corpses by the hundreds, piling them atop each other like ship's cargo with only a thin layer of dirt over each, until each pit was filled.

In addition to all the calamities we suffered in the city, I ought to make clear for you that the dreadful things happening in the city were suffered in the countryside as well. In all the fortified towns the situation was just as in Florence, although on a smaller scale, but in the rural villages and the countryside proper the poor miserable peasants and their families, having no physicians or servants to help them in any way, collapsed in the dirt lanes, in their fields and cottages at all hours of day and night, dying more like animals than human beings. Like the townspeople, they paid no attention to their duties or possessions, believing each day might be their last, and so they did not bother to till the fields or tend to their animals or do anything to prepare for a future. Instead they just abandoned what they had, with the result that their oxen, asses, sheep, goats, pigs, chickens—even their faithful dogs—were driven away and allowed to roam at will through the fields, where the unreaped and ungathered crops were simply neglected. . . .

What more can be said, except that the cruelty of heaven (and possibly, to some degree, the cruelty of mankind) was so terrible that between March and June of that year, by the fierceness of the plague and the fact that so many of the sick were poorly cared for or flat-out abandoned at their neediest moment because the healthy were too frightened to approach them, more than one hundred thousand people died within the walls of Florence.

STUDY QUESTIONS

1. What makes Boccaccio's description of the plague "modern"?
2. What effects does the plague have on Florentine society?

11.4. JULIAN OF NORWICH, *REVELATIONS OF DIVINE LOVE*, AFTER 1373

Julian of Norwich (1342–ca. 1416) was an English anchoress who, near the age of thirty, received mystical visions of Jesus during a near-death experience. She recorded these visions in an English text that brought the message of God's unlimited love during a time of plague, war, and suffering. The main message of Julian's work is the unity of love from God—a notion often meditated on by Christian mystics, which floods the soul with light and warmth. Though she was never canonized, Julian remains a model of mystical devotion, particularly for those who suffer.

2

And when I was thirty and a half years old, God sent me a bodily sickness in which I lay for three days and three nights; and on the fourth night I received all the rites of the Holy Church and did not believe that I would live until morning. And after this I lingered on for two days and two nights. And on the third night I often thought that I was dying, and so did those who were with me. But at this time I was very sorry and reluctant to die, not because there was anything on earth that I wanted to live for, nor because I feared anything, for I trusted in God, but because I wanted to live so as to love God better and for longer, so that through the grace of longer life I might know and love God better in the bliss of heaven. For it seemed to me that all the short time I could live here was as nothing compared with that heavenly bliss. So I thought, "My good Lord, may my ceasing to live be to your glory!" And I was answered in my reason, and by the pains I felt, that I was dying. And I fully accepted the will of God with all the will of my heart.

So I endured till day, and by then my body was dead to all sensation from the waist down. Then I felt I wanted to be in a sitting position, leaning with my head back against the bedding, so that my heart could be more freely at God's disposition, and so that I could think of God while I was still alive; and those who were with me sent for the parson, my parish priest, to be present at my death. He came, and a boy with him, and brought a cross, and by the time he came my eyes were fixed and I could not speak. The parson set the cross before my face and said, "Daughter, I have brought you the image of your Saviour. Look upon it and be comforted, in reverence to him that died for you and me." It seemed to me that I was well as I was, for my eyes were looking fixedly upwards into heaven, where I trusted that I was going. But nevertheless I consented to fix my eyes on the face of the crucifix if I could, so as to be able to do so for longer until the moment of my death; because I thought that I might be able to bear looking straight ahead for longer than I could manage to look upwards. After this my sight began to fail and the room was dim all around me, as dark as if it had been night, except that in the image of the cross an ordinary, household light remained—I could not understand how. Everything except the cross was ugly to me, as if crowded with fiends. After this I felt as if the upper part of my body was beginning to die. My hands fell down on either side, and my head settled down sideways for weakness. The greatest pain that I felt was shortness of breath and failing of life. Then I truly believed that I was at the point of death. And at this moment all my suffering suddenly left me, and I was as completely well, especially the upper part of my body, as I ever was before or after. I marveled at this change, for it seemed to me a mysterious work of

From Julian of Norwich, *Revelations of Divine Love*, translated by Elizabeth Spearing. London: Penguin, 1998, pp. 5–8.

God, not a natural one. And yet, although I felt comfortable, I still did not expect to live, nor did feeling more comfortable comfort me entirely, for I felt that I would rather have been released from this world, for in my heart I was willing to die.

3

And it suddenly occurred to me that I should entreat our Lord graciously to give me the second wound, so that he would fill my whole body with remembrance of the feeling of his blessed Passion, as I had prayed before; for I wanted his pains to be my pains, with compassion, and then longing for God. Yet in this I never asked for a bodily sight or any kind of showing of God, but for fellow-suffering, such as it seemed to me a naturally kind soul might feel for our Lord Jesus, who was willing to become a moral man for love. I wanted to suffer with him, while living in my mortal body, as God would give me grace.

And I suddenly saw the red blood trickling down from under the crown of thorns, all hot, freshly, plentifully and vividly, just as I imagined it was at the moment when the crown of thorns was thrust on to his blessed head—he who was both God and man, the same who suffered for me. I believed truly and strongly that it was he himself who showed me this, without any intermediary, and then I said, "Benedicite dominus!" Because I meant this with such deep veneration, I said it in a very loud voice; and I was astounded, feeling wonder and admiration that he was willing to be so familiar with a sinful being living in this wretched flesh. I supposed at the time that our Lord Jesus of his courteous love would show me comfort before the time of my temptation. For I thought it might well be, by God's permission and under his protection, that I would be tempted by fiends before I died. With this sight of the blessed Passion, along with the Godhead that I saw in my mind, I saw that I, yes, and every creature living that would be saved, could have strength to resist all the fiends of hell and all spiritual enemies.

4

And at the same time I saw this bodily sight, our Lord showed me a spiritual vision of his familiar love.

I saw that for us he is everything that is good and comforting and helpful. He is our clothing, wrapping and enveloping us for love, embracing us and guiding us in all things, handing about us in tender love, so that he can never leave us. And so in this vision, as I understand it, I saw truly that he is everything that is good for us.

And in this vision he showed me a little thing, the size of a hazel-nut, lying in the palm of my hand, and to my mind's eye it was as round as any ball. I looked at it and thought, "What can this be?" And the answer came to me, "It is all that is made," I wondered how it could last, for it was so small I thought it might suddenly disappear. And the answer in my mind was, "It lasts and will last for ever because God loves it; and in the same way everything exists through the love of God." In this little thing I saw three attributed: the first is that God made it, the second is that he loves it, the third is that God cares for it. But what does that mean to me? Truly, the maker, the lover, the carer; for until I become one substance with him, I can never have love, rest or true bliss; that is to say, until I am so bound to him that there may be no created thing between my God and me. And who shall do this deed? Truly, himself, by his mercy and his grave, for he has made me and blessedly restored me to that end.

Then God brought our Lady into my mind. I saw her spiritually in bodily likeness, a meek and simple maid, young of age, in the same bodily form as when she conceived. God also showed me part of the wisdom and truth of her soul so that I understood with what reverence she beheld her God who is her maker, and how reverently she marveled that he chose to be born of her, a simple creature of his own making. For what made her marvel was that he who was her Maker chose to be born of the creature he had made. And the wisdom of her faithfulness, and knowledge of the greatness of her Maker and the littleness of her who was made, moved her to say very humbly to the angel Gabriel, "Behold, the handmaid of the Lord." With this sight I really understood that she is greater in worthiness and fullness of grace than all that God made below her; for nothing that is made is above her except the blessed Manhood of Christ. This little thing that is made that is below our

Lady Saint Mary, God showed it to me as small as if it had been a hazel-nut. It was so small I thought it might have disappeared.

In this blessed revelation God showed me three nothings. Of these nothings this was the first I was shown, and all men and women who wish to lead the contemplative life need to have knowledge of it: they should choose to set at nothing everything that is made so as to have the love of God who is unmade. This is why those who choose to occupy themselves with earthly business and are always pursuing worldly success have nothing here of God in their hearts and souls: because they love and seek their rest in this little thing where there is no rest, and know nothing of God, who is almighty, all wise and all good, for he is true rest. God wishes to be known, and is pleased that we should rest in him; for all that is below him does nothing to satisfy us. And this is why, until all that is made seems as nothing, no soul can be at rest. When a soul sets all at nothing for love, to have him who is everything that is good, then it is able to receive spiritual rest.

STUDY QUESTIONS

1. In what specific ways does Julian "experience" the suffering of Jesus in his Passion?
2. Does her vision of the Virgin Mary underscore the different experiences of a *female* mystic?

11.5. FROM FROISSART, "ON FLAGELLANTS," 1369–1400

A contemporary chronicler, Jean Froissart (ca. 1337–ca. 1405) offers a glimpse of the horrific world of the Black Death, which ravaged Europe in a virulent first bout in 1348–1350, killing perhaps as much as 40 percent of the population. The Flagellants (from the Latin "to whip") were a penitential group that traveled in procession from city to city—unwittingly spreading the very disease they hoped to alleviate. Froissart's account reveals the panic that beset people in the face of chronic and inexplicable death and helps us understand how rational 14th-century citizens could turn to such drastic actions.

ON THE FLAGELLANTS

In the year of grace 1349 of Our Lord a group of penitents appeared, coming initially from Germany—wild people who performed their penance in public by scourging their backs with whips studded with small iron points. With these whips they lashed themselves mercilessly between their shoulders. Some few of them were women who dressed in bloodstained rags; they feared for their souls and despaired of what the world might come to in the absence of a miracle. In doing their penance they chanted the most pitiable dirges about the birth and holy suffering of Our Lord, and implored God to end the plague. For it was a time of death, suffering, and

Translation by Clifford Backman.

plague, with people dropping dead all of a sudden throughout the whole world—at least a third of the human population.

The penitents I just mentioned travelled in companies from village to village, city to city, wearing hoods made of felt. Each company had its own color. By custom, law, and ordinance they could stay in each village only a single night and were pledged to proceed on their pilgrimage for thirty-three and a half days—one day for each year of Jesus Christ's earthly life, as the Holy Scriptures testify. Each company, therefore, processed for the prescribed thirty-three and a half days, after which it returned again to whatever village, city, or castle from which it had originally set out. They lacked for nothing throughout their pilgrimages, for the good people of each village and town they passed through provided them with food and refreshment. They never lodged in these places, though, out of fear that doing so might spread the malady even faster. Instead, whenever they entered anyone's home for food or refreshment they first kneeled as a group, out of humility, and recited three Our Fathers and three Hail Marys, and they always repeated the gesture when they took their leave.

They resolved countless conflicts and established fair peace continuously, these penitents and the good people who supported them; wherever there were people of differing opinions who could come to no agreement, they found compromise after the penitents intervened.

Included in their ordinances were many intelligent and useful things, and it was either these sound ideas or simple human nature that inclined these companies' members to go on these penitential processions. Whatever the case, they did not enter the kingdom of France, for Pope Innocent, who was then in office and living in Avignon, and his cardinals had given these companies some thought and had come to a firm decision about the penitents. They declared that public penance, and public support for it, was neither permissible nor acceptable; in fact, they declared that it was forbidden. Henceforth any clergy who was among them or was a member of their company or who served them as a curate, canon, or chaplain, or who shared their opinions was to be deprived of his benefice—and if he desired absolution, he would have to request it directly from Avignon. If one contrasts this decree with all that is generally known, one can see that the popes and the kings of France regarded them as enemies and rebels, and would not suffer another Hainault. For if the penitents were to make it to Cambrai or Saint-Quentin they would be able to reach the coast. If it should happen that the penitents got that far, and if any new people joined them, the Jews [in those cities] might fear for their lives and flee, being gone for more than two hundred years. For they have a saying:

> And there will come knights carrying iron mallets who will be terribly cruel, but lacking a leader they will not be able to exert their might or perform deeds outside the German empire. Nevertheless, when they come, we will all be killed.

So they'll flee, and truly at that time countless Jews will be slaughtered in land after land until at last the popes and the kings of Spain, Aragon, and Navarre, with great effort, will re-establish peace for them.

STUDY QUESTIONS

1. What did the flagellants see as the primary cause of the Black Death?
2. How and why did they encounter opposition from Church authorities?

11.6. JAKOB TWINGER, *CHRONICLE*, CA. 1382–1420

Jakob Twinger (1346–1420) was born at Königshofen, a small village near the city of Strasbourg. Ordained a priest in 1382, he began to write his *Chronicle* in the same year of his ordination and continued to add to it until his death, by which time he had brought the narrative forward to 1415. In 1395 he was appointed a canon of the church of St. Thomas in Strasbourg and placed in charge of maintaining its archives—a source from which he regularly drew for his history. The passage below recounts the massacres visited on the Jews of Strasbourg in the wake of the Black Death.

In the year of Our Lord 1349 the most terrible pestilence in history occurred, spreading death from one end of the Earth to the other. Rampaging both on this side and the far side of the sea—it was in fact even deadlier among the Muslims than among the Christians—it killed so many people that in some places hardly a single person was left alive. Ships floated adrift on the sea, their holds bulging with goods, but with the entire crew dead and no one left to steer the ship. In Marseilles, the bishop and all the priests and monks died, taking more than half the city's population with them. In other cities and districts so many people perished that the desolation can hardly be described. The pope in Avignon cancelled the entire court's activities and locked himself in his chamber; no one was granted admission to him at all, and he kept a fire roaring in his room day and night. What had caused the epidemic? Even the wisest scholars and physicians could say only that it had to be the will of God. The effect of the plague here in Strasbourg was the same as elsewhere, and it lasted more than an entire year. Arriving in the summer of 1349, it killed approximately sixteen thousand people.

Everywhere throughout the world blame for the plague fell upon the Jews, who were loathed for supposedly causing the pestilence by poisoning the water-wells, and so they were thrown to the flames everywhere from the Mediterranean to Germany (except for in the city of Avignon, where the pope protected them). In the Swiss towns of Berne and Zofingen a number of Jews admitted, after being tortured, to poisoning the wells—and the poison was even found, so the townsmen burned the Jews throughout the region and wrote of their actions to the people in Strasbourg, Freiburg, and Basel, so that they might do the same.

Officials in the first two cities refused to take similar action—although in Basel the populace marched on the city hall and forced the town council to swear that they would in fact burn the Jews living there and never allow another Jew into the city for two hundred years; all the Jews of Basel were therefore arrested, and a hearing was scheduled to meet at Benfeld. The bishop of Strasbourg, all the nobility of Alsace, and representatives of the townsmen of Strasbourg, Freiburg, and Basel were in attendance, and they asked the Strasbourg officials what they intended to do with the arrested Jews. The officials replied that they had no cause to take action against the Jews, and demanded to know why the citizens of the city had closed up the wells and put away all the buckets. A huge, indignant roar rose from the crowd, and in the end it was the bishop and nobles of Strasbourg, and the people of the imperial cities, who decided to do

Translation by Clifford Backman.

away with the Jews—and as a result of their resolve, Jews throughout the region were fed to the flames. Jews who were merely expelled from their towns were invariably captured by the nearby peasant and were either cut down or drowned. . . .

In Strasbourg, the officials who had refused to punish the Jews were deposed and replaced by a new council that gave in to the demands of the mob.

On St. Valentine's Day, a Saturday, the new council had the Jews burned to death atop a wooden platform that they had ordered built in the Jews' cemetery; there were about two thousand of them, and they were all put to death, except for the few who declared themselves willing to receive baptism. Some children were pulled from the flames at the last moment and were forcibly baptized, against the will of their fathers and mothers who looked on. All debts to the Jews were cancelled, first, so the Jews were forced to surrender all pledges and bonds that they had taken as collateral. The town council seized all the Jews' cash, and divided it among the commoners. The money, of course, was the Jews' downfall. If they had been poor, and if the nobles had not been in debt to them, they would never have been killed. Once their money was distributed to the citizens, some of them gave a share of it to the local cathedral or some other church, on the advice of their confessors.

That is how the Jews of Strasbourg came to be burned. Much the same thing happened to the Jews in all the Rhineland cities, whether Free or Imperial or belonging to the nobles. Some places gave the Jews a trial, first; others, not. And in some places the Jews set fire to their own homes and cremated themselves. Afterwards, officials in Strasbourg decided that no Jew should be allowed to enter the city for a hundred years, but less than twenty years later a new council voted to permit Jews back. Thus did Jews return to Strasbourg in the year 1368 after the Incarnation of Our Lord.

STUDY QUESTIONS

1. According to Twinger, how are the Jews to blame for the plague?
2. Compare Twinger's account of the plague with Boccaccio's (Document 11.3). How are they different?

CHAPTER 12

RENAISSANCES AND REFORMATIONS

12.1. PETRARCA, "LETTER TO POSTERITY"

This letter, which Petrarca (1304–1374) never finished, represents something of an autobiographical obituary. In it he offers a summary of his life and achievements, which, interestingly, does not include the vernacular love poetry. He wanted above all to be remembered as a scholar, a lover of classical antiquity, and a Latin poet—above all, as the author of the (paralyzingly dull) epic poem *Africa*, about the Roman general Scipio Africanus. Petrarca carries his life story as far forward as 1341; he left no notes about what he intended to include in the presumed second half of the letter.

It is possible that you may have heard of me, but I doubt it; a name as obscure and insignificant as mine cannot have travelled far in either time or space. But if you have heard of me, it may interest you to know the kind of man I was, or the results of my long labors—especially those you may have heard of them, or, at any rate, whose titles may have reached you.

To begin with myself, then, I should warn you that the things men say about me will differ considerably, since men are usually more influenced by whim than by truth whenever they are passing judgment on another; there is no limit to either praise or blame. The truth is that I was one of you, a poor mortal, of no exalted origin but neither of terribly lowly birth. I simply belonged, as Augustus Caesar once said of himself, to an ancient family. In disposition, I was not naturally perverse, nor was I wanting in modesty except as the contagion of custom may have corrupted me. My youth was gone before I realized it, and young manhood carried me away. Maturity

eventually brought me to my senses and taught me, through experience, the truth I had long before read in books—namely, that youth and pleasure are vain. . . . In my prime I was blessed with an agile and active, though not particularly strong, body, and although I cannot boast of having been terribly handsome, I was good-looking enough in those days. I had a clear complexion, somewhere between light and dark, and I had lively eyes. For many years I enjoyed keen vision, but it deserted me all of a sudden around my sixtieth birthday and forced me, reluctantly, to wear glasses. I had always been perfectly healthy, but old age brought its usual array of complaints.

My parents were good people, Florentines both, and not very well off. I may as well admit it: they were in fact on the verge of poverty. They had been expelled from their native city, which is why I was born in exile at Arezzo, in 1304. . . . I have always been contemptuous of wealth; but it is not that I would not

Translation by Clifford R. Backman.

175

have liked to be rich—I simply hate the work and worry that seems always to accompany wealth. I never cared to give great banquets, and have led a much happier life with a plain diet and ordinary foods. . . . On the other hand, the pleasure of dining with friends is great, and nothing gives me more delight than the unexpected arrival of a friend. Nothing irks me more than ostentation, for not only is it bad in itself, being opposed to humility, but it is distracting and annoying.

In my younger years I struggled constantly with an all-consuming but pure love affair, my only one, and I would have struggled with it even longer had not my love's premature death (bitter, but in the end, salutary for me) extinguished the last flames. I wish I could say that I have been free of the lusts of the flesh, but I would be lying if I did. I can at least say this, though: even while I was occasionally swept away by the ardor of my youth and temperament, I always detested such sins from the very depths of my soul. . . .

I have taken pride in others, though never in myself, and even as insignificant as I have been, I have also thought myself even more so. In anger I have often injured myself but never another. I have always had the greatest desire for honorable friendships, and have cherished them faithfully. I can make the following boast without fear, for I know I am speaking sincerely: while I am prone to taking offense, I am quick to forget—and I never fail to remember acts of generosity. I have had the good fortune to associate with kings and princes, and to enjoy the friendship of nobles, to such a point as to excite envy. But it is the cruel fate of aging that eventually we weep for friends who have passed away. Some of the greatest kings of this age have courted and cherished my friendship. They may know why. I certainly do not. With some of them I was on such terms that they seemed, in some way, to be my guests, rather than I theirs. Their eminence in no way discomforted me; in fact, it brought me many advantages. I kept well away from many others of whom I was quite fond, for my innate longing for freedom was so strong that I carefully avoided those whose eminence seemed to threaten the liberty I loved so much.

I had more of a well-balanced mind than a keen one, one suited to many kinds of good and wholesome study but especially inclined to moral philosophy and poetry. Over time I paid less and less attention to the latter and found delight in sacred literature, discovering in it a hidden sweetness that I had earlier failed to appreciate. I came to regard works of poetry as mere amenities. I found many subjects interesting, yet focused especially on the study of antiquity, for I have always disliked our own age so much that, were it not for the love of those dearest to me, I would have preferred to live in any other period than our own. To forget the world in which we live, I have always striven to place my mind in other ages—and thus I came to love history. The conflicting opinions of people about the past have never offended me. When in doubt, I have made it a point to accept what seems to me the most probable explanation, or simply to yield to the authority of the historian I was reading. . . .

Along the breezy banks of the Rhône river I spent my boyhood, under the care of my parents, and then I spent my adolescence under the guidance of my own vanities. There were some long intervals spent abroad, though. I spent four years in the little town of Carpentras, which lies a little to the east of Avignon. In these two places I learned all that I could, considering my age, of grammar, logic, and rhetoric; or rather, I learned as much as is usually taught in school—and you, dear reader, will know how little that is. I then moved on to Montpellier for four years, to study law, and then to Bologna for three years more. . . . I was twenty-two when I finally returned home. Since habit has nearly the force of nature to it, I call Avignon—my place of exile—home. I was already beginning to make a name for myself there, and my friendship was sought by a number of prominent people. Why? I do not really know. I confess that it is now a source of surprise to me, although it seemed a natural enough thing then, when I was at the age when we are used to thinking ourselves deserving of the highest respect. I was courted first and foremost by the eminent and noble Colonna family, which then adorned the Roman Curia with their presence. . . . I spent many years in the house of Cardinal Giovanni Colonna, the brother of Giacomo, living not like a servant to Giovanni's lord but as if he were my father, or even better, my loving brother. It felt like living in my very own home. In time, though, youthful curiosity drove me to visit France and Germany. I invented a number of reasons to justify the journey to my elders, but the real impulse was simply my burning desire to see new sights. I went first to Paris, since I wanted to learn what was true in what I had heard about the city, and what was nonsense. Returning from this journey I went straightaway to Rome, which I had wanted to see ever since I was a child. There I soon came to revere Stefano Colonna, the great family's noble patriarch, an ancient hero who welcomed me in every possible way, as though I were his own son. The love and good will with which this marvelous man treated me lasted until the end of his life, and it lives on in my heart, where it will never fade until I myself cease to be.

Upon returning, I instantly felt the revulsion I have always had for city life, especially for the disgusting city of Avignon, which I truly abhorred. Seeking some means of escape, I was lucky enough to discover, about fifteen miles away, a delightful valley, narrow and secluded, called Vaucluse, where the Sorgue river (that prince of streams!) has its source. The charm of the site captivated me, and so I moved there together with all my books. If I were to tell you all that I did during my many years there, it would be a long story indeed. Almost every bit of writing I produced [in those years] was either done or begun there, or was at least conceived there; and those writings have been so numerous that even today they keep me busy and weary. My mind is like my body—more agile than strong; and while it was quite easy for me to think up new projects, I dropped many when they proved too difficult to carry out.

Inspired by the beauty of my surroundings, I undertook to write a pastoral or bucolic song: my *Bucolicum Carmen*. I also wrote *The Life of Solitude* (*De vita solitaria*), in two books, which I dedicated to the great man who is now Cardinal-Bishop Philip of Sabina, although at that time he was still the humble bishop of Cavaillon. He is the only one of my old friends who is still alive, and he has always loved me and treated me not as a bishop (as Ambrose did to Augustine) but as a brother. One Friday during Holy Week as I was hiking through those mountains I developed a powerful urge to write an epic poem, one based on Scipio Africanus the Great, who had been a favorite of mine since childhood. I began the project in a rush of enthusiasm, but because of a number of distractions I was forced to put it aside. The poem was called *Africa*, after its hero, and by some fate—my own or the poem's?—it did not fail to rouse the interest of many readers even before I published it. . . .

In a long passage, omitted here, he describes how he was summoned to Rome by the members of the Senate, to receive the laurel crown—the highest honor for a poet in Roman tradition.

I was very much pre-occupied with the honor I had just received, worried and fretful that I was unworthy of it, and as a result, when I was hiking through the hills again one day, I happened to cross the river Enza, in the area of Reggio Selvapiana and all of a sudden the beauty of the spot inspired me to finish writing my incomplete *Africa*. My enthusiasm for the project revived as from the dead and I wrote a number of lines that very day. More lines followed every day until I made it all the way to Parma, where I found a quiet, secluded house—which I later bought, and still own—and devoted myself to the poem with such energy that I completed it in no time at all, a fact that still amazes me to this day.

I was thirty-four years old. I returned to my home at the source of the Sorgue, to my beloved trans-Alpine solitude, after that long stay in Parma and Verona, where everyone I met, I am thankful to say, welcomed me with much greater honor that I deserved. Not long afterward, however, my reputation attracted the attention of Giacomo the Younger, of Carrara, an extraordinary man whose equal I doubt could be found even among the rulers of the age. He sent a constant stream of messengers and letters to me for years, no matter if I was in Italy or on the other side of the Alps, begging me to accept his friendship until at last, expecting little good to come of it, I decided to visit him and see what this persistence on the part of so eminent a man, a stranger to me, was all about. So I made my way to Parma, where I was received by him, who is now so dear to my memory, not as a mere mortal might be received but as the saints are received in Heaven—with so much joy and astonishing affection and respect that I cannot put it into words. Therefore, let me be silent. Among the many honors he gave me, he made me a canon of the cathedral of Padua (after he learned that I had been a cleric from boyhood) in order to strengthen my connection to him and his city. To put it bluntly, if he had not died so soon he would have put an end to all my wanderings. But alas, nothing mortal lasts forever, and everything that is sweet eventually turns bitter. Giacomo had scarcely given two years to me, to his city, and to the entire world when God, Who had given him to us, took him away. It is not out of blind love for him that I believe neither I, the city, nor the world were worthy of him. Giacomo's son and successor, a man of genuine sensibility and distinction, was likewise very friendly and respectful to me, but I could not remain with him after the death of one to whom I was so intimately connected. (We were even of the same age.) I returned to France, not because I was wanting to see again the old familiar place but because I wanted to get free of my misery, like a sick man wants, by a change of scene.

STUDY QUESTIONS

1. How does Petrarca come to love the past? What are the reasons he gives for his desire to "place my mind in other ages"?
2. What role do important men like Stefano Colonna and Giaccomo the Younger of Carrara play in Petrarca's life? What does this say about the role of friendship in his scholarly career?

12.2. FROM ARIOSTO, *ORLANDO FURIOSO* (*MAD ORLANDO*), PUBLISHED 1516

Ludovico Ariosto (1474–1533) reprises the familiar characters from the "Song of Roland" (Document 10.6) in his epic romance, *Orlando Furioso*, itself a continuation of another poem (*Orlando Innamorato*). Occurring in a dreamy Renaissance version of the medieval world—including trips to Japan and the moon!—the plot centers on Orlando (a new Roland) who embodies the conflict between Muslims and Charlemagne's army by helplessly loving a pagan princess, Angelica. When Orlando discovers that Angelica has fallen in love with a Saracen named Medoro, he tips headfirst into a mania that leaves a trail of destruction across Europe. He can be saved only by his friends who bring him a flask with his "wits" inside—when he breathes it, he simultaneously falls out of love and regains his sanity.

The day, the night to him were both alike;
Abroad upon the cold bare earth he lies;
No sleep, no food he takes, nor none would seek;
All sustenance he to himself denies.

Thus he began and ended half the week,
And he himself doth marvel whence his eyes
Are fed so long with such a spring of water,
And to himself thus reasons on the matter:

Rudolf Gottfried, *Ariosto's Orlando Furioso*. Bloomington: Indiana University Press, 1964, pp. 184–6, 190–1, 343–7. Reprinted with permission of Indiana University Press.

"No, no, these be no tears that now I shed;
These be no tears, nor can tears run so rife;
But fire of frenzy draw'th up to my head
My vital humor that should keep my life;
This stream will never cease till I be dead.
Then welcome, death, and end my fatal strife;
No comfort in this life my woe can minish
But thou, who canst both life and sorrow finish.

"These are not sighs, for sighs some respite
    have;
My gripes, my pangs no respite do permit;
The blindfold boy made me a seeing slave
When from her eyes my heart he first did hit.
Now all inflamed, I burn, I rage and rave
And in the midst of flame consume no whit:
Love sitting in my heart, a master cruel,
Blows with his wings, feeds with his will the fuel.

"I am not I, the man that erst I was;
Orlando, he is burièd and dead;
His most ungrateful love (ah, foolish lass)
Hath killed Orlando and cut off his head;
I am his ghost that up and down must pass
In this tormenting hell forever led,
To be a fearful sample and a just
To all such fools as put in love their trust."

Straightways he draweth forth his fatal blade
And hews the stones; to heave'n the shivers flee;
Accursèd was that fountain, cave, and shade,
The arbor and the flowers and every tree;
Orlando of all places havoc made
Where he those names together joined may see;
Yea, to the spring he did perpetual hurt
By filling it with leaves, boughs, stones, and dirt.

And having done this foolish, frantic feat,
He lays him down all weary on the ground,
Distempered in his body with much heat,
In mind with pains that no tongue can expound;
Three days he doth not sleep nor drink nor eat,
But lay with open eyes as in a sound;
The fourth, with rage and not with reason
    wakèd,
He rents his clothes and runs about stark naked.

His helmet here he flings, his pouldrons there;
He casts away his curats and his shield;
His sword he throws away, he cares not where;
He scatters all his armor in the field;
No rag about his body he doth bear
As might from cold or might from shame him
    shield;
And save he left behind this fatal blade,
No doubt he had therewith great havoc made.

But his surpassing force did so exceed
All common men that neither sword nor bill
Nor any other weapon he did need;
Mere strength sufficed him to do what he will.
He roots up trees as one would root a weed;
And e'en as birders laying nets with skill
Pare slender thorns away with easy strokes,
So he did play with ashes, elms, and oaks.
. . .
Away they fled, but he pursued so fast
That some he caught, and some surprised with
    fear
Stood still, as oft it happens, all aghast,
Not knowing how to hide themselves nor where;
Some other ploughmen, seeing what had passed,
Thought it but little wit to tarry there,
But climbed, for fear, their houses and their
    churches,
Not trusting strength of elms, of beech and
    birches.

Among the rest he takes one by his heel
And with his head knocks out another's brain,
Which causèd both of them such pain to feel
As till Doomsday they never shall complain;
Another with his fist he made to reel
Till pain itself made him past sense of pain;
And when the men fled all away afeard,
Then with like rage he set upon their herd.
. . .
And finding no man there, nor small nor great,
For all were fled away from thence for awe,
As famine forced him, he sought out some meat;
And were it fine or coarse, the first he saw
In greedy sort he doth devour and eat,
Not caring if it roasted were or raw;

And when thus homely he had ta'en repast,
About the country bedlamlike he passed.

Then kneeling down as if he asked some boon
Of God or some great saint, that pot he brought
Which he had carried from beyond the moon,
The jar in which Orlando's wit was caught,
And closed it to his nostrils; and eftsoon
He drawing breath, this miracle was wrought:
The jar was void and emptied every whit,
And he restored unto his perfect wit.

As one that in some dream or fearful vision
Hath dreamt of monstrous beasts and ugly fiends
Is troubled, when he wakes, with superstition
And feareth what such ugly sight intends
And lying wake thinks of that apparition
And long time after in that fancy spends:
So now Orlando lay, not little musing
At this his present state and uncouth using.

He holds his peace, but lifting up his eyes
He sees his ancient friends King Brandimart

And Oliver and him that made him wise,
All whom he knew and lovèd from his heart;
He thinks, but cannot with himself devise
How he should come to play so mad a part;
He wonders he is nak'd and that he feels
Such store of cords about his hands and heels.

At last he said, as erst Sileno said
To those that took him napping in the cave,
"Release me!" with countenance so staid
And with a sheer so sober and so grave
That they unloosèd him as he them prayed
And suffered him his liberty to have
And clothèd him and comforted his sadness
That he conceivèd of his former madness.
Thus being to his former wits restored,
He was likewise delivered clean from love;
The lady whom he erst so much adored
And did esteem all earthly joys above
Now he despised, yea rather quite abhorred;
Now only he applies his wits to prove
That fame and former glory to recover
Which he had not lost the while he was a lover.

STUDY QUESTIONS

1. In what specific respects does Orlando's passion appear as madness?
2. Is Orlando still the ideal type of a Christian knight, even before he is released from his enchantment?

12.3. MACHIAVELLI, *DISCOURSES ON LIVY*, CA. 1517?

The humanist and statesman Niccolò Machiavelli (1469–1527) is best known for his Italian treatise, *The Prince*, on Renaissance city-state rulers—but his *Discourses on Livy* better clarify his republican ideals. In the response to Roman historian Livy, Machiavelli traces the origins of "good" republics. He comments on the maintenance of liberties, the role of religion, and the danger of societal fragmentation through conspiracy.

Discourses on Livy translated by Bondanella and Bondanella (2010) 1666w from pp. 31–32, 53–56, 256–258, 275. By permission of Oxford University Press.

CHAPTER 5

WHETHER THE GUARDIANSHIP OF LIBERTY MAY BE MORE SECURELY LODGED IN THE PEOPLE OR IN THE UPPER CLASSES; AND WHO HAS MORE REASON TO CREATE AN UPRISING, HE WHO WISHES TO ACQUIRE OR HE WHO WISHES TO MAINTAIN

Among the most necessary things established by those who have founded a republic in a prudent fashion is a safeguard for liberty, and according to whether it is well established or not, that free way of life is more or less enduring. Because in every republic there are men of prominence and men of the people, some doubt has arisen over whose hands into which this guardianship would best be placed. Among the Spartans and, in our own times, among the Venetians, it was placed in the hands of the nobles, but among the Romans it was placed in the hands of the plebeians.

For this reason, it is necessary to examine which of these republics made the best choice. If we were to explore the reasons, something could be said for both sides, but if we examine the results, we would choose the side of the nobles, since the liberty of Sparta and Venice endured longer than that of Rome. Turning to the causes, let me say, while first taking the side of the Romans, that the guardianship must be given to those who have less of an appetite to usurp it. No doubt, if we consider the goal of the nobles and that of the common people, we shall see in the former a strong desire to dominate and in the latter only the desire not to be dominated, and, as a consequence, a stronger will to live in liberty, since they have less hope of usurping it than men of prominence; just so, since the common people are set up as guardians of this liberty, it is reasonable to think that they will take better care of it, and, being incapable of appropriating it for themselves, they will not permit others to do so. On the other hand, those who defend the organization of Sparta and Venice declare that those who place the guardianship in the hands of the powerful accomplish two good things: first they better satisfy their ambition, and since they have a larger part to play in the republic with this club in their hands, they have more reason to be content; second

they remove a kind of authority from the restless minds of the plebeians that is the cause of countless conflicts and disagreements in any republic and is likely to drive the nobility to despair, which, in the passing of time, will produce harmful consequences. As an example they offer Rome itself, where, once the tribunes of the people had this authority in their hands, they did not consider it sufficient to have one plebeian consul and wanted two of them. After this, they wanted the censorship, the praetorship, and all the other positions of power in the city; nor did this suffice, for led by this same consuming desire, they then began in time to idolize those men they saw capable of beating down the nobility; and from this arose the power of Marius and the ruin of Rome. Truly, anyone who properly considers one side or the other could remain in doubt about which of the two should be chosen as the guardian of such liberty, not knowing which human disposition is more harmful in a republic: either that which wishes to preserve honour already acquired, or that which wishes to acquire honour yet to be possessed.

. . .

CHAPTER 12

HOW IMPORTANT IT IS TO TAKE ACCOUNT OF RELIGION, AND HOW ITALY, LACKING IN RELIGION THANKS TO THE ROMAN CHURCH, HAS BEEN RUINED

Those princes or republics that wish to maintain their integrity must, above all else, maintain the integrity of their religious ceremonies, and must always hold them in veneration, because there can be no greater indication of the ruin of a state than to see a disregard for its divine worship. This is easy to understand if one knows how the religion in the place where a man is born has been founded, because the life of every religion has its foundations in one of its principal institutions. The existence of the pagan religion was founded upon the responses of the oracles and the sect of diviners and soothsayers; all the other ceremonies, sacrifices, and rites depended upon them, because they simply believed that the god who could predict your future good or evil could also grant it to you.

. . .

Since many are of the opinion that the well-being of the Italian cities arises from the Roman church, I want to discuss the arguments that occur to me against this opinion, and I shall cite as evidence two very powerful ones which, in my view, cannot be refuted. The first is that because of the evil examples set by this court, this land has lost all piety and religion; this brings with it countless disadvantages and countless disorders, because just as we take for granted every good thing where religion exists, so, where it is lacking, we take for granted the contrary. We Italians have, therefore, this initial debt to the church and to the priests, that we have become irreligious and wicked, but we have an even greater debt to them, which is the second cause of our ruin: that is, the church has kept and still keeps this land divided, and truly, no land is ever united or happy unless it comes completely under the obedience of a single republic or a single prince, as has occurred in France and Spain. The reason why Italy is not in the same condition and why it, too, does not have either a single republic or a single prince to govern it lies solely with the church, because although the church has its place of residence in Italy and has held temporal power there, it has not been so powerful nor has it possessed enough skill to be able to occupy the remaining parts of Italy and make itself ruler of this country, and, on the other hand, it has not been so weak that, for fear of losing control over its temporal affairs, it has been unable to bring in someone powerful to defend it against anyone in Italy who had become too powerful: this is seen to have happened in ancient times through a number of examples, as when with Charlemagne's assistance, the Lombards, already kings of almost all of Italy, were driven out, and when in our own times the church took power away from the Venetians with the aid of France and then chased out the French with the aid of the Swiss. Since it has not, therefore, been powerful enough to take possession of all of Italy, nor has it permitted anyone else to do so, the church has been the reason why Italy has been unable to unite under a single leader and has remained under a number of princes and lords, who have produced so much disunity and

weakness that it has come to be easy prey not only to powerful barbarians but to anyone who might attack it. For this we Italians are indebted to the church and to no one else. Anyone who might wish to see this truth more clearly through actual experience needs to possess sufficient power to send the Roman court, with all the authority it possesses in Italy, to live in the lands of the Swiss, who are today the only people who live, with respect to religion and military institutions, as the ancients did, and he would observe that in a brief time the wicked customs of that court would create more disorder in that land than any other event that could at any time take place there.

. . .

CHAPTER 6

ON CONSPIRACIES

I did not think I should omit an analysis of conspiracies, since they represent a grave danger for princes and for private citizens. It is evident that many more princes have lost their lives and their states through conspiracies than through open warfare, because being able to wage open war against a prince is within the reach of very few, while the possibility of conspiring against him is open to everyone. . . . Truly golden is that maxim of Tacitus, which declares that men must honour past affairs and endure present ones, and that they should desire good princes, but regardless of what they are like, should tolerate them. And truly, anyone who does otherwise most often ruins himself and his native land.

. . .

Injuries must either be against property, lifeblood, or honour. To threaten someone's lifeblood is more dangerous than to execute him; or rather, making threats is extremely dangerous, while ordering executions involves no danger whatsoever, because a dead man cannot think about a vendetta, while those who remain alive most often leave the thinking to the dead. But anyone who is threatened and forced by necessity either to act or to suffer will become a very dangerous man to the prince, as we shall discuss in detail in the proper place. Besides this kind of necessity, injuries to property and honour are the two things that offend men more than any other kind of attack, and the prince must protect himself against them, because he can never strip a man of so much that he will not have a knife left with which to take his revenge; nor can he ever dishonour a man so much that he does not retain a heart and mind stubbornly intent on revenge.

. . .

Princes, therefore, have no greater enemy than a conspiracy, because if a conspiracy is organized against them, it either kills them or disgraces them; if it succeeds, they die, and if it is discovered and they kill the conspirators, people always believe that the conspiracy was an invention of the prince to give vent to his avarice and cruelty against their lives and property of those whom he has killed.

STUDY QUESTIONS

1. Does Machiavelli employ examples from the pre-Christian and his contemporary world equally?
2. Why does he see the Church as an "impediment" to the political ambitions of Italians?

12.4. ERASMUS, "LETTER TO A FRIEND," "JULIUS EXCLUDED FROM HEAVEN," AND *INTRODUCTION TO THE GOSPELS*, FIRST PUBLISHED 1522

Desiderius Erasmus (ca. 1466–1536) was a Catholic priest who has also been called the Prince of the Humanists for his application of humanist principles to the religious disruption of the Reformation—he created new editions of the New Testament and wrote a handful of satires and other texts on Christian life. Although Erasmus was appalled by the abuses of the Catholic Church, he chose to try to address them while remaining a staunch Catholic. In 1512, Erasmus began work on a fresh Greek edition of the New Testament (with the Latin in parallel columns) that would share a beautified, holistic, and purified Word of God with Catholics in a time of religious turmoil. Interestingly, this would be the version used by Luther to make his own German translation (Document 12.5).

LETTER TO A FRIEND ON PRESENT CONDITIONS

It is no part of my nature, most learned Wolfgang, to be excessively fond of life; whether it is, that I have, to

my own mind, lived nearly long enough, having entered my fifty-first year, or that I see nothing in this life so splendid or delightful, that it should be desired by one who is convinced by the Christian faith, that

From Erasmi Opuscula, ed. W. K. Fergison. The Hague: Martinus Nijhoff, 1933, pp. 65–8, trans. M. P. Gilmore; From De Libero Arbitrio (1524), in J. Clericus, ed., Desiderii Erasmi Roterodami Opera Omnia. Lugduni Batavorum: Petri Vander Aa, 1703–1706, IX, 1240, 1244, 1248, trans. Brice M. Clagett.; De Libero Arbitrio (1524), in J. Clericus, ed., Desiderii Erasmi Roterodami Opera Omnia. Lugduni Batavorum: Petri Vander Aa, 1703–1706, IX, 1215, 1219–20, trans. Brice M. Clagett.

a happier life awaits those who in this world earnestly attach themselves to piety. But at the present moment I could almost wish to be young again, for no other reason but this, that I anticipate the near approach of a golden age; so clearly do we see the minds of princes, as if changed by inspiration, devoting all their energies to the pursuit of peace. The chief movers in this matter are Pope Leo, and Francis, King of France.

There is nothing this king does not do or does not suffer, in his desire to avert war and consolidate peace; submitting, of his own accord, to conditions which might be deemed unfair, if he preferred to have regard to his own greatness and dignity, rather than to the general advantage of the world; and exhibiting in this, as in every thing else, a magnanimous and truly royal character. Therefore, when I see that the highest sovereigns of Europe, Francis of France, Charles the Catholic King, Henry of England and the Emperor Maximillian have set all their warlike preparations aside, and established peace upon solid, and as I trust adamantine foundations, I am led to a confident hope, that not only morality and Christian piety, but also a genuine and purer literature may come to renewed life or greater splendor; especially as this object is pursued with equal zeal in various regions of the world,—at Rome by Pope Leo, in Spain by the Cardinal of Toledo, in England by Henry, eighth of the name, himself not unskilled in Letters, and among ourselves by our young king Charles. In France King Francis, who seems as it were born for this object, invites and entices from all countries men that excel in merit or in learning. Among the Germans the same object is pursued by many of their excellent princes and bishops, and especially by Maximillian Caesar, whose old age, weary of so many wars, has determined to seek rest in the employments of peace, a resolution more becoming to his own years, while it is fortunate for the Christian world. To the piety of these princes it is due, that we see everywhere, as if upon a given signal, men of genius are arising and conspiring together to restore the best literature.

Polite letters, which were almost extinct, are now cultivated and embraced by Scots, by Danes and by Irishmen. Medicine has a host of champions; at Rome Nicolas of Leonice; at Venice Ambrosius Leo of Nola, in France William Cop, and John Ruelle, and in England Thomas Linacre. The Imperial Law is restored at Paris by William Budé, in Germany by Udalris Zasy; and Mathematics at Basel by Henry of Glaris. In the theological sphere there was no little to be done, because this science has been hitherto mainly professed by those who are most pertinacious in the abhorrence of the better literature, and are the more successful in defending their own ignorance as they do it under pretext of piety, the unlearned vulgar being induced to believe, that violence is offered to Religion, if any one begins an assault upon their barbarism. For in the presence of an ignorant mob they are always ready to scream and excite their followers to stone-throwing, if they see any risk of not being thought omniscient. But even here I am confident of success, if the knowledge of the three languages continues to be received in schools, as it has now begun. For the most learned and least churlish men of the profession do in some measure assist and favour the new system; and in this matter we are especially indebted to the vigorous exertions of James Lefèvrew of Étaples, whom you resemble not only in name, but in a number of accomplishments.

The humblest part of the work has naturally fallen to my lot. Whether my contribution has been worth anything, I cannot say; at any rate those who object to the world regaining its senses, are as angry with me, as if my small industry had had some influence, although the work was not undertaken by me with any confidence that I could myself teach anything magnificent; but I wanted to construct a road for other persons of higher aims, so that they might be less impeded by pools and stumbling-blocks in carrying home those fair and glorious treasures.

* * *

JULIUS II EXCLUDED FROM HEAVEN: JULIUS, HIS TUTELARY SPIRIT, AND SAINT PETER

JULIUS: What's the trouble here? Won't the doors open? The lock must have been changed or at least tampered with.

SPIRIT: Perhaps you haven't brought the right key, for this door will never be opened by the same key as you use for your money-box. So why haven't you brought both keys here, for this one that you have is the key of power not of knowledge?

JULIUS: This is the only one I ever had and I see no need of another as long as I have this.

SPIRIT: Nor indeed do I except that in the meantime we are shut out.

JULIUS: I am getting very angry. I will beat down these gates. Hey, someone in there, open this door at once! What is the matter? Will no one come? Why does the porter dally like this? No doubt he's snoring and probably drunk.

SPIRIT: (As always he judges everyone else by himself!)

SAINT PETER: It's a good thing we have adamantine doors here; otherwise this man would have broken in. he must be some giant or satrap, a conqueror of cities. But, O immortal God, what stench! I will not open the door at once, but by looking out this little barred window find out what kind of a monster this may be. Who are you and what do you want?

JULIUS: Open as quickly as you can. If you had done your duty, you ought to have come out and meet me with all the pomp due an emperor.

SAINT PETER: Spoken imperiously enough. But first explain to me who you are.

JULIUS: As if you could not see for yourself!

SAINT PETER: See? Indeed I see a strange and hitherto unknown, not to say monstrous, spectacle.

JULIUS: Unless you are wholly blind, you must recognize this key even if you don't know the golden oak. And you see the triple crown and the pallium gleaming with gems and with gold.

SAINT PETER: Indeed I see a key silvered all over although it is only one and very different from those keys which Christ as the true pastor of the Church once gave over to me. And how should I recognize this proud crown? No barbarian tyrant ever worse such a one still less anyone who demanded to be admitted here. Nor does this pallium in the least move me who have always scorned and despised gold and gems as

rubbish. But what is this? I see everywhere on key and crown and pallium the signs of that most wicked rogue and impostor Simon [Magus] who shares my name but not my way of life, and whom I long ago turned out of the temple of Christ.

JULIUS: If you are wise you will put aside this joking, for, in case you don't know, I am Julius the Ligurian and you will surely recognize the two letters P. M. if you learned to read at all.

SAINT PETER: I believe they stand for "Pestis Maxima" [Supreme Plague].

SPIRIT: Ha ha ha! How this soothsayer has hit the nail on the head!

JULIUS: No, "Pontifex Maximus" [Supreme Pontiff].

SAINT PETER: If you were three times "Maximus" and more even than Mercury Trismegistus, you would not come in here unless you were also "optimus," that is holy [*sanctus*].

JULIUS: If in fact it matters at all to be called "sanctus," you who are delaying the opening the doors for me have passed the bounds of imprudence since you during so many centuries have been called only "sanctus," while no one has ever called me anything but "sanctissimus." And there are six thousand bulls . . . in which I am not only named "most sacred lord" but am described by the very name of holiness itself, not *sanctus*, so that I did whatever I pleased.

SPIRIT: Even indulging in drunkenness.

JULIUS: They said that that made the sanctity of the most sacred lord Julius.

SAINT PETER: Then ask admission of those flatterers who made you most sacred and let them give you happiness who gave you sanctity. Although you think this is a question of no concern, will you be called "sanctus" whether you are or not?

JULIUS: I am exasperated. If I were only permitted to live, I should envy you neither that sanctity nor that felicity.

SAINT PETER: O what a revelation of a "most sacred mind"! Although I have now for some time been inspecting you from all sides, I notice in you many signs of impiety and none of holiness: And what does this strange crowd so very unpontifical want for itself? You bring some twenty thousand with you nor do I see anyone in such a great mob who has the countenance of a Christian. I see the loathsome dregs of men, smelling of nothing but brothels, drink-shops and gunpowder: It seems to me that hired robbers or rather infernal skeletons have rushed hither from hell to make war on heaven. Also the more I contemplate you yourself, the less do I see any vestige of an apostle. In the first place what kind of monster are you who, although you wear outside the garments of a priest, underneath bristle and clink with a covering of bloody armor? In addition to this how savage are your eyes, how stubborn your mouth, how threatening your brow and how haughty and arrogant your glance! It is shameful to have to say and at the same time disgusting to see that no part of your body is not defiled by the signs of your unrestrained and abominable lust: Not to speak of the fact that you always belch and smell of inebriation and drunkenness and indeed seem to me to have just vomited. This is so truly the condition of your whole body that you seem withered, wasted, and broken not so much by age and disease as by drunkenness.

SPIRIT: How graphically he has depicted him in all his colors.

SAINT PETER: Although I see that you have long been threatening me with your look, yet I cannot keep back what I feel. I suspect that you are that most pestilential heathen Julius returned from hell to make sport of me.

* * *

PARACLESIS: INTRODUCTION TO THE GOSPELS

I strongly dissent from those who are unwilling to have the Scriptures translated into the vernacular and read by the ignorant, as if Christ taught so complicated a doctrine that it can hardly be understood even by a handful of theologians or as if the arcanum of the Christian religion consisted in its not being known. It is perhaps reasonable to conceal the mysteries of kings but Christ seeks to divulge his mysteries as much as possible. I should like to have even the most humble women read the Evangel and the Epistles of St. Paul. And these ought also to be translated into all languages so that they might be read and known not only by Scots and Irishmen but also by Turks and Saracens. The first step is certainly to know the Scriptures in whatever manner. Although many will mock at them some will be captivated. Would that the ploughboy recited something from them at his ploughshare, that the weaver sang from them at his shuttle and that the traveler whiled away the tedium of his journey with their tales, indeed would that the converse of Christian men were drawn from them, for we are on the whole what our daily discourse reveals us to be. Let each attain what he can and express what he can. Let him who is behind not envy him who is ahead and let the leader encourage the follower without making him despair. Why should we restrict to a few a profession which is common to all? For since baptism in which the first profession of the philosophy of Christ is made is equally common to all Christians, since they share alike the other sacraments and finally the supreme reward of immortality, it is not fitting that the possession of dogma be relegated to those few whom we call theologians or monks. Although these latter constitute only a minute proportion of the Christian people nevertheless I could wish that they confirm more closely to what they head. For I fear lest there be found among the theologians those who are far from deserving this title, who discourse of earthly not of divine things and among the monks who profess poverty and contempt for the world you may find instead even more of the world. To me he is truly a theologian who teaches not with syllogisms and contorted arguments but with compassion in his eyes and his whole countenance, who teaches indeed by the example of his own life that riches are to be despised, that the Christian man must not put his faith in the defenses of this world but depend entirely on heaven, that he is not to return an injury for an injury, that he is to pray well for those who pray badly and do his best for those who deserve ill, that all good men ought to love and cherish each other as members of the same body and evil men tolerated if they cannot be corrected. Those who lose their goods, who are deposited of their possessions, who mourn—these are not to be pitied for they are the blessed and death is even to be desired by the pious for it is the passage to immortality. If anyone inspired by the spirit of Christ preaches things of this kind, if he inculcates, urges, invites, encourages, then he is a true theologian even if he should be a ditch digger or a weaver.

. . . For that which is especially according to nature easily comes into the minds of all. And what else is the philosophy of Christ which he himself calls a re-birth (*renascentia*) but a restoration of a nature which was originally created good?

* * *

ERASMUS ATTACKS LUTHER (1524)

What shall I say of the prodigal son? How could he have wasted his share of the inheritance had it not been his to do with as he pleased? But what he had, he held of his father; and we, too, remember that all our natural qualities are so many gifts of God. Besides, he enjoyed his share even when it was in his father's possession, and then it was in safer hands. What does it mean, then—his departure from his father after suddenly having demanded his share? Quite simply, to give oneself credit for one's natural qualities, and to use them, not in obeying the commandments of God, but in satisfying carnal lusts. And what means the hunger of the prodigal son? It is the sickness by which God directs the mind of the sinner towards self-knowledge, self-hatred, and regret for having left his Father. What is the meaning of the son's inner questioning, when he envisions confession and return? It is the human will adapting itself to the motivating grace that is also called, as we have said, "prevenient" grace. What about this Father who goes before his son on the way? It is the grace of God, which allows our will do to the good when we have determined to do it.

Besides, I ask, what merit could a man claim for himself who is indebted to Him from whom he received natural intelligence and free will for all he can do with these faculties? And yet God considers it meritorious in us not to turn our soul from His grace, and to enlist our talents in His service. That is enough to show that we make no mistake in attributing something to man, although we refer all his works to God as to their author: it is from Him, in fact, that man derives the power of making his strivings one with the operations of divine grace. . . . [The divine wisdom assists man] as guide and advisor, just as an architect directs his workman, draws his plans for him, explains the reason for them, corrects his faulty beginnings, and bolsters him if he loses courage: the work is attributed to the architect, without whose aid nothing would have been created, but no one pretends that the worker and pupil were worthless. What the architect is to his pupil, grace is to our will. That is why Paul writes to the Romans (8.26): "Even so His Spirit cometh to aid our weakness." Now no one calls a person who does nothing weak; that term, rather, is applied to him who lacks strength sufficient to accomplish what he undertakes; in the same sense, you do not say that some one helps you when he does everything. Now Scripture continually speaks of aid, support, succor, shelter. In order for there to be aid, the person aided has to do something. You would not say that the potter helps the clay to become a pot, or that the carpenter aids the axe in making a stool.

That is why, when our opponents declare that man can do nothing without the grace of God, therefore there are no good works by men, we confront them with this proof, which I believe more probable, that men can do everything with the aid of grace, therefore all human works can be good. As many passages as there are in Holy Scripture which mention succor, there are an equal number to establish free will, and they are countless; and I shall carry the day without any possible disagreement if the matter is judged by the number of proofs. . . .

In my opinion, similarly, free will could be preserved while completely avoiding this flagrant confidence in our own merits and the other dangers seen by Luther, without even considering those which we have cited above, and while retaining the main advantages of Lutheran teaching. This is what the doctrine means to me which attributes to grace all the first inspiration which enflames the soul, but which leaves to the human will, when it is not devoid of divine grace, a certain place in the unfolding of the drama. Now since this drama has three parts, the beginning, the development, and the fulfillment, we give the two extremities to grace and let free will enter only into the development. Thus two causes collaborate in the same given action, divine grace and the human will; but grace is the principal cause, the will a secondary one which could do nothing without the first, while grace is sufficient in itself—thus fire burns by its natural virtue, although God is the essential cause which sustains its action, without which the fire would lose all its power, if God happened to withdraw his support. . . .

But why, we are asked, leave a place for free will? In order to have something with which justly to accuse the impious who by their own decision stand outside divine grace; to acquit God of false charges of cruelty or injustice; to drive despair or arrogance far from us; to inspire us to effort. These are the reasons which have led almost all writers to admit free will; but it would remain ineffective without the perpetual aid of the grace of God, which justly prevents us from pride. But still it will be said: what good, then, is free will, if it can do nothing by itself? I shall only reply, "And what would be the use of man himself and all his faculties, if God acted on him as the potter on the clay, or even as He might act on a pebble?"

* * *

I take so little pleasure in dogmatizing that I should rather rank myself with the sceptics, whenever I am justified in so doing by the inviolable authority of Holy Scripture and by the decisions of the Church, to which I always submit my judgment quite willingly, whether or not I understand the reasons for what she

decrees. And this temper of mind appears to me preferable to that of certain others, who, narrowly attached to their own views, never let any one deviate from them in anything, and who violently twist all the texts of Scripture in support of the position they have embraced once and for all. . . .

Here it will be objected: "Why the need of interpretation, when Scripture itself is perfectly clear?" But if it is as clear as all that, why, over the centuries, have such eminent men been blind on so important a point, as our opponents contend? If Scripture is without obscurity, why was there need for prophecies in apostolic times? That, I shall be told, was a gift of the Holy Spirit. But I should like to know whether, just as the gift of healing and the gift of tongues have ceased, this divine gift has not ceased also. And if it has not ceased, we must seek to learn to whom it could have passed. If it has passed to merely anyone at all, then every interpretation will be uncertain; if it has been received by no one, since today so many obscurities still torment the learned, no interpretation will be more certain. If I maintain that it resides in the successors of the apostles, it will be objected that over the centuries many men have succeeded the apostles who nevertheless had none of the apostolic spirit. And yet, everything else being equal, it will be sought in them, for it is more probably that God has infused His Spirit in those to whom He has given holy orders; just as we believe that grace is more clearly given to the baptized than to the unbaptized.

But, as we must, we shall admit no less than the possibility that the Spirit may actually reveal to some humble and illiterate person truths withheld from a host of learned men, as when Christ thanked His Father for the things He made known to the simple, to those whom the world thought mad—things he had hidden from the wise and the judicious, from the knowledge of scribes, Pharissees, and philosophers. And perhaps Dominic, perhaps Francis [the thirteenth century saints], were the kind of madmen who are allowed to follow their inspirations. But if Paul, in the day when this gift of the Spirit was in its full vigor, already warns men to check on whether these inspirations really come from God, what must we do in our worldly age? By what standard shall we judge opinions? By learning? But there are none but master scholars in both parties. By conduct? On both sides, likewise, there are only sinners. But we find the chorus of saints all on the same side, defending free will. I am told, it is true, "They were nothing but men." But I only meant to compare men with one another, never with God. I am asked, what does the majority prove, with regard to spiritual insight? I answer, what does the minority prove? I am asked, how can a bishop's mitre be of use in understanding Holy Scripture? I answer, what good is a mantle or cowl? Again, how can philosophical studies make it easier to understand Holy Writ? And I reply, what use is ignorance? And again, how is the comprehension of texts connected with the meeting of a council, where it might be that no member had received the Spirit of God? I answer, what then is the value of private pseudo-councils of a few individuals, where there is only too clearly no possessor of the Spirit?

Do we remember this plea of Paul's, "Don't ask for proof that Christ lives in me"? Then the apostles were only believed to the extent to which their miracles confirmed their teaching. These days, on the contrary, anyone at all demands credence just because he declares he is filled with the spirit of the Gospel. Because the apostles drove out serpents, cured the sick, brought the dead to life, and gave the gift of tongues by the laying on of hands, men decided to believe, and not without difficulty, the paradoxes they taught. And today, when we see new teachers declaring things that common sense cannot even class as paradoxes, we have not yet seen one of them capable of curing a lame horse. And would to Heaven that, if they cannot work miracles, some of them would at least show the purity and simplicity of apostolic life, which to us, poor late-comers, would be miraculous enough!

I am not speaking specifically of Luther, whom I have never met and whose works give me a confused impression, but of certain others whom I have known more closely. It is they who in biblical controversies reject the interpretation of the Fathers which we suggest to them, they who cry unrestrainedly, "The Fathers were only men!" If they are asked what criterion can be used to establish the true interpretation of Scripture, since there are only men on both sides, they rely on the revelations of the Spirit. But if they are asked why the Spirit should favor them rather than those whose miracles have shone forth throughout the world, they answer if the Gospel had disappeared from the earth thirteen centuries ago. If you insist that their life be worthy of the Spirit, they retort that they are justified by faith, not by works. If you require miracles, they tell you that the time for them has long passed, and that there is no longer any need for them, now that the Scriptures are fully clarified. And then if you doubt that Scripture is clear precisely on the point where so many great minds have erred, you fall back into the same vicious circle.

Besides if we admit that he who possesses the Spirit is sure of understanding the Scriptures, how shall I be certain of what he has seen only partially? What shall I do when several learned men bring me different interpretations, each one swearing all the time that he has the Spirit? Especially, if we add that the Spirit does not reveal all truth to them fully, even he who has the Spirit can go wrong, and err on some point.

These are my objections to those who so easily reject the traditional interpretation of the Holy Books, and who propose their own as if it had plummeted from Heaven. Finally, assuming that the Spirit of Christ could have left His people in error on some secondary point without immediate repercussions on human salvation, how can we admit that for thirteen hundred years He abandoned His Church to error, and that in all the host of holy people not one could reveal to the Church that truth which, our recent arrivals pretend, constitutes the heart of all the Gospel teaching?

But to finish this matter: whatever others may arrogate to themselves is their own affair; as for me, I claim for myself neither wisdom nor sanctity, and I take no pride in my intellect, but I shall simply and carefully set forth the views which capture my allegiance. If any one wishes to teach me, I shall not meet the truth with a closed mind.

STUDY QUESTIONS

1. What lessons, particularly concerning warfare, does Erasmus hope that the kings of Europe will draw from reading his edition of the Gospels?
2. Did the behavior of the "Warrior Pope" Julius II warrant his being "excluded" from Heaven?
3. How did Erasmus reconcile the reading of Scripture and its interpretation in the correct, Christian spirit? Can every Christian interpret what s/he reads correctly?

12.5. MARTIN LUTHER, "PREFACE TO THE NEW TESTAMENT," FIRST PUBLISHED 1522

Martin Luther (1483–1546), known for his unplanned split from the Catholic Church, was a theologian and monk. Among other major points, Luther condemned the Catholic notion that priests enjoyed special spiritual status over other Christians that enabled them to intercede for ordinary sinners; he rejected the use of *indulgences* to purchase forgiveness for sins; and he claimed that only God's grace, and not something a Christian could "earn," would bring him salvation. He translated the Bible into German to make it accessible to his literate compatriots. For these actions, he was excommunicated, threatened with death, and ultimately became the unwitting founder of the first Protestant sect, Lutheranism. In this introduction to his German translation, Luther guides his readers through Jesus's teachings so that they may come to experience them on their own.

D. PREFACE TO LUTHER'S COLLECTED WORKS, 1545

[While working on the Psalms] I was absorbed by a passionate desire to understand Paul in his Epistle to the Romans. Nothing stood in my way but that one expression, "The justice of God is revealed in the Gospel" (Romans 1:17). For I hated these words, "the justice of God," because I had been taught to understand them in the scholastic sense as the formal or active justice whereby God, who is righteous, punishes unrighteous sinners. I was in the frame of mind of feeling that although I was living a blameless life as a monk, I was still a sinner with a troubled conscience before God, and I had no confidence that I could appease Him by my efforts. I did not love—nay, I hated the righteous God who punishes sinners, and I murmured with unbridled resentment, if not with unspoken blasphemy, against Him, saying, "As if it were not enough for miserable sinners who are eternally lost through original sin to be afflicted with every kind of

From Preserved Smith, *Luther's Correspondence*. Philadelphia: Lutheran Publishing Co., 1913, I, pp. 91–3; (A) From Luther, The Bondage of Will (1525). Trans. Henry Cole. Grand Rapids, Mich.: W. B. Eerdmans Publishing Co., 1931, pp. 74, 231, 384–5, 391. Original in WA, XVIII, 551 ff.; From Luther, *To the Christian Nobility of the German Nation* (1520). Eds. Henry Wace and C. A. Buchheim. *In Luther's Primary Works*. London: Hodder and Stoughton, 1896, pp. 162–75, pas-sim.

calamity through the law of the Ten Commandments, without God's adding woe to woe through the Gospel and even threatening us with His justice and wrath in the Gospel." Thus I raged, my conscience wild and disturbed. Still I kept hammering away at those words of Paul, wishing passionately to know what he meant.

After I had pondered the problem for days and nights, God took pity on me and I saw the inner connection between the two phrases, "The justice of God is revealed in the Gospel" and "The just shall live by faith." Then I began to understand that this "justice of God" is the righteousness by which the just man lives through the free gift of God, that is to say "by faith"; and that the justice "revealed in the Gospel" is the passive justice of God by which He takes pity on us and justifies us by our faith, as it is written, "The just shall live by faith." Thereupon I felt as if I had been born again and had entered Paradise through wide-open gates. Immediately the whole of Scripture took on a new meaning for me. I raced through the Scriptures, so far as my memory went, and found analogies in other expressions: "the work of God," i.e., what God works in us; "the strength of God," by which He gives us strength; "the wisdom of God," by which He makes us wise; "the power of God," "the blessing of God," "the glory of God."

Whereas the expression "justice of God" had filled me with hate before, I now exalted it as the sweetest of phrases with all the more love. And so this verse of Paul's became in truth the gate to Paradise for me.

* * *

G. LETTER TO STAUPITZ, MAY 30, 1518

I remember, reverend Father, among those happy and wholesome stories of yours, by which the Lord used wonderfully to console me, that you often mentioned the word *poenitentia*, whereupon, distressed by our consciences and by those torturers who with endless and intolerable precept taught nothing but what they called a method of confession, we received you as a messenger from Heaven, for penitence is not genuine save when it begins

from the love of justice and of God, and this which they consider the end and consummation of repentance is rather its commencement.

Your words on this subject pierced me like the sharp arrows of the mighty, so that I began to see what the Scriptures had to say about penitence, and behold the happy result: the texts all supported and favored your doctrine, in so much that, while there had formerly been no word in almost all the Bible more bitter to me than *poenitentia* (although I zealously simulated it before God and tried to express an assumed and forced love), now no word sounds sweeter or more pleasant to me than that. For thus do the commands of God become sweet when we understand that they are not to be read in books only, but in the wounds of the sweetest Saviour.

After this it happened by the favor of the learned men who taught me Hebrew and Greek that I learned [from Erasmus' edition of the New Testament in Greek, note on Matthew 3:2] that the Greek word is *metanoia* from *meta* and *noun*, i.e., from "afterwards" and "mind," so that penitence or *metanoia* is "coming to one's right mind, afterwards," that is, comprehension of your own evil, after you had accepted loss and found out your error. This is impossible without a change in your affections. All this agrees so well with Paul's theology, that, in my opinion, at least, nothing is more characteristically Pauline.

Then I progressed and saw that *metanoia* meant not only "afterwards" and "mind," but also "change" and "mind," so that *metanoia* means change of mind and affection. . . .

Sticking fast to this conclusion, I dared to think that they were wrong who attributed so much to works of repentance that they have left us nothing of it but formal penances and elaborate confession. They were seduced by the Latin, for *poenitentiam agere* means rather a work than a change of affection and in no wise agrees with the Greek.

When I was glowing with this thought, behold indulgences and remissions of sins began to be trumpeted abroad with tremendous clangor, but their trumpets animated no one to real struggle. In short, the doctrine of true repentance was neglected, and only the cheapest part of it, that called penance, was magnified. . . . As I was not able to oppose the fury of these preachers, I determined modestly to take issue with them and to call their theories in doubt, relying as I did on the opinion of all the doctors and of the whole Church, who all say that it is better to perform the penance than to buy it, that is an indulgence. . . . This is the reason why I, reverend Father, who always love retirement, have unhappily been forced into the public view.

* * *

B. LUTHER REPLIES TO ERASMUS (1525)

You [Erasmus] alone in pre-eminent distinction from all others, have entered upon the thing itself; that is, the grand turning point of the cause; and have not wearied me with those irrelevant points about popery, purgatory, indulgences, and other like baubles, rather than causes, with which all have hitherto tried to hunt me down,—though in vain! You, and you alone, saw what was the grand hinge upon which the whole turned, and therefore you attacked the vital part at once; for which, from my heart, I thank you. . . .

The human will is, as it were, a beast between [God and Satan]. If God sit thereon, it wills and goes where God will; as the Psalm saith, "I am become as it were a beast before thee, and I am continually with thee." (Ps. 73:22–23.) If Satan sit thereon, it wills and goes as Satan will. Nor is it in the power of its own will to choose, to which rider it will run, nor which it will seek; but the riders themselves contend, which shall have and hold it. . . .

God is that Being, for whose will no cause or reason is to be assigned, as a rule or standard by which it acts; seeing that, nothing is superior or equal to it, but it is itself the rule of all things. For if it acted by any rule or standard, or from any cause or reason, it would be no longer the will of God. Wherefore, what God wills is not therefore right, because He ought or ever was bound so to will; but on the contrary, what takes place is therefore right, because He so wills. A cause and reason are assigned for the will

of the creature, but not for the will of the Creator; unless you set up, over Him, another Creator. . . .

As to myself, I openly confess, that I should not wish "free-will" to be granted me, even if it could be so, nor anything else to be left in my own hands, whereby I might endeavor something towards my own salvation. And that, not merely because in so many opposing dangers, and so many assaulting devils, I could not stand and hold it fast (in which state no man could be saved, seeing that one devil is stronger than all men); but because, even though there were no dangers, no conflicts, no devils, I should be compelled to labour under a continual uncertainty, and to beat the air only. Nor would my conscience, even if I should live and work to all eternity, ever come to a settled certainty, how much it ought to do in order to satisfy God. For whatever work should be done, there would still remain a scrupling, whether or not it pleased God, or whether He required any thing more; as I proved in the experience of all those who believe in words, and as I myself learned to my bitter cost, through so many years of my own experience.

But now, since God has put my salvation out of the way of *my* will, and has taken it under *His own*, and has promised to save me, not according to my working or manner of life, but according to His own grace and mercy, I rest fully assured and persuaded that He is faithful, and will not lie, and moreover great and powerful, so that no devils, no adversaries can destroy Him or pluck me out of His hand. "No one (saith He) shall pluck them out of My hand, because My Father which gave them Me is greater than all" (John, 10:27–8). Hence it is certain, that in this way, if all are not saved, yet some, yea, many shall be saved; whereas by the power of "free-will" no one whatever could be saved, but all must perish together. And moreover, we are certain and persuaded, that in this way, we please God, not from the merit of our own works, but from the favour of His mercy promised unto us; and that, if we work less, or work badly, He does not impute it unto us, but, as a Father, pardons us and makes us better.

* * *

A. LUTHER CHALLENGES THE AUTHORITY OF THE ROMAN CHURCH (1520–1521)

The Romanists have, with great adroitness, drawn three walls round themselves, with which they have hitherto protected themselves, so that no one could reform them, whereby all Christendom has fallen terribly.

Firstly, if pressed by the temporal power, they have affirmed and maintained that the temporal power has no jurisdiction over them, but, on the contrary, that the spiritual power is above the temporal.

Secondly, if it were proposed to admonish them with the Scriptures, they objected that no one may interpret the Scriptures but the Pope.

Thirdly, if they are threatened with a council, they pretend that no one may call a council but the Pope.

Thus they have secretly stolen our three rods, so that they may be unpunished, and intrenched themselves behind these three walls, to act with all the wickedness and malice, which we now witness. . . .

Let us, in the first place, attack the first wall: [that the temporal power has no jurisdiction over the spiritual].

It has been devised that the Pope, bishops, priests, and monks are called the *spiritual estate*; princes, lords, artificers, and peasants are the *temporal estate*. This is an artful lie and hypocritical device, but let no one be made afraid by it, and that for this reason: that all Christians are truly of the spiritual estate, and there is no difference among them, save of office alone. As St. Paul says (I Cor. 12), we are all one body, though each member does its own work, to serve the others. This is because we have one baptism, one Gospel, one faith, and are all Christians alike; for baptism, Gospel, and faith, these alone make spiritual and Christian people.

As for the unction by a Pope or a bishop, tonsure, ordination, consecration, and clothes differing from those of laymen—all this may make a hypocrite or an anointed puppet, but never a Christian or a spiritual man. Thus we are all consecrated as priests by baptism. . . .

Therefore a priest should be nothing in Christendom but a functionary; as long as he holds his office, he has precedence of others; if he is deprived of it, he is a peasant or a citizen like the rest. Therefore a priest is verily no longer a priest after deposition. But now they have invented *characteres indelibiles*, and pretend that a priest after deprivation still differs from a simple layman. They even imagine that a priest can never be anything but a priest—that is, that he can never become a layman. All this is nothing but mere talk and ordinance of human invention.

It follows, then, that between laymen and priests, princes and bishops, or, as they call it, between spiritual and temporal persons, the only real difference is one of office and function, and not of estate. . . .

Now see what a Christian doctrine is this: that the temporal authority is not above the clergy, and may not punish it. This is as if one were to say the hand may not help, though the eye is in grievous suffering. It is not unnatural, not to say unchristian, that one member may not help another, or guard it against harm? Nay, the nobler the member, the more the rest are bound to help it. Therefore I say, Forasmuch as the temporal power has been ordained by God for the punishment of the bad and the protection of the good, therefore we must let it do its duty throughout the whole Christian body, without respect of persons, whether it strike Popes, bishops, priests, monks, nuns, or whoever it may be. . . .

The second wall is even more tottering and weak: that they alone pretend to be considered masters of the Scriptures; although they learn nothing of them all their life. They assume authority, and juggle before us with impudent words, saying that the Pope cannot err in matters of faith, whether he be evil or good, albeit they cannot prove it by a single letter. That is why the canon law contains so many heretical and unchristian, nay unnatural laws; but of these we need not speak now. For whereas they imagine the Holy Ghost never leaves them, however unlearned and wicked they may be, they grow bold enough to decree whatever they like. But were this true, where were the need and use of the Holy Scriptures? Let us burn them, and content ourselves with the unlearned gentlemen at Rome, in whom the Holy Ghost dwells, who, however, can dwell in pious souls only. If I had not read it, I could never have believed that the devil should have put forth such follies at Rome and find a following. . . .

Therefore it is a wickedly devised fable—and they cannot quote a single letter to confirm it—that it is for the Pope alone to interpret the Scriptures or to confirm the interpretation of them. They have assumed the authority of their own selves. And though they say that this authority was given to St. Peter when the keys were given to him, it is plain enough that the keys were not given to St. Peter alone, but to the whole community. Besides, the keys were not ordained for doctrine or authority, but for sin, to bind of loose; and what they claim besides this from the keys is mere invention. . . .

Only consider the matter. They must needs acknowledge that there are pious Christians among us that have the true faith, spirit, understanding, word, and mind of Christ; why then should we reject their word and understanding and follow a pope who has neither understanding nor spirit? Surely this were to deny our whole faith and the Christian Church. Moreover, if the article of our faith is right, "I believe in the holy Christian Church," the Pope cannot alone be right; else we must say, "I believe in the Pope of Rome," and reduce the Christian Church to one man, which is a devilish and damnable heresy. Besides that, we are all priests, as I have said, and have all one faith, one Gospel, one Sacrament; how then should we not have the power of discerning and judging what is right or wrong in matters of faith? . . . Balaam's ass was wiser than the prophet. If God spoke by an ass against a prophet, why should He not speak by a pious man against the Pope?

The third wall falls of itself, as soon as the first two have fallen. . . .

When need requires, and the pope is a cause of offence to Christendom, in these cases whoever can best do so, as a faithful member of the whole body, must do what he can to produce a true free council. This no one can do so well as the temporal authorities, especially since they are fellow-Christians, fellow-priests, sharing one spirit and one power in all things, and since they should exercise the office that they have received from God without hinderance, whenever it is necessary and useful that is should be exercised. . . .

As for their boasts of their authority, that no one must oppose it, this is idle talk. No one in Christendom has any authority to do harm, or to forbid others to prevent harm being done. There is no authority in the Church but for reformation. Therefore if the Pope wished to use his power to prevent the reformation of the Church, we must not respect him or his power; and if he should begin to excommunicate and fulminate, we must despise this as the doings of a madman, and, trusting in God excommunicate and repel him as best we may. . . .

And now I hope the false, lying spectre will be laid with which the Romanists have long terrified and stupefied our consciences. And it will be seen that, like all the rest of us, they are subject to the temporal sword; that they have no authority to interpret the Scriptures by force without skill; and that they have no power to prevent a council, or to pledge it in accordance with their pleasure, or to bind it beforehand, and deprive it of its freedom; and that if they do this, they are verily of the fellowship of antichrist and the devil, and have nothing of Christ but the name.

STUDY QUESTIONS

1. How did Luther find release from his torments by reading, closely, the book of Romans?
2. How did Luther recall developing his ideas concerning the doctrine of salvation by faith?
3. Is Luther's tone in writing excessively violent? Could his words be used to endorse actual violence?

12.6. FRANCESCO GUICCIARDINI, FLORENCE UNDER LORENZO DE' MEDICI

Francesco Guicciardini (1483–1540) was a wealthy lawyer with good political connections. Like many such figures in the Renaissance, he also had cultural and intellectual ambitions. In his later years he wrote a brilliant *History of Italy* that was one of the first works of history to combine the use of extensive archival records and a critical attitude toward political motivations and intentions. His *History of Florence*, however, is the work of a young man trying to feel his way in an unfamiliar discipline. Its most incisive passage is translated below and provides a closely observed portrait of Lorenzo de' Medici (1449–1492), who ruled Florence from 1469 until his death. (Guicciardini, of course, did not know Lorenzo personally, being only nine years old when the ruler died.)

Lorenzo de' Medici was only forty-three years old when he died, after having ruled Florence for twenty-three years. He was only twenty when his father Piero died in 1469 and was still being advised by Messer Tommasso Soderini and some other elder politicians, but it took only a short time for him to come into his full strength and stature, such that he was able to govern the city just as he saw fit. . . .

RD1>Until he died in 1492 Lorenzo controlled and ran Florence as completely as if he were a Greek *tyrannos*. His renown was as widespread before his death as it has become after it. His greatness was so remarkable, and indeed without parallel in all of Florence's history, in fact, that I think it is not a mistake—and in fact may prove quite useful—if I describe his manner and character is some detail. I do not speak from my own experience, for I was still a mere boy when he died, but my information comes from reliable and trustworthy sources. Unless I have been lied to, what I am about to say is completely true.

Lorenzo had many extraordinary virtues and a fair share of vices; some of the latter came to him naturally, while some others arose from necessity. His authority in the city was so complete that it is fair to say that Florence was not free in his time, but it enjoyed as many blessings and as much happiness as there could be in any other city that we call "free" but which is in fact under a *tyrannos*. Although not everything he did was admirable, most of his actions were so tremendous and noble that the more one studies them the more impressive they appear. Glory in arms and feats of military achievement do not figure among his successes, as they do among the great figures of antiquity, but that was more the circumstance of the times in which he lived than of his own failure. You will not read here of any brave defense of the city, a celebrated capture of a fortress, a brilliant strategy on the field of battle, or a glorious upset over enemies; Lorenzo's claim to fame includes no such military splendor. What one does find in his record is every possible sign of the virtues of civic life—no one, not even his enemies and rivals, would deny his brilliance in that regard. Who could? The simple fact that he ruled Florence for twenty-three years, always increasing its power and glory, proves the point. Bear in mind that Florence is an opinionated place, full of calculating and ambitious people, and since the city is small and cannot provide for everyone, to benefit some means to skip over others. Finally, the roster of great Italian and foreign princes who counted themselves as his friend attests to his reputation. . . .

He was generally of sound judgment and wise, but his intellect transcended politics. He committed a number of ill-considered actions, such as his war

Translation by Clifford R. Backman.

against Volterra in 1473, when he conspired to get the people of that town to rebel against him so that he could have an excuse to seize their alum mines; in so doing he ignited a fire that could have engulfed all of Italy, although things turned out well in the end. And he could have avoided the civil war of 1478 if he had handled relations with the pope [Sixtus IV, r. 1471–1484] and the king [Ferrante of Naples, r. 1458–1494] more skillfully, instead of playing the role of the aggrieved innocent for all it was worth and thereby causing the war and nearly costing himself and the city their lives. His subsequent trip to Naples, also, was too rash and hurried a decision, one that placed him directly in the hands of his enemy, an untrustworthy and traitorous king. The desperate need for peace partially excuses him, but many still live who think he could have achieved it much more safely and no less effectively had he negotiated from Florence.

He dreamed of glory and renown, and indeed he desired these more than anyone else of his time. His desire for them influenced his actions even in the most minor matters—for which he may justly be criticized. Whether he was penning verses, playing a game, or doing any little thing at all, he became enraged if someone else matched or bettered him. Even in matters of real importance his lust for glory influenced him excessively. He conspired and struggled against every prince in Italy, to the great displeasure of Duke Ludovico [Sforza of Milan, r. 1489–1500]. On the whole, his ambitions were admirable and in the end they did bring him fame and renown, both within Italy and elsewhere. He worked diligently to make Florence pre-eminent in all the arts. He founded the University of Pisa as a center for the humanities. When his advisors argued that the university would never have as many students as the universities in Padua or Pavia, he replied that he would be satisfied to have more professors than they, and indeed all the most famous and brilliant scholars in Italy taught there for a time. Lorenzo spared no expense or effort to hire them, and consequently they received extraordinarily high salaries. The humanities flourished in Florence under the tutelage of Messer Agnolo Poliziano; the study of Greek advanced under Messer Demetrios [Chalcondylas] and [Konstantinos] Lascaris; philosophy and art were the

domain of Marsilio Ficino, Giorgio Benigno, Count [Giovanni] Pico della Mirandola, and other notable men. He was equally generous to the fields of vernacular poetry, music, architecture, painting, sculpture, and all other arts and disciplines. The city overflowed with superior talent, and all because Lorenzo, a universal man, was such an excellent judge of skilled men—all of whom competed with one another for his favor. In his infinite generosity, he lavished them with salaries and everything they needed for their work. For example, when he decided to establish a Greek library, he sent the learned Lascaris back to Greece to search for books of antiquity.

He employed the same liberality with princes everywhere in order to further his reputation; no expense, however great, was too much to pay if it helped him to keep the friendship of powerful people. Consequently, in places like Lyons, Milan, and Bruges, where he had business interests, his habit of spreading money everywhere made his expenses rise and his profits fall; the real fault, though, lay with some of his underlings, who did not have his talent. . . .

Lorenzo had a haughty personality. He disliked it when anyone contradicted him, and he spoke in few words, even in matters of importance, because he expected people to understand him intuitively. In casual conversation, though, he could be quite pleasant if somewhat facetious. His private home life was simple, not luxurious at all except for the banquets he threw, in which he lavished hospitality on his noble guests who visited Florence. He was lusty in his carnal appetites, and engaged in love affairs with real abandon. Some of these relationships lasted for years. So persistent was he in his conquests that many people think his extreme carnality weakened his body and brought on his early death. . . .

Many people thought him cruel and vindictive by nature, citing especially the case of the Pazzi Rebellion [of 1478], in which, after the shedding of so much blood he threw many innocents into prison and forbade the girls [of the Pazzi family] ever to marry, but one must remember how bitterly he resented the family's attempt to overthrow him, and so such harshness can hardly be surprising. Besides, he did eventually allow the Pazzi girls to marry, and freed the Pazzi boys on condition they left Florence forever. In other instances too we can see that he was not truly cruel or bloodthirsty, but simply had the flaw of excessive suspicion of others. This troublesome suspiciousness arose not from his intrinsic nature but from the fact that he had a city-state to keep under control and had to do it by means of magistrates and laws in order to maintain the appearance that Florence was a free republic. . . .

His constant distrust of others forced him not to allow powerful families to form marriage alliances. He aimed always at pairing people off in a way that did not pose any threat to his power. Sometimes he did this by forcing some young man of standing to marry a woman who was not really acceptable. In fact, the truth is that soon enough hardly any marriages took place among the important classes without his direct permission. The same suspiciousness inspired him to appoint permanent chancellors at the courts in Rome, Naples, and Milan, in order to keep an eye on the ambassadors he sent to those places. These well-paid chancellors were present to lend assistance to the various ambassadors but their real purpose was to keep Lorenzo informed of their actions.

It is true that he kept himself constantly surrounded by a large number of armed guards, who were well rewarded for their service (in fact, he even bestowed a number of hospitals and holy shrines upon some of them). He did this not out of intrinsic distrust of people, however; the truth is that the Pazzi conspiracy was to blame. Even so, it was hardly the sort of thing proper to a republic and to a private citizen; it smacked more of a tyrant ruling his subjects. In the end, one has to conclude that although Florence under Lorenzo was not a free city, it was a city that could hardly have wished for a better and more pleasing tyrant. His good qualities and virtues produced an infinity of blessings, and while the nature of his tyranny occasioned some ill-doings, these were relatively minor and never worse than they needed to be. . . .

STUDY QUESTIONS

1. According to Guicciardini, what were the virtues of Lorenzo de' Medici? Were his virtues confined to politics? What picture of court patronage and the arts emerges from Guicciardini's portrait of Lorenzo?
2. Based on this description, would you say that Guicciardini preferred strong leaders like Lorenzo over popularly elected governments? Why?

12.7. CELLINI, *MY LIFE*, 1558–1563

Benvenuto Cellini (1500–1571) was an Italian goldsmith and sculptor—and part-time soldier— who inhabited the thrilling art world dominated by masters like Michelangelo and Da Vinci. A member of the Mannerist school, Cellini was patronized by dukes, popes, and the French king; his "artistic temperament" meant that he was often in trouble with his fellow artists—he was accused of four homicides over the course of his life. This selection from his autobiography illustrates the way in which his artistic excellence framed his every experience and relationship, both personal and professional.

My Life translated by Bondanella and Bondanella (2010) 1968w from pp. 24–29, 66–69, 124–125. By permission of Oxford University Press.

15. Continuing to work with Master Pagolo Arsago, I earned a great deal of money, always sending the largest part of it to my good father. By the end of two years, following my father's entreaties, I returned to Florence, and once again I went to work with Francesco Salinbene, with whom I earned a good deal and worked very hard at learning. I started going around with Francesco di Filippo again, given that I was intent upon the pursuit of some pleasure, thanks to practicing that damned music, and I always saved certain hours of the day or night which I gave over to my studies. In that period I created a silver "heart-key," which is what these objects were called at that time. This was a belt three fingers in width that new bridges were in the custom of wearing, and it was made in low relief with some little figures in the round among the others. I made it for a man who was called Raffaello Lapaccini. Although I was very poorly paid, I gained so much honour from it that it was worth much more than the recompense I justly earned. During this period I had worked with many different people in Florence, where I had made the acquaintance of some very worthy men among the goldsmiths, such as that Marcone who was my first master, as well as others who had very good reputations but who did me down in my work and blatantly robbed me whenever they could. Once I saw this, I kept away from them and considered them wicked men and thieves.

. . .

16. One day it happened that as I was leaning against the shop of one of these goldsmiths he called out to me, partly reproaching and partly threatening me; to his remarks I responded that if they had done their duty towards me, I would have said of them what one says about honest and worthy men. But, since they had done the contrary they should complain about themselves and not about me. While I was standing there talking, one of them, their cousin, who was called Gherardo Guasconti, perhaps compelled by all of them together, waited until a pack-animal with a load passed by. This was a load of bricks. When the load was near me, this Gherardo pushed it against me so forcefully that he hurt me very badly. I immediately turned on him, and when I saw that he was laughing I gave him such a hard blow with my fist on his temple that he fell down unconscious, like a dead man; then I turned to his cousins and announced: "This is how to treat thieving cowards like you!" And because they were about to make some move, since there were several of them, incensed, I put my hand on a small knife that I had and said: "Whichever one of you leaves his shop, the other will go fetch his confessor, because there'll be no use for a doctor." These words so terrified them that no one went to the assistance of his cousin. Immediately after I had left, their fathers and children ran to the Eight and claimed that I had assaulted them with a weapon in their own shops, something which was unheard of in Florence. The Eight had me summoned before them, whereupon I appeared; they gave me a severe reprimand and scolding, since they saw me dressed in a cloak, while the Guasconts wore the mantle and hood of well-bred people, but they did so also because while my adversaries had gone to speak with all these magistrates at their homes in private, I, lacking experience, had not spoken to any of them, since I relied upon being entirely in the right.

. . .

I felt as if I had been totally discredited, and it was not long before I sent for my cousin, who was called Master Annibale the surgeon, the father of Messer Librodoro Librodori, wanting him to serve as my guarantee. Annibale refused to come: for this reason, I became very indignant and, puffing myself up like an asp, decided to do something desperate. In all of this it is obvious how much the stars not so much influence us as force us into certain courses of action. Knowing how much this Annibale owed my family, my anger became so great that it turned toward a harmful course of action—being also somewhat hot-blooded by nature—and I stood waiting until the members of the Eight had gone out to dinner, then, while I remained there alone, seeing that the guards of the Eight were no longer keeping an eye on me, and inflamed with anger, I left the Palazzo, ran to my workshop, where I seized a large dagger, and bounded into the home of my adversaries, which served as both home and workplace. I found them at table, and that young Gherardo, who had been the main cause of my interrogation, threw himself upon me: I responded by stabbing him in the chest, piercing his tunic and vest through to the shirt without touching his flesh or doing him even the slightest harm. I thought, by the way in which my hand entered his garments and by the sound his clothes made, that I had hurt him very seriously, and when he fell terrified onto the floor, I shouted: "You traitor, today is the day I kill you all." Believing that the Day of Judgment had arrived, his father, mother, and sisters threw themselves down on their knees, and at the top of their lungs they called out for mercy; once I saw that they had no defence against me and that Gherardo was stretched out on the floor like a dead man, I thought it too cowardly an act to attack them, but still furious, I ran down the stairs, and when I reached the street I came upon the rest of the clan, more than twelve of them: one of them held an iron shovel, another a huge iron pipe, while others carried hammers, anvils, and cudgels. I attacked them, like an enraged bull, throwing four or five to the ground, and I fell along with them, always striking out with my dagger, now at one, now at another. Those who had remained standing hastened as best they could to deal me some blows with both hands, with their hammers, cudgels, and anvils, and because God in His mercy sometimes intervenes in such matters, He kept us from doing each other any harm whatsoever. All I left there was my hat, captured by my adversaries although previously they had fled from it, which each one struck with his weapon; then they looked around them for their dead and wounded, but nobody had been harmed.

. . . .

38. Skipping over a few things, I shall describe how Pope Clement, in order to save the papal tiaras, with all of the numerous large jewels belonging to the Apostolic Chamber, had me summoned, and he shut himself up alone in a room with me and Cavalierino. This Cavalierino had once worked in the stable of Filippo Strozzi: he was a Frenchman, a person of very humble origins, and since he was a very faithful servant, Pope Clement had made him an extremely rich man and trusted him as he did himself. This, with the Pope, Cavalierino, and me locked inside this room, they placed me before the tiaras with that large number of jewels belonging to the Apostolic Chamber, and I was given the commission of extracting

them all from the gold in which they were set. And I did so: then I wrapped each of them up in small pieces of paper and sewed them up in the linings of some garments worn by the Pope and this Cavalierino. Then they gave me all the gold, which was around two hundred pounds, and they told me to melt it down in as much secrecy as I could. I went to the Angel where my own room was located, and where I could lock the door so that no one would disturb me, and once I had built a small brick blast-furnace in the bottom of which I set a fairly large ash-tray shaped like a dish, I tossed the gold on the charcoal, which little by little dripped down into the dish. While this furnace was in operation, I constantly studied on how I could do our enemies harm, and since we had the enemy's trenches beneath us less than stone's throw away, I did them a great deal of damage in those trenches using some bits of old scrap, of which there were several piles, formerly used in the Castello as ammunition. Taking a saker and a falconet, both of which were broken a bit at the muzzle, I filled them with this scrap metal, and then as I opened fire with these weapons my shots flew down like mad, causing many unexpected injuries in the trenches. And so, keeping these weapons constantly loaded while I melted down that gold, a short time before the hour of vespers I saw a man mounted on a mule riding on the edge of the trench. This mule was moving along very swiftly, and the man was speaking to the men in the trenches. I stood ready to fire my artillery before he arrived in front of me. So, with good judgment, I commenced firing and hit him, knocking him directly in the face with one of those scraps of metal, while the rest hit the mule which fell down dead; I heard a tremendous uproar from the trench, and I fired another piece, not without doing them great damage. This man was the Prince of Orange, who was carried along the trenches to a certain inn nearby, where all the noblemen in the army quickly gathered. When Pope Clement learned what I had done, he immediately sent for me and asked about the affair, and I explained everything to him and, moreover, I told him that he must have been a man of very great importance, since all the leaders of the army, as far as one could determine, immediately gathered at the inn to which they had carried him.

. . .

After I returned to Cornaro's home, a few days later Cardinal Farnese was elected Pope, and after immediately settling matters of the greatest importance, the Pope next asked me, saying that he did not want anyone else to make his coins. Hearing these words, a certain gentleman named Messer Latino Iuvinale, who was on intimate terms with the Pope, stated that I was a fugitive from a homicide I had committed on the person of a Milanese named Pompeo, and he put all my motives in the most favourable light. At those words, the Pope said: "I didn't know about the death of Pompeo, but I knew of Benvenuto's motives perfectly well, so write him out an order of safe conduct immediately, with which he will be completely secure." There was present a great friend of that Pompeo and close confidant of the Pope named Messer Ambruogio, a Milanese, and he said: "During the first days of your papacy, it would not be good to grant pardons of this sort." Turning toward him, the Pope said: "You don't understand the matter as well as I do. You should know that men like Benvenuto, unique in their profession, need not be subject to the law: especially not Benvenuto, since I know what good reasons he had." And after my safe-conduct was made out, I immediately began to serve the new Pope and was treated with the greatest favour.

STUDY QUESTIONS

1. How does Benvenuto use violence to reinforce his sense of honor?
2. Are the endorsements of Cellini offered by the Popes surprising?

12.8. VASARI, *LIVES OF ARTISTS*, FIRST PUBLISHED IN 1550, REVISED AND ADDED TO UNTIL 1568

An architect and fresco-painter in his own right—and even an apprentice to Michelangelo in his youth—Giorgio Vasari (1511–1574) is most fondly remembered for his personal accounts of roughly two hundred celebrated artists of Renaissance Italy. Using art historical analysis, Vasari talks capably about the production and technical elements of paintings, ambitious architectural projects, metalworking, and sculpture. Charming anecdotes about the greats—Giotto, Michelangelo, Botticelli, etc.—bring to life the world inhabited by these incredibly talented individuals. *The Life of Donatello* (1386–1466) provides glimpses into the artistic temperament exemplified by Cellini (Document 12.7), and the Preface to Part III provides an overview of artistic development throughout the Renaissance.

Lives of the Artists translated by Bondanella and Bondanella (2009) 2731w from pp. 147–149, 153–154, 159–160, 277–279, 281–283. By permission of Oxford University Press.

THE LIFE OF DONATELLO, FLORENTINE SCULPTOR

[1386–1466]

Donato, who was called Donatello by his relatives and thus signed some of his works this way, was born in Florence in the year 1303. And devoting himself to the art of design, he became not only an unusually fine sculptor and a marvellous statue-maker, but also grew experienced in stucco, quite skilled in perspective, and highly esteemed in architecture. His works possessed so much grace and excellence and such a fine sense of design that they were considered to be more like the distinguished works of the ancient Greeks and Romans than those of any other artist who has ever existed, and he is therefore quite rightly recognized as the first artisan who properly used the device of scenes in bas-relief. He worked out these scenes with such careful thought, true facility, and expert skill that it was obvious he possessed a true understanding of them and executed them with extraordinary beauty. Thus, no other artisan surpassed him in this field, and even in our own times, there is no one who is his equal.

Donatello was raised from childhood in the home of Ruberto Martelli, and with his fine qualities and the diligence with which he refined his skill, he not only earned Martelli's affection but that of this entire noble family. In his youth, he worked upon so many things that they were not very highly regarded because there were so many of them. But the thing which earned him a name and brought him recognition was an Annunciation in blue-grey stone which was placed in the church of Santa Croce in Florence at the altar in the chapel of the Cavalcanti family, for which he made a decoration in the grotesque style. Its base was varied and twisted, completed by a quarter-circle to which were added six putti carrying several garlands who seem to be steadying themselves by embracing each other as if they were afraid of the height. But Donatello demonstrated above all his great ingenuity and artistry in the figure of the Virgin, who, frightened by the sudden appearance of the angel, timidly but gently moves Her body in a very chaste bow, turning towards the angel greeting Her with the most beautiful grace, so that Her face reflects the humility and gratitude one owes to the giver of an unexpected gift, and even more so when the gift is so great. Besides this, Donatello proved his ability to carve masterful folds and turns in the robes of this Madonna and the angel, and in suggesting the nude forms of his figures, he showed just how he was attempting to rediscover the beauty of the ancients which had already remained hidden for so many years. And he exhibited so much facility and skill in this work that no one could really expect more from him in design and judgement, or from the way he carved and executed the work.

In the same church below the choir screen beside the scenes frescoed by Taddeo Gaddi, Donatello took extraordinary pains in carving a wooden crucifix which, upon completing it and believing that he had produced a very rare object, he showed to Filippo di Ser Brunellesco, his very dear friend, in order to have his opinion of it. Filippo, who expected to see something much better from Donatello's description of it, smiled a bit when he saw it. When Donatello saw this, he begged Filippo for the sake of their friendship to give him his honest opinion of it, and so, Filippo, who was very candid, replied that it seemed to him as if Donatello had placed a peasant upon the cross and not a body like that of Jesus Christ, which was most delicate and represented, in all its parts, the most perfect human being born. Hearing himself criticized—and even more sharply than he had imagined—rather than receiving the praise he had hoped for, Donatello answered: "If it were as simple to create something as to criticize, my Christ would look like Christ to you and not like a peasant; take some wood and try to make one yourself." Without saying another word, Filippo returned home, and without anyone knowing, he set his hand to making a crucifix, seeking to surpass Donatello in order to vindicate his own judgement, and after many months he brought it to the highest degree of perfection. And once this was finished, he invited Donatello one morning to have lunch with him, and Donatello accepted the invitation. And so, they went together towards Filippo's home, and when they reached the Old Market, Filippo bought a few things and gave them to Donatello, saying: "Go on home with these things and wait for me there, and I'll be along shortly." Donatello therefore entered the house and, on the ground-floor, saw Filippo's crucifix in a perfect light, and stopping to examine it, he found it so perfectly finished that, realizing Filippo had outdone him, and completely stupefied, as if he had lost his wits, he relaxing his grip on his apron; whereupon, the eggs, the cheese, and everything else fell out, breaking into pieces and spilling all over, and as he stood there stunned and amazed, Filippo caught up with him, and said with a laugh: "What's your plan, Donatello? How can we have lunch if you have spilled everything?" Donatello replied: "Personally, I've had enough for this morning, but if you want your share, take it. But no more, thank you: it's for you to make Christs and for me to make peasants."

. . .

It was said that a Genoese merchant had Donatello execute a very handsome life-size bronze head which was thin and light so that it could be carried over a long distance, and it was through Cosimo that Donatello received the commission for such a work. When it was finished and the merchant wanted to pay Donatello, he thought that the sculptor was asking too high a price. So the deal was referred to Cosimo, who had the bust carried to a courtyard above his palace and had it placed between the battlements overlooking the street so that it could be better seen. Wishing to settle the matter, Cosimo, who found the merchant far from the price asked by Donatello, turned to the merchant and declared that Donatello's price was too low. At this, the merchant, who thought it too high, declared that Donatello had worked upon it for only a month or a little more, and that this added up to more than half a florin per day. Donatello then turned angrily away, thinking himself too greatly offended, and told the merchant that in one hundredth of an hour he could spoil the labour and value of an entire year, and he gave the bust a shove, immediately breaking it upon the street below into many pieces and telling the merchant he proved himself more accustomed to bargaining for beans than for statues. The merchant regretted what he had done and wanted to give Donatello more than double his price if he would only recast the bust, but neither the merchant's promises nor Cosimo's entreaties could ever convince Donatello to redo it.

. . .

It is said that when Cosimo was about to die, he commended Donatello to the care of his son Piero who, as a most conscientious executor of his father's will, gave Donatello a farm in Cafaggiulo with enough income for him to live comfortably. Donatello was delighted by this, for he felt that with this more than secure income he would not risk dying from hunger. But he had only held it for a year when he returned to Piero and gave it back to him by means of a written contract, declaring that he did not wish to lose his peace of mind having to dwell upon domestic concerns or the troubles of his peasant tenant, who was underfoot every third day—first, because the wind blew the roof off his doves' hitch; next, because the Commune seized his livestock for taxes; and then, because the storm deprived him of wine and fruit. He was so fed up and disgusted with all these things that he preferred to die from hunger rather than to think about them.

Piero laughed at Donatello's simple ways, but in order to free Donatello from this worry he accepted the farm at Donatello's insistence, and he assigned him from his own bank an allowance of the same amount or more but in cash, which was paid to Donatello every week in appropriate installments. This made Donatello exceedingly content.

PREFACE TO PART THREE

Those excellent masters we have described up to this point in the Second part of these *Lives* truly made great advances in the arts of architecture, painting, and sculpture, adding to the accomplishments of the early artists rule, order, proportion, design, and style, and if they were not perfect in every way, they drew so near to the truth that artists in the third group, whom we shall now discuss, were able, through that illumination, to rise up and reach complete perfection, the proof of which we have in the finest and most celebrated modern works. But to clarify the quality of the improvements that these artists made, it will not be out of place to explain briefly the five qualities I mentioned above and to discuss succinctly the origins of that true goodness which has surpassed that of the ancient world and rendered the modern ago so glorious.

. . . Design is the imitation of the most beautiful things in Nature in all forms, both in sculpture and in painting, and this quality depends upon having the hand and the skill to transfer with great accuracy and precision everything the eye sees to a plan or drawing or to a sheet of paper, a panel, or another flat surface, and the same is true for relief in sculpture. And then the most beautiful style comes from constantly copying the most beautiful things, combining the most beautiful hands, heads, bodies, or legs together to create from all these beautiful qualities the most perfect figure possible, and using it as a model for all the figures in each one's works; an on account of this, it is said to be beautiful style.

Neither Giotto nor those artisans did this, even though they had discovered the principles underlying all such difficulties and had resolved them superficially, as in the case of drawing, which became more lifelike than it had been before and more true to Nature, and in the blending of colours and the composition of the figures in scenes, and in many other things, about which enough has already been said. And although the artists of the second period made extraordinary efforts in these crafts in all the areas mentioned above, they were not, however, sufficient to achieve complete perfection. They still lacked, within the boundaries of the rules, a freedom which—not being part of the rules—was nevertheless ordained by the rules and which could coexist with order without causing confusion or spoiling it; and this freedom required copious invention in every particular and a certain beauty even in the smallest details which could demonstrate all of this order with more decoration. In proportion, they lacked good judgement which, without measuring the figures, would bestow upon them, no matter what their dimensions a grace that goes beyond proportion. In design they did not reach the ultimate goal, for even when they made a rounded arm or a straight leg, they had not fully examined how to depict the muscles with that soft and graceful facility which is partially seen and partially concealed in the flesh of living things, and their figures were crude and clumsy, offensive to the eye and harsh in style. Moreover, they lacked a lightness in touch in making all their figures slender and graceful, especially those of women and children, whose bodies should be as natural as those of men and yet possess a volume of softness which are produced by design and good judgement rather than by the awkward example of real bodies. They also lacked an abundance of beautiful costumes, variety in imaginative details, charm in their colours, diversity in their buildings, and distance and variety in their landscapes.

. . .

The artisans who followed them succeeded after seeing the excavation of some of the most famous antiquities mentioned by Pliny: the Laocoon, the Hercules, the great torso of Belvedere, the Venus, the Cleopatra, the Apollo, and countless others, which exhibit in their softness and harshness the expressions of real flesh copied from the most beautiful details of living models and endowed with certain movements which do not distort them but lend them motion and the utmost grace. And these statues caused the disappearance of a certain dry, crude, and clear-cut style which bequeathed to this craft.

. . .

But what matters most is that the artisans of today have made their craft so perfect and so easy for anyone who possesses a proper sense of design, invention, and colouring that whereas previously our older masters could produce one panel in six years, the masters of today can produce six of them in a year. And I bear witness to this both from personal observation and from practice, and these works are obviously much more finished and perfected than those of the other reputable masters who worked before them.

But the man who wins the palm among artists both living and dead, who transcends and surpasses them all, is the divine Michelangelo Buonarroti, who reigns supreme not merely in one of these arts but in all three at once. This man surpasses and triumphs over not only all those artists who have almost surpassed Nature but even those most celebrated ancient artists themselves, who beyond all doubt surpassed Nature: and alone he has triumphed over ancient artists, modern artists, and even Nature herself, without ever imagining anything so strange or so difficult that he could not surpass it by far with the power of his most divine genius through his diligence, sense of design, artistry, judgement, and grace. And not only in painting and colouring, categories which include all the shapes and bodies, straight and curved, tangible and intangible, visible and invisible, but also in bodies completely in the round; and through the point of his chisel and his untiring labour, this beautiful and fruitful plant has already spread so many honourable branches that they have not only filled the entire world in such an unaccustomed fashion with the most luscious fruits possible, but they have also brought these three most noble arts to their final stage of development with such wondrous perfection that one might well and safely declare that his statues are, in every respect, much more beautiful than those of the ancients. When the heads, hands, arms, and feet they created are compared to those he fashioned, it is obvious his works contain a more solid foundation, a more complete grace, and a much more absolute perfection, executed at a certain level of difficulty rendered so easily in his style that it would never be possible to see anything better. The same things can be said of his paintings. If it were possible to place any of them beside the most famous Greek or Roman paintings, they would be held in even greater esteem and more highly honoured than his sculptures, which appear superior to all those of the ancients.

But if we have admired those most celebrated artists who, inspired by excessive rewards and great happiness, have given life to their works, how much more should we admire and praise to the skies those even rarer geniuses who, living not only without rewards but in a miserable state of poverty, produced such precious fruits? It may be believed and therefore affirmed that, if just remuneration existed in our century, even greater and better works than the ancients ever executed would, without a doubt, he created. But being forced to struggle more with Hunger than with Fame, impoverished geniuses are buried and unable to earn a reputation (which is a shame and a disgrace for those who might be able to help them but take no care to do so).

STUDY QUESTIONS

1. Did Donatello gain more from his relationship to his patrons Cosimo and Piero de Medici than they received from him?
2. Does Vasari claim that artists in his day can surpass the achievements of the Greeks and Romans?

CHAPTER 13

WORLDS OLD AND NEW

13.1. BARTOLOMÉ DE LAS CASAS, *A SHORT ACCOUNT*, WRITTEN 1542; PUBLISHED 1552

A Dominican friar, Bartolomé de las Casas (ca. 1484–1566) wrote his *Short Account* to open the eyes of King Philip II of Spain as to the atrocities committed in newly discovered Latin America. For this early devotion to the protection of what would be called "human rights," de las Casas was appointed "Protector of the Indians." The text itself can be difficult to read—the crimes against the indigenous populations are recounted with a matter-of-fact tone that seems at odds with the level of horrific detail provided. De las Casas argues that this inhumane activity must cease for two reasons: first, because "Indian" souls would not be saved through conversion; second, because Spain would suffer God's wrath as a result of these sins.

PREFACE

The Americas were discovered in 1492, and the first Christian settlements established by the Spanish the following year. It is accordingly forty-nine years from now since Spaniards began arriving in numbers in this part of the world. They first settled the large and fertile island of Hispaniola, which boasts six hundred leagues of coastline and is surrounded by a great many other large islands, all of them, as I saw for myself, with as high a native population as anywhere on earth. Of the coast of the mainland which, at its nearest point, is a little over two hundred and fifty leagues from Hispaniola, more than ten thousand leagues had been explored by 1541, and more are being discovered every day. This coastline, too, swarming with people and it would seem, if we are to judge by those areas so far explored, that the Almighty selected this part of the world as home to the greater part of the human race.

God made all the peoples of this area, many and varied as they are, as open and as innocent as can be imagined. The simple people in the world—unassuming, long-suffering, unassertive, and submissive—they are without malice or guile, and are utterly faithful and obedient both to their own native lords and to the Spaniards in whose service they now find themselves. Never quarrelsome or belligerent or boisterous, they harbour no grudges and

From Bartolomé de Las Casas, *A Short Account of the Destruction of the Indies*. Trans. Nigel Griffin. London: Penguin Classics, 1993, pp. 9–13, 15–7, 127–8.

do not seek to settle old scores; indeed, the notions of revenge, rancor, and hatred are quite foreign to them. At the same time, they are among the least robust of human beings: their delicate constitutions make them unable to withstand hard work or suffering and render them liable to succumb to almost any illness, no matter how mild. Even the common people are no tougher than princes or than other Europeans born with a silver spoon in their mouths and who spend their lives shielded from the rigours of the outside world. They are also among the poorest people on the face of the earth; they own next to nothing and have no urge to acquire material possessions. As a result they are neither ambitious nor greedy, and are totally uninterested in worldly power. Their diet is every bit as poor and as monotonous, in quantity and in kind, as that enjoyed by the Desert Fathers. Most of them go naked, save for a loincloth to cover their modesty; at best they may wrap themselves in a piece of cotton material a yard or two square. Most sleep on matting, although a few possess a kind of hanging net, known in the language of Hispaniola as a hammock. They are innocent and pure in mind and have a lively intelligence, all of which makes them particularly receptive to learning and understanding the truths of our Catholic faith and to being instructed in virtue; indeed, God has invested them with fewer impediments in this regard than any other people on earth. Once they begin to learn of the Christian faith they become so keen to know more, to receive the Sacraments, and to worship God, that the missionaries who instruct them do truly regard them men of exceptional patience and forbearance; and over the years I have time and again met Spanish laymen who have been so struck by the natural goodness that shines through these people that they frequently can be heard to exclaim: "These would be the most blessed people on earth if only they were given the chance to convert to Christianity."

It was upon these gentle lambs, imbued by the Creator with all the qualities we have mentioned, that from the very first day they clapped eyes on them the Spanish fell like ravening wolves upon the fold, or like tigers and savage lions who have not eaten meat for days. The pattern established at the outset has remained unchanged to this day, and the Spaniards still do nothing save tear the natives to shreds, murder them and inflict upon them untold misery, suffering and distress, tormenting, harrying and persecuting them mercilessly. We shall in due course describe some of the many ingenious methods of torture they have invented and refined for this purpose, but one can get some idea of the effectiveness of their methods from the figures alone. When the Spanish first journeyed there, the indigenous population of the island of Hispaniola stood at some three million; today only two hundred survive.

. . .

One God-fearing individual was moved to mount an expedition to seek out those who had escaped the Spanish trawl and were still living in the Bahamas and to save their souls by converting them to Christianity, but, by the end of a search lasting three whole years, they had found only the eleven survivors I saw with my own eyes. A further thirty or so islands in the region of Puerto Rico are also now uninhabited and left to go to rack and ruin as a direct result of the same practices. All these islands, which together must run over two thousand leagues, are now abandoned and desolate.

On the mainland, we know for sure that our fellow-countrymen have, through their cruelty and wickedness, depopulated and laid waste an area which once boasted more than ten kingdoms, each of them larger in area than the whole of the Iberian Peninsula. The whole region, once teeming with human beings, is now deserted over a distance of more than two thousand leagues: a distance, that is, greater than the journey from Seville to Jerusalem and back again.

At a conservative estimate, the despotic and diabolical behaviour of the Christians has, over the last forty years, led to the unjust and totally unwarranted deaths of more than twelve million souls, women and children among them, and there are grounds for believing my own estimate of more than fifteen million to be nearer the mark.

. . .

They spared no one, erecting especially wide gibbets on which they could string their victims up with their feet just off the ground and then burn them alive thirteen at a time, in honour of our Saviour and the twelve Apostles, or tie dry straw to their bodies and set fire to it. Some they chose to keep alive and simply cut their wrists, leaving their hands dangling, saying to them: "Take this letter"—meaning that their sorry condition would act as a warning to those hiding in the hills. The way they normally dealt with the native leaders and nobles was to tie them to a kind of griddle consisting of sticks resting on pitchforks driven into the ground and then grill them over a slow fire, with the result that they howled in agony and despair as they died a lingering death.

It once happened that I myself witnessed their grilling of four or five local leaders in this fashion (and I believe they had set up two or three pairs of grills alongside so that they might process other victims at the same time) when the poor creatures' howls came between the Spanish commander and his sleep. He gave orders that the prisoners were to be throttled, but the man in charge of the execution detail, who was more bloodthirsty than the average common hangman (I know his identity and even met some relatives of his in Seville), was loath to cut short his private entertainment by throttling them so he personally went round ramming wooden bungs into their mouths to stop them making such a racket and deliberately stoked the fire so that they would take just as long to die as he himself chose. I saw all these things for myself and many others besides. And, since all those who could do so took to the hills and mountains in order to escape the clutches of these merciless and inhuman butchers, these mortal enemies of human kind trained hunting dogs to track them down—wild dogs who would savage a native to death as soon as look at him, tearing him to shreds and devouring his flesh as though he were a pig. These dogs wrought havoc among the natives and were responsible for much carnage. And when, as happened on the odd occasion, the locals did kill a European, as, given the enormity of the crimes committed against them, they were in all justice fully entitled to, the Spanish came to an unofficial agreement among themselves that for every European killed one hundred natives would be executed.

. . .

CONCLUSION

I, Bartolomé de Las Casas, or Casaus, a brother in the Dominican Order, was, by the grace of God, persuaded by a number of people here at the Spanish court, out of their concern for the Christian faith and their compassion towards the afflictions and calamities that befall their fellow-men, to write the work you have before you in order to help ensure that the teeming millions in the New World, for whose sins Christ gave His life, do not continue to die in ignorance, but rather are brought to knowledge of God and thereby saved. My deep love of Castile has also been a spur, for I do not wish to see my country destroyed as a divine punishment for sins against the honour of God and the True Faith. It has always been my intention to pen this account, although it has been long delayed by my being taken up with so many other tasks. I completed it in Valencia on the eighth day of December 1542, at a time when the violence, the oppression, the despotism, the killing, the plunder, the depopulation, the outrages, the agonies and the calamities we have described were at their height throughout the New World wherever Christians have set foot. It may be that some areas are worse than others: Mexico City and the surrounding territories are a little better than most, for there, at least, outrages cannot be committed so publicly, as there is justice of a sort, despite the crippling taxation unjustly imposed on the people. Yet I do see hope for the future, for, as the Emperor and King of Spain, Charles V (whose person and whose Empire may God preserve), learns of the crimes committed against his will and against that of God by his servants in the New World and of their treachery towards the people of the continent (for, until now, there has been an effective conspiracy of silence about what has really been happening), he will, as one wedded to the concept of justice and avid to see it prevail, put a stop to the wickedness and undertake a total reform of the administration of this New World that God has bestowed upon him and will do so for the greater glory of the Holy Catholic Church and for the salvation of his own royal soul. Amen.

STUDY QUESTIONS

1. In what terms does de las Casas argue for the humanity of the Native Americans?
2. Is his principal interest in their souls, which can be converted if they are reached in time and by the right agents?

13.2. GALILEO GALILEI, LETTER TO DON BENEDETTO CASTELLI, DECEMBER 21, 1613

An Italian astronomer, physicist, and mathematician, Galileo Galilei (1564–1642) made many significant contributions to science—such as improvements to the telescope and work with sunspots—but is remembered for his support of a heliocentric model of the solar system. His conviction led him into conflict with the Catholic Church; he was accused of heresy and finished his days under house arrest. Aside from his astronomical texts, Galileo also corresponded with leading figures of his day. This letter, to the Benedictine mathematician Benedetto Castelli, addresses one of the main articles of the problem with Galileo's heliocentrism: how to reconcile observable scientific fact with the words of the Bible, held to be literal and inviolable in 17th-century Italy.

SCIENCE AND RELIGION

LETTER TO DON BENEDETTO CASTELLI

Very Reverend Father and most worth Signore,

I received a visit yesterday from Signor Niccolò Arrighetti, who brought me news of your Reverence. I was delighted to hear what I never doubted, namely the high opinion in which you are held by the whole university, both the governors and the teachers and students of all nations. . . . But what set the seal on my pleasure was hearing his account of the arguments which you were able to put forward, thanks to the great kindness of their Serene Highnesses, first at their dinner table and later in Madame's drawing-room, in the presence of the Grand Duke and the Archduchess and the distinguished and excellent gentleman Don Antonio and Don Paolo Giordano and other excellent philosophers. What greater favour could you wish for than that their Highnesses should be pleased to hold conversation with you, to put their doubts to you, to hear you resolve them and finally to be satisfied with your Reverence's replies?

The points which you made, as signor Arrighetti reported them to me, have prompted me to think afresh about some general principles concerning the citing of Holy Scripture in disputes on matters of natural science, and in particular on the passage in Joshua which was put forward by the Dowager Grand Duchess, and to which the Archduchess offered some rejoinders, as evidence against the motion of the Earth and the fixed position of the Sun.

As regards the first general question raised by Madame, it seems to me that both she and you were entirely prudent when she asserted and you agreed that the Holy Scripture can never lie or be in error, but that its decrees are absolutely and inviolably true.

Selected Writings translated by Shea and Davie (2013), pp. 55–61. By permission of Oxford University Press.

I would simply have added that, although Scripture cannot err, nonetheless some of its interpreters and expositors can, and in various ways. One error in particular, which is especially serious and frequent, is to insist always on the literal meaning of the words, for this can lead not only to many contradictions but also to grave heresies and blasphemies; for it would mean attributing to God feet and hands and eyes, not to mention physical human affectations such as anger, repentance, hatred, and sometimes even forgetfulness of past events and ignorance of the future. So, since Scripture contains many statements which, if taken at their face value, appear to be at variance with the truth, but which are couched in these terms so as to be comprehensible to the ignorant, it is up to wise expositors to explain their true meaning to those few who deserve to be set apart from the common herd, and to point out the particular reasons why they have been expressed as they have.

Given, then, that Scripture in many places not only admits but necessarily requires an interpretation which differs from the apparent meaning of the words, it seems to me that it should be brought into scientific disputes only as a last resort. For while Holy Scripture and nature proceed alike from the divine Word—Scripture as dictated by the Holy Spirit, and nature as the faithful executor of God's commands—it is agreed that Scripture, in order to be understood by the multitude, says many things which are apparently and in the literal sense of the words at variance with absolute truth. But nature never transgresses the laws to which it is subject, but is inexorable and unchanging, quite indifferent to whether its hidden reasons and ways of working are accessible to human understanding or not. Hence, any effect in nature which the experience of our senses places before our eyes, or to which we are led by necessary demonstrations, should on no account be called into question because of a passage of Scripture whose words appear to suggest something different, because not every statement of Scripture is bound by such strict rules as every effect of nature.

. . .

I believe that the purpose of the authority of Holy Scripture is solely to persuade men of those articles and propositions which are necessary to their salvation and which, being beyond the scope of human reasoning, could not be made credible to us by science or by any other means, but only through the mouth of the Holy Spirit himself. I do not consider it necessary to believe that the same God who has endowed us with sense, and with the power of reasoning and intellect, should have chosen to set these aside and to convey to us by some other means those facts which we are capable of finding out by exercising these faculties. This is especially the case with those sciences of which only a tiny part is to be found in scattered references in Scripture, which as astronomy, of which Scripture contains so little that it does not even mention the planets. For if the sacred writers had intended to persuade the people of the order and motions of the heavenly bodies, they would not have said so little about them—almost nothing compared to the infinite, profound, and wonderful truths which this science contains.

So you can see, Father, if I am not mistaken, how flawed is the procedure of those who, in debating the questions of natural science which are not directly matters of faith, give priority to verses of Scripture—often verses which they have misunderstood.

. . .

To confirm this, I come now to the particular case of Joshua, about which you presented three statements to their Highnesses; and specifically to the third of these, which you rightly attributed to me, but to which I now want to add some further considerations, which I do not believe I have yet explained to you.

So let me first concede to my adversary that the words of the sacred text should be taken in exactly their literal sense, namely that God made the Sun stand still in response to Joshua's prayers, so that the day was prolonged and Joshua was able to complete his victory. But let me claim the same concession for myself, lest my adversary should tie me down while remaining free himself to change or modify the meanings of words; and I will show that this passage of Scripture clearly demonstrates the impossibility of the Aristotelian and Ptolemaic world system, and on the contrary fits perfectly well with the system of Copernicus.

I ask first, does my adversary know in what ways the Sun moves? If he does, he must perforce reply that it has two motions, an annual motion from west to east, and a daily one in the opposite direction, from east to west.

My second question then is, do these two different and almost contrary motions both belong to the Sun, and are they both proper to it? To this the answer must be no: only the annual motion is specific and proper to the Sun, while the other belongs to the highest heaven or Primum Mobile, which draws the Sun, the other planets, and the sphere of the fixed stars along with it, making them complete a revolution around the Earth every twenty-four hours, with a motion which is, as I have said, contrary to their own natural and proper motion.

So to the third question: which of these two motions of the Sun produces day and night, the Sun's own real motion or that of the Primum Mobile? The answer has to be that day and night are the result of the motion of the Primum Mobile, and that the Sun's own motion produces not day and night but the changing seasons, and the year itself.

Hence it is clear that, if the length of the day depends not on the motion of the Sun but on that of the Primum Mobile, in order to prolong the day it is the Primum Mobile which must be made to stop, not the Sun. Indeed, anyone who understands these first elements of astronomy will realize that if God had stopped the motion of the Sun, the effect would have been to shorten the day, not to lengthen it. The motion of the Sun being in the opposite direction to the daily revolution of the heavens, the more the Sun moved towards the east, the more its progress towards the west would be held back; and if the Sun's motion were diminished or stopped altogether, it would reach the point where it sets all the more quickly. This effect can be clearly seen in the case of the Moon, whose daily revolution is slower than the Sun's by the same amount as its own proper motion is faster than the Sun's. So it is simply impossible, according to the system of Ptolemy and Aristotle, to prolong the day by stopping the motion of the Sun, as Scripture says happened. It follows therefore that either the motions of the heavens are not as Ptolemy says, or we must change the sense of the words of Scripture and say that, when Scripture says that God stopped the Sun, what it meant was that God stopped the Primum Mobile.

. . .

However, since we have agreed that we should not change the meaning of the words of Scripture, we must have recourse to another arrangement of the world to see whether it agreed with the plain meaning of the words, as indeed we shall see that it does.

I have discovered and rigorously demonstrated that the globe of the Sun turns on its own axis, making a complete revolution in all the space of roughly one lunar month, in the same direction as all the other revolutions of the heavens. Moreover, it is very probable and reasonable to suppose that the Sun, as the instrument and the highest minister of nature—the heart of the world, so to speak—imparts not only light (as it clearly does) but also motion to the planets which revolve around it. So if we follow Copernicus in attributing first of all a daily rotation to the Earth, it is clear that, to bring the whole system to a stop solely in order to prolong the extent and time of daylight without disrupting all the other relations between the planets, it was enough that the Sun should stand still, just as the words of Holy Writ say. This, then, is how the length of the day on Earth can be extended by making the Sun stand still, without introducing any confusion among the parts of the world and without altering the words of Scripture.

I have written much more than my indisposition allows, so I close by offering myself as your servant, kissing your hand and praying our Lord that you may have a joyful festive season and every happiness.

In Florence, 21 December 1613, your Reverence's devoted servant, Galileo Galilei.

STUDY QUESTIONS

1. How does Galileo, with specific reference to the story of Joshua making the sun stand still, illustrate the danger of reading Scripture in *literal* terms?
2. How does he contrast the various purposes of Scripture and science in this respect?

13.3. JOHN DONNE, SERMON (DECEMBER 12, 1626); "TO HIS MISTRESS GOING TO BED" (1633)

John Donne (1572–1631) was a Catholic-turned-Anglican priest, poet, and satirist. Donne spanned the literary scale, writing hundreds of texts ranging from erotic love poems to sermonic meditations on God. After love pushed him into a ruinous marriage (that ultimately yielded twelve children), Donne endured fourteen years of destitution and depression—during which time he wrote some of his most poignant poetry. The sermon included here explores the lofty topics of true knowledge and change, whereas the almost bawdy poem revels in the exploration of his lover's body.

FROM A SERMON PREACHED 12 DECEMBER 1626

[THE STATE OF KNOWLEDGE]

How imperfect is all our knowledge? What one thing do we know perfectly? Whether we considered arts, or sciences, the servant knows but according to the proportion of his master's knowledge in that art, and the scholar knows but according to the proportion of his master's knowledge in that science; Young men mend not their sight by using old men's spectacles; and yet we look upon nature, but with Aristotle's spectacles, upon the body of man, but with Galen's, and upon the frame of the world, but with Ptolomey's spectacles. Almost all knowledge is rather like a child that is embalmed to make a mummy, than that is nursed to make a man; rather conserved in the stature of the first age, than grown to be greater; And if there be any addition to knowledge, it is rather new knowledge, than a greater knowledge; rather a singularity in a desire of proposing something that was not known at all before, than an improving, an advancing, a multiplying of former inceptions; and by that means, no knowledge comes to be perfect. One philosopher thinks he is dived to the bottom, when he says, he knows nothing but this, That he knows nothing; and yet another thinks, that he hath expressed more knowledge than he, in saying, That he knows not so much as that, That he knows nothing. St. Paul found that to be all knowledge, To know Christ; And Mahomet thinks himself wise therefore, because he knows not, acknowledges not Christ, as St. Paul does. Though a man knew not, that every sin casts another shovel of brimstone upon him in Hell, yet if he knew that every riotous feast cuts off a year, and every wanton night even years of his seventy in this world, it were some degree towards perfection in knowledge. He that purchases a manor, will think to have an exact survey of the land: But who thinks of taking so exact a survey of his conscience, how that money was got, that purchased that manor? We call that a man's means, which he hath; But that is truly his means, what way he came by it. And yet how few are there, (when a state comes to any great proportion) that know that; that know what they have, what they are worth?

. . .

[MUTABILITY]

I need not call in new philosophy, that denies a settledness, an acquiescence in the very body of the earth, but makes the earth to move in that place, where we thought the sun had moved; I need not that help, that the earth itself is in motion, to prove this, That nothing upon earth is permanent; The assertion

John Donne, *The Major Works, Including Songs and Sonnets and Sermons*, ed. John Carey (New York: Oxford University Press, 2008), pp. 12–13, 372–374.

will stand of itself, till some man assign me some instance, something that a man may rely upon, and find permanent. Consider the greatest bodies upon earth, The monarchies; Objects, which one would think, destiny might stand and stare at, but not shake; Consider the smallest bodies upon earth, the hairs of our head, objects, which one would think, destiny would not observe, or could not discern; And yet destiny, (to speak to a natural man) and God, (to speak to a Christian) is no more troubled to make a monarchy ruinous, than to make a hair gray. Nay, nothing needs to be done to either, by God, or destiny; a monarchy will ruin, as a hair will grow gray, of itself. In the elements themselves, of which all sub-elementary things are composed, there is no acquiescence, but a vicissitudinary transmutation into one another; air condensed becomes water, a more solid body, And air rarified becomes fire, a body more disputable, and in-apparent. It is so in the conditions of men too; a merchant condensed, kneaded and packed up in a great estate, becomes a Lord; And a merchant rarified, blown up by a perfidious factor, or by riotous son, evaporates into air, into nothing, and is not seen. And if there were anything permanent and durable in this world, yet we got nothing by it, because howsoever that might last in itself, yet we could not last to enjoy it; If our goods were not amongst moveables, yet we ourselves are; if they could stay with us, yet we cannot stay with them.

. . .

ELEGY: TO HIS MISTRESS GOING TO BED

Come, Madam, come, all rest my powers defy,
Until I labour, I in labour lie.
The foe oft-times, having the foe in sight.
Is tired with standing though they never fight.
Off with that girdle, like heaven's zone glistening,
But a far fairer world encompassing.
Unpin that spangled breastplate, which you wear
That th'eyes of busy fools may be stopped there:
Unlace yourself, for that harmonious chime

Tells me from you that now 'tis your bed-time.
Off what that happy busk, which I envy,
That still can be, and still can stand so nigh.
Your gown going off, such beauteous state reveals,
As when from flowery means th'hill's shadow
    steals.
Off with your wiry coronet and show
The hairy diadem which on you doth grow.
Off with those shoes: and then safely tread
In this love's hallowed temple, this soft bed.
In such white robes heaven's angels used to be
Received by men; thou angel bring'st with thee
A heaven like Mahomet's paradise; and though
Ill spirits walk in white, we easily know
By this these angels from an evil sprite,
They set our hairs, but these our flesh upright.
    Licence my roving hands, and let them go
Behind, before, above, between, below.
O my America, my new found land,
My kingdom, safeliest when with one man manned,
My mine of precious stones, my empery,
How blessed am I in the discovering thee.
To enter in these bonds is to be free,
Then where my hand is set my seal shall be.
    Full nakedness, all joys are due to thee.
As souls unbodied, bodies unclothed must be,
To taste whole joys. Gems which you women use
Are like Atalanta's balls, cast in men's views,
That when a fool's eye lighteth on a gem
His earthly soul may covet theirs, not them.
Like pictures, or like books' gay coverings made
For laymen, are all women thus arrayed;
Themselves are mystic books, which only we
Whom their imputed grace will dignify
Must see revealed. Then since I may know,
As liberally as to a midwife show
Thyself; case all, yea this white linen hence,
Here is no penance, much less innocence.
    To teach thee, I am naked first: why then

What needest thou have more covering than a man?

STUDY QUESTIONS

1. Does Donne seem to believe that perfect knowledge of anything can exist?
2. What do his references to "Mahomet" and "America" reveal about his time and place?

13.4. DESCARTES, *A DISCOURSE ON METHOD*, 1637

René Descartes (1596–1650) has been called the Father of Modern Philosophy because of his work in philosophy, metaphysics, theology, and mathematics. Perhaps best known for the groundbreaking maxim "I think, therefore I am," Descartes lays out a method for creating solid foundations upon which he can build theoretical arguments—an epistemology known as Cartesianism. The *Discourse* moves from autobiography to philosophical tract and recounts how Descartes came to the thoughts and processes that redefined philosophy.

PART ONE

Good sense is the most evenly distributed thing in the world; for everyone believes himself to be so well provided with it that even those who are the hardest to please in every other way do not usually want more of it than they already have. Nor is it likely that everyone is wrong about this; rather, what this shows is that the power of judging correctly and of distinguishing the true from the false (which is what is properly called good sense or reason) is naturally equal in all men, and that consequently the diversity of our opinions arises not from the fact that some of us are more reasonable than others, but solely that we have different ways of directing our thoughts, and do not take into account the same things. For it is not enough to possess a good mind; the most important thing is to apply it correctly. The greatest minds are capable of the greatest vices as well as the greatest virtues; those who go forward but very slowly can get further, if they always follow the right road, than those who are in too much of a hurry and stray of it.

For myself, I have never presumed my mind to be any way more accomplished than that of the common man. Indeed, I have often wished that my mind was as fast, my imagination as clear and precise, and my memory as well stocked and sharp as those of certain other people. And I personally know of no any other mental attributes that go to make up an accomplished mind; for, as regards reason or good sense (insofar as it is the only thing that makes us human and distinguishes us from brute beasts), I am ready to believe that it is altogether complete in every one of us, . . .

But I venture to claim that since my early youth I have had the great fortune of finding myself taking certain paths that have led me to reflections and maxims from which I have fashioned a method by which, it seems to me, I have a way of adding progressively to my knowledge and raising it by degrees to the highest point that the limitations of my mind and the short span of life allotted to me will permit it to reach. For I have already reaped so many fruits from the method that I derive the highest satisfaction from the progress that I believe myself already to have made in my pursuit of truth, . . .

. . .

So my aim here is not to teach the method that everyone must follow for the right conduct of his reason, but only to show in what way I have tried to conduct mine. . . .

I was educated in classical studies from my earliest years, and because I was given to believe that through them one could acquire clear and sure knowledge of everything that one needed in life, I was extremely eager to acquire them. But as soon as I had finished my course of study, at which time it is usual to be admitted to the ranks of the well educated,

A Discourse on the Method of Correctly Conducting One's Reason and Seeking Truth in the Sciences translated by Maclean (2009) 2178w from pp. 5–11, 28–30, 374. By permission of Oxford University Press.

I completely changed my opinion, for I found myself bogged down in so many doubts and errors, that it seemed to me that having set out to become learned, I have derived no benefit from my studies, other than that of progressively revealing to myself how ignorant I was. And yet I was a pupil of one of the most famous schools in Europe, in which I believed that there must be as learned men as are to be found anywhere on earth. There I had learnt everything that others were learning; and not just content with the subjects that we were taught, I had even read all the books that fell into my hands on subjects that are considered the most occult and recondite. Moreover, I knew what assessment others had made of me, and realized that I was not thought inferior to my fellow pupils, even though several among them had already been singled out to take the place of our teachers. And finally, our age seemed to me to be as flourishing as any preceding age, and to abound in as many great minds. This emboldened me to judge all others by myself, and to think that there was no body of knowledge on earth that lived up to the expectations I had been given of it.

I did not, however, cease to hold the school curriculum in esteem. I know that the Greek and Latin that are taught there are necessary for understanding the writings of the ancients; that fables stimulate the mind through their charm; that the memorable deeds recorded in histories uplift it, and they help form our judgment when read in a discerning way; that reading good books is like engaging in conversation with the most cultivated minds of the past centuries who had composed them, or rather, taking part in a well-conducted dialogue in which such minds reveal to us only the best of their thoughts; that oratory is incomparably powerful and beautiful, and that poetry possesses delightful delicacy and charm; that mathematics has very subtle techniques that can be of great use in satisfying minds as well as in coming to the aid of the arts and reducing human labour; that books on morals contain highly instructive teachings and exhortations to virtue; that theology charts our path to heaven; that philosophy provides us with the means of speaking *plausibly* about anything and impressing those who are less well instructed; that law; medicine, and other disciplines bring to those who profess them riches and honours; . . .

. . .

I was most keen on mathematics, because of its certainty and the *incontrovertibility* of its proofs; but I did not yet see its true use. Believing as I did that its only application was to the mechanical arts, I was astonished that nothing more exalted had been built on such sure and solid foundations; whereas, on the other hand, I compared the moral works of ancient pagan writers to splendid and magnificent palaces built on nothing more than sand and mud. They exalt the virtues, and make them seem more worthy of esteem than anything else on earth; but they do not give sufficient indication of how to learn about them; and what they call by such a fine name is in many cases no more than lack of human feeling, pride, despair, or parricide.

. . .

But after having spent several years studying the book of the world and trying to acquire some experience of life, I took the decision one day to look into myself and use all my mental powers to choose the paths I should follow. In this it seems to me that I have had much more success than if I had never left either my country or my books.

. . .

PART FOUR

. . . because I wished at the time to concentrate on the pursuit of truth, I came to think that I should do the exact opposite and reject as completely false everything in which I could detect the least doubt, in order to see if anything thereafter remained in my belief that was completely indubitable. And so, because our senses sometimes deceive us, I decided to suppose that nothing was such as they lead us to imagine it to be. And because there are men who make mistakes in reasoning, even about the simplest elements of geometry, and commit logical fallacies, I judged that I was as prone to error as anyone else, and I rejected as false all the reasoning I had hitherto accepted as valid proof. Finally, considering that all the same thoughts which we have while awake can come to us while asleep without any one of them then being true, I resolved to pretend that everything that had ever entered my head was no more true than the illusions of my dreams. But immediately afterwards I noted that, while I was trying to think of all things being false in this way, it was necessarily the case that I, who was thinking them, had to be something; and observing this truth: *I am thinking therefore I exist*, was so secure and certain that it could not be shaken by any of the most extravagant suppositions of the sceptics, I judged that I could accept it without scruple, as the first principle of the philosophy I was seeking.

Next, examining attentively what I was, I saw that I could pretend that I had no body and that there was no world or place for me to be in, but that I could not for all that pretend that I did not exist; on the contrary, from the very fact that I thought of doubting the truth of other things, it followed *incontrovertibly* and certainly that I myself existed, whereas, if I had merely ceased thinking, I would have no reason to believe that I existed, even if everything else I had ever imagined had been true. I thereby concluded that I was a *substance* whose whole *essence* or nature resides only in thinking, and which, in order to exist, had no need of place and is not dependent on any material thing. Accordingly this "I," that is to say, the Soul by which I am what I am, is entirely distinct from the body and is even easier to know than the body; and would not stop being everything it is, even if the body were not to exist.

After this, I came to think in general about what is required for a proposition to be true and certain; for since I had just found one such proposition, I thought that I ought also to know in what this certainty consists. And having observed that there was nothing in this proposition, *I am thinking therefore I exist*, which makes me sure that I am telling the truth, except that I can see very clearly that, in order to think, one has to exist, I concluded that I could take it to be a general rule that things we conceived of very clearly and distinctly are all true, but that there is some difficulty in being able to identify those which we conceive of distinctly.

As a result of which, as I thought about the fact that I was doubting and that consequently my being was not altogether perfect (for I saw clearly that it was a greater perfection to know than to doubt), I decided to look for the source from which I had learned to think of something more perfect than I was myself, and I came to the *incontrovertible* realization that this must be from some nature that was in fact more perfect. As for the thoughts I had about many other things outside myself, such as the heavens, the earth, light, heat, and numerous others, I had no such difficulty in knowing where they came from, because, seeing nothing in them which seemed to make them superior to myself, I could believe that if they were true, they depended on my nature in so far as it contained some perfection; and if they were not true, I held them from nothing, that is to say, that they were in me because I was lacking something. But this could not be true of the idea of a being more perfect than mine; for it was manifestly impossible that I should hold this from nothing; and because it was no less contradictory that the more perfect should proceed from and depend on the less perfect than it is that something should proceed from nothing, I could not hold it from myself either. So that there remained only the possibility that it had been put into me by a nature which was truly more perfect than mine, and one which even had in itself all the perfections of which I could have any idea, that is to say, in a word, which was God. To which thought I added that, because I knew some perfections that I did not myself have, I was not the only being who existed (I shall here freely employ, with your permission, some scholastic terminology), but that *of necessity* there must be some other, more perfect being upon whom I depended and from whom I had acquired all that I possessed. For if I had been the sole being and had been independent of every other being so as to *have, of myself*, that small degree of *participation* in the perfection which I shared with the perfect being, I could have been able to *have to myself*, by the same reason, all the remaining perfection that I knew myself to lack, and so be myself infinite, eternal, unchanging, omniscient, in a word, to have all the perfections which I could observe in God.

STUDY QUESTIONS

1. How does Descartes account for the general perception of equal knowledge among people?
2. How does he find enlightenment through introspection, rather than through trusting conventional authorities of wisdom?

13.5. *THE JESUIT RELATIONS*, FRENCH NORTH AMERICA, 1649

The *Jesuit Relations* are the most important set of documents attesting the encounter between Europeans and native North Americans in the 17th century. These annual reports of French missionaries from the Society of Jesus document the conversions—or attempted conversions—of the various native peoples in what is today the St. Lawrence River basin and the Great Lakes region. When they arrived on the banks of the St. Lawrence in 1625, French Jesuits were entering a continent still very much under the control of First Nations peoples, who were divided by their own ethnic and linguistic differences. Even the catch-all terms "Huron" and "Iroquois" masked the existence of confederacies, composed of several distinct nations, who had joined together prior to the arrival of Europeans.

When the Jesuits made headway with one group, they usually lost initiative with the group's rivals—and sometimes found themselves in the midst of a conflict that they could barely understand or appreciate. This section of one of the *Relations* concerns the torture and murder of Jean Brébeuf, who had lived among the Hurons at various points from the 1620s through the 1640s, observing their culture and systematically attempting to convert them to Catholicism. However, when an Iroquois raiding party invaded his settlement, the depth of the Hurons' Christian commitment—and his own—would be tested.

The sixteenth day of March in the present year, 1649, marked the beginning of our misfortunes—if an event, which no doubt has been the salvation of many of God's elect, can be called a misfortune.

The Iroquois, enemies of the Hurons, arrived by night at the frontier of this country. They numbered about a thousand men, well furnished with weapons, most of them carrying firearms obtained from their allies, the Dutch. We had no knowledge of their approach, although they had started from their country in the autumn, hunting in the forests throughout the winter, and had made a difficult journey of nearly two hundred leagues over the snow in order to take us by surprise. By night, they reconnoitered the condition of the first place upon which they had designs. It was surrounded by a pine stockade fifteen or sixteen feet in height, and a deep ditch with which nature had strongly fortified this place on three sides.

There remained only a small space that was weaker than the others.

It was at this weak point that the enemy made a breach at daybreak, but so secretly and promptly that he was master of the place before anyone could mount a defense. All were then sleeping deeply, and they had no time to recognize the danger. Thus this village was taken, almost without striking a blow and with only ten Iroquois killed. Part of the Hurons—men, women, and children—were massacred then and there, while the others were made captives and were reserved for cruelties more terrible than death.

. . .

The enemy did not stop there, but followed up his victory, and before sunrise he appeared in arms to attack the town of St. Louis, which was fortified with a fairly good stockade. Most of the women and the

Paul Ragueneau, *Relation of 1648–49*, from Allan Greer, The Jesuit Relations: Natives and Missionaries in Seventeenth-Century North America (Bedford/St. Martin's, 2000), pp. 112–115.

children had just gone from it upon hearing the news which had arrived regarding the approach of the Iroquois. The people of greatest courage, about eighty persons, being resolved to defend themselves well, courageously repulsed the first and the second assaults, killing about thirty of the enemy's boldest men, in addition to many wounded. But finally, the larger number prevailed, as the Iroquois used their hatchets to undermine the palisade of stakes and opened a passage for themselves through some considerable breaches.

About nine o'clock in the morning, we perceived from our house at St. Marie the fire which was consuming the cabins of that town, where the enemy, after entering victoriously, had reduced everything to desolation. They cast into the flames the old, the sick, the children who had not been able to escape, and all those who, being too severely wounded, could not have followed them into captivity. At the sight of those flames, and by the color of the smoke which issued from them, we understood sufficiently what was happening, for this town of St. Louis was no more than a league distant from us. Two Christians who escaped the fire arrived about this time and confirmed this.

In this town of St. Louis were at that time two of our fathers, Father Jean de Brébeuf and Father Gabriel Lalemant, who had charge of a cluster of five towns. These formed but one of the eleven missions of which we have spoken above, and we call it the mission of St. Ignace.

Some Christians had begged the fathers to preserve their lives for the glory of God, which would have been as easy for them as for the more than five hundred persons who went away at the first alarm, for there was more than enough time to reach a place of safety. But their zeal could not permit such a thing, and the salvation of their flock was dearer to them than the love of their own lives. They employed the moments left to them as the most previous which they had ever had in the world, and through the heat of the battle their hearts were on fire for the salvation of souls. One was at the breach, baptizing the catechumens, [native converts who had not yet been baptized] and the other was giving absolution to the neophytes. [recently baptized Christians] Both of them urged the Christians to die in the sentiments of piety with which they consoled them in their miseries. Never was their faith more alive, nor their love for their good fathers and pastors more keenly felt.

An infidel, seeing the desperate situation, spoke of taking flight, but a Christian named Etienne Annaotaha, the most esteemed in the country for his courage and his exploits against the enemy, would never allow it. "What!" he said. "Could we ever abandon these two good fathers, who have exposed their lives for us? Their love for our salvation will be the cause of their death, for there is no longer time for them to flee across the snows. Let us then die with them, and we shall go together to heaven." This man had made a general confession a few days previously, having had a presentiment of the danger awaiting him and saying that he wished that death should find him disposed for Heaven. And indeed he, as well as many other Christians, had abandoned themselves to fervor in a manner so extraordinary that we shall never be sufficiently able to bless the guidance of God over so many predestinated souls. His divine providence continues lovingly to guide them in death as in life.

STUDY QUESTIONS

1. How well do the Jesuits seem to have understood the conflicts among native peoples in this region?
2. How was Ragueneau's reporting of the battle designed to highlight the "success" of the mission, despite an apparent setback?

13.6. THOMAS HOBBES, "ON NATURAL LAW," *LEVIATHAN*, 1651

Thomas Hobbes (1588–1679) was an English political philosopher who examined the idea of a "social contract" existing between a ruler and society. Although he upheld absolutism as a political system, his liberal ideas—such as the belief in the natural equality for all men and the idea that rule should emerge from the needs of society—helped frame early American political thought. His massive work *Leviathan*, named for the Biblical sea-beast, explores and explains this theory of social contract during the English civil war that challenged traditional monarchy. This selection outlines Hobbes's views on natural law and the liberties it demands.

CHAPTER XIII

OF THE NATURAL CONDITION OF MANKIND AS CONCERNING THEIR FELICITY, AND MISERY

1. NATURE hath made men so equal, in the faculties of the body, and mind; as that though there be found one man sometimes manifestly stronger in body, or of quicker mind than another; yet when all are reckoned together, the difference between man, and man, is not so considerable, as that one man can thereupon claim to himself any benefit, to which another may not pretend, as well as he. For as to the strength of body, the weakest has strength enough to kill the strongest, either by secret machination, or by confederacy with others, that are in the same danger with himself.

2. And as to the faculties of the mind, (setting aside the arts grounded upon words, and especially that skill of proceeding upon general, and infallible rules, called science; which very few have, and but in few things; as being not a native faculty, born with us; nor attained (as prudence,) while we look after somewhat else,) I find yet a greater equality amongst men, than that of strength. For prudence, is but experience; which equal time, equally bestows on all men, in those things they equally apply themselves unto. That which may perhaps make such equality incredible, is but a vain conceit of one's own wisdom, which almost all men think they have in a greater degree, than the vulgar; that is, than all men but themselves, and a few others, whom by fame, or for concurring with themselves, they approve. For such is the nature of men, that howsoever they may acknowledge many others to be more witty, or more eloquent, or more learned; yet they will hardly believe there be many so wise as themselves; for they see their own wit at hand, and other men's at a distance. But this proveth rather that men are in that point equal, than unequal. For there is not ordinarily a greater sign of the equal distribution of any thing, than that every man is contented with his share.

3. From this equality of ability, ariseth equality of hope in the attaining of our ends. And therefore if any two men desire the same thing, which nevertheless they cannot both enjoy, they become enemies; and in the way to their end, (which principally their own conservation, and sometimes their delectation only,) endeavor to destroy, or subdue one another. And from hence it comes to pass, that where an invader hath no more to fear, than another man's single power; if one plant, sow, build, or possess a convenient seat, others may probably be expected to come prepared with forces united, to dispossess, and deprive him, not only

From Thomas Hobbes, *Leviathan*. ed. J. C. A. Gaskin. New York: Oxford University Press, 2010, pp. 82–6, 132–3, 138–9, 141–3.

of the fruit of his labour, but also of his life, or liberty. And the invader again is in the like danger of another.

4. And from this diffidence of one another, there is no way for any man to secure himself, so reasonable, as anticipation; that is, by force, or wiles, to master the persons of all men he can, so long, till he see no other power great enough to endanger him: and this is no more than his own conservation requireth, and is generally allowed. Also because there be some, that taking pleasure in contemplating their own power in the acts of conquest, which they pursue farther than their security requires; if others, that otherwise would be glad to be at ease within modest bounds, should not by invasion increase their power, they would not be able, long time, by standing only their defence, to subsist. And by consequence, such augmentation of dominion over men, being necessary to a man's conservation, it ought to be allowed him.

5. Again, men have no pleasure, (but on the contrary a great deal of grief) in keeping company, where there is no power able to over-awe them all. For every man looketh that his companion should value him, at the same rate he sets upon himself: and upon all signs of contempt, or undervaluing, naturally endeavours, as far as he dares (which amongst them that have no common power to keep them in quiet, is far enough to make them destroy each other,) to extort a greater value from his contemners, by damage; and from others, by the example.

6. So that in the nature of man, we find three principal causes of quarrel. First, competition; secondly, diffidence; thirdly, glory.

7. The first, maketh men invade for gain; the second, for safety; and the third, for reputation. The first use violence, to make themselves masters of other men's persons, wives, children, and cattle; the second, to defend them; the third, for trifles, as a word, a smile, a different opinion, and any other sign of undervalue, either direct in their persons, or by reflection in their kindred, their friends, their nation, their profession, or their name.

8. Hereby it is manifest, that during the time men live without a common power to keep them all in awe, they are in that condition which is called war; and such a war, as is of every man, against every man. For WAR, consisteth not in battle only, or the act of fighting; but in a tract of time, wherein the will to contend by battle is sufficiently known: and therefore the notion of *time*, is to be considered in the nature of war; as it is in the nature of weather. For as the nature of foul weather, lieth not in a shower or two of rain; but in an inclination thereto of many days together: so the nature of war consisteth not in actual fighting; but in the known disposition thereto, during all the time there is no assurance to the contrary. All other time is PEACE.

9. Whatsoever therefore is consequent to a time of war, where every man is enemy to every man; the same is consequent to the time, wherein men live without other security, than what their own strength, and their own invention shall furnish them withal. In such condition, there is no place for industry; because the fruit thereof is uncertain: and consequently no culture of the earth; no navigation, nor use of the commodities that may be imported by sea; no commodious building; no instruments of moving, and removing such things as require much force; no knowledge of the face of the earth; no account of time; no arts; no letters; no society; and which is worst of all, continual fear, and danger of violent death; and the life of man, solitary, poor, nasty, brutish, and short.

10. It may seem strange to some man, that has not well weighed these things; that nature should thus dissociate, and render men apt to invade, and destroy one another: he may therefore, not trusting to this inference, made from the passions, desire perhaps to have the same confirmed by experience. Let him therefore consider with himself, when taking a journey, he arms himself, and seeks to go well accompanied; when going to sleep, he locks his doors; when even in his house he locks his chests; and this when he knows there be laws, and public officers, armed, to revenge all injuries shall be done him; what opinion he has of his fellow-subjects, when he rides armed; of his fellow citizens, when he locks his doors; and of his children, and servants, when he locks his chests. Does he not there as much accuse mankind by his actions, as I do by my words? But neither of us accuse man's nature in it. The desires, and other passions of man, are in themselves no sin. No more are the actions, that proceed from those

passions, till they know a law that forbids them: which till laws be made they cannot know: nor can any law be made, till they have agreed upon the person that shall make it.

11. It may peradventure be thought, there was never such a time, not condition of war as this; and I believe it was never generally so, over all the world: but there are many places, where they live so now. For the savage people in many places of America, except the government of small families, the concord whereof dependeth on natural lust, have no government at all; and live at this day in that brutish manner, as I said before. Howsoever, it may be perceived what manner of life there would be, where there were no common power to fear; by the manner of life, which men that have formerly lived under a peaceful government, use to degenerate into, in a civil war.

12. But though there had never been any time, wherein particular men were in a condition of war one against another; yet in all times, kings, and persons of sovereign authority, because of their independency, are in continual jealousies, and in the state and posture of gladiators; having their weapons pointing, and their eyes fixed on one another; that is, their forts, garrisons, and guns upon the frontiers of their kingdoms; and continual spies upon their neighbours; which is a posture of war. But because they uphold thereby, the industry of their subjects; there does not follow from it, that misery, which accompanies the liberty of particular men.

13. To this war of every man against every man, this also is consequent; that nothing can be unjust. The notions of right and wrong, justice and injustice have there no place. Where there is no common power, there is no law: where no law, no injustice. Force, and fraud, are in war the two cardinal virtues. Justice, and injustice are none of the faculties neither of the body, nor mind. If they were, they might be in a man that were alone in the world, as well as his senses, and passions. They are qualities, that relate to men in society, not in solitude. It is consequent also to the same condition, that there be no property, no dominion, no *mine* and *thine* distinct; but one that to be every man's, that he can get; and for so long, as he can keep it. And thus much for the ill condition, which man by mere nature is actually placed in;

though with a possibility to come out of it, consisting partly in the passions, partly in his reason.

14. The passions that incline men to peace, are fear of death; desire of such things as are necessary to commodious living; and a hope by their industry to obtain them. And reason suggesteth convenient articles of peace, upon which men may be drawn to agreement. These articles, are they, which otherwise are called the Laws of Nature: whereof I shall speak more particularly, in the two following chapters.

. . .

CHAPTER XX

OF DOMINION PATERNAL, AND DESPOTICAL

1. A COMMONWEALTH *by acquisition*, is that, where the sovereign power is acquired by force; and it is acquired by force, when men singly, or many together by plurality of voices, for fear of death, or bonds, do authorize all the actions of that man, or assembly, that hath their lives and liberty in his power.

2. And this kind of dominion, or sovereignty, differeth from sovereignty by institution, only in this, that men who choose their sovereign, do it for fear of one another, and not of him whom they institute: but in this case, they subject themselves, to him they are afraid of. In both cases they do it for fear: which is to be noted by them, that hold all such covenants, as proceed from fear of death, or violence, void: which if it were true, no man, in any kind of commonwealth, could be obliged to obedience. It is true, that in a commonwealth once instituted, or acquired, promises proceeding from fear of death, or violence, are no covenants, nor obliging, when the thing promised is contrary to the laws; but the reason is not, because it was made upon fear, but because he that promiseth, hath no right in the thing promised. Also, when he may lawfully perform, and doth not, it is not the invalidity of the covenant, that absolveth him, but the sentence of the sovereign. Otherwise, whensoever a man lawfully promiseth, he unlawfully breaketh: but when the sovereign, who is the actor, acquitteth him, then he is acquitted by him than extorted the promise, as by the author of such absolution.

3. But the rights, and consequences of sovereignty, are the same in both. His power cannot,

without his consent, be transferred to another: he cannot be punished by them: he is judge of what is necessary for peace; and judge of doctrines: he is sole legislator; and supreme judge of controversies; and of the times, and occasions of war, and peace: to him it belongeth to choose magistrates, counselors, commanders, and all other officers, and ministers; and to determine of rewards, and punishments, honour, and order. The reasons whereof, are the same which are alleged in the precedent chapter, for the same rights, and consequences of sovereignty by institution.

. . .

18. So that it appeareth plainly, to my understanding, both from reason, and Scripture, that the sovereign power, whether placed in one man, as in monarchy, or in one assembly of men, as in popular and aristocratical commonwealths, is as great, as possibly men can be imagined to make it. And though of so unlimited a power, men may fancy many evil consequences, yet the consequences of the want of it, which is perpetual war of every man against his neighbor, are much worse. The condition of man in this life shall never be without inconveniences; but there happeneth in no commonwealth any great inconvenience, but what proceeds from the subject's disobedience, and breach of those covenants, from which the commonwealth hath its being. And whosoever thinking sovereign power too great, will seek to make it less, must subject himself, to the power that can limit it; that is to say, to a greater.

19. The greatest objection is, that of the practice; when men ask, where, and when, such power has by subjects been acknowledged. But one may ask them again, when, or where has there been a kingdom long free from sedition and civil war. In those nations, those commonwealths have been long-lived, and not been destroyed but by foreign war, the subjects never did dispute of the sovereign power. But howsoever, an argument from the practice of men, that have not been sifted to the bottom, and with exact reason weighed the causes, and nature of commonwealths, and suffer daily those miseries, that proceed from the ignorance thereof, is invalid. For though in all places of the world, men should lay the foundation of their houses on the sand, it could not thence be inferred,

that so it ought to be. The skill of making, and maintaining commonwealths, consisteth in certain rules, as doth arithmetic and geometry; not (as tennis-play) on practice only: which rules, neither poor men have the leisure, nor men that have had the leisure, have hitherto had the curiosity, or the method to find out.

. . .

5. But as men, for the attaining of peace, and conservation of themselves thereby, have made an artificial man, which we call a commonwealth; so also have they made artificial chains, called *civil laws*, which they themselves, by mutual covenants, have fastened at one end, to the lips of that man, or assembly, to whom they have given the sovereign power; and at the other end to their own ears. These bonds in their own nature but weak, may nevertheless be made to hold, by the danger, though not by the difficulty of breaking them.

6. In relation to these bonds only it is, that I am to speak now, of the *liberty of subjects*. For seeing there is no commonwealth in the world, wherein there be rules enough to set down, for the regulating of all the actions, and words of men; (as being a thing impossible:) it followeth necessarily, that in all kinds of actions, by the laws praetermitted [passed over], men have the liberty, of doing what their own reasons shall suggest, for the most profitable to themselves. For if we take liberty from chains and prison, it were very absurd for men to clamour as they do, for the liberty they so manifestly enjoy. Again, if we take liberty, for an exemption from laws, it is no less absurd, for men to demand as they do, that liberty, by which all other men may be masters of their lives. And yet as absurd as it is, this is it they demand; not knowing that the laws are of no power to protect them, without a sword in the hands of a man, or men, to cause those laws to be put into execution. The liberty of a subject, lieth therefore only in those things, which in regulating their actions, the sovereign hath praetermitted: such as is the liberty to buy, and sell, and otherwise contract with one another; to choose their own abode, their own diet, their own trade of life, and institute their children as they themselves think fit; and the like.

7. Nevertheless we are not to understand, that by such liberty, the sovereign power of life, and death, is

either abolished, or limited. For it has been already shown, that nothing the sovereign representative can do to a subject, on what pretence soever, can properly be called injustice, or injury; because every subject is author of every act the sovereign doth; so that he never wanteth right to any thing, otherwise, than as he himself is the subject of God, and bound thereby to observe the laws of nature. And therefore it may, and doth often happen in commonwealths, that a subject may be put to death by the command of the sovereign power; and yet neither do the other wrong: as when Jeptha caused his daughter to be sacrificed: in which, and the like cases, he that so dieth, had liberty to do the action, for which he is nevertheless, without injury put to death. And the same holdeth also in a sovereign prince, that putteth to death an innocent subject. For though the action be against the law of nature, as being contrary to equity, (as was the killing of Uriah, by David;) yet it was not an injury to Uriah, but to God. Not to Uriah, because the right to do what he pleased, was given him by Uriah himself: and yet to God, because David was God's subject; and prohibited all iniquity by the law of nature. Which distinction, David himself, when he repented the fact, evidently confirmed, saying, *To thee only have I sinned*. In the same manner, the people of Athens, when they banished the most potent of their commonwealth for ten years, thought they committed no injustice; and yet they never questioned what crime he had done; but what hurt he would do: nay they commanded the banishment of they knew not whom; and every citizen bringing his oystershell into the market place, written with the name of him he desired should be banished, without actually accusing him, sometimes banished an Aristides, for his reputation of justice; and sometimes a scurrilous jester, as Hyperbolus, to make a jest of it. And yet a man cannot say, the sovereign people of Athens wanted right to banish them; or an Athenian the liberty to jest, or to be just.

8. The liberty, whereof there is so frequent, and honourable mention, in the histories, and philosophy of the ancient Greeks, and Romans, and in the writings, and discourse of those that from them have received all their learning in the politics, is not the liberty of particular men; but the liberty of the commonwealth: which is the same with that, which every man then should have, if there were no civil laws, no commonwealth at all. And the effects of it also be the same. For as amongst his neighbor; no inheritance, to transmit to the son, nor to expect from the father; no propriety of goods, or lands; no security; but a full and absolute liberty in every particular man: so in states, and commonwealths not dependent on one another, every commonwealth, (not every man) has an absolute liberty, to do what it shall judge (that is to say, what that man, or assembly that representeth it, shall judge) most conducing to their benefit. But withal, they live in the condition of a perpetual war, and upon the confines of battle, with their frontiers armed, and cannons planted against their neighbours round about. The Athenians, and Romans were free; that is, free commonwealths: not that any particular man had the liberty to resist their own representative; but that their representative had the liberty to resist, or invade other people. There is written on the turrets of the city of Lucca in great characters at this day, the word LIBERTAS; yet no man can thence infer, that a particular man has more liberty, or immunity from the service of the commonwealth there, than in Constantinople. Whether a commonwealth be monarchical, or popular, the freedom is still the same.

STUDY QUESTIONS

1. Does Hobbes see war as a natural and even necessary experience for humanity?
2. How does he contrast the "freedom" of the individual with the freedom of the commonwealth as a whole?

CHAPTER 14

THE WAR OF ALL AGAINST ALL

14.1. JOHN FOXE, *FOXE'S BOOK OF MARTYRS*, TRIAL OF ANNE ASKEW

John Foxe (1517–1587) authored this martyrology that especially focuses on the martyrdoms of 16th-century Protestants at the hands of Catholic inquisitors. This selection recounts the trial against Anne Askew, an Englishwoman who became actively involved in propagating Protestant beliefs—even being rejected by her husband as a result of her zeal. As in medieval inquisitions, the questions asked to Anne are aimed at clarifying where the error arises; here, she rejects the doctrine of transubstantiation and challenges the authority of "improper" priests. Her answers are logical and coherent as she unwittingly condemns herself. Anne was tortured in the Tower of London and burned at the stake in 1546 at the age of twenty-five.

To satisfy your expectation: good people (saith she) this was my first examination in the year of our Lord 1545 and in the month of March.

First Christopher Dare examined me at Sadler's Hall; being one of the quest, and asked if I did not believe that the sacrament, hanging over the altar, was the very body of Christ really. Then I demanded this question of him: wherefore Saint Stephen was stoned to death, and he said, he could not tell. Then I answered that no more would I assoil his vain question.

Secondly, he said that there was a woman, which did not testify that I should read, how God was not in temples made with hands. Then I showed him the seventh and seventeenth chapters of the Acts of Apostles, what Stephen and Paul had said therein. Whereupon he asked me how I took those sentences?

I answered, "I would not throw pearls among swine, for acorns were good enough."

Thirdly, he asked me wherefore I said that I had rather read five lines in the Bible, than to hear five masses in the temple? I confessed, that I had said no less: not for the dispraise of either the epistle or the gospel, but because the one did greatly edify me, and the other nothing at all. As Saint Paul doth witness in the fourteenth chapter of his first epistle to the Corinthians, whereas he saith, "If the trumpet giveth an uncertain sound who will prepare himself to the battle?"

Fourthly: he laid unto my charge that I should say: "If an ill priest ministered, it was the devil and not God."

My answer was, that I never spake any such thing. But this was my saying: that whosoever he were that ministered unto me, his ill conditions could not hurt

"Foxe's Book of Martyrs: Select Narratives," ed. John N. King. (New York: Oxford University Press, 2009), pp. 22–35.

my faith, but in spirit I received nevertheless, the body and blood of Christ.

He asked me what I said concerning confession? I answered him my meaning, which was as Saint James saith, that every man ought to acknowledge his faults to other, and the one to pray for the other.

Sixthly, he asked me what I said to the King's Book? And I answered him, that I could say nothing to it, because I never saw it.

Seventhly, he asked me if I had the spirit of God in me? I answered, "If I had not, I was but a reprobate or castaway." Then he said he had sent for a priest to examine me, which was here at hand.

The priest asked me what I said to the sacrament of the altar, and required much to know therein my meaning. But I desired him again, to hold me excused concerning that matter. None other answer would I make him, because I perceived him to be a papist.

Eighthly he asked me, if I did not think that private Masses did help souls departed? I said it was great idolatry to believe more in them, than in the death which Christ died for us.

Then they had me thence unto my Lord Mayor, and he examined me, as they had before, and I answered him directly in all things I answered the quest before. Besides this my Lord Mayor laid one thing to my charge, which was never spoken of me, but of them: and that was, whether a mouse eating the host, received God or no? This question did I never ask, but indeed they asked it of me, whereunto I made them no answer but smiled.

Then the bishop's chancellor rebuked me and said, that I was much to blame for uttering the scriptures. For Saint Paul (he said) forbade women to speak, or to talk of the word of God. I answered him that I knew Paul's meaning as well as he, which is in 1 Corinthians 14, that a woman ought not to speak in the congregation by the way of teaching. And then I asked him, how many women he had seen go into the pulpit and preach? He said he never saw none. Then I said he ought to find no fault in poor women, except they had offended the law.

Then the Lord Mayor commanded me to ward, I asked him if sureties would not serve me, and he made me short answer, that he would take none. Then was I had to the Counter, and there remained eleven days, no friend admitted to speak with me. But in the mean time there was a priest sent to me, which said that he was commanded of the bishop to examine me, and to give me good counsel, which he did not. But first he asked me for what cause I was put in the Counter, and I told him, I could not tell. Then he said it was great pity that I should be there without cause, and concluded that he was very sorry for me.

Secondly, he said, it was told him, that I should deny the sacrament of the altar. And I answered again that, that I have said, I have said.

Thirdly he asked me if I were shriven, I told him, so that I might have one of these three, that is to say, Doctor Crome, Sir Guillam, or Huntington. I was contented because I knew them to be men of wisdom, "as for you or any other I will not dispraise, because I know you not." Then he said, "I would not have you think, but that I, or another that shall be brought to you, shall be as honest as they, for if we were not, you may be sure the kind would not suffer us to preach." Then I answered by the saying of Solomon: "By communing with the wise, I may learn wisdom, but by talking with a fool, I shall take scathe." Pro[verbs, ch. 1].

Fourthly he asked, "If the host should fall and a beast did eat it, whether the beast did receive God or no?" I answered, "Seeing you have taken the pains to ask the question, I desire you also to assoil it yourself: for I will not do it, because I perceive you come to tempt me." And he said, "It was against the order of schools that he which asked the question should answer it." I told him [that] I was but a woman and knew not the course of schools.

Fifthly he asked me, if I intended to receive the sacrament at Easter, or no? I answered, that else I were not Christian woman, and thereat I did rejoice, that the time was so near at hand, and then he departed thence with many fair words.

The twenty-third day of March, my cousin Brittain came into the Counter unto me, and asked me whether I might be put to bail or no? Then went he immediately unto my Lord Mayor, desiring of him to be so good unto me. That I might be bailed. My Lord answered him, and said that he would be glad to do the best that in him lay. Howbeit he could not bail me, without the consent of a spiritual officer: requiring him to go and speak with the chancellor of London. For he said, like as he could not commit me to prison without the consent of a spiritual officer, no more could he bail me without consent of the same.

. . .

On the morrow after, the Bishop of London sent for me, at one of the clock, his hour being appointed at three, and as I came before him, he said he was very sorry for my trouble, and desired to know my opinion in such matters as were laid against me.

. . .

In the mean while he commanded his archdeacon to common with me, who said unto me: "Mistress wherefore are you accused and thus troubled here before the bishop?" To whom I answered again and said: "Sir, ask I pray you my accusers, for I know not as yet." Then took he my book out of my hand, and said: "Such books as this, have brought you to the trouble you are in. Beware," (saith he), "beware, for he that made this book and was the author thereof, was an heretic I warrant you, and burnt in Smithfield." Then I asked him, if he were certain and sure, that it was true that he had spoken. And he said he knew well the book was of John Frith's making. Then I asked him if he were not ashamed for to judge of the book before he saw it within, or yet knew the truth thereof. I said also, that such unadvised and hasty judgement is a token apparent of a very slender wit. Then I opened the book and showed it to him. He said he thought it had been another, for he could find no fault therein. Then I desired him no more to be so unadvisedly rash and swift judgement, till he thoroughly knew the truth, and so he departed from me.

. . .

Then brought he forth this unsavoury similitude: that if a man had a wound, no wise surgeon would minister help unto it before he had seen it uncovered. "In like case," saith he, "can I give you no good counsel, unless I know wherewith your conscience is burdened." I answered, that my conscience was clear in all things: and for to lay a plaster unto the whole skin, it might appear much folly.

. . .

Then said my Lord unto me, that I had alleged a certain text of the scripture. I answered that I alleged none other but Saint Paul's own saying to the Athenians in the eighteenth chapter in the Apostle's acts, that God dwelleth not in temples made with hands. Then asked he me what my faith and belief was in that matter? I answered him, "I believe as the scripture doth teach me."

Then enquired he of me, "What if the scripture do say that it is the body of Christ?" "I believe," said I, "as

the scripture doth teach me." Then asked he again, "What if the scripture do say that it is not the body of Christ?" My answer was still, "I believe as the scripture informeth me." And upon this argument he tarried a great while, to have driven me to make him an answer to his mind. Howbeit I would not: but concluded this with him, that I believe therein and in all other things as Christ and his holy apostles did leave them.

Then he asked me why I had so few words? And I answered, "God hath given me the gift of knowledge, but not of utterance. And Solomon saith: "That a woman of few words is a gift of God." Proverbs nineteen.

. . .

"Be it known," (saith he), "of all men, that I Anne Askew do confess this to be my faith and belief, notwithstanding my reports made afore to the contrary. I believe that they which are houseled at the hands of a priest, whether his conversation be good or not, do receive the body and blood of Christ in substance really. Also I do believe, that after the consecration, whether it be received or reserved, it is no less than the very body and blood of Christ in substance. Finally I do believe in this and in all other sacraments of holy church, in all points according to the old Catholic faith of the same. In witness whereof I the said Anne have subscribed my name."

There was somewhat more in it, which because I had not the copy, I cannot not remember. Then he read it to me and asked me if I did agree to it. And I said again, "I believe so much thereof, as the holy scripture both agree unto: wherefore I desire you, that ye will add that thereunto." Then he answered, that I should not teach him what he should write. With that, he went forth into his great chamber, and read the same bill before the audience, which inveigled and willed me to set to my hand, saying also, that I have favour showed me.

. . .

"The true copy of the confession and belief of Anne Askew, otherwise called Anne Kime, made before the Bishop of London, the twentieth day of March, in the year of our Lord God after the computation of the Church of England, 1545, and subscribed with her own hand, in the presence of the said bishop and other, whose names hereafter are recited, set forth and published at this present, to the intent the world may see what credence is now to be given unto the same woman, who in so short a time hath most damnably altered and changed her opinion and belief, and therefore rightfully in open court arraigned and condemned," *Ex. Registrum.*

"Be it known to all faithful people, that as touching the blessed sacrament of the altar, I do firmly and undoubtedly believe, that after the words of consecration be spoken by the priest, according to the common usage of this Church of England, there is present really the body and blood of our saviour Jesus Christ, whether the minister which both consecrate, be a good man, or a bad man, and that also whensoever the said sacrament is received, whether the receiver be a good man or a bad man, he doth receive it really and corporally. And moreover, I do believe, that whether the said sacrament then received of the minister, or else reserved to be put into the pix, or to be brought to any person that is impotent or sick, yet there is the very body and blood of our said saviour: so that whether the minister or the receiver be good or bad, yea whether the sacrament be received or reserved, always there is the blessed body of Christ really.

"And this thing with all other things touching the sacrament and other sacraments of the church, and all things else touching the Christian belief, which are taught and declared in the king's majesty's book lately set forth for the erudition of the Christian people, I Anne Askew, otherwise called Anne Kime, do truly and perfectly believe, and so here presently confess and knowledge. And here I do promise that henceforth I shall never say or do anything against the promises, or against any of them. In witness whereof, I the said Anne have subscribed my name unto these presents. Written the twentieth day of March, in the year of our Lord God 1545." *Ex Registrum.*

By me Anne Askew, otherwise called Anne Kime. . . .

Here mayest thou note gentle Reader in this confession, both in the bishop and his register: a double sleight of false conveyance. For although the confession purporteth the words of the bishop's writing, whereunto she did not set her hand, yet by the title prefixed before, mayest thou see that both she was arraigned and condemned before this was registered, and also that she is falsely reported to have put to her hand, which indeed by this her own book appeareth not so to be, but after this manner and condition: "I Anne Askew do believe all manner things contained in the faith of the Catholic Church, and not otherwise." It followeth more in the story.

Then because I did add unto it the Catholic Church he flang into his chamber in a great fury. With that my cousin Brittain followed him, desiring him for God's sake to be good Lord unto me. He answered that I was a woman, and that he was nothing deceived in me. Then my cousin Brittain desired him to take me as a woman, and not to set my weak woman's wit to his lordship's great wisdom.

Then went in unto him Doctor Weston, and said, that the cause why I did write there "the Catholic Church," was that I understood not "the church" written afore. So with much ado, they persuaded my Lord to come out again, and to take my name with the names of my sureties, which were my cousin Brittain, and Master Spilman of Gray's Inn.

This being done, we thought that I should have been put to bail immediately according to the order of the law. Howbeit, he would not suffer it, but committed me from thence to prison again, until the next morrow, and then he willed me to appear in the Guildhall, and so I did. Notwithstanding, they would not put me to bail there neither, but read the bishop['s] writing unto me, as before, and so commanded me again to prison.

Then were my sureties appointed to come before them on the next morrow in Paul's Church: which did do indeed. Notwithstanding they would once again have broken off with them because they would not be bound also for another woman at their pleasure, whom they knew not nor yet what matter was laid unto her charge. Notwithstanding at the last, after much ado and reasoning to and fro, they took a bond of them recognizance for my forthcoming. And thus I was at the last delivered.

Written by me Anne Askew.

. . .

Hitherto we have entreated of this good woman. Now it remaineth that we touch somewhat as concerning her end and martyrdom. After that she, being born of such stock and kindred, that she might have lived in great wealth and prosperity, if she would rather have followed the world, than Christ, now had been so tormented, that she could neither live long in so great distress, neither yet by her adversaries be suffered to die in secret: the day of her execution being appointed, she was brought into Smithfield in a chain, because she could not go on her feet, by means of her great torments. When she was brought unto the stake, she was tied by the middle with a chain that held up her body. When all things were thus prepared to the fire, Doctor Shaxton who was then appointed to preach, began his sermon. Anne Askew hearing, and answering again unto him, where he said well, confirmed the same: where he said amiss, there said she, "He misseth, and speaketh without the book."

The sermon being finished, the martyrs standing there tied at three stakes ready to their martyrdom, began their prayers. The multitude and concourse of the people was exceeding, the place where they stood being railed about to keep out the press. Upon the bench under Saint Bartholomew's Church, sat Wriothesley Chancellor of England, the old Duke of Norfolk, the old Earl of Bedford, the Lord Mayor with diverse other more. Before the fire should be set unto them, one of the bench hearing that they had gunpowder about them, and being afraid lest the faggots by strength of the gunpowder would come flying about their ears, began to be afraid, but the Earl of Bedford declaring unto him how the gunpowder was not laid under the faggots, but only about their bodies to rid them out of their pain, which having vent, there was no danger to them of the faggots, so diminished that fear.

Then Wriothesley Lord Chancellor, sent to Anne Askew letters, offering to her the king's pardon, if she would recant. Who refusing once to look upon them, made this answer again: that she came not thither to deny her lord and master. Then were the letters likewise offered unto the other, who in like manner, following the constancy of the woman, denied not only to receive them, but also to look upon them. Whereupon the Lord Mayor commanding fire to be put unto them, cried with a loud voice, "*Fiat justitia.*"

And thus the good Anne Askew with these blessed martyrs, being troubled so many manner of ways, and having passed through so many torments, having now ended the long course of her agonies, being compassed in with flames of fire, as a blessed sacrifice unto God, she slept in the Lord, anno 1546, leaving behind her singular example of Christian constancy for all men to follow.

STUDY QUESTIONS

1. How does Anne Askew appeal to her own reading of the Bible throughout her interrogation?
2. Why were her interrogators so insistent on the point of transubstantiation, and how does this reflect the larger goals of Henry VIII's Church of England in the 1540s?

14.2. OGIER GHISELIN DE BUSBECQ, "THE COURT OF SULEIMAN THE MAGNIFICENT," 1581

Ghiselin (1522–1592) was a Flemish ambassador who represented the Austrian Habsburgs at the court of Suleiman the Magnificent (1520–1566) in Istanbul. In 1581, he published an account of his time among the Ottomans as *Itinera Constantinopolitanum et Amasianum* (*Travels in Constantinople and Asia Minor*). A polymath, a sensitive observer of court politics, and an adventurous intellectual, Ghiselin also discovered a nearly intact copy of the autobiography of the Roman emperor Augustus that had been inscribed at Ankara, and he publicized the contents of this *Monumentum Ancyranum* for scholars around the world—and up to the present day. However, in this segment of his travel narrative, he draws attention to the personal habits and behaviors of a contemporary emperor—and one who saw himself as the heir to the Romans as well as to the other monarchs who had held Constantinople/Istanbul.

Wayne S. Vucinich, *The Ottoman Empire: Its Record and Legacy* (Princeton: Van Nostrand, 1965), pp. 127–129.

The Sultan was seated on a very low ottoman, not more than a foot from the ground, which was covered with a quantity of costly rugs and cushions of exquisite workmanship; near him lay his bow and arrows. His air, as I said, was by no means gracious, and his face wore a stern, though dignified, expression. On entering we were separately conducted into the royal presence by the chamberlains, who grasped our arms. . . . After having gone through a pretense of kissing his hand, we were conducted backwards to the wall opposite his seat, care being taken that we should never turn our backs on him. The Sultan then listened to what I had to say; but the language I held was not at all to his taste, for the demands of his Majesty breathed a spirit of independence and dignity . . . and so he made no answer beyond saying in a tetchy way, "Giusel, giusel," i.e. well, well. . .

. . .

With all this luxury great simplicity and economy are combined; every man's dress, whatever his position may be, is of the same pattern; no fringes or useless points are sewn on, as is the case with us. . . . They were quite as much surprised at our manner of dressing as we were at theirs. They use long robes reaching down to the ankles, which have a stately effect and add to the wearer's height, while our dress is so short and scanty that it leaves exposed to view more than is comely of the human shape; . . .

I was greatly struck with the silence and order that prevailed in this great crowd. There were no cries, no hum of voices, the usual accompaniments of a motley gathering, neither was there any jostling; without the slightest disturbance each man took his proper place according to his rank. The Agas, as they call their chiefs, were seated, to wit, generals, colonels (*bimbashi*), and captains (*soubashi*). Men of a lower position stood. The most interesting sight in this assembly was a body of several thousand Janissaries, who were drawn up in a long line apart from the rest; their array was so steady and motionless that, being at a little distance, it was some time before I could make up my mind as to whether they were human beings or statues; at last I received a hint to salute them, and saw all their heads bending at the same moment to return my bow.

. . .

When the cavalry had ridden past, they were followed by a long procession of Janissaries, but few of whom carried any arms except their regular weapon, the musket. They were dressed in uniforms of almost the same shape and colour, so that you might recognize them to be the slaves, . . . There is only one thing in which they are extravagant, viz., plumes, headdresses, etc., and veterans who formed the rear guard were specially distinguished by ornaments of this kind. The plumes which they insert in their frontlets might well be mistaken for a walking forst.

STUDY QUESTIONS

1. Why were order and discipline apparently so important at Suleiman's court?
2. Why might Ghiselin have found the Janissaries so particularly impressive?

14.3. FROM CHRISTOPHER MARLOWE, *THE MASSACRE AT PARIS*, CA. 1593

Christopher Marlowe (before 1564–1593) was an Elizabethan poet and playwright, historically connected with Shakespeare's work—until his mysterious assassination, Marlowe was England's most celebrated dramatist, a title Shakespeare then inherited. His play *Massacre at Paris* describes

Marlowe, *The Massacre at Paris*. (Oxford: The Malone Society Reprints, 1928), lines 504–542, 578–633.

the horrific event known as the Saint Bartholomew's Day massacre (beginning on 23 August 1572), in which the ruling Catholic majority arranged the simultaneous assassination of the leaders of the dissenting Protestant (Huguenot) party. The surviving manuscript is most likely reconstructed from the memory of the play's actors, but nonetheless gives a glimpse into how deadly religious disagreement could become in early modern France. These scenes show the Catholic Duke of Guise's attempts to limit Huguenot survivors; attitudes toward "heretical" corpses; and concerns about inheritance of the French throne in this era of dramatic turmoil.

GUISE: My Lord of *Anjoy*, there are a hundred Protestants.
 Which we have chased into the river rene,
 That swim about and so preserve their lives:
 How may we do? I fear me they will live.
DUMAINE: go place some men upon the bridge,
 With bows and darts to shoot at them as they flee, 510
 And sink them in the river as they swim.
 Guise.
GUISE: Tis well advice *Dumaine*, go see that it be done.
 And in the meantime my Lord, could we devise
 To get those pedants from the King *Navarre*,
 that are tutors to him and the prince of *Condy.*
ANJOY. For that let me alone, Cousin stay you here,
 And when you see me in, then follow hard.
 He knocks, and enter the King of Navarre *and Prince of* Condy, *with their schoolmasters.*
 How now my Lords, how fare you? 521
NAVARRE: My Lord, they say that all the Protestants are massacred.
ANJOY: I, so they are, but yet what remedy:
 I have done what I could to stay this broil.
NAVARRE. But yet my Lord the report does run,
 That you were one that made this Massacre.
AN: Who I, you are deceived, I rose but now.
ENTER GUISE. (HENCE.
GUISE: Murder the Hugonets, take those pedants 530
NA: Thou traitor *Guise*, lay off thy bloody hands.
CONDY: Come let us go tell the King.*Exeunt.*
GUISE: Come sirs, I'll whip you to death with my Dagger's point. *he kills them.*
AN: Away with them both. *Exit* Anjoy.
GUISE. And now sirs for this night let our fury stay.
 Yet will we not that the Massacre shall end,
 Gonzago posse you to Orleance,
 Retes to Deep, *Mountsorrell* unto Roan,

and spare not one that you suspect of heresy. 540
And now stay that bell that to the devils Mattins rings.
   Now.
 . . .

Enter two with the Admirals *body.* *sc. vii*
1. Now sirra, what shall we do with the Admiral? 580
2. Why let us burn him for a heretic.
1. O no, his body will infect the fire, and the fire the air, and so we shall be poisoned with him.
2. What shall we do then?
1. Let's throw him into the river.
2. Oh it will corrupt the water, and the water the fish, and by the fish ourselves when we eat them.
1. Then throw him into the ditch. 590
2. No, no, to decide all doubts, be ruled by me, let's hang him here upon this tree.
1. Agreed. *They hang him.*

Enter the Duke of Guise, and Queen Mother, *and the Cardinal.*
GUISE: Now Madame, how like you our lusty Admiral?
[B 5] *Queen.*
QUEEN: Believe me *Guise* he becomes the place so well,
 As I could long before this have wished him there. 600
 But come let's walk aside, the air is not very sweet.
GUISE: No by my faith Madam.
 Sire, take him away and throw him in some ditch.
 carry away the dead body.
 And now Madam as I understand,
 There are a hundred Hugonets and more,

Which in the woods do horde their synagogue:
And daily meet about this time of day,
And thither will I to put them to the sword.

QU: Do so sweet *Guise*, let us delay no time,   610
For if these stragglers gather head again,
And disperse themselves throughout the Realm of France,
It will be hard for us to work their deaths.
Be gone, delay no time sweet *Guise*.

GUISE: Madam I go as whirl-winds rage
before a storm.   *Exit* Guise.

QU: My Lord of Loraine have you marked of late,
How *Charles* our son begins for to lament:
For the late nights work which my Lord of
Guise   620

Did make in Paris amongst the Hugonites?

CARD: Madam, I have heard him solemnly vow,
With the rebellious King of *Navarre*,
For to revenge their deaths upon us all.

QU: I, but my Lord let me alone for that,
For *Katherine* must have her will in France:
As I do live, for surely he die.
                                     And
The Massacre
And *Henry* then shall wear the diadem.
And if he grudge or cross his Mothers will,
I'll disinherit him and all the rest:(crown: 630
For I'll rule France, but they shall wear the
And if they storm, I then may pull them down.
Come my Lord lets us go.   *Exeunt.*

STUDY QUESTIONS

1. What seems to be motivating Guise, Anjou, and the Queen Mother Catherine in their deliberations about the impending massacre?
2. How might this play have appealed to Elizabethan English audiences, who had not experienced the French Wars of Religion in the 1570s and 1580s?

14.4. JOHANNES JUNIUS, LETTER TO HIS DAUGHTER AND TRIAL TRANSCRIPT, 1628[1]

Johannes Junius (1573–1628), the mayor of Bamberg, Germany, was accused of witchcraft during the craze of 1628. Before his tragic execution, Junius wrote a moving letter to his daughter Veronica so that she would understand the charges brought against him and the torture he endured. Amid prayers to keep him in God's care, Junius describes false witnesses brought against him, his sufferings, and the lies that he finally "confessed" to no avail. The transcript of his trial has survived as well and permits a glimpse into the terrifying machinery of the witch-hunts.

From Johannes Junius, "Letter from Prison." Bamberg, 1628. Trans. Clifford R. Backman.

[1] http://books.google.com/books?id=wHW7AAAAIAAJ&pg=PA159&lpg=PA159&dq=johannes+junius&source=bl&ots=9 1EOUoCn2T&sig=7mVYuNIPTADtXHHO4WcCCzEiIxE&hl=en&sa=X&ei=voVxUPmAHLOP0QGYsYGACQ&ved=0 CDYQ6AEwAQ#v=onepage&q=johannes%20junius&f=false/

Ahundred thousand Good Nights, my darling Veronica, my daughter. Innocent have I been imprisoned, innocent have I been tortured, and innocent must I die—for whoever comes into this place must become a witch, or else he will be tortured until he invents something (may God have mercy) and confesses to it. I will tell you everything that has happened to me. The first time I was brought before the court Doctor Braun, Doctor Kötzendorffer, and two other doctors whom I did not know were there [SEVERAL WORDS MISSING] Then Doctor Braun asked me from the gallery, "How did you end up here, brother?" "Bad luck," I answered. "Listen!" he said, "You are a witch! Will you confess it freely? If not, they will put witnesses and the executioner in front of you." I said, "I've been betrayed! My conscience is clean. Even if they bring a thousand witnesses, I'm not worried. I'll gladly listen to their witnesses." Then the Chancellor's son was brought forth. I asked him, "Herr Doctor, what do you know about me? I have never seen you before in all my life, whether for good or for bad." And he gave me in answer, "Friend, I know you from the district court. I asked you for a pardon when I appeared before you in court." "Yes, but so what?" He said nothing. So I asked the Lord Commissioner to question him under oath. Doctor Braun said that "he need not do what he does not wish to do; it is enough that he has stated he saw you. Step down now, Herr Doctor!" I said, "My lords, what kind of evidence is that? If that is how this process goes, then how can you be any more sure it was me [he saw] than some other honest man?" But no one would listen to me. Then the Chancellor came up and said that he too, just like his son, had seen me [at a witch-gathering]. But he knew me only by reputation, nothing more. Then came Hopfen-Else, who said she had seen me dance on the Hauptmoor. "With whom?" I asked. She replied that she didn't know. I then swore on oath to the lord justices that what they had heard was all pure lies, so help me God, and that they should ask these witnesses of theirs to be truthful and honest. But they did not wish to know the truth, or else they would have said so; instead they wanted me to confess freely, or else the executioner would drag it out of me. I answered, "I have never renounced God and will never do so. May God in His grace keep me from such a thing! I would rather suffer anything, than that." And

that was when—O God in Highest Heaven have pity!—in came the executioner, who tied my hands together and twisted thumbscrews on them until blood flowed out from my nails and all over; for four weeks I couldn't use my hands, as you can see by my writing. I thought about the five Holy Wounds suffered by God and said, since as far as the name and glory of God was concerned I had not renounced them, I would commend my innocence and all my agony and suffering to His Five Wounds. He would ease my pain, so that I could endure any amount of it. But then they hauled me up, hands bound behind my back, and lifted me in the hanging torture. I thought then that heaven and earth were ending. Six times they hoisted me up in this way, and then let me fall. The pain was horrible.

All of this happened while I was stark naked, since they had stripped me and left me that way. Since no one but Our Lord God could help me, I called out to Him, saying, "Forgive them. O God, for they are hurting an innocent man! They care nothing for my life and soul! They only want to seize my wealth and possessions!" Then Doctor Braun said, "You are a devil!" I answered, "I'm no devil or any such thing. I'm as innocent as any one of you! And if anyone doubts me, then no honest man in all of Bamberg is safe—not you, not me, not anyone else!"

The Doctor then cried out that he would not be challenged by a devil. "Neither will I!" I shouted. "But these false witnesses are the devil, and so is this wretched torture of yours—for it lets no one go free, and no one can endure it."

All of this occurred on Friday, 30 June, when I was forced to endure, with God's help, the torture. Throughout that entire time I was strung up and could not use my hands, but suffered pain upon pain despite my innocence. When the executioner finally led me back to my prison cell he said to me, "I beg you, sir! For God's sake, confess to something, whether it's true or not! Invent something—for you won't be able to survive the torturing they plan for you. Even if you do survive, you'll never go free. Not even if you were an earl. It will just be one torture after another, until you confess and say that you are a witch. Only then will they let you go free. That's how all these trials go, each one just like the other."

Sometime after this, Georg came and told me that the Commissioner had declared he wanted to make such an example of me that people would talk about it for a long time. They had already brought in several more torturers, just for me. Georg too pleaded with me, for God's sake, to confess to something, for even if I were entirely innocent I would never again go free. The candle-maker, the lamplighter, and a few others, too, told me the same thing. Since I was in such a sad plight, I asked to be granted a day to think things over and consult with a priest. They denied me a priest but allowed me some time to think.

So now, dear daughter, what do you think about the danger I was in, and still am in? I have to confess to being a witch even though I am not one, and must do for the first time something that I have never before considered—renounce God. I wrestled with myself day and night over this, until finally an idea came to me one night as I was praying, showing how I need not be troubled: since I was denied a priest, with whom I could take counsel, I would simply invent something and say it. How much better it would be to simply confess something by the words of my mouth even though it was not actually true. I could confess my lie later, and the fault would be on those who had forced me to do it. I could explain that I had asked to see a priest from the Dominican cloister but had been refused. And so, here follows my sworn statement—the entire thing a lie. Dearest child, what follows is the affidavit I made on account of the horrible pain, the cruel torture, I suffered and could endure no longer.

In 1624 or 1625 I had gone on city business to the town of Rottweil, and had to carry about six hundred florins with me in order to conduct some legal affairs on behalf of Doctor Braun and the city—which is why I had taken counsel with so many honest people who had helped me out. Everything that follows appears in my affidavit, but is nothing but a pure lie—a lie I told in light of the horrible, monstrous torture that compelled me, and for which I now must die. In my affidavit it says that I went into my field at Friedrichsbrunnen, and was so troubled that I had to sit down. While I was there a peasant girl approached and asked, "What's wrong, sir? Why are you so sad?" "I don't know," I replied. She drew closer to me and did several things to me that resulted in my lying with her, and no sooner was this done than she turned into a goat and said, "Behold, now you can see who you've been dealing

with." Then he grabbed me by the throat and said, "You must be mine now, or else I'll kill you!" "God save me!" I cried. He disappeared suddenly, then just as suddenly he reappeared with two women and two men at his side. I was forced to renounce God, which I did, and at the same time I renounced the Lord of Heaven. After this, he baptized me—and the two women he had brought became my godmothers. Then they gave me a gold coin as a token, but it was really just a potsherd. It seemed to me that I had survived, for they then led me to stand alongside the executioner. Where was I during the dances? I confessed then and there, after giving it some thought, what I had heard from the Chancellor, his son, and Hopfen-Else, and all the elders of the court, the council-room: the Hauptmoor—just as I had heard in the reading of the initial charges against me. So that was the name of the site that I gave.

Next I was told to identify the people I had seen there. I said that I had not recognized anyone. "You devil! I'll put the executioner at your throat! Tell us! Wasn't the Chancellor there?" I said he was. "Who else?" I said I hadn't recognized anyone else. So he said, "Take one street after another; start at the market then go up one street and down the next." I had to name a few people at least. Then came the long street—I had to name at least one person there. Next the Zinkenwörth—one person more. Then over the upper bridge to both sides of the Bergtor. I knew nobody. Did I recognize anyone from the castle, anyone at all? I should speak without fear. They carried on this way for street after street, but there was nothing more I could or would say, so they handed me over to the executioner, saying that he should strip me, cut off all my hair, and start to torture me again. "This devil knows someone in the market, sees him every day, and yet refuses to identify him!" They meant Dietmeyer—so I had to identify him too.

Then they made me tell what evils I had committed. "None," I replied, "the Devil had wanted me to do something, but I had refused, and so he beat me." "Haul the fellow up!" So I said that I was supposed to murder my own children, but I had killed a horse instead. That didn't help, though, [so I said that] I had also taken a piece of the Host and had desecrated it. Once I had said this, they left me in peace.

Dear child, you now have my entire confession and the reasons for which I must die. They are nothing but lies and imaginings, so help me God. I said all these things out of fear of the wretched torture that was threatened beyond what I had already suffered; they never stop with the torturing until one confesses something. No matter how pious a man might be, he will confess to being a witch. No one escapes, not even a lord. If God allows no remedy that would let the light of day shine through, the whole family is done for. One has to denounce other people, even if one knows nothing at all about them, as I have had to do—and God in Heaven knows that I know next to nothing about [the people I accused]. I die an innocent man, like a martyr. Dearest child, I know that you are every bit as devout as I am, but even you have told a few lies in your time, and if I may be permitted to give you some advice: take all the money and letters you have [SEVERAL WORDS MISSING] and devote half a year to a holy pilgrimage, and do everything you can, in that time period, to [SEVERAL WORDS MISSING]. I recommend doing this until it becomes clear that your resources have run out. This way, at least, there will be some honest men and women in Bamberg, both in the church and in the world of business—people who do not know evil and who have clean consciences, as I once was (as you know) before my arrest. Nevertheless, they very well may find themselves in the witch-prison; for all it takes is for a rumor about an individual to go around, no matter if he is honest or not. Herr Neudecker, the Chancellor, his son, the candle-maker, the daughter of Wolff Hoffmeister, and Hopfen-Else have all testified against me, all at the same time. Their testimony was all false, drawn out of them by force, as they all told me later when they begged my forgiveness in God's name before they were executed. Their last words to me were that they knew nothing but good of me. They had been forced to lie, just as I was. I am done for, for sure. That's how it is for many people now, and will be for many more yet to come, if God does not shine a path out of this darkness. I have nothing more to say.

Dear child, hide this letter so that no one ever sees it. Or else I will be tortured yet again, and piteously; more than that, my jailers would be beheaded—so strongly is it forbidden [to smuggle out letters]. Herr Steiner, my cousin, is familiar to you—you can trust him and [SEVERAL WORDS MISSING] him read it. He is a discreet man.

Dear child, pay this man a Reichstaler [SEVERAL WORDS MISSING].

It has taken me several days to write this, since my hands are broken. I am in a wretched state. I beg you, in the light of Judgment Day, to keep this letter safe, and to pray for me, your father, as you would for a true martyr. After my death, do as you wish but be careful not to let anyone see this letter. Please ask Anna Maria also to pray for me. You can swear it on oath that I was not a witch but a martyr, and that I died as such.

A thousand times Good Night. Your father, Johannes Junius, will never see you again. 24 July 1628.

STUDY QUESTION

1. Why does Junius fail to convince his accusers of his innocence of witchcraft?

CHAPTER 15

FROM WESTPHALIA TO PARIS: REGIMES OLD AND NEW

15.1. ANNE OF FRANCE, *LESSONS FOR MY DAUGHTER* (END 16TH CENTURY)

"Madame la Grande," as she was called, was the daughter of King Louis XI of France and briefly the regent for her brother Charles VIII. Anne (1461–1522) was an able stateswoman who managed royal lands and the ducal territories of her husband and oversaw the education and raising of aristocratic offspring. In this vein, Anne wrote a handbook for her only daughter, Suzanne, guiding her through the courtly gauntlet. Like Dhuoda's handbook to her son (Document 8.5), Anne attempts to help her daughter avoid the pitfalls of courtly life—but in this case, a woman's worst enemies are frivolity, immodesty, and a quick tongue. The Dr. Lienard referred to several times in this passage cannot be identified.

And so, my daughter, devote yourself completely to acquiring virtue. Behave so that your reputation may be worthy of perpetual memory: whatever you do, above all, be truly honest, humble, courteous, and loyal. Believe firmly that if even a small fault or lie were to be found in you, it would be a great reproach. As Doctor Lienard writes in his argument about lying, it is the worst of all the vices, foul and dishonest to God and the world. Now then, my daughter, if you would like to be numbered among worthy women and to have a good and honest reputation, be very careful to avoid it. And as Socrates says, do not like those foolish idlers who, in their idiocy, think themselves wise and worthy when they deceive and abuse many people with their evil and venomous cunning, which is detestable

to God and abominable to the world. And as the aforementioned Doctor Lienard says, no man or woman of great rank who has good judgment wants to have such a reputation. And he also says there are many dishonest and evil nobles in the world today who come from good families and have a large following, but, to speak frankly and truthfully, those who follow them are either fools or have business with them. Be assured, as the aforesaid doctor says, that if their followers flatter them to their faces, they damn them behind their backs. Finally, as Saint Ambrose says, whatever pretences they make and however long it takes, in the end such people are neither loved by God nor the world. Wise men say you should fly from them as if they were poison no matter how pleasing their greetings and no matter

Translation by Clifford R. Backman.

how charming their pastimes—in the end, associating with them is too perilous. And so, my daughter, protect yourself from them and their deceptive company.

. . .

And so, my daughter, because virtues and good works are as well praised, loved, and valued in this world as they are in the next, you should take great pains to be virtuous; to this end, make sure that your conversation is always honest and good, that you are courteous and amiable in all things, and that you are pleasant to all and loved by all. And, truly, when it comes to love, the Philosopher says honesty must be its foundation because any other "love" is only false treachery and hypocrisy—with all the authority and power that a mother can and should have over a daughter, I command you to flee from such love. It is important to control your bearing, your expressions, your words, your sentiments, your thoughts, your desires, your wishes, and your passions. As Saint Paul says, of all the temptations and subtle deceptions in the world, this is one of the worst, and from "love" comes great evil, so dishonestly is it practiced today. As many doctors agree, there is no man of worth, however, noble he may be, who does not use treachery, nor to whom it does not seem good sport to deceive or trick women of rank from one good family or another, it doesn't matter which. And Doctor Lienard says there is no man so perfect who, in matters of love, is truthful or keeps his word, however firm or fervent—which I certainly believe. One time I heard a noble woman of great rank tell about a knight she knew who, in such a situation, took a solemn oath of his own free will, on his honor as a gentleman, on the altar and on a missal where Mass is said everyday—and this knight did not keep his oath for more than four hours! And, as she told me, the oath was very reasonable and, with all respect to his honor and conscience, he had no excuse whatsoever for breaking it except his own lust, weak will, and sudden change of heart. Therefore, my daughter, whatever flattering speeches or great signs of love that someone may make you, trust none of them. As Doctor Lienard says, those who are wisest and think they are following the right path are often the first to be misled. . . . Although, certainly, it must be said that when those of virtuous character come together, by one means or another, love can be marvelously great and, in the end, good and honest.

But when this does happen, as Doctor Lienard says at the end of his argument about true love, the enemy, who is full of venomous subtlety, uses his power to break and distance such love because of the great goods and honors that result from it. . . . Therefore, for the greatest certainty in such situations, I advise you to avoid all private meetings, no matter how pleasant they are, because, as you have seen, many an honest beginning comes to dishonest and harmful end. And even when it seems all is for the best, you must also fear the foolish and the irresponsible opinions others often express, to the prejudice of women and at their expense. As Doctor Lienard says, in this situation and in others, the world is so vile and so corrupt that true love is hardly understood or recognized.

. . .

For this reason, my daughter, heed this example and, wherever you are, avoid making any unpleasant faces and shaking or turning your head this way and that, and do not stare, peer around you, or let your eyes wander. Also, make sure you do not laugh too much for any reason because it is very unbecoming, especially for young noblewomen, whose manners should be more solemn, gentler, and more controlled than the manners of others. Nor should you talk too much or too sharply like many foolish and conceited women who want to attract attention and, to be more admired, speak boldly and in a flighty way, responding to everyone and on all topics, which is very unbecoming in all women, whatever their state, but especially so for young virgins, rich and poor alike, who must protect their reputations. Because of their careless talk, many young women are judged to be foolish and unchaste; as one philosopher says, the way a woman minds her eyes and her tongue is an indication of her chastity. For this reason, my daughter, always use your eyes and tongue cautiously and carefully; that is, know when to speak and where your eyes belong, never be the first or the last to talk, and do not be a tale-teller, especially of something unpleasant or prejudicial. Also, be slow and cool in all your responses because, as wise men say, on some subjects a reply cannot be avoided. Also, take care not to run or jump, and do not pinch or hit anyone. Likewise suffer no man to touch your body, no matter who he is, no holding of hands or pressing of feet. In conclusion, my daughter, remember those three aforementioned daughters who were the cause of their mother's death, and do not behave so that your bad conduct is the cause of mine.

. . .

I do not wish to say that . . . in hearing, speaking, and responding to honest questions and proposals you might not sometimes encounter the bad as well as the good. But, suppose a castle is beautiful and so well-guarded that it is never assailed—then it is not to be praised, nor is a knight who has never proven himself to be commended for his prowess. To the contrary, the thing most highly commended is that which has been in the fire yet cannot be scorched (or worse) or that which has been in the terrible depths of the sea yet cannot be drowned or that which has been in the mire of this world yet cannot be soiled in any way. Worthy of being praised, therefore, are women who in this miserable world know to live in purity of conscience and chastity; they are worthy of eternal glory because by their steadfast chastity and good virtue they redirect fools, disordered in their carnality, to the good road. As the saying goes, the habit does not make the monk, and sometimes those you think are the biggest deceivers and the most worldly are easiest to convert and greatly to be commended. Nevertheless, in this situation there is no certainty, and I counsel more doubt than surety. As Saint Paul says, the assaults and stings of this world are hard to endure except with the help of God, with which nothing is impossible.

STUDY QUESTIONS

1. Is it even more essential for women to channel their thoughts and words into virtuous paths than for their male counterparts?
2. How can a woman avoid scandalous talk, even if standards of behavior are applied unequally to females?

15.2. MOLIÈRE, *THE MISANTHROPE,* FIRST PERFORMED 1666

An actor who abandoned social prestige for the stage, Jean-Baptiste Poquelin (1622–1673), better known as Molière, numbers among the greatest comedy playwrights. His French plays incorporated traits of Commedia dell'arte while poking fun at the foibles of mankind—such as the hypochondriac obsessions of the Imaginary Invalid. The Misanthrope, a comedy of manners, centers around the plight of Alceste, who adores the flirt Célimène while simultaneously condemning her for blindly obeying social niceties, such as politeness toward strangers. When he ultimately discovers that Célimène has led him on, Alceste decides that self-imposed exile from society to be the only solution to his misanthropic loathing.

ACT I

SCENE 1

Alceste, Philinte

PHILINTE: Oh, what's the matter? What's wrong now?

ALCESTE: Leave me alone.
　　Go away.

PHILINTE: But why must you adopt this angry tone? . . .

ALCESTE: Oh, leave me here, I said. Go, run away
　　and hide.

The Misanthrope, Tartuffe, and Other Plays, translated by Slater (2009) 1397w from pp. 209–213. By permission of Oxford University Press.

PHILINTE: Alceste, don't lose your temper. Listen, then decide.

ALCESTE: I want to lose my temper, and to make a stand.

PHILINTE: I find your angry rantings hard to understand.
Although we're still good friends, I really must insist . . .

ALCESTE: What? Me, your friend? Why don't you cross me off your list?
It's true I've always made a show of liking you;
But now I've witnessed your behaviour, we're through.
I tell you, I don't want your friendship any more—
I hate you, now I know you're rotten to the core.

PHILINTE: You seem to have decided I'm the one to blame . . .

ALCESTE: That's right. Why don't you crawl away and die of shame?
I'mtellingyou,there'snoexcuseforwhatyou'vedone—
Your antics must seem scandalous to everyone.
You met a man, you treated him as your best friend,
You were all over him, you hugged him without end,
You said he mattered to you, swore by Heaven above
That what you felt for him was liking, even love.
I asked you for the fellow's name, when he had gone,
And you scarcely remembered who he was—come on!
No sooner had he turned his back on you, I swear,
You spoke of him to me, as if you didn't care.
Good grief! The way you carry on is a disgrace.
You worthless coward, must you really be so base?
If I had done what you've just done, do you know what
I'd do? I'd go and hang myself, right on the spot.

PHILINTE: Come on, it's not a hanging matter, so don't tease.
I beg leave to appeal against my sentence, please.
It's time you showed some mercy. Don't be quite so hard.
What, make me hang myself for that? What a charade!

ALCESTE: Oh, very funny! That was typical of you.

PHILINTE: But, seriously, what am I supposed to do?

ALCESTE: You should be honourable, honest, without art,
And everything you say should come straight from the heart.

PHILINTE: But when a stranger rushes up and hugs you tight,
You have to hug him back—it seems only polite;
You can't keep him at arm's length, you must play the game,
And if he swears you're his best friend, you do the same.

ALCESTE: No. Your hypocrisy disgusts me, and that's flat.
You fashionable types, you all behave like that.
I tell you, I can't stand the phoney posturing
Of men who claim they like you more than anything,
And fling their arms around you, kiss you on the cheek,
Insist that they adore you, every time they speak.
They've perfect manners, and they obey the rules,
But decent men are treated on a par with fool.
Look, I mean, what's the point of someone kissing you,
And swearing he appreciates and loves you too,
Proclaiming to the world that you're the only one,
Then rushing off to do the same to everyone?
No. If a man who has the slightest self-respect
Is faced with such hypocrisy, he must object.
For very little's added to our sense of worth
If we're the same as all the others on this earth.
If you respect a man, believing he's the best,
Don't put him on an equal footing with the rest.
Now you're no different from the other fellows, so,
Damn it, you're not the sort of man I want to know.
I can't value a friend who puts himself about,
And doesn't see why merit should be singled out.
I want to be distinguished from the rest, you see:
The friend of all humanity's no friend to me.

PHILINTE: But, in polite society, you have to do
Your bit, or people won't think very well of you.

ALCESTE: Nonsense! I say, the time has come to make a stand
Against these hypocrites. I want them to be banned.
I want us to be proper men, and when we meet,

To show our secret, inner thoughts, without deceit.
We must speak from the heart, lay bare our sentiments,
Not hide the truth with empty, formal compliments.

PHILINTE: It won't work. There are times when total frankness would
Be idiotic, totally misunderstood.
And sometimes, even if we find it an ordeal,
It's better to suppress the truth of what we feel.
Truth can be inappropriate; most people shrink
From telling everyone precisely what they think.
Whatifweknowsomeonewehate,orfinduncouth—
Are we supposed to tell the whole, unvarnished truth?

ALCESTE: Yes.

PHILINTE: What, you want to go to poor old Emilie,
And tell her she's too old to dress so prettily—
With all that make-up, she looks like a painted whore?

ALCESTE: That's right.

PHILINTE: Should we tell Dorilas he's a great bore?
The courtiers hate the way he shows off endlessly,
And boasts about his courage, and his pedigree.

ALCESTE: We should.

PHILINTE: You must be joking.

ALCESTE: Joking? not at all.
I tell you, we must spare nobody, great or small.
My eyes are never spared, at court or in the town:
I'm always shaving to see sights that make me frown.
It puts me in a rage, to see what I detest:
The way men treat each other makes me so depressed.
Hypocrisy is everywhere, and flattery,
And crude self-interest, and even treachery.
I've had enough. Mankind's an absolute disgrace.
I'll make a stand, alone against the human race.

PHILINTE: Your grim philosophy is too morose by half.
Your fits of black depression simply make me laugh.
It strikes me we resemble, in a curious way,
The brothers in The School for Husbands, Molière's play,
Who . . .

ALCESTE: Good God! Some comparison. Please, let that drop.

PHILINTE: Fine. Let's be serious. I'm asking you to stop
This madness. You won't change the world with what you do,
And since this frankness seems to have such charms for you,
I tell you, frankly, you've become so querulous,
That, nowadays, the world finds you ridiculous.
You turn your nose up, claim our modern manners shock,
But everyone around thinks you're a laughing stock.

ALCESTE: Well, good, damn it! Yes, good! I ask for nothing more.
I'm quite delighted, that's what I've been hoping for.
Since everyone I know seems hateful in my eyes,
I'd be disgusted, if they thought that I was wise.

PHILINTE: Why blame the human race? You're eaten up with hate.

ALCESTE: It overwhelms me totally—I'm desperate.

PHILINTE: You say you loathe us all, without exception, and
There's not a single human being you can stand?
Can't you imagine any situation when . . . ?

ALCESTE: No. My disgust is general. I hate all men—
Hate some of them because they are in an evil crew,
And others for condoning what the villains do,
Instead of treating them with loathing and contempt,
As they deserve. They might at least make an attempt
To judge that fellow who's no better than he ought,
I mean the filthy beast who's taken me to court:
His wickedness shines out behind his bland façade,
And everybody knows his manner's a charade.
He sighs and rolls his eyes, and mouths his platitudes,
But no one's taken in, save idiots or prudes.
Confound him! He's got his flat foot in every door.
He gets on in the world by dirty tricks, what's more.
He does so well, living off his ill-gotten gains,
Ironically, he's rewarded for his pains—
He has some sort of title, which he likes to use,
But all his posturing can't alter people's views.
Call him confounded liar, no one will object;

Say he's a fraud, and nobody will contradict.
Yet, with his smirking face, he gets himself received
In the best circles, though his hosts are not deceived.
He knows all the right people, so he always wins.

He beats his rivals, though he can't conceal his sins.
Yes, curse him, every time! It cuts me to the quick
To see him get away with every dirty trick.
Sometimes, it overwhelms me. I feel mortified
By all mankind, and long to run away and hide.

STUDY QUESTIONS

1. How does Alceste skewer the phoniness and hypocrisy of "polite society"?
2. What does he believe will happen, even if the essentially fraudulent nature of this society is exposed?

15.3. CARDINAL RICHELIEU, "THE ROLE OF THE KING," *POLITICAL TESTAMENT,* CA. 1638, FIRST PUBLISHED 1688

Armand Jean du Plessis (1585–1642), the Duke of Richelieu and a Catholic bishop, became the First Minister for King Louis XIII. He worked to centralize the French state at the expense of the nobility and factions; this included curtailing the political liberties of the Huguenots but supporting them in the Thirty Years' War (1618–1648) to limit Austrian and Spanish power before a strong French king. His *Political Testament*, one of many works, would have served as a guide for the young Louis XIII in case Richelieu fell prey to his frequent illnesses—which explains its hasty, jotted-down feel. This selection outlines the proper role of the king in Richelieu's vision of a strongly centralized France.

CHAPTER VI

THE ROLE OF THE KING

God is the principle of all things, the sovereign master of kings, and the only one who can make their reigns happy. If the devotion of Your Majesty were not known to all, I would begin this chapter, which is concerned with your person, by stating to you that should you not follow the wishes of your Creator and submit to His laws you could not hope to have yours observed by subjects obedient to your orders.

But it would be a superfluous gesture to exhort Your Majesty in the matter of devotion. You are so bent toward it by inclination and so confirmed in it by virtuous habit that there is no reason to fear you might turn away from it. It is because of this that in place of showing you the advantage religious principles have over others I will content myself with observing that although devotion is necessary for kings, it ought to be devoid of all over-scrupulousness. I say this, Sire, because the sensitiveness of Your Majesty's conscience has often made you fear to offend God in

Hill, Henry Bertram, *The Political Testament of Cardinal Richelieu*. © 1961 by the Board of Regents of the University of Wisconsin System. Reprinted by permission of The University of Wisconsin Press.

reaching even those decisions which you cannot abstain from making without sin.

I well know that faults of such a nature in a prince are much less dangerous for a state than those which lean in the direction of presumption and disrespect toward that which a monarch should revere. But since they are faults, it is necessary to correct them, as it is most certain that they have resulted in many inconveniences prejudicial to the interests of the state. I beseech you, in this matter, to try to fortify yourself against your scruples, reminding yourself that you can never be guilty in the eyes of God if, on occasions involving difficult discussions of matters of conscience, you follow the advice of your council, confirmed by that of several competent theologians not suspected of having an interest in the question.

The basic problem recognized, there remains nothing else of a personal nature intrinsically necessary to the successful conducting of your affairs save the preservation of your health, and I cannot go on without giving it special emphasis. Long, thorough, and persistent observation of your conduct in all sorts of circumstances emboldens me to say that nothing is more important than the proper direction of your will, which otherwise can be a most powerful enemy, as it so often is with princes who cannot be prevailed upon to do not only what is useful but what is even absolutely necessary. Your Majesty's mind so completely dominates your body that the slightest emotional upset affects your whole being. Many occurrences of this have made me so certain of the truth of my diagnosis that I am convinced I have never seen you ill in any other way.

God has seen fit to give Your Majesty the force of character necessary to act with firmness when confronted with business of the greatest importance. But as a balance to this noble quality He has often allowed you to be sensitive to matters so small that no one in advance would suspect they might trouble you and thus try to protect you from their bothersomeness. So far, time alone has provided the only remedy for these overwhelming experiences of which the inward consequence has always been a bodily indisposition. You are, in this regard, much like those whose great courage makes them disdain the blows of a sword but who cannot, because of a certain natural antipathy, stand the puncture of the scalpel. It is impossible for many men to anticipate the surprises which will come from their emotions. I do not think, however, that such is the case with Your Majesty, who has many excellent qualities most people do not have. I believe that, in all likelihood, the first ebullience of your ardent youth having passed, the stability of a greater maturity will help you protect yourself by forethought in the future from an enemy which is all the more dangerous because it is internal and domestic, and which has already caused you misfortune serious enough on two or three occasions to have brought your life in jeopardy.

Just as this is a matter of great importance for your health, so is it also for your reputation and glory, for which it should always appear that reason prevailed over your emotions. I cannot help repeating again a plea that I have made many times before to Your Majesty, begging you to apply yourself to the matters of greatest importance to your country, disdaining the little ones as beneath your thought and interest. It would be useful and inspiring for you to dwell often upon the vast prospects of the trend of events. If you preoccupy yourself with the small matters, you will not only fail to gain benefit therefrom, you will even bring misfortune upon yourself. Not only does such a preoccupation divert you from a better one. Just as little thorns are more capable of pricking than larger ones, which are more easily seen, so it would be impossible for you to protect yourself from many unpleasant happenings inconsequential for public business and bad for your own health.

The great emotional outbursts to which you have been subject on several occasions urge me to tell you here, as I have earlier done more than once, that while there are certain public charges necessary to the furtherance of state affairs which you much perform, there are others the performance of which can do no less than destroy the good disposition of whoever plunges into them. This in turn so adversely affects those charged with carrying out decisions that they too are less able to do what is expected of them. The experience of governing that Your Majesty has acquired from a reign which thus far has lasted twenty-five years makes you well aware of the fact that the outcome of large undertakings rarely confirms directly with the orders initially given. It also teaches you that you might better have compassion for those charged with the execution of your commands when their efforts do not succeed, rather than to blame them for the poor results for which they may not be responsible. It is only God whose acts are infallible, and yet His goodness is such that, letting men act as their weakness directs, He even so overlooks the gulf between their deeds and His standards. This should teach kings to tolerate with patient reasonableness what the Creator endured assuredly because of His benevolence.

Your Majesty being by nature delicate, with a weak constitution, and a restless, impatient disposition, particularly when you are with the army where you always insist on taking the command, I believe it would be committing a crime if I did not beseech you to avoid war in the future in as far as it is possible. This plea I base upon the fact that the frivolousness and unreliability of the French can generally be overcome only by their master's presence and that Your Majesty cannot, without endangering your health, commit yourself to a program of long duration with the hope of success. You have made the valor and strength of your arms well enough known to entitle you in the future to think only of how to enjoy the peace your efforts have brought to the realm, while ever being on the alert to defend it against all those who might break their pledge and attack it again.

Although it is common enough with many men to act only when driven by some emotion, so that one may conceive of them as being like incense which smells sweet only when it is being burned, I cannot help reminding Your Majesty that such a character trait is dangerous in any kind of person, and it is particularly so in kings, who more than all others should be motivated by reason. If emotion once in a while does in fact bring good results, it is only a matter of luck, since by its very nature it misleads men so much that it blinds those who are possessed by it. If a man so deprived of sight occasionally does find the proper course, it is a marvel if he does not stray and get lost completely. And if he does not fall down he will certainly need the best of good fortune not to falter many times. Often indeed have evils befallen princes and their countries when they have been more

inclined to follow their emotions than their minds, especially when guided by their whims rather than by considerations of the public interest. Because of this is it impossible for me not to beg Your Majesty to reflect frequently on this matter in order to confirm more and more in yourself your natural tendency to do the right thing.

I also plead with you to think often of how I have reminded you many times that there is no prince in a worse position than he who, not always able to do those things by himself which it is nevertheless his duty to perform, finds it even harder to let others do them for him. The capability of allowing himself to be served is not one of the least qualities a great king should have. Without this quality, opportunities are often quickly and senselessly lost when favorable action could be taken in settling matters for the advancement of the state.

The late king, your father, being in dire extremity, paid with kind words those who served him, accomplishing with caresses what his lack of funds would not permit him to encourage by other means. Your Majesty is unable to follow the late king in this practice, not being of the same make-up, having instead a natural dryness which you inherited from your mother the Queen, who herself has told you this in my presence several times. I cannot help reminding you that the public interest requires that you treat with consideration those who serve you, and at the least it is wise for you to be particularly careful not to say anything that would offend them.

Since I am going to deal later with the subject of the liberality princes should exercise I will say no more about it here, but I will dwell a bit on the bad effects which result from the remarks of those who speak too loosely about their subjects. The blows from a sword are easily healed. But it is not the same with blows of the tongue, especially if they be from the tongue of a king, whose authority renders the pain almost without remedy unless it be provided by the king himself. The higher a stone is thrown, the greater its striking force when it returns. There are many who would give no thought to being cut to pieces by the enemies of their master but who cannot suffer the slightest scratch from his hand. Just as flies do not constitute the diet of the eagle, so the lion is contemptuous of all animals with less than his strength. Likewise a man who attacked a child would be blamed by everyone. In similar fashion, I make bold to say, a great king should never insult his subordinates since they too are relatively weak. History is full of the unfortunate episodes which have resulted from the excessively free rein great men have given to their tongues, causing the unhappiness of those they considered beneath them.

God has seen fit to so endow Your Majesty as to make it natural for you not to do evil, and such being the case, it is only reasonable that you should carefully guard what you say, so that even your words will give no offense. I am sure, in this matter, that you will not by intent speak offensively, but it is difficult for you not to act impulsively, and sudden waves of emotion occasionally overtake you when you least expect them. I would not be your loyal servant if I did not warn you that both your reputation and your interests require that you have a particular care with regard to them, because such looseness of the tongue, while it may not disturb your conscience, can do much harm to your affairs. Just as to speak well of your enemies is an heroic virtue, so also a prince cannot speak offensively about those who would lay down their lives a thousand times for him and his interests without committing a great fault against the laws of Christianity, to say nothing of those of political wisdom.

A king who has clean hands, a pure heart, and a gentle tongue is not of little virtue, and he who has the first two qualities so eminently as Your Majesty, can with great facility acquire the third. As it is part of the grandeur of kings to be so reserved in their speech that nothing comes out of their mouths which could give offense to their subordinates, so too it is prudent to say nothing derogatory about the principal governmental agencies. Indeed they should be so spoken of as to give occasion for the belief they are held in high regard. The most important undertakings of state so frequently require that they be thwarted that prudence itself indicates they should be pampered in lesser matters.

It is not enough for great princes to resolve never to speak evil of anyone. Good sense requires that they also close their ears to slander and false information, pursuing and even banishing the authors as most dangerous plagues, often capable of poisoning the hearts of princes, as well as the minds of all those who approach them. All those who have free access to the ears of kings, without meriting it, are dangerous, and those who possess their hearts out of pure favoritism are even more so, for in order to preserve such a great treasure it is necessary to have recourse to artifice and malice, in default of the true virtues which invariably are lacking in such people.

I am compelled to say further in this matter that I have always been more apprehensive about the power of such influences over Your Majesty than of the world's greatest kings, and you have more need to guard yourself from the artifice of a valet who wants to take you by surprise than of all the factions the high nobles might form within your realm, even if they should have a common goal. When I first entered your service I learned that those who previously had the honor of serving you were absolutely convinced you were easily persuaded to suspect them, and having such a conviction their principal care was ever to keep their agents close to you to counteract the suspected evil. The fact of the firmness of Your Majesty in supporting me obliges me to recognize either that this judgment was without foundation or else that mature reflection has erased your youthful weakness. Even so, I cannot help beseeching you to strengthen this trait in your character so that the attitude you have been pleased to take toward me will be the one naturally expected by anyone who may succeed me. In addition I must also say to you that just as the ears of princes ought to be closed to calumny, so also should they be open to all truths useful to the state, and in like manner just as their tongues should never give utterance to words prejudicial to the reputation of others, so they should be able to speak freely and boldly when questions of public interest are at stake.

STUDY QUESTIONS

1. How does the cardinal mix flattery with sound advice?
2. Did Richelieu have an interest in warning the king against listening to gossip about his subordinates?

15.4. JEAN DOMAT, *CIVIL LAWS ACCORDING TO THE NATURAL ORDER*, 1697

Jean Domat (1625–1696) was a lawyer and legal scholar who served as Royal Prosecutor in the city of Clermont from 1655 to 1683, after which he retired to his study and dedicated himself to compiling his massive legal code. Apart from reordering the bulk of the Roman law tradition, Domat's work is significant for its concern to emphasize natural law as the basis for civil law—that is, the idea that law arises from, and represents, the innate moral values of a society. Although he accepted the then popular idea of the divine right of kings to rule, Domat presents law as an organic system over which the king presides but which does not emanate from him.

It is well-known that human society forms a kind of organic body, of which each person forms a part—and this truth, as the Bible has shown and the light of reason makes clear, is the foundation upon which all the duties and obligations that govern all men's actions toward one another individually and toward the body as a whole is based. These duties, moreover, are nothing less than the prescribed functions expected of each person, whatever his position in society. In this principle we find the origin of those laws that determine the duties of those who govern and of those who are governed. . . . As the Lord commands everyone to faithfully obey the precepts of His law that pertain to everyone, so does He command every person to faithfully obey the precepts that pertain to whatever specific condition or status he holds in the body politic. . . . But since, in their fundamental nature, all men are equal simply by virtue of being human, nature does not decree that any one person is subject to another. . . . Within this state of natural equality, however, individuals are differentiated by various qualities that result in their being of unequal status, and thus people must develop relationships and dependencies that determine their duties toward each other. Thus government is made necessary.

And since government, as established by God, is necessary for the good of society, it is therefore also incumbent upon all who are subject to it to submit to it and obey it—for if not, they would be resisting God Himself, and government (which ought to be the guarantor of peace and unity and the mainstay of the public good) would become the cause of division and conflict, and thus bring about its own downfall. . . .

To obey a government entails accepting its laws as laws, not attempting any action that runs counter to them, performing whatever action it requires, avoiding all that it forbids, shouldering the public responsibilities it assigns—whether in terms of serving in office or in payment of taxes—and in general to accept the obligation not to disturb public order but to endorse and assist it as one's circumstances allow.

Such obedience being necessary to maintain the harmonious order that should unite the head and other members that make up the state, it remains an essential duty for all subjects to obey without question the ruler's commands, without presuming to judge which orders they will or will not obey. For if everyone had the right to determine what is or is not justice, then every person would in effect be his own master—and sedition would arise. . . .

Among the rights given to the sovereign by the law is the right to possess and display whatever accoutrements of grandeur and majesty he needs to make

Jean Domat: Le droit public, suite des lois civiles dans leur ordre naturel, vol. 3, Oeuvres completes, nouvelle edition revue corrigée, ed. Joseph Remy (Paris: Firmin-Didot, 1829), pp. 1–2, 15–21, 26–27, 35, 39, 40, 44–45.

Translation by Clifford R. Backman.

known the tremendous authority and dignity of the all-encompassing power he possesses, in order to impress upon the minds of his subjects a proper attitude of veneration. . . . For it is by God's grace that He invests His power in sovereigns, and He permits rulers to adorn the authority He gives them with whatever seems to them to be appropriate, as a means of assuring the people's respect. This can be best achieved by having an aura of splendor radiate from their magnificent palaces, amid other visible signs of that splendor. . . .

The primary and most absolute of all the duties owed by those to whom God has entrusted the power of government is this: to acknowledge that they hold all of their power from God Himself, that it is His place they are taking, that it is through Him that they govern, and that it is God to Whom they should turn for guidance and wisdom in the matter of governing. May these truths form the foundation of all their conduct, and guide all of their actions in the performance of their duties. . . . [duties which include]: maintaining public order throughout the state, the peaceful lives of his subjects and the peace of mind of their families, care for every matter that pertains to the common good, the selection of capable ministers who love justice and truth, the appointment of worthy men to all public offices. . . . the discreet application of either severity or mercy in cases where the strong hand of justice may perhaps be restrained. . . . the good administration of public finances, prudence in relations with foreign states—in all, everything that can make government a blessing to good people, a terror to the wicked, and a worthy exemplar to Heaven's mandate to govern.

STUDY QUESTIONS

1. What metaphor does Domat use to present natural law?
2. How would Louis XIV—who ruled France when Domat composed *Civil Laws According to the Natural Order*—have responded to Domat's view of law as an organic system over which the king presides but which does not emanate from him?

15.5. FRANÇOIS FÉNELON, *THE ADVENTURES OF TELEMACHUS*, 1699

A Catholic priest and writer, François Fénelon (1651–1715) was enlisted by the church to preach to French Protestants (Huguenots) to bring them back to orthodox belief. His bestseller work, *The Adventures of Telemachus*, adds to the story of the Odyssey (Document 4.1) by describing the travels of Odysseus' son, Telemachus. Guiding Telemachus is his tutor, simply called Mentor (but later revealed as Diana, goddess of wisdom), who explains the tenets of a truly good society—one that abolished government, upheld the brotherhood of citizens, and looked back to ancient Greece as a model. Thus, Telemachus served as a fierce criticism of the rule of the Sun King, Louis XIV of France (1638–1715).

From François Fénelon, *The Adventures of Telemachus*. Trans Dr. Hawkesworth. New York: Hurd and Houghton, 1872, pp. 450–8.

The bark now touched the dominions of Pluto, and the shades ran down in crowds to the shore, gazing, with the utmost curiosity and wonder, at the living mortal who stood distinguished among the dead in the boat; but, the moment Telemachus set his foot on the shore, they vanished like the darkness of night before the first beams of morning. Then Charon, turning towards him, with a brow less contracted into frowns than usual, said to him: "O favored of heaven, since thou art permitted to enter the realms of darkness, which to all the living, besides thyself, are interdicted, make haste to go whithersoever the Fates have called thee; proceed by this gloomy path to the palace of Pluto, whom thou wilt find sitting upon his throne, who will permit thee to enter those recesses of his dominion, the secrets of which I am not permitted to reveal."

Telemachus, immediately pressing forward with a hasty step, discovered the shades gliding about on every side, more numerous than the sands on a seashore; and he was struck with a religious dread to perceive that, in the midst of the tumult and hurry of this incredible multitude, all was silent as the grave. He sees, at length, the gloomy residence of unrelenting Pluto: his hair stands erect, his legs tremble, and his voice fails him. "Tremendous power!" said he, with faltering and interrupted speech, "the son of unhappy Ulysses now stands before thee. I come to inquire whether my father is descended into your dominions, or whether he is still a wanderer upon the earth?"

Pluto was seated upon a throne of ebony: his countenance was pale and severe, his eyes hollow and ardent, and his brow contracted and menacing. The sight of a mortal still breathing the breath of life was hateful to his eyes, as the day is hateful to those animals that leave their recesses only by night. At his side sat Proserpine, who was the only object of his attention, and seemed to soften him into some degree of complacency. She enjoyed a beauty that was perpetually renewed but there was mingled with her immortal charms something of her lord's inflexible severity.

At the foot of the throne sat the pale father of destruction, Death, incessantly whetting a scythe which he held in his hand. Around this horrid spectre hovered repining Cares and injurious Suspicions; Vengeance, distained with blood and covered with wounds; causeless Hatred; Avarice, gnawing her own flesh; Despair,

the victim of her own rage; Ambition, whose fury overturns all things like a whirlwind; Treason, thirsting for blood, and not able to enjoy the mischief she produces; Envy, shedding round her the venom that corrodes her heart, and sickening with rage at the impotence of her malice; Impiety, that opens for herself a gulf without bottom, in which she shall plunge at last without hope; Spectres, all hideous to behold; Phantoms, that represent the dead to terrify the living; frightful Dreams; and the horrid Vigils of disease and pain. By these images of woe was Pluto surrounded: such were the attendants that filled his palace. He replied to the son of Ulysses in a hollow tone, and the depths of Erebus remurmured to the sound: "If it is by fate, young mortal, that thou hast violated this sacred asylum of the dead, that fate, which has thus distinguished thee, fulfill. Of thy father I will tell thee nothing; it is enough that here thou art permitted to seek him. As upon the earth he was a king, thy search may be confined, on one side, to that part of Tartarus where wicked kings are consigned to punishment, and, on the other, to that part of Elysium, where the good receive their reward. But, from hence thou canst not enter the fields of Elysium till thou hast passed through Tartarus. Make haste thither, and linger not in my dominions."

Telemachus instantly obeyed, and passed through the dreary vacuity that surrounded him with such speed that he seemed almost to fly; such was his impatience to behold his father and to quit the presence of a tyrant equally the terror of the living and the dead. He soon perceived the gloomy tract of Tartarus at a small distance before him: from this place ascended a black cloud of pestilential smoke, which would have been fatal in the realms of life. This smoke hovered over a river of fire, the flames of which, returning upon themselves, roared in a burning vortex with a noise like that of an impetuous torrent precipitated from the highest rock, so that in this region of woe no other sound could be distinctly heard.

Telemachus, secretly animated by Minerva, entered the gulf without fear. He first saw a great number of men, who, born in a mean condition, were now punished for having sought to acquire riches by fraud, treachery, and violence. Among them he remarked many of the impious hypocrites, who, affecting a zeal for religion, played upon the credulity of others and gratified their own ambition. These wretches, who had abused virtue itself, the best gift of heaven, to dishonest purposes, were punished as the most criminal of men. Children who had murdered their parents, wives who had sold their country in violation of every tie, were punished with less severity than these. Such was the decree pronounced by the judges of the dead, because hypocrites are not content to be wicked upon the common terms; they would be vicious, with the reputation of virtue; and by an appearance of virtue, which at length is found to be false, they prevent mankind from putting confidence in the true. The gods, whose omniscience they mock and whose honor they degrade, take pleasure in the exertion of all their power to avenge the insult.

After these appeared others, to whom the world scarcely imputes guilt, but whom the divine vengeance pursues without pity—the liar, the ingrate, the parasite who lavishes adulation upon vice, and the slanderer who falsely detracts from virtue—all those who judge rashly of what they know but in part, and thus injure the reputation of the innocent.

But, among all who suffered for ingratitude, those were punished with most severity who had been ungrateful to the gods. "What!" said Minos, "is he considered as a monster who is guilty of ingratitude to his father or his friend, from whom he has received some such benefits as mortals can bestow, and shall the wretch glory in his crime who is ungrateful to the gods, the givers of life and of every blessing it includes? Does he not owe his existence rather to the authors of nature than to the parents through whom his existence was derived? The less these crimes are censured and punished upon earth, the more are they obnoxious in hell to implacable vengeance, which no force can resist and no subtlety elude."

Telemachus, seeing a man condemned by the judges, whom he found sitting, ventured to ask them what was his crime. He was immediately answered by the offender himself. "I have done," said he, "no evil; my pleasure consisted wholly in doing good. I have been just, munificent, liberal, and compassionate; of what crime, then, can I be accused?" "With respect to man," replied Minos, "thou art accused of none; but didst thou not owe less to man than to the gods? If so, what are thy pretensions to justice? Thou hast

punctually fulfilled thy duty to men, who are but dust; thou hast been virtuous, but thy virtue terminated wholly in thyself, without reference to the gods who gave it: thy virtue was to be thy own felicity, and to thyself thou wast all in all. Thou hast, indeed, been thy own deity. But the gods, by whom all things have been created, and who have created all things for themselves, cannot give up their rights: thou hast forgotten them, and they will forget thee. Since thou hast desired to exist for thyself, and not for them, to thyself they will deliver thee up. Seek, then, thy consolation in thine own heart. Thou art separated forever from man, whom, for thy own sake, thou hast desired to please, and art left to thyself alone, that idol of thy heart. Learn now, at least, that piety is that virtue of which the gods are the object, and that without this no virtue can deserve the name. The false lustre of that which thou hast long dazzled the eyes of men, who are easily deceived, will deceive no more. Men distinguish that only from which they derive pain or pleasure, into virtue and vice, and are, therefore, alike ignorant both of good and evil: but here the perspicacity of divine wisdom discerns all things as they are; the judgment of men, from external appearance, is reversed; what they have admired is frequently condemned, and what they have condemned, approved.

These words, to the boaster of philosophic virtue, were like a stroke of thunder, and he was unable to sustain the shock. The self-complaisance with which he had been used to contemplate his moderation, his fortitude, his generosity, was now changed to despair. The view of his own heart, at enmity with the gods, became his punishment. He now saw, and was doomed forever to see, himself by the light of truth. He perceived that the approbation of men, which all his actions had been directed to acquire, was erroneous and vain. When he looked inward, he found every thing totally changed; he was no longer the same being, and all comfort was eradicated from his heart. His conscience, which had hitherto witnessed in his favor, now rose up against him, and reproached him even with his virtues, which, not having deity for their principle and end, were erroneous and illusive. He was overwhelmed with consternation and trouble, with shame, remorse, and despair. The Furies, indeed, forbore to torment him; he was delivered over to himself, and they were satisfied; his own heart was the avenger of the gods, whom he had despised. As he could not escape from himself, he retired to the most gloomy recesses, that he might be concealed from others: he sought for darkness, but he found it not; light still persecuted and pursued him: the light of truth, which he had not followed, now punished him for neglect. All that he had beheld with pleasure became odious in his eyes, as the source of misery that could never end. "O fool!" said he, "I have known neither the gods, men, nor myself; I have, indeed, known nothing, since I have not known the only and true good. All my steps have deviated from the path I should have trodden; all my wisdom was folly and all my virtue was pride, which sacrificed, with a blind impiety, only to that vile idol, myself!"

The next objects that Telemachus perceived, as he went on, were the kings that had abused their power. An avenging Fury held up before them a mirror which reflected their vices in all their deformity. In this they beheld their undistinguishing vanity, that was gratified by the grossest adulation; their want of feeling for mankind, whose happiness should have been the first object of their attention; their insensibility to virtue, their dread of truth, their partiality to flatterers, their dissipation, effeminacy, and indolence; their causeless suspicions; their vain parade and ostentatious splendor, an idle blaze, in which the public welfare is consumed; their ambition of false honor, procured at the expense of blood; and their inhuman luxury, which extorted a perpetual supply of superfluous delicacies from the wretched victims of grief and anguish. When they looked into this mirror, they saw themselves faithfully represented; and they found the picture more monstrous and horrid than the Chimera vanquished by Bellerophon, the Lernaean hydra slain by Hercules, and even Cerebus himself, though from his three howling mouths he disgorges a stream of black venomous blood, that is sufficient to infect the whole race of mortals that breathe upon the earth.

At the same time another Fury tauntingly repeated all the praises which sycophants had lavished upon them in their lives, and held up another mirror, in which they appeared as flattery had represented them. The contrast of these pictures, widely different, was the punishment of their vanity. It was remarkable that the most wicked were the objects of the most extravagant praise; because the most wicked are most to be feared, and because they exact, with less shame, the servile adulation of the poets and orators of their time.

Their groans perpetually ascended from this dreadful abyss, where they saw nothing but the derision and insult of which they were themselves the objects—where every thing repulsed, opposed, and confounded them. As they sported with the lives of mankind upon the earth, and pretended that the whole species were created for their use, they were, in Tartarus, delivered over to the capricious tyranny of slaves, who made them taste all the bitterness of servitude in their turn. They obeyed with unutterable anguish, and without hope that the iron hand of oppression would lie lighter upon them. Under the strokes of these slaves, now their merciless tyrants, they lay passive and impotent, like an anvil under the hammers of the Cyclops, when Vulcan urges their labor at the flaming furnaces of Mount Aetna.

Telemachus observed the countenance of these criminals to be pale and ghastly, strongly expressive of the torment they suffered at the heart. They looked inward with a self-abhorrence, now inseparable from their existence. Their crimes themselves had become their punishment, and it was not necessary that greater should be inflicted. They haunted them like hideous spectres, and continually started up before them in all their enormity. They wished for a second death, that might separate them from these ministers of vengeance, as the first had separated their spirits from the body—a death that might at once extinguish all consciousness and sensibility. They called upon the depths of hell to hide them from the persecuting beams of truth, in impenetrable darkness; but they are reserved for the cup of vengeance, which, though they drink it forever, shall be ever full. The truth, from which they fled, has overtaken them, an invincible and unrelenting enemy. The ray which once might have illuminated them, like the mild radiance of the day, now pierces them like lightning—a fierce and fatal fire, that, without injury to the external parts, infixes a burning torment at the heart. By truth, now, an avenging flame, the very soul is melted, like metal in a furnace; it dissolves all, but destroys nothing; it disunites the first elements of life, yet the sufferer can never die. He is, as it were, divided against himself, without rest and without comfort; animated by no vital principle, but the rage that kindles at his own misconduct, and the dreadful madness that results from despair.

Among these objects, at the sight of which the hair of Telemachus stood erect, he beheld many of the ancient kings of Lydia who were punished for having preferred the selfish gratification of others, which, to royalty, is a duty of indispensable obligation.

These kings mutually reproached each other with their folly. "Did I not often recommend to you," said one of them to his son, "during the last years of my life, when old age had given weight to my counsel, the reparation of the mischiefs that my negligence had produced?" "Unhappy father!" replied the son, "thou art the cause of my perdition; it was thy example that made me vain-glorious, proud, voluptuous, and cruel. While I saw thee surrounded with flattery, and relaxed into luxury and sloth, I also insensibly acquired the love of pleasure and adulation. I thought the rest of men were to kings what horses and other beasts of burden are to men—animals wholly unworthy of regard, except for the drudgery they perform and the conveniences they procure. This was my opinion, and I learnt it of thee. I followed thy example, and share thy misery." These reproaches were mingled with the most horrid execrations: mutual rage and indignation aggravated the torments of hell.

Around these wretched princes there still hovered, like owls in the twilight, causeless Jealousies and vain Alarms, Mistrust and Dread, which revenge upon kings their disregard of mankind; Avarice, insatiable of wealth; False-Honor, ever tyrannical and oppressive; and effeminate Luxury, a deceitful demon that aggravated every evil, and bestows only imaginary good.

Many kings were also severely punished, not for the mischief they had done, but for the good they had neglected to do. Every crime that is committed by the subject in consequence of laws not enforced, is the crime of the kings, for kings reign only as ministers of the law. To kings also are imputed all the disorders that arise from pomp, luxury, and every other excess which excites irregular and impetuous passions that cannot be gratified but by the violation of the common rights of mankind. But the princes who, instead of watching over their people as a shepherd watches over his flock, worried and devoured them like the wolf were punished with the most exemplary severity.

In this abyss of darkness and misery, Telemachus beheld, with yet greater astonishment, many kings who had been honored for their personal virtues upon earth, but were, notwithstanding, condemned to the pains of Tartarus for having left the administration of government to wicked and crafty men. They were punished for mischiefs which they had suffered to be perpetrated under the sanction of their authority. The greater part of them, indeed, had been by principle neither virtuous nor vicious; supinely taking the color impressed upon them from without, they did not shun the truth when it presented itself, but they had no relish for virtue, no delight in doing good.

When Telemachus left Tartarus, he felt himself relieved, as if a mountain had been removed from his breast. This relief, so sudden and so great, impressed him with a strong sense of the misery of those who are confined there without hope of deliverance. He was terrified at having seen so many kings punished with much greater severity than any other offenders. "Have kings, then," said he, "so many duties to fulfill, so many difficulties to surmount, and so many dangers to avoid? Is the knowledge that is necessary to put them upon their guard, as well against themselves as others, so difficult to be acquired? and, after all the envy, tumult, and opposition of a transitory life, are they consigned to the intolerable and eternal pains of hell? What folly, then, to wish for royalty! How happy the peaceful private station, in which the practice of virtue is comparatively easy!"

STUDY QUESTIONS

1. How are the tribunals and monarchs of Hades modeled on those of Louis XIV's France?
2. Does the document serve as a warning to kings against the powers of sycophants and the long-term consequences of poor decisions?